THE DIVINE
DECEPTION

Also by Keith Laidler

The Head of God

THE DIVINE DECEPTION

THE CHURCH, THE SHROUD AND THE CREATION OF A HOLY FRAUD

KEITH LAIDLER

HEADLINE

First published in 2000
by HEADLINE BOOK PUBLISHING

10 9 8 7 6 5 4 3 2 1

British Library Cataloguing in Publication Data

Laidler, Keith, 1949-
    The divine deception : the Church the Shroud and the
    creation of a holy fraud
    1.Holy Shroud
    I.Title
    232.9'66[F]

    ISBN 0 7472 7484 3 (hardback)
    ISBN 0 7472 7485 1 (softback)

Typeset by
Letterpart Limited, Reigate, Surrey

Printed and bound in Great Britain by
Mackays of Chatham PLC, Chatham, Kent

HEADLINE BOOK PUBLISHING
A division of the Hodder Headline Group
338 Euston Road
London NW1 3BH

www.headline.co.uk
www.hodderheadline.com

CONTENTS

PREFACE

The road that led me to study the origins of the Shroud of Turin began with the findings of my book *The Head of God*. Here I gave reasons for believing that Jesus had belonged to the royal line that descended from the Pharaoh Akhenaten, that the Jewish cult of the Nazarites had carried on the religious heritage of 'the Heretic Pharaoh', and that these rites had included the worship of the head. I discovered that on his death Jesus, as the leader of the Nazarites, had been ritually decapitated and his head embalmed. It was this embalmed head of Christ that had been discovered by the Knights Templar beneath the Temple of Solomon in Jerusalem and had been worshipped by them as Baphomet, the Father of Wisdom. The relic had been held by this order of warrior-monks as a sacred relic, and had been finally laid to rest beneath the Templar 'Grail Chapel' at Rosslyn, Scotland.[1]

The book stimulated much controversy, and not a few brickbats, but it resulted in far less open debate on the basic propositions of the theory than I would have wished. Moreover, the trustees of Rosslyn Chapel proved more willing to open their doors to the many visitors my book generated than to open the chapel itself to a true investigation of what lay in the ashlar vaults beneath its stone floor. Frustratingly, they declined all my requests to excavate beneath the building. I was told that radar sweeps of the ground (which in any case would reveal only the surface details of the chapel) might be possible 'a year or two from now'. The director of Rosslyn Chapel gave it as his opinion that any object of great value 'would have been buried forty to fifty feet down', immediately casting doubt on the value of any such superficial investigations even supposing permission was granted.[2] Nevertheless, as far as the trustees were concerned a full excavation was out of the question in the foreseeable future. Nothing I could do would change their minds. The discovery, from a Templar informant, that there was a concealed passageway connecting Rosslyn Castle to the chapel further increased my concern – was it possible that the relic might be spirited away from the chapel with no overt signs of excavation?[3] Had it already been removed?

Frustrated in my hope of quickly holding Christendom's most precious relic in my hands, I began casting round for further proof of the existence of the head of Christ. Apart from the records of the Inquisition, the carvings at Rosslyn Chapel and paintings of a bearded head, had the Templars left any other evidence of their possession of the head of Christ? The Order of the Temple contained within its ranks some of the most intelligent and broad-minded men of their time, men whose interests ranged widely and absorbed useful and practical knowledge no matter what its provenance might be – Jew, Arab or pagan. Was there anything from Templar times that would allow me to look, as it were 'by proxy', on the relic that I am certain lies beneath Rosslyn? In short, was there any way of seeing the true features of Jesus, of looking on the face of Christ?

I discovered that there was. My researches opened a window into a forgotten past that encompassed the original Christian beliefs, the lost history of Christ's disciples and the tale of vanished technologies. And I discovered a deception that had been practised successfully on the whole of the Christian world for over 600 years. But this was no ordinary fraud; it had not been perpetrated for either of the two usual motives: lust for power or greed of gold. It was a Divine Deception, needful because the medieval Zeitgeist, the spirit of the time, would not allow the truth to be spoken openly. Even today, as I have discovered, to write of such matters was to bring down the wrath and derision of a vociferous section of orthodox Christianity, with churchmen still ready to accuse dissenters of 'heresy'.

Nevertheless, the sacred relic was accessible without recourse to excavations beneath Rosslyn Chapel. Incredible as it first appears, there is an actual photographic record of the embalmed head of Christ. And it had been quite literally staring everyone in the face for over 600 years.

A TIMELESS MYSTERY

A Hideous Death

O N A COLD evening in early spring, in the centre of the Ile-des-Javiaux in Paris, two high officials of a religious order were slowly roasted to death on the orders of the French king, Philip le Bel. Jacques de Molay, the Grand Master of the Poor Knights of the Temple of Solomon, and Geoffrey de Charnay, the Order's Preceptor of Normandy, were the last victims of a process that had begun seven years before and which had reduced the most powerful religious and military Order in Christendom to ruin. The charges that had destroyed the Order were bizarre, even for the devil-obsessed tenor of the time. The Templars were accused of heresy. They were said to have spat on the cross, denied that Christ was God, and to have worshipped idols, chief among them a severed, embalmed human head, long-haired and bearded and known as Baphomet.[1]

The existence of the Baphomet is not seriously in doubt; too many of the Knights confessed to having seen this object, which was held in the greatest secrecy and shown at the major Chapters of the Order. But when the officers of the Inquisition searched the Templar properties, no trace was ever found of the Order's vast riches, or of its records, or of the Baphomet. There is very good reason to believe that some members of the Order had prior warning of the attack,[2] and that the embalmed head was spirited away just before the blow fell and taken to Scotland, where it remains to this day. It is the existence of this head, and the history of the de Charnay family, that holds the key to the mysterious origin of the Shroud of Turin.

Sacred or Sham?

Exactly 50 years after the destruction of the Templar Order, in 1357, there occurred the first unveiling of a religious relic that was to become both a focus of veneration and a source of acrimonious dispute for the next six centuries. Its owner was another Geoffrey de Charnay, lord of the lands surrounding the Lirey Church. He was a famous knight in his time and is known to history as Geoffrey I de Charnay, to distinguish him from his son, yet another Geoffrey, who is known as Geoffrey II de Charnay. Geoffrey I was the nephew of the Templar Preceptor roasted to death during the suppression of the Order by Pope Clement V.[3] As I was later to discover, this family connection was to prove a vital clue in the story of the provenance of the Holy Shroud.

The first, uncontested exposition of the Shroud took place in Lirey, an insignificant hamlet in Champagne. We know of this from an irate letter written in 1389, more than three decades after the event, by Pierre d'Arcis, then Bishop of Troyes, and addressed to Pope Clement VII. The hamlet of Lirey was the family seat of the de Charnays, and the good bishop castigates the head of the family, Geoffrey II de Charnay, for allowing the canons of the Lirey Church to exhibit a cloth displaying 'the two-fold image of one man, that is to say, the back and the front' which they claimed to be the gravecloth in which Christ was wrapped. According to d'Arcis, the Dean of Lirey 'was consumed with the passion of avarice'; he was paying men and women to pose as crippled pilgrims so that they might be 'miraculously' cured whenever this 'fake' Shroud was exposed.[4] These alleged shenanigans were taking place at the time the bishop was writing (1389). But it had, he claimed, all begun a generation before. D'Arcis goes on to state that this same Shroud had been exhibited previously, 'thirty-four years or thereabouts' earlier, and that his predecessor, Henri of Poitiers had investigated the cloth and discovered that it had been painted. The bishop claims that Henri de Poitiers had even apprehended a painter who had confessed to producing the counterfeit. D'Arcis appealed to the Pope to prevent further expositions and to reject the authenticity of the supposed Holy Shroud. In response, Geoffrey II de Charnay appealed directly to the Pope, and at the same time petitioned the king of France, Charles VII, to allow the expositions to proceed.

Here again, I discovered that Templar and family connections came to the fore. Geoffrey II de Charnay was not unknown to Pope Clement; the nobleman was quite closely related to the Holy Father (de Charnay's stepfather was the Pope's uncle). In addition, Pope Clement VII was the spiritual heir of Pope Clement v, by whose orders, less than a hundred years before, the Templars had been suppressed. The king of France, Charles vii, was a Capetian monarch, a descendant of Hugh Capet, who had founded the dynasty in 987. And Charles was closely related to Philip le Bel, the monarch who had instigated the attack on the Temple on 13 October 1307, claiming the suppression of heresy and the worship of an embalmed head as his motive for the attack. For both Charles and Clement the spectre of the destroyed Order of the Temple must have been too close for comfort. There may have been much concerning the Temple that these two kings, one religious, one secular, wished to remain concealed.

And so it seems, for both sided with Geoffrey ii de Charnay. King Charles of France granted de Charnay the right to show the Shroud, making no restrictions on the expositions. Pope Clement was more subtle, as well he might be. After all, Charles had not been asked to adjudicate on the Shroud's authenticity (although his acquiescence to its exposition certainly gave the Shroud a favourable odour of sanctity). Pope Clement had to pronounce a definitive judgement on the Holy Cloth. And his answer was very telling. Clement replied by threatening d'Arcis with excommunication if he took his accusations further. He followed this up with a letter to Geoffrey ii, insisting that the Shroud be called an 'impression' of Jesus but forbidding it to be named as the true gravecloth of Christ.[5] This is very clear: with all the strength of papal authority, Clement is saying that the cloth is emphatically not the Shroud from Jesus' tomb, and yet, at the same time, he is forcibly threatening excommunication on Bishop d'Arcis and those attempting to prove that the impression was fraudulent. The Pope was essentially giving notice that the impression of the figure on the Shroud was off limits. The first time I read of the Shroud's history I found the Pope's statement astonishing. Why this ambivalent attitude? Surely the question is simple: the Shroud is either what it purports to be, the burial cloth of Jesus, with a unique portrait of Jesus imprinted on its fibres, or it is not. And it is therefore counterfeit. A fake. There could, as far as I could see, be no middle way.

Of course, the plain Shroud might just conceivably have been the genuine article, with (as d'Arcis claimed) a counterfeit image painted on it. But the papal pronouncement took a diametrically opposite position: the image was to be allowed, but the cloth as the Shroud of the Crucifixion was proscribed. How could this be?

Later, the more I considered this apparently incomprehensible papal statement, the more convinced I became that the Vicar of Christ was attempting to strike a balance between what he knew to be the truth and what he did not dare admit. The Pope was signalling that, while the Shroud was not the gravecloth of Jesus, it did nevertheless carry upon it a true impression of Jesus, an impression that was so important that excommunication was the price to be exacted on anyone attempting to prove the likeness a fraud.

But this threw up other, apparently intractable problems. If the impression *was* that of Jesus, then (as it showed a bloody and crucified Christ) it could have been made only postmortem, presumably by wrapping the cloth around the body after the Crucifixion. In other words, if the image was true it simply *had to be* the gravecloth of Christ, made while he lay in the tomb of Joseph of Arimathea. At that time there did not appear to be any possible way in which the two opinions could be reconciled.

It was only later that the puzzle became clear. And then I could only marvel at the subtlety of Pope Clement's statement.

History of the Shroud

Following its debut on to the world stage in 1357, the history of the Shroud is well documented. But it is the identity of the first known owner of the Shroud that holds another important clue to the origin of the relic. Tradition has it that the Shroud was first shown by Geoffrey I de Charnay, but the truth is that there is no documentary evidence of his owning the Shroud. What we do know is that following his death in the battle of Poitiers, it was his wife, Jeanne de Vergy, who claimed ownership of the relic. This has led some researchers to the conclusion that, during his lifetime, Geoffrey I de Charnay took pains to keep his possession of the Shroud secret, and that it was only on his death that his wife, Jeanne de Vergy, began the expositions mentioned in the letter of Bishop d'Arcis.[6] As Ian Wilson has commented: '. . . until the very first Lirey expositions of the 1350s . . . no one was prepared to shout their ownership of the Shroud to the rooftops'. It seems that, at least initially, the relic was perceived as a dangerous commodity. As a secret that must be kept hidden.

When Geoffrey I's son, Geoffrey II de Charnay, died in 1398, the Shroud passed to his daughter Margaret, who was married twice, first to Jean de Baufremont (1400) and then, 18 years later, to Humbert de Villersexel. Due to the exigencies of the Hundred Years War, the canons of the Lirey Church handed over the Shroud to Humbert for safekeeping. Margaret seems to have considered the Shroud her own property, as she refused to return it to the Lirey canons, despite repeated requests. Margaret's reason for believing she was the rightful possessor of the Shroud has puzzled historians for decades. In a deposition Margaret claims that her title to the Shroud rested on the fact that the relic was 'conquis par feu messire Geoffrey de Charnay'.[7]

'Conquis par feu'? The most likely translation for this phrase is 'conquered by, or through, fire', which, on the face of it, is a nonsense. How could the Shroud be conquered by fire? The phrase has no relevance when applied to the history of her father, Geoffrey II de Charnay (to whom most historians believe the phrase 'messire Geoffrey de Charnay' refers). It is equally meaningless with regard to her grandfather, Geoffrey I de Charnay. It struck me that the word 'messire' is strangely vague (it carries the same meaning as 'monsieur' in modern French or 'mister' in English) especially for a legal deposition where the need for verbal precision is paramount. 'Mon père' or 'mon grandpère' would have made the question of ownership crystal clear. Margaret cannot have been unaware of the potential for confusion that could occur because of the abundance of Geoffreys in the de Charnay family. Might the word have been chosen for this very reason, just because it did introduce a note of confusion? Was it Margaret's intention to be purposely obtuse, to throw a veil over the actual identity of the 'messire'? In short, could Margaret had been referring to an earlier Geoffrey de Charnay, to the Templar Preceptor of Normandy, roasted to death on the Ile-des-Javiaux in 1314? If so, then her enigmatic phrase 'conquis par feu' takes on a startling relevance. She is telling us that Geoffrey de Charnay conquered through the flames, that he kept faith with the Order of the Temple unto death, that he won the right to hold the Holy Shroud by enduring the fire without revealing the sacred secret of the Order.

Margaret seems to have kept the Shroud with her as a talisman wherever she lived, and she exhibited it at various sites, including St Hippo sur Doubs, Chimay, in Belgium, and at Germolles, near Mâcon, in France.[8] However, in 1453, either because of a lack of financial resources or because she was nearing the end of her life and wished to secure the Shroud's future (she died without issue), Margaret transferred ownership of the Shroud to her distant relation, the Duke of Savoy. Eleven years later the Lirey canons (still claiming ownership of the relic) waived their rights in return for an annual rent, paid by Duke Louis I of Savoy. Several authors have noted that this agreement spells out specifically that the Shroud was first owned by Geoffrey de Charnay, Lord of Savoisy and Lirey. This is firm confirmation that the Shroud was owned by the de Charnay family before being bequeathed to the Lirey canons. But it may prove more than that. The Templar Preceptor Geoffrey de Charnay had also been lord of these lands. So here again, as with Margaret de Charnay's enigmatic deposition, there appears to be a sound reason for suspecting that the de Charnay family gained possession of the

Shroud by reason of their link to the Order of the Temple.

From this time forward until 1983, the Shroud was the property of the Dukes of Savoy. At first it led a peripatetic existence. For example, between 1471 and 1478 the relic was moved on at least eight occasions. Thereafter it continued to wander with the Savoy family between their holdings in Italy and France until it was finally housed 'permanently' at Chambéry, high in the French Alps. Here it stayed for almost 80 years, until a French invasion of Savoy lands sent it on its travels once more. Over the next eight years, always just one step ahead of the French raiders, it was moved to Piedmont, Turin, Milan, Vercelli, Nice, Aosta and finally, in 1561, it was returned in a triumphant torch-lit procession to Chambéry and its place in Sainte Chapelle. With the Dukes of Savoy making Turin the new capital of their dominions, the Shroud was transferred to Turn Cathedral on 14 September 1578. Since that date, it has never left the city. The Shroud remained the property of the Savoy family for over 500 years, until 1983 and the death of ex-King Umberto ɪɪ. In his will, Umberto ɪɪ bequeathed the Shroud to the Popes of the Roman Catholic Church on condition that the relic remains in its traditional home, Turin.

'Pre-History' of the Shroud

Despite the rigorously well-documented history of the Shroud since 1357, the origins of this enigmatic relic have remained a mystery for the past 600 years. How did it come into the possession of the de Charnay family? If it was produced in the Middle Ages, when, where and how was it made? If it is genuine, where was the Shroud for the 13 long centuries before its exposition at Lirey?

Various researchers have tried to reconstruct a 'prior history' for the relic, attempting to follow a trail that precedes the de Charnays of Lirey and winds back into the first millennium. Most of these workers are 'believers', convinced of the Shroud's authenticity; their stated aim is to track the linen cloth to its ultimate point of origin in the tomb of the crucified Christ. This is a valid quest and one that should be taken seriously. If there is a path leading back to first-century Palestine, then it would provide good evidence that the Shroud is indeed the cloth that was wrapped around Jesus' body in the tomb. Unfortunately, it is a quest that, despite valiant efforts, has so far produced no real convincing evidence of the Shroud's existence very much earlier than its first documented showing in the 1350s.

Perhaps the most accomplished exponent of the pre-history procedure is Ian Wilson, a veteran Shroud scholar whose book *The Turin Shroud* was in large measure responsible for bringing the relic to the attention of the public in 1978.[9] Ian Wilson's researches have led him to suggest a pre-1357 history for the Shroud that includes a 300-year disappearance with the Shroud hidden in the walls of the city of Edessa (present-day Urfa in southern Turkey). Following this, the cloth is said to have been taken to Byzantium, where it stayed until the sack of that city in the Fourth Crusade. After this there is a second 150-year 'disappearance', with the Shroud finally surfacing at Lirey sometime in the mid-1350s. So, in this historical scenario, for 450 years – a full third of the time between the death of Jesus and the 1357 exposition – the whereabouts of the cloth are admitted to be unknown. For the rest, we are asked to believe that the Shroud is to be identified first with the 'Cloth of Edessa', the earliest descriptions of which state that it was an image of the head or face of Jesus. Later identifications of the Shroud are similarly tenuous: for example, the Mandylion, another head of Christ, is said to have been the Shroud folded in such a way that only the face was visible. Unfortunately, such a folding would have produced an extremely bulky object, whereas the Mandylion is known to have been carried as a standard into battle. In a similar fashion, many early paintings of the face of Jesus are said to reproduce the salient features of the head on the Shroud. However, it is just as likely (and it certainly requires less tortuous logic and leaps of faith) to see such symbols of the head of Jesus (and there are many others) as reflecting a knowledge of the existence of an embalmed head of Christ. Even when ancient records of a 'full body' Shroud are noted, the exponents of the pre-history scenarios omit one extremely important fact. During the first millennium (and after), several Shrouds of Christ are known to have existed.[10] This makes it certain that some 'Holy Shrouds', if not all of them, were fakes. And this in turn increases the likelihood that it is one of these fake Shrouds that is being misidentified in the first-millennium records as the object we now know as the Shroud of Turin. All in all, it is neither very satisfactory nor very convincing.

The brutal truth is that we have no real evidence that the Shroud existed before the medieval period. All we know for certain is that the first record of the Shroud that now lies in Turin is dated 1389 and mentions a prior date for the same object of around 1357.

Was There Ever a Shroud?

One major point glossed over in these exercises in myth-making is that, although much time is spent poring over ancient manuscripts, the most directly pertinent of all ancient records are given scant attention. The Gospels and Acts of the Apostles in the New Testament are the most detailed accounts we have of the life and death of Jesus, and they are by no means unanimous that a Shroud (let alone a Shroud with an image imprinted on it) even existed.

Enshrouding is certainly not a universal custom: the dead body can be placed in a coffin, naked or fully clothed and surrounded by possessions, or it may be laid in a foetal position, or burned, or wrapped in linen strips (as in Egyptian mummification), or cut up and fed to birds of prey (the Tibetan 'sky burial'), or any other of scores of different rites for the dead. Of the Gospel writers, it is Matthew who comes closest to describing a Shroud, saying that Joseph of Arimathea wrapped Jesus' body in 'a fine linen cloth'. This use of the singular to describe the linen cloth certainly carries with it the implication of a Shroud. However, when we come to the other Gospels, the situation is far less clear. Mark is much more equivocal, saying Joseph 'brought fine linen' to cover the body, which while it could mean a Shroud could equally indicate a number of cloth pieces, or even linen strips for the burial. Luke seems to favour these latter two suggestions, mentioning the plural 'linen clothes' (Luke xxiv, 12), as does the Gospel of John: after Joseph of Arimathea has received the body of Jesus, he 'wound it in linen clothes' (John xix, 40), which clearly suggests strips of material wound around the body. The phrase certainly states clearly that more than one piece of cloth was involved. In the next chapter, this information is repeated. After the open tomb is discovered by Mary Magdalene, the disciple Peter looked into the tomb and 'saw the linen clothes lying; yet went he not in' (John xx, 5). Simon Peter has more courage and boldly enters the sepulchre '. . . and seeth the linen clothes lie, And the napkin that was about his head, not lying with the linen clothes, but wrapped together in a place by itself' (John xx, 6, 7). Verse 7 is especially interesting here. Until now, the possibility remained that the term 'linen clothes' or graveclothes was a reference to the Shroud, together with the napkin that went over the face of the deceased in certain Jewish burial rites (as is mentioned in the raising of Lazarus, for example). But this interpretation is specifically excluded in verse 7. Simon Peter sees the napkin laid to one side, but the remaining linen is still referred to in the plural as 'linen clothes'.

In sum, then, if we grant equal authority to each Gospel writer on this question, the balance of probabilities must fall on the side of several pieces of cloth being used in the burial and away from a whole-body, single shroud. On this basis, there is little likelihood that a Turin shroud-style gravecloth was present in the tomb of Jesus.

Compounding this strong doubt that a shroud, as a single long sheet, even existed, it is undeniable that one of the few points concerning the resurrection that the four Gospels do see eye to eye on is that they make no mention whatsoever of any miraculous image on the gravecloths.

Both the New Testament and the Apocryphal Gospels are replete with miracle-tales concerning the Master. And yet all of them, without exception, maintain a deafening silence on the existence of anything remotely resembling the Shroud of Turin. This is a most embarrassing fact for 'believers'. Surely, if the gravecloth of Jesus was found to bear an impression of the risen Christ, this fact would have been trumpeted in triumph across the pages of every one of the Gospels. In the Middle Ages the Shroud was seen as proof positive of Christ's resurrection – it would have been just as effective an instrument of propaganda during the early days of Christianity, when the fledgling religion was struggling to find converts. As the sole physical reminder of Jesus, its fame would have spread far and wide, and we might reasonably expect to find evidence of its existence among the very earliest writings of the Church. And yet there is no word of this miraculous cloth. Why? The most likely explanation must be because it was not in existence at that time.

The Evidence of the Image

One of the main spurs for this historical myth-making is the Shroud itself, or rather the image imprinted on it. Anyone who looks at the cloth, believer or sceptic, cannot fail to be moved by the image on it, the tragic impression of an executed man, scourged and done to death by that most horrible of tortures, crucifixion. The realism of the image is all too apparent and horrific. And, of course, the indignities and tortures to which the Man on the Shroud has been subjected correspond exactly with the Gospel stories of the Crucifixion of Christ, making identification of the figure with Jesus almost irresistible.

But the veracity of the image becomes even more striking and impressive when its fine details are examined. Despite claims to the contrary,[11] the vast majority of Shroud researchers, no matter on which side of the fence they sit, are confident that the image has not been produced by any normal painting method. In fact, it would have been extremely counter-productive for a forger to produce a 'painting' whose true value could be discerned only centuries later, after the invention of a method (photography) that allowed the viewing of a negative image of his work. The image on the Shroud has less to do with painting than with a subtle process that has in some way altered the structure of the linen that makes up the Shroud.[12] It is almost as if the image had been burned into the fibres of the surface layers of the linen by some mysterious process. This has led to the theory that the image was created at the very moment of resurrection by a powerful unknown (and perhaps unknowable) radiation that burst from the revivified body of Jesus.[13] We will have cause to return to this 'radiation hypothesis' later in the book.

Just as impressive as the origin of the mysterious marks that make up this remarkable portrait is the utter realism of the image. There are a wealth of anatomical and forensic details on the Shroud which speak most forcefully for its being genuine. It is this constellation of detail, unknown in the history of Western art at the time the Shroud might have been faked, that has been a major factor in convincing many researchers of the Shroud's authenticity.

Perhaps the most dramatic features of the Shroud are the blood flows, which in the case of the hands and arms show a striking parallel to what one would expect of a crucified man. As the believers have been quick to point out, for a forger to have so carefully thought out and incorporated such naturalistic details into his fake (when contemporary paintings make no effort at verisimilitude) indicates very strongly that the Shroud image is that of a genuinely crucified man. And the constellation of injuries points unmistakably towards an identification with Jesus.

Blood flows from hands and feet   There is no doubt that the direction of blood flow along the hands and arms is impressively realistic. This corresponds exactly with what one might expect of an actual crucifixion victim. There is even an inverted V-shaped blood flow on the back of the left wrist which may indicate two separate positions adopted by the crucified in an attempt to ease his agony, or which perhaps reveals the premortem and postmortem posture of the victim.[14] The wounds on the feet are not as clear as those of the hands, but do nevertheless show a very naturalistic rendition of copious bleeding, apparently the result of nails driven through the front of both feet.

Blood flows from scalp   Slightly less convincing are the blood flows seen on both the front and the back of the head. These are seemingly the result of a 'helmet' containing numerous sharp pointed 'tines' that have punctured the scalp in many places, with resultant bleeding from numerous points. This has been widely interpreted as evidence of the biblical 'crown of thorns' that Jesus was forced to wear. The flows down the forehead are quite remarkable, with one forming a '3-shape' as it runs from the hairline into the left eyebrow. This corresponds in every way to a flow of venous blood across the characteristic 'pain ridges' that form on the forehead as a result of extreme agony.[15]

Blood flows from spear thrust   On the front image of the Shroud, blood can be seen issuing from a piercing wound that has entered the body just beneath the fifth rib. The fluid flow reveals that there has been a separation of the liquid into a clear and a more viscous component. This has been taken as evidence that a haemothorax took place, with blood leaking into the right pleural cavity of the chest. Moreover, the man on the Shroud must have been dead when the wound was inflicted, as it could only be after death that the blood would have separated into cellular and serous components. Such a condition would, of course, also account for the passage in John where it is said that '. . . one of the soldiers with a spear pierced his side, and forthwith came there out blood and water' (John xix, 34).

Postmortem blood flows   The lance wound appears to have bled again during the movement of the corpse, presumably after it had been taken down from the cross. The flow first collected beneath the right elbow. From there, in two rivulets, it crosses the lumbar region of the back and pools again in a second stain directly opposite the first. This is interpreted as showing how the corpse was laid first on its right side and then on the left during the preparation for burial.

Other undeniably impressive features include the position of the entry of the nails used to crucify the victim. These pass out through the wrist bones, unlike other contemporary images that show the wounds in their normal 'stigmata' positions in the palm of the hands. The thumbs are not visible in the image, which is said to correspond to damage to the median nerve by the passage of the nail through the wrist, such trauma causing the thumb to snap into the hand, rendering it invisible.[16] Scourge marks are also visible on the body of the man of the Shroud, the number, over a hundred, bearing witness to a severe whipping. These dumbbell-shaped wounds are identical to the Roman scourges used in first-century Palestine, but also, it must be said, to some medieval scourges. The scourging, together with what appears to be bruising to the face (the right cheek especially seems deformed, and the nose may be broken) mirror with uncanny exactness the indignities we are told Jesus suffered before his execution, and make it almost impossible to doubt that the image on the Shroud is that of Jesus.

Limestone and Pollen

Other non-image aspects of the Shroud go far in supporting this identification. Deposits of calcium carbonate on the Shroud have been identified as travertine aragonite, far rarer than the more common form of limestone, known as calcite. Work by Dr Eugenia Nitowski and Dr Joseph Kohlbeck have shown that the limestone from Jerusalem tombs is also composed of travertine aragonite.[17] In addition, a scanning ion microprobe analysis by Dr Ricardo Levi-Setti of the University of Chicago has revealed the Shroud calcium samples to be all but indistinguishable from the limestone of the Jerusalem tombs.[18] So while it is impossible to say that there are no other areas in the world with limestone of a similar chemical 'fingerprint', this evidence does seem to show that the Shroud fabric has been located at one period in Jerusalem, and that it was stored for some time in a vault constructed of Jerusalem limestone. Once again, these facts call to mind the story of Jesus' burial in the tomb of Joseph of Arimathea.

In 1973 a respected forensic scientist, Dr Max Frei, discovered yet another piece of pro-authenticity evidence in the form of pollen grains harvested from the Shroud. Dr Frei was the founder of the central scientific department of the Zurich police, lectured in criminology and was scientific editor of the German review Kriminalistik. He had for many years used the technique of pollen analysis to assist his criminal investigation.[19] Many plants have a restricted geographical distribution and grow only in certain well-defined habitats: in mountain forests, for example. If a crime has been committed at such a site, the presence of pollen from mountain plants on the clothing of a suspect can help to determine if he had ever been in such an area. Pollen is virtually indestructible, and intact pollen has been collected from sites more than 10,000 years old. Dr Frei reasoned that, just like a suspect's clothes, the Shroud should also have picked up pollen from whatever regions it had travelled through. In the hope of tracing these travels, he asked for, and was granted, permission to collect samples of detritus from the Shroud fabric, using lengths of sticky tape. Twelve tape samples were taken in 1973 and additional samples in 1978. At the same time, a second set of tapes was obtained by an American team, and further sampling was undertaken by Professor Giovanni Riggi using a mini-vacuum on the underside of the Shroud.

A great amount of microscopic debris was collected. This included fly-ash from power stations and metal fragments – gold, silver and bronze – presumably from the containers of precious metal which have held the relic from time to time. There was fabric in abundance: cotton, linen, wool, silk and pink nylon, this last being identical to that used for ladies' tights![20] But among all this detritus, as Dr Frei had hoped, was a veritable treasure-trove of pollen. When this was subject to analysis, it gave great impetus to the idea that the Shroud was indeed the gravecloth of Christ.

Along with a large number of pollen grains from Western Europe (which corresponds to the Shroud's known history of travel between France and Italy), Dr Frei identified many species who provenance lay much further to the east. Two pollen species derived from Turkey, in particular the Anatolian plateau. But by far the greater number of pollen species were from further east again, in Israel, with eight halophytic (salt-loving) plant species native to the Dead Sea region and a further six species characteristic of Jerusalem.[21] While there is some question as to whether each pollen can be confidently identified to the species level, given the number of species found, this is good evidence that the Shroud was, at some time in its career, present in Israel, and (though this is more doubtful) perhaps also in Anatolia. As Dr Frei stated: 'Consequently, a forgery, produced somewhere in France during the Middle Ages in a country lacking these typical halophytes, could not contain such characteristic pollen grains from the desert regions of Palestine.' This is an incontestable deduction. But it holds true only if the forgery was produced in Western Europe.

Scientific Enquiry

Despite the immediacy and plausibility of the Shroud portrait, the forensic evidence contained in the image, and the pollen and other fragments recovered from the fabric, there remained no definite scientific proof that the Shroud could be dated to the first century AD, that it did truly belong to the time of Jesus. However, one test could be applied to the cloth which would, in theory, give a cast-iron verdict on its age – carbon dating.

Discovered and developed in the late 1940s by the American chemist Willard F. Libby, carbon dating is dependent on two very simple principles. First, the carbon atom (on which all life is based) is composed of two different forms or isotopes, C^{12} and C^{14}. The former isotope is very stable, while C^{14} is subject to radioactive decay. In living organisms these two isotopes remain in a constant proportion throughout the life of the animal or plant, as a result of feeding, growth and repair. But on death, no more carbon 14 is absorbed from the environment and, as a result of radioactive decay, the proportion of C^{14} in the organism's remains gradually declines.[22]

Fortunately for those interested in dating early organic remains, carbon 14 decays at a known steady rate (it decreases by half every 5,570 years). So by measuring the amount of C^{14} still present in a sample of unknown age, and knowing the original amount of C^{14} present when the animal was alive, it is a simple calculation to determine the actual age of the animal or plant concerned. Carbon 14 dating has been used in dating literally hundreds of thousands of samples over the past 40 years, and although it has produced some real dating howlers on rare occasions[23] it is now accepted as one of the most reliable dating tools in the armoury of the archaeologist and palaeobiologist. Willard F. Libby's services to science were recognised in 1960, when he received the Nobel Prize for Chemistry for his innovative work.

The Shroud is composed of linen fibres, harvested from flax plants at an unknown date. At the exact moment that the flax fell to the scythe, carbon 14 ceased to be incorporated into the plant and radioactive decay of the isotope in the plant began. Therefore, it should be possible to tell with a very good degree of accuracy the date of the linen fibres making up the Shroud. This would give an absolute date, a *terminus a quo*, for the production of the earliest image on the Shroud.

It seemed, then, that carbon dating could at last provide a definite answer on the most crucial of all Shroud questions. Unfortunately, in these early days a large section of the Shroud material (a little under 900 square centimetres) would have been needed to perform the carbon dating. As the sample is destroyed by the test, the owners of the Shroud, the Savoy family, were understandably unwilling to sacrifice so large a proportion of the Holy Relic. Willard Libby himself approached the owners of the Shroud soon after the technique was perfected, but like several others his request was denied.

However, by the late 1980s two things had changed. With the death of the Shroud's owner, ex-King Umberto II of Italy, ownership of the Shroud had been transferred to the Holy See. Perhaps more important, the carbon dating method had been revolutionised. Professor Harry Gove and his co-workers at the University of Rochester had devised a way of actually counting the individual carbon 14 atoms in a sample, leading to results that, while just as accurate, took minutes rather than months to achieve and required relatively tiny sample sizes.[24] Pressure now began to mount on the Vatican to allow the Shroud to be dated by this method, especially when, at an international conference on the Shroud in Turin, Harry Gove called for the use of his method on the Shroud and let it be known that Oxford University's prestigious Research Laboratory for Art and Archaeology was also keen to participate.

Several meetings followed, and after much bickering over precedent and protocol (and, it must be said, accusations of back-stabbing), agreement was finally given for the testing of the Shroud on 10 October 1987. Science would at last be given its chance to solve the mystery. However, instead of the original seven laboratories originally envisaged as performing the test, only three – Oxford, Arizona and Zurich – were chosen to proceed. The remaining laboratories were excluded, for reasons that remain unclear to this day. All the 'chosen three' laboratories would use the accelerator mass spectrometer method devised by Professor Gove. The methodology of the experiment was also altered at this time. So as to avoid even unconscious bias, scientific tests are conducted with the participants having no knowledge of the samples or (if possible) the required outcome. Unfortunately, because of a lack of suitable ancient fabric with which to conduct 'blind' testing (with each of the laboratories unaware of the identity of the cloth it was handling until after carbon dating was completed), the procedure was to be undertaken with the Shroud material alone. Despite this, the fact that there would be three separate investigations, each undertaken by a laboratory of international reputation, gave grounds for confidence that the test results obtained would be accurate and reliable.

The samples were obtained on 21 April 1988: three 1.3-centimetre pieces of cloth taken from a 1-centimetre-wide strip 8 centimetres long (the remaining half of the sample has not, so far, been tested). After an expectant delay of nearly six months, the scientists were ready to announce their findings. This long delay struck many commentators as odd, considering that the accelerator mass spectrometer dating could be performed in less than a week. It was almost as if the researchers, or more likely the Church authorities, were purposely delaying the announcement, waiting for a specific time or day to reveal the findings on the Shroud. And intriguingly (in the light of my later findings) they chose to announce their conclusions to the world on 13 October, a date that coincided with a quite remarkable anniversary. The thirteenth of October 1307 was the very day that saw the attack on the Order of the Temple in France, an attack that was to result in the destruction of this powerful Order of warrior-monks and the disappearance of the embalmed head known as the Baphomet. Strangely, the only other major investigation into the Turin Shroud, the 1978 examination by members of the Shroud of Turin Research Project (STURP), was also made to conclude on precisely the same date. The choice of 13 October in both these cases has never been explained, but it can hardly have been coincidence. It looks very like a covert admission by those high in the Catholic hierarchy of some sort of Templar involvement in Shroud history.

When the results were announced it was found that all three laboratories, in the USA, England and Switzerland, had produced essentially the same date from their tests. Their combined results gave a date for the linen fibres of the Shroud of no earlier than 1260. There was a splay of possible dates, ranging from 1260 to 1390, 130 years, with a central date of AD 1325. With 95 per cent probability, the flax that produced the linen was harvested between these dates.[25] The conclusion was obvious: the Shroud was a fake. That the carbon dating married precisely with the time of the first documented exposition of the Shroud at Lirey served only to reinforce this judgement. On the basis of this analysis, the Holy Cloth was undoubtedly a sham, the work of a clever forger working during the medieval period. One of the British team, Professor Hall, was blunt in his comments: 'Somebody just got a piece of cloth, faked it and flogged it. I don't think the Shroud of Turin is of much interest any longer.'[26]

But for a great number of people, the results made the Shroud even more interesting. Many researchers refused to accept the radiocarbon dates, insisting that the evidence of the image on the Shroud could not have been fabricated. But just as many took an opposing view, believing the carbon dating to be definite evidence of fraud.

This is where the subject still stands at the present time: two opposing camps, one crying 'Fraud!' and citing the radiocarbon dates as proof positive of forgery, the other shouting equally loudly that no forger could ever have produced an image so anatomically perfect and so full of incontestable forensic evidence. And here is the dilemma, the absolute crux of the mystery. The cloth reveals the Shroud as a fake, the image proclaims its authenticity. Until now, no theory has emerged that can reconcile both camps. However, new evidence concerning the story of Jesus, and a new analysis of the Shroud itself, point to a solution that will harmonise the opposing views. And strangely, it is the undoubted medieval date for the Shroud, and its Templar connection, combined with discoveries concerning the Cult of the Head, which give the strongest proof yet that the Shroud does reveal a true likeness of Jesus.

Pope Clement VII was correct. Paradoxically, the Shroud is both 'fake' and 'authentic'. A fourteenth-century fabrication that carries upon it a genuine image of the face of Christ.

PART ONE

THE HEAD

CHAPTER ONE

JESUS AND THE CULT OF THE HEAD

Baphomet – the Forbidden Relic

ONE PART of the Templar story that had always puzzled me was the enormous secrecy that surrounded the worship of their enigmatic relic, the severed head known as Baphomet. It seemed an unnecessary precaution as, at the very time the Knights Templar were adoring the Baphomet in Chapters held at the dead of night, tens of thousands of other Christians were making pilgrimages to numerous holy sites to pay homage to the relics of an enormous cast of saints and holy men. This was the time of the medieval Cult of Relics, when the demand for sainted remains reached such a height that monks stole holy remains from other monks, archbishops took to biting pieces from sainted corpses to carry back to their own diocese, and the bodies of saints were routinely dismembered so that the benefit of their holy parts could reach the greatest number of recipients.[1] Things became so bad that the remains of saints multiplied 'miraculously'. One researcher has calculated that there are two bodies of Saint Thomas, three bodies of Saint Teilo, and that Saint Gregory is the proud possessor of four bodies and two heads![2]

But behind all this hysteria lies a genuine and deeply felt religious need. The Cult of Relics and the adoration of holy remains were actively encouraged by the medieval Church as an act of true Christian devotion. Embalmed heads and skulls were an essential focal point in much of this ritual: at least 20 heads are known to have been venerated during the medieval period, and all with the approval and active encouragement of the Church.[3] And this is the point: why, when there was no opprobrium or risk attached to the worship of the head of a holy man, was the Baphomet adored in such complete secrecy? What was it about the Templar severed head that produced such paranoia in the Knights? It was as if possession of the relic was a crime against the established Church, as if the object itself constituted a heresy. I began to research the subject more deeply. Was there any category of relic, or any specific relic that remained taboo?

Despite the licence granted by the Church to worship any and all body parts of just about any holy man, it turned out that there was one relic that remained wholly proscribed. The object that orthodox Christianity could never accept, the 'forbidden relic', was the body of Jesus.

According to Church dogma, Jesus' body had physically ascended into heaven. So it followed that there never was, nor could there ever be, any question of a relic of Christ; for the whole of Jesus' earthly body was already in heaven. The inventive medieval mind circumvented this restriction to some degree by providing various 'true' secondary relics: the crown of thorns, pieces of the 'true' cross, the nails of the Crucifixion, the hammer that drove in the nails, the pliers that removed them, and so on.[4] And later it was realised that some body parts of Jesus could have remained on earth without contradicting accepted dogma or antagonising the guardians of Church orthodoxy. And so they duly appeared: the milk teeth of Jesus, his tears, his blood, even his foreskin, removed during the Jewish rite of circumcision. It was, however, difficult to know which foreskin of Jesus was genuine – in total 13 prepuces claimed the privilege.[5]

Despite all such religious loopholes, the essential dogma remained crystal clear: Jesus had ascended into heaven in the body. No part of the adult Jesus could therefore have remained on earth. By the beginning of the fourteenth century, the Church had promulgated such a belief as sacred truth for well over a thousand years. Should anyone have discovered a true relic of Jesus, then the authority and credibility of the Church would have been undermined. It would have initiated a crisis of faith of such proportions that the whole edifice of the Catholic Church could have been swept away. Such a relic would have been perceived as a great danger by the established Church hierarchy. It would have been an even greater danger to those possessing it. They would have been swiftly eliminated, and the relic itself would never have been allowed to see the light of day.

Here, then, was a reason for the Templars' passionate desire for secrecy. If they had possessed such a relic, then all the apparently paranoid steps they took to keep their ceremonies hidden immediately become intelligible.

Could it be, then, that the Baphomet was actually the severed embalmed head of Christ? The very thought seemed blasphemous. But as I researched, I discovered that many early Christians had also denied the resurrection of Jesus in the body. And once this single dogmatic point was put aside, the problem of what *did* happen to Jesus' earthly remains became a valid point of research. The question now was: could I find any evidence that linked Jesus to a Palestinian or Jewish Cult of the Head?

This apparently simple query proved to be the starting point for a quest that drew me inexorably further and further back into history. It took me far past the time of the Templars to an era 2,000 years before the birth of Christ. To the age of the biblical patriarch Abraham and his dealings with Egypt.

Isaac's True Father?

We are all accustomed to thinking of Abraham in terms of some poor ragged nomad struggling through the desert, living in a Bedouin tent and earning a meagre living from his small flock of goats. Nothing could be further from the truth. Documents discovered in Mesopotamia in 1934 show that many of the major cities in the region were named after Abraham's forebears. It is obvious from this that Abraham and the patriarchs who followed him were no ordinary family but a dynasty of some note.[6] The fallacy is pointed up by the biblical account of Abraham (or Abram, as he was then known) visiting the Pharaoh. The Egyptian Pharaoh was god on earth, a divine being, the son of the sun-god, Ra. His presence was sacred, and an audience with Pharaoh was not granted lightly. And yet we find that Abram is able to visit the Pharaoh and is allowed to meet and talk to this human 'god'. This is something only the most august of foreign ambassadors were allowed, and it gives the lie to the commonly held view of Abram as a poor herdsman.

In fact, Abram appears to have been so highly regarded that his sister was considered a fit bride for the Pharaoh. Except that Abram's 'sister' was in fact his wife. This confusing love triangle quite literally engendered the true beginning of our story. The Bible tells us that Abram, on approaching Egypt, tells his wife Sarai that she must pretend to be his sister. The reason he gives is that Sarai is so beautiful that the Egyptian lords may kill him in order to possess her. Why Sarai being Abram's sister should make any difference is not explained. He would surely defend his sister's honour as vigorously as he would his wife's. Unless, of course, it was Abram's plan to 'marry' off his wife to his *own* advantage. At that time it would be perfectly allowable for a man to marry off a sister, whereas to do the same for a wife would be absolutely taboo.

Sure enough, no less a person than Pharaoh himself is seduced by Sarai's charms, 'and the woman was taken into Pharaoh's house', a biblical euphemism for marriage. God finds this offensive and visits various calamities on the Egyptian king until, discovering he has been duped, the Pharaoh sends both Sarai and Abram out of his kingdom. Abram does not go empty-handed, however; he had already received what appears to be a bride-price for Sarai: 'sheep and oxen and he-asses and menservants, and maidservants, and she-asses and camels.' And the Pharaoh sends him away with even more material wealth, for we are told that 'Abram was very rich in cattle, in silver and in gold'.

As the Egyptologist Ahmed Osman has pointed out, the subsequent birth of Isaac may well have been the fruit of the union not of Abram and Sarai but of the Pharaoh and Abram's 'sister'.[7] He identifies the Pharaoh as Tutmosis III. By the time the Bible was written in its present form, the Egyptians had long been cast in the role of villain, the enemy of the Hebrew race, and the truth of Isaac's parentage was suppressed. Sarai is even said to have given birth at 90 years of age, a patently ridiculous proposition, and seemingly a clumsy attempt to put as much time as possible between her bigamous marriage to Pharaoh and the birth of a son. However, several clues have slipped through.

At the very moment Abram is told by God that his wife will bear a son, God demands that they both change their names. Abram becomes the better-known Abraham. Sarai's name-change is very significant: she becomes Sarah, a name meaning 'queen'. This makes no sense unless Sarai was, or had been, married to a king.

Nor is the Bible the only ancient book that hints at Isaac's natural father. The Jewish Talmud notes that most of Abraham's contemporaries derided the claim that Isaac was his son, believing instead that the boy was a foundling.[8] Abraham's famous willingness to use Isaac as a human sacrifice to Yahweh also becomes more understandable if the two were not genetically related. A genealogical passage in the Qur'an (Sura xix, 58) seems to confirm this. It gives both Abraham and Isaac's son Jacob equal status as ancestors of Ishmael, Moses and Aaron. But if Abraham *was* Isaac's father, then Jacob (as Isaac's son) should have been numbered alongside Ishmael, Moses and Aaron, as all four are descendants of Abraham. In short, Jacob should never have been placed in the same category as Abraham. And why the reluctance to mention Isaac himself?

Abraham had seven sons, born to other women, and all older than Isaac. Yet, strangely, it is solely to Isaac that God gives his promise of greatness

(Genesis, xvii, 20). Isaac's descendants alone are guaranteed a return to Egypt. They are also promised that they will rule 'from the river of Egypt unto the great river, the river Euphrates', a dominion that precisely mirrors the realm over which Tutmosis III had ruled.

The idea that Tutmosis III was the beginning of a line of royal Hebrews also explains the prominence given to the House of David in the scriptures. The Jewish King David was a petty king ruling a small kingdom from Jerusalem in the tenth century BC. And yet the Old Testament scribes have assigned to this David an enormous realm, an empire stretching from the Nile to the Euphrates. Biblical scholars, historians and archaeologists all agree that the Jewish tribal king never reigned over such an enormous empire. They have been forced to conclude that these biblical reports are a work of fiction, an attempt to inflate the importance of a petty monarch. However, Egyptologist Ahmed Osman has shown that the realm ascribed to David is exactly that ruled by Tutmosis III. Even more telling, Osman has demonstrated that a transliteration of David from the Hebrew 'dvd', gives 'twt' in Egyptian. And 'Twt' is the first segment of the name Tutmosis. It seems, then, that there have been two Davids in Jewish history, both of them kings, and that the memory of the first 'David', Tutmosis III, who held sway over an extensive domain and fathered Isaac, has been conflated with that of a much less exalted monarch.

Jesus was also a member of the House of David. Could this mean, I wondered, that he was of the royal house of the Egyptian Pharaoh? It seemed incredible, but a number of factors pointed to this conclusion.

Jesus the Pharaoh

The New Testament tells us that the Saviour spent time in Egypt in his youth, fleeing southwards to escape the wrath of King Herod. The slaughter of the innocents which is said to have followed the Holy Family's escape (Matthew, ii, 16) has not a shred of evidence to support it. Josephus, who lost no opportunity to castigate Herod, makes no mention of it in his copious writings. Today, the reported atrocity is seen by many as a piece of Christian propaganda, a pretext, a means of explaining away the Lord's time in the land of the Pharaohs. Strangely, the Jewish Talmud agrees with the New Testament in placing Jesus in Egypt in his youth, but for a far more specific purpose than simple escape from enemies. One of the most persistent accusations in the Jewish corpus of Jesus stories is that he had spent much time in Egypt 'studying magic'. This is not so pejorative a statement as it first appears. For the Hebrews of Jesus' time, 'magic' was a name given to any religion that was not Jewish. So what we have here is a memory of Jesus spending time in the Black Land, studying the secret lore of the Egyptians.

The Jewish writings also deny the Virgin Birth of Jesus. In fact (perhaps in response to the persecution they received at the hands of the Christians), they have a number of tales concerning Jesus which are less than complimentary. Perhaps the most offensive to Christian ears is the tale of Jesus' bastardy. Here, the father of Jesus is neither God, nor even Joseph, the husband of Mary. Instead, it is claimed than another man fathered Jesus by visiting Mary in the dead of night just before she was to be married. In the darkness, Mary believed that it was Joseph, her intended, who was with her, and she submitted to his demand for intercourse. While the story therefore clears Mary of any blame for the offence, it nevertheless marks Jesus with the stigma of bastardy.[9] But what is really interesting about this tale is the name of the 'true' father. He is said to be called ben Pandira (and indeed many stories in the Talmud refer to Christ as 'Jesus ben Pandira'). But ben Pandira is not a Jewish name, so how did this name arise? The most plausible explanation gives Pandira an Egyptian origin and an extremely interesting derivation. In Hebrew the word breaks down as 'Pa-ndi-ra', which in Egyptian is transliterated as 'Pa-ntr-ra'. What is absolutely astounding is that this is a title of the Egyptian sun-god, Ra. The 'ben' portion of the name is a Jewish patronymic, similar to the Scottish 'Mac' and meaning 'son of'. So Jesus, as ben Pandira, is being identified as 'Jesus, son of the sun-god'. This epithet, son of Ra, has been an indispensable title of the Egyptian Pharaoh since the time of the Fourth Dynasty, almost 3,000 years before Jesus. Jesus, son of Ra, is in effect Jesus the Pharaoh.[10]

Two manuscripts in the Vatican Library point to the truth of this. Both contain the story of Jesus' bastardy and both have been edited by hands unknown, with sections deleted from the text. But it is not the imputation of bastardy (which one might reasonably assume to have caused most offence) which has been excised. The anonymous editor has removed only the name ben Pandira. The reason for such very specific mutilation can only be that the name itself contains important information about Jesus that certain vested interests would prefer to keep hidden.[11]

Joseph

This idea of a Hebrew royal bloodline extending back to the Pharaohs is given an enormous boost when the story of Joseph (of the coat of many colours) is considered. The tale of Joseph as a lowly slave sold into bondage and who is raised to the status of second-in-command of all Egypt is familiar to most people. His elevation to the Egyptian nobility is said to have occurred on the strength of Joseph's interpretation of a single dream. But a moment's reflection reveals that this explanation does not hold water; it is quite simply incredible. The interpretation that Joseph gives of Pharaoh's dreams of 'seven fat and seven thin cows, and seven full and seven empty ears of corn' is that there will be seven years of plenty followed by seven of famine. For this, the Bible tells us that Joseph is immediately placed above all other courtiers; he is given the Pharaoh's ring and is told by the Egyptian monarch that 'only in respect of the throne will I be greater than you'. This is more like the welcome for a long-lost brother or kinsman than for a stranger. And yet we are asked to believe that all this is bestowed upon Joseph solely on the basis of a dream interpretation that could not be fully verified for a full fourteen years, and which could not even be partially confirmed for eight years. Surely there is a more credible explanation?

If Ahmed Osman is right and Joseph's grandfather Isaac was a son of the Pharaoh Tutmosis III, then this would explain the new Pharaoh's eagerness and his apparent irresponsibility in elevating the untried Joseph to high rank. Joseph, a slave, is discovered to be a close kinsman of the Egyptian king, almost literally a long-lost brother, and he was treated as such and recompensed for the time he had spent in prison and in servitude. But Osman has gone further and has identified Joseph with an actual historical figure, the only 'commoner' ever to be buried in the Valley of the Kings. This enigmatic figure was Yuya, who held the post of vizier under Pharaoh Amenhotep III.[12] The parallels between Yuya and Joseph are many and impressive. But what proved even more interesting, from the point of view of my quest, was a cult prevalent in Palestine at the time of Joseph, the Cult of the Head.

The Cult of the Head

Worship of the severed head has existed in the Levant for at least 9,000 years. In Palestine there have been many finds of severed heads, usually cached beneath the ground, as for example at 'Ain Ghazal, in Jericho, and at Nahal Hemar, a cave site in the Judaean desert.[13] Most of these skulls are covered with plaster (asphalt in some cases) in an obvious attempt to model the soft tissue of the face, and so re-create the individual whose skull has been taken. Several researchers in this field believe that the rite may be linked to a cult of heroes, where outstanding individuals were, after death, ritually beheaded. As such men and women were considered to be favourites of the gods, the heads may have been used as intermediaries, as a link with the supernal regions, as mediators who could intercede with the gods on behalf of those still living, and obtain for them the blessings of abundant rain, good harvests, etc.[14]

It appeared possible that Joseph (or perhaps one of the many Hebrews who later followed) had brought the secret teachings of this cult to Egypt. If so, then (as preservation of the soft tissue was deemed so important) Egyptian embalming techniques would undoubtedly have been seized upon and incorporated into the belief system. Joseph is known to have been on very friendly terms with the priests of On (he married the daughter of the high priest of On), members of the sun cult based in Heliopolis. It seemed likely that the Cult of the Head had merged with the sun religion of the priests of On to produce a syncretised system that incorporated aspects of both (this would be a quite natural evolution – the head has long been a solar symbol). The hypothesis became even more probable when I followed the story of the most famous of Yuya's descendants, his grandson 'the Heretic Pharaoh'.

Akhenaten

In a love story worthy of a Hollywood epic, the Pharaoh Amenhotep III fell in love with Yuya's daughter, whose name was Tiye. So strong was this attraction that he married her, and instead of bestowing the title of Great Royal Wife on his sister (whom, in line with tradition, he had previously married) he gave it to Yuya's daughter.[15] This provoked a constitutional crisis of unprecedented proportions, and for a very good reason. The Egyptian royal descent was through the female line – which was why the Pharaoh married his sister, and why she was given the title Great Royal Wife. It was her children alone (and the Pharaoh had many wives) who could inherit the throne. Naming Tiye as Great Royal Wife carried with it the implication that her children might one day sit upon the throne of the Black Land. And to make matters worse, Tiye was the daughter of a Hebrew. This was intolerable to most Egyptians, who less than a century before had suffered the depredations of the Hyksos, the Canaanite 'Shepherd Kings', whom they identified as kin to the Hebrews.[16] Despite this, Amenhotep III would not be moved. Tiye remained Great Royal Wife, and continued as Amenhotep's favourite. The priests of the god Amun, the state religion, protested at Tiye's status, apparently because they felt that the Hebrew Yuya had brought to Egypt religious beliefs that might threaten their supremacy. Their misgivings proved to be well founded. The fruit of this unique marriage was a Hebrew-Egyptian who was to shake the very foundations of Egyptian, and world, beliefs. His original name was Amenhotep IV, but he is known to history as Akhenaten, 'the Heretic Pharaoh'.[17]

Akhenaten's early life was charged with danger. His father, Amenhotep III, in an apparent attempt to appease the priests of Amun, had ordered that any male child of Tiye was to be stifled at birth. Akhenaten's elder brother simply disappeared, and he himself seems to have survived an attack on his life, for he later gave himself the title 'He Who Lived Long'. He was sent away from Thebes, the capital, probably to protect him from further assassination attempts, and he spent most of his childhood in the Eastern Delta, where many Hebrew relatives of his mother Tiye lived. Here, he was close to Heliopolis, the City of the Sun, and to the solar religion of the priests of On.

On his return to Thebes as co-regent, Akhenaten immediately alienated the established priesthood by his open, exuberant devotion to a new god, the Aten. Akhenaten's innovative conception was to see the Aten as a universal creator, as an unseen force that gave life to the whole of creation. The Aten was the One, the universal essence of existence. Before the Aten, all other gods (including the gods of Egypt) were imaginary deities, shams, shadow figures without substance. By Akhenaten's command, the temples of all other gods were closed, their goods forfeited, their monuments defaced. So single-minded was the Pharaoh's devotion to the Aten that Akhenaten's men scoured every monument for signs of polytheism. Wherever the word 'gods' was discovered, it was blotted out. There was, in Akhenaten's system of philosophy, room for only the One God. In brief, Akhenaten was the world's first monotheist.

He was also, I knew from my own studies in mysticism, much more than this. Occult tradition credits Akhenaten with the creation of the Great White Brotherhood, one of the first 'mystery schools', whose initiates were credited with knowledge of the universe withheld from other men.[18] It was from the Great White Brotherhood that other occult groups, such as the Rosicrucians and various Jewish mystical orders, were said to spring. The Templars, too, shared many aspects of their philosophy with such groups.

This was interesting indeed, as I knew that in these esoteric organisations the head, or heads, formed a potent symbol. Templar head-worship is an acknowledged fact, and, as I was aware from personal experience, the head plays an important part in certain Rosicrucian rituals. In the Jewish Kabbalah, God, the Absolute, is termed 'En Soph', a title meaning 'Endless' or

'Boundless'. He is also called the Ancient of Days, or Aged of the Aged, and, most significantly, is pictured as one enormous head containing within it several other heads or skulls.[19] In addition, one of the seven titles of the first *sephira*, or emanation, from En Soph 'which contained within itself the plan of the universe in its infinity of time and space, in its endless variety of form and colour and movement', is the White Head.[20] In short, the head appears to be the emblem of the creator, the ultimate, arcane symbol of the All.

The True Identity of Moses

There remained yet another twist in the tale of this remarkable Pharaoh. In 1937 the renowned psychiatrist Sigmund Freud, father of psychoanalysis, shocked the world with his book *Moses and Monotheism*.[21] The book documents Freud's belief that Moses was an Egyptian of high rank, who had embraced the teachings of Akhenaten and had led a band of Hebrew followers out of Egypt. Freud proved that the name Moses was not, as the Bible would have it, a Hebrew name meaning 'he that was drawn out of the water'; it was instead an Egyptian word for 'child'. Freud also discovered that circumcision, to most people the most quintessential of Jewish customs, was in fact of Egyptian origin. And, as he forcefully pointed out, it made no sense for the biblical Moses (intent as he was on removing his people from the yoke of the hated Egyptians) to impose on them a custom that was a defining ritual of the Egyptian race. Even the Jewish word for God, Adonai ('Lord'), was revealed as Egyptian. 'Adonai' is actually two words. 'Ai' is the Hebrew possessive pronoun, so 'Adon-ai' is more correctly translated as 'my Lord'. But what of 'Adon', what is the derivation of this word? It turns out that, transliterated to the Egyptian, 'Ad-on' becomes 'At-en', the very name of Akhenaten's solar deity.[22]

Freud showed that the biblical story of Moses was a mirror image of many similar myths. In these stories (for example, Sargon of Agade, Romulus and Remus, Perseus the Destroyer), the hero is of royal blood who through misfortune is brought up by peasants, and later, in manhood, regains his true status as king.[23] It is accepted that such tales have arisen in order to legitimise the right of the hero (who was in all probability a commoner) to the honours of kingship. In Moses' case the opposite is true: he is portrayed as a poor man's son, brought by chance to the riches of the Pharaoh's family, and then returned once again to his true people. Freud believed that this myth had the same purpose as the story of Sargon and the other heroes, but with an important difference. Moses had originally been of royal Egyptian stock, and the purpose of the myth was to remove this aura of royalty, to give him a Hebrew origin, and make him one with the people he came to lead.

Freud's reasoning is very persuasive. He claimed an analytical reading of the Bible proved his case, and that it was what he called 'the awe of biblical tradition' that prevented others from seeing what he had seen. But Freud himself was guilty of this same biblical blindness. He had theorised that a 'high official' of Akhenaten's court had led the Hebrews out of Egypt. And yet, as he himself had shown, the scriptural story revealed Moses as not simply of Egyptian blood but as a blood member of the family that 'adopted' him, the royal house of Egypt. If his theory was correct, then Moses was a true son of the Pharaoh, quite literally a 'prince of Egypt'.

The Egyptologist Ahmed Osman has taken Freud's theory to its logical conclusion. Osman believes that Akhenaten did not merely inspire an unnamed Egyptian to lead the Hebrews into exile. He insists that Akhenaten and Moses are one and the same man.[24] He has pointed out numerous correspondences between the life of Moses and that of Akhenaten, not least of which was that both men 'invented' monotheism and vehemently insisted on the belief in a single omnipotent creator to the exclusion of all other gods.

It was Akhenaten's single-minded pursuit of his faith that precipitated a series of events that mesh with the biblical story of Moses. The Heretic Pharaoh's devotion to his god resulted in a backlash from the established priesthood of Egypt. Exactly what occurred has not been recorded, but after ruling for 17 years Akhenaten simply vanishes from history. In a vengeful echo of his treatment of their gods, the priesthood attempted to totally obliterate any knowledge of his existence from the annals of Egypt. His name was cut from every monument. It was forbidden even to speak his name, and he was referred to by such pejorative terms as 'the Heretic' or 'the Rebel'.[25] Nor did the remainder of this Egyptian-Hebrew dynasty long outlast his disappearance. His brother Semenkhare ruled for only months after Akhenaten's eclipse and seems to have been murdered. Akhenaten's son, the famous Tutankhamun, also perished by foul play after a brief rule of nine years. The last of the line, Akhenaten's uncle Aye, kept a tenuous hold on power for another few years, until he, too, was done to death, by Horemheb, a general who usurped the throne and initiated the rule of the Nineteenth Dynasty.[26]

Strangely, Akhenaten's body was never found. His tomb exists, discovered in 1891 by Alessandro Basanti, an Italian archaeologist, but it had never contained the Pharaoh's body. Several other factors suggest that Akhenaten was deposed and sent into exile.[27] Other evidence points to this place of exile as being the same as that of Moses, the Sinai Peninsula. And later research has given a new rationale linking the name Moses (which Freud correctly interpreted as 'child') to Akhenaten. In an ancient Egyptian legal case, inscribed on the walls of a tomb in Saqqara, the word 'Mos' has been shown to possess a second meaning: it designates the 'rightful son and heir'.[28] This is an apt title for Akhenaten, who was heir to the throne of Egypt, had been wrongfully deposed, and whose real name it was forbidden to utter. On the death of his uncle Aye, Akhenaten would have been the last of his line, and he is believed to have returned from exile to press his case for reinstatement. However, Ramses had already usurped the throne and, faced with the overwhelming power of the Egyptian army, Akhenaten was once again forced into exile, this time taking with him the bulk of his mother Tiye's people, the Hebrews, and those renegade Egyptians who held his own monotheistic beliefs.

The parallels to the biblical Moses tale are compelling. In the Bible, Moses returns from exile to meet the Pharaoh, carrying with him a bronze serpent staff which was the symbol of Pharaonic authority. The Egyptian priests acknowledge Moses' authority, bowing down to him in submission. But the Pharaoh, backed by the army, is intransigent. After a series of miraculous plagues, Moses leaves Egypt with the captive Hebrews, en route for Canaan. This retreat, with the Egyptian army at their back, is the biblical Exodus.

If this reading of history was correct, and it had much to commend it, then it provided a link between the Cult of the Head, the mystery schools of Egypt and the occult schools that developed in Israel, many of which held esoteric beliefs concerning the head. I later discovered that one important group of Jewish mystics followed the teachings of Akhenaten, venerated the head, and also possessed a strong connection with Jesus. They were known as the Nazarites.

The Nazarites

The word 'Nazarite' derives from 'nâzîr', which signifies separation. Members of the sect deliberately divided themselves off from the rest of the populace and dedicated themselves to Adonai. Unusually for the Jewish culture of that time, the Nazarite could be of either sex. They were forbidden alcohol, and especially wine (fresh grapes were also taboo); they were not allowed to come close to dead bodies, even of their kinfolk. But by far the most rigorously enforced taboo seems to have been the prohibition on cutting the hair of the head. The biblical book of Numbers makes it plain that it is the head itself which is holy. If a Nazarite was defiled by a dead body then he had 'defiled the head of his consecration'. Atonement was made and the priest 'shall hallow his head the same day' (Numbers vi, 9, 11). For the Nazarite, the hair was merely the outward manifestation of the power that resided in the holy head.

The Nazarites as a sect are as old as Israel itself, or perhaps even older. Joseph in Egypt was given a Nazarite consecration: his head was blessed and he is called 'separate' (Genesis xlix, 26).

Judah, Samson and the prophet Samuel were all Nazarites, and there is evidence to suggest that the sect was a powerful political grouping during certain periods in Jewish history, including the time of Jesus. The Nazarites were in the vanguard of what might be termed mystical Israel, a movement violently opposed to the doctrines of anti-mystical Israel (the Sadducees and some segments of the Pharisee sect), who interpreted the Holy Books in the most literal manner and who had no time for mystical speculation or practice. So deep was the schism between these two groups that, during the first century AD, the Sadducean establishment enjoined all pious Jews of their following to exclaim three times each day: 'Oh God, send thy curse upon the Nazarites.'[29] But what I found of even greater interest was the specific religious attitude of the Nazarite community. Although they regarded themselves as Jews, were circumcised and kept the major feast days, they rejected all prophets after Moses. They further claimed that the Pentateuch (the first five books of the Bible, reputedly written by Moses) was false. There was a secret teaching of Moses, but this was known only to the Nazarites, not to the bulk of the Jews.[30] It is important to understand the significance of this: what we have here is a group of Jews who revere the head as holy, who reject all the prophets after Moses (who is to be identified as Akhenaten) and who claim knowledge of a secret teaching derived from the Heretic Pharaoh. As if this was not enough, Epiphanius, the Bishop of Constantia, tells of a sub-sect of Nazarites called Sampsaei, whose name is derived from a word for the solar disc, the same symbol as that of Akhenaten's Aten. But the Sampsaei were not simple sun-worshippers; instead they regarded the solar disc merely as an outward manifestation, as a symbol, of the universal creator. This concept is identical to Akhenaten's own beliefs.[31]

The Nazarite sect had continued until Jesus' own time, and they were linked, if not synonymous with, the groups known collectively as Essenes. Jesus himself had been crucified as 'Jesus the Nazarite' ['ὁ Ναξωραῖος'] (the title 'Jesus of Nazareth' is a mistranslation of this term). Moreover, the whole of Jesus' immediate family seem to have been deeply involved in the Nazarite cause. His cousin John the Baptist was a Nazarite, and Jesus' brother James (who took over the leadership of the Jerusalem Church after the Crucifixion) was also of the sect. Tellingly, throughout the biblical Acts of the Apostles, 'Nazarite' is the only term used for the early 'Christians', and the primitive Church has rightly been called 'the Nazarite Church'.

A pattern was emerging from this long trail of seemingly disconnected events. Isaac had been conceived as the result of a 'bigamous' marriage between the Pharaoh Tutmosis III and Abraham's wife Sarah. Isaac's grandson Joseph (Yuya) had returned to Egypt and (as a member of the 'House of David') had been elevated to the position of vice-king of the Black Land. Here, the Palestinian Cult of the Head was merged with the Egyptian sun cult of Heliopolis, later giving rise to the first monotheistic religion. Joseph's grandson Akhenaten attempted to foist this belief in the one god on to the Egyptian populace, with the head cult known only to those initiated into the deeper mysteries. Unfortunately, the common people were too attached to their pantheon of jackal- and ram-headed gods. Akhenaten's beliefs were rejected, he was forced to abdicate and to flee to Palestine, taking with him the Cult of the Head, whose mysteries were perpetuated for over a thousand years by the Nazarite sect. Jesus was named as the son of Ra, he was a scion of the House of David, that is, a true priest-king of the Egyptian royal line. He was also a leader of the Nazarites, a sect that revered the head and held to the precepts of Akhenaten. It followed, then, that Jesus' links to the Cult of the Head would have been strong. And the esteem in which he was held might well make him worthy of the ritual of head-preservation.

CHAPTER TWO

THE HEAD OF GOD

I F THE CULT of the Head had survived into Jesus' time among the Nazarites, and members of this sect continued the ritual removal and embalming of heads 'touched by God', then (as the leader of the sect, and as the acknowledged Messiah) it is logical to assume that Jesus' own head would have been taken after his death and kept as a relic. Logical, yes. But is there any proof that such a bizarre ritual had taken place? To my surprise, I discovered that the evidence was there, and that perhaps the most compelling proof was to be found in the New Testament itself.

In the Gospel of Saint John we are told of the events that occurred immediately after Jesus' death and the laying of his body in the nearby tomb of his uncle, Joseph of Arimathea. Joseph and Nicodemus (a fellow member of the Sanhedrin, the Jewish Council) visited the tomb on the night of the Crucifixion, presumably to attend to the laying out of the body. 'And there came also Nicodemus, which at first came to Jesus by night, and brought a mixture of myrrh and aloes, about an hundred pound weight' (John xix, 39). This is an enormous quantity of spices, and the question arises: did aloes and myrrh form a part of the laying-out procedures in an orthodox Jewish burial? The answer is an emphatic no. According to Dr Joseph Zias, the foremost authority on Palestinian first-century burials, 'spices formed no part of orthodox Jewish burial at that time, not a single ounce, much less the amount mentioned in the New Testament'.[1] So, whereas we have all been brought up to regard these verses as the story of a Jewish community honouring its leader with the proper and time-honoured rites of burial, in truth it is nothing of the sort. It is a very improper burial, using spices that were invaluable in the ritual of embalming. Given these facts, we are entitled to ask: just what was happening here?

An additional complication is that both Mark and Luke report that Mary Magdalene, Mary mother of James, and others also 'brought sweet spices that they might anoint him'. This occurred on the day after the Sabbath, three days after Jesus' Crucifixion. It is obvious from this that the women did not know that Joseph of Arimathea and Nicodemus had previously visited the sepulchre with almost 50 kilogrammes of aloes and myrrh, for otherwise they would have been aware that their work was unnecessary, and that spices had already been brought to the body. We have to conclude that these women, close confidantes of Jesus (the Magdalene may well have been his wife), were therefore unaware of the ritual that had been carried out by Joseph and Nicodemus. These reports also show that, while the women were unable to perform their rites because of the beginning of the Sabbath, and keeping to the Jewish law had waited until after the Sabbath to bring spices, Nicodemus and Joseph had visited the sepulchre, and performed their work there, *during the Sabbath*, actions that were anathema to an orthodox Jew. But just what sort of secret ritual required 100 pounds of embalming spices?

A medieval manuscript, the *Continuation* of the Old French *Perceval*, seems to hold the answer to this riddle. This book draws heavily on the Gospel of Nicodemus, one of the Apocryphal Gospels excluded from the New Testament. The Gospel of Nicodemus informs us that after Christ's Crucifixion the Jews imprisoned Joseph. However, he miraculously escapes his incarceration and returns to Arimathea. The *Continuation* takes up this story and tells us that the Jews (presumably Joseph's enemies in the Sanhedrin) took counsel together and decided to banish both Joseph and Nicodemus. Then, astoundingly, it goes on to say that:

> Nicodemus had carved and fashioned a head in the likeness of the Lord on the day that he had seen Him on the cross. But of this I am sure, that the Lord God set his hand to the shaping of it, as they say: for no man ever saw one like it nor could it be made by human hands . . .[2]

When I first read this it was hard to suppress a shudder of excitement. Jesus the Nazarite, whose sect believed that the head is holy, is crucified. Two of his followers visit the sepulchre at the dead of night, carrying large quantities of embalming spices. The body vanishes, and one of the two men has in his possession a head of Jesus, so lifelike that 'the Lord God set his hand to the shaping of it . . . nor could it be made by human hands . . .'. The conclusion seemed obvious. If God himself had made the head, if it could not be made by human hands, then this 'carved' head of Jesus must be real. It was, quite literally, the head of Christ.

The Templar Connection

It was one thing to discover that Jesus' head had been preserved as a relic in the first century AD. It was quite another to link this to the Baphomet, the embalmed, severed head worshipped by the elite of the Order of the Temple. A space of over a thousand years divided the two relics. Baphomet was a corruption of the Moorish word 'Bufihimat', meaning 'Father of Wisdom'.[3] Was it possible to show that 'Baphomet', the 'Father of Wisdom', was a title bestowed by the Templars on the head of Christ? Could a connection be found?

The answer lay in the full title of the Templars, the Order of Poor Knights of the Temple of Solomon, and the story of the Order's inception during the First Crusade. The chroniclers recount that after Jerusalem fell to the Christian armies, nine knights, led by one Hugues de Payens, presented themselves before King Baldwin of Jerusalem. They asked permission to form an order of warrior-monks, whose job would be to keep safe the pilgrim routes between the Mediterranean coast and the Holy City. Baldwin acceded to their request and granted them lodgings in the al-Aqsa Mosque, on the site of the Temple of Solomon.[4] This seemed a plausible enough tale, but what followed made the story more than a little suspect. Contemporary annals insist that the Holy Land at that time was a very dangerous place, with kidnapping and killing of pilgrims an almost daily occurrence.[5] And yet for nine long years the knights of this fledgling Order, ostensibly formed solely to protect these same pilgrims, took in no new members! Nor is there any record of the nine original knights scouring the highways of the Holy Land in search of Christian travellers at the mercy of Islamic raiders. What was so important, so essential, that it caused the nine to remain in seclusion, ignoring the outside world, on the site of the Temple of Solomon?

The Templars were apparently less interested in events above ground than in what was to be found beneath the sacred soil of the Temple Mount. There is no doubt that there are caves and tunnels cut from the rock beneath the temple,[6] and that several of them are the result of Templar excavations. Exploration undertaken in the 1860s resulted in the recovery of several Templar artefacts from these tunnels: spurs, a sword hilt, a spearhead and a lead pattée cross, the last an incontrovertible symbol of the Poor Knights.[7]

It seems clear that the protecting pilgrims' story was just that – a cover story to mask covert excavations beneath the temple. There is evidence that the Templars were controlled, at least in part, by a shadowy group who have achieved fame in our own time as the Priory of Sion but who were probably known in the twelfth century as the Order of Sion.[8] These men, and in all likelihood the leaders of the Templar Knights, seem to have been privy to a secret, to have had special knowledge of a treasure of some sort that had been secreted beneath the temple. This hoard had been untouchable for over a thousand years following the expulsion of the Jews from their homeland, after the destruction of the temple by the legions of Titus in AD 70. Several of the members of the Order of Sion would appear to have had Jewish ancestry, and to have been linked to the House of David. In this context, I found it very telling that the leader of the Templars, Hugues de Payens, had chosen as his heraldic symbol three severed heads.[9]

A further item of evidence strengthened the severed head connection. It made me believe that the Templars had discovered the 'treasure' they sought beneath Mount Mariah, and that it was none other than the relic I had named the head of Christ.

Sometime after the excavations on the Temple Mount, certain members of the Order began to be buried in a manner wholly out of keeping with Christian orthodoxy. Throughout Christendom, whether wrapped in a rough winding sheet or lying within a bejewelled sepulchre, the body was always buried intact.[10] To defile or disfigure a cadaver was regarded as a great sin. And yet certain Templar corpses of high rank were buried in a purposely mutilated condition, in tiny coffins that seemed more appropriate for a child than a full-grown warrior. The reason for such small coffins was that the bodies were beheaded and partially dismembered. The lower limbs were removed and placed crosswise on the trunk with the severed head laid just above them. This macabre pattern is, of course, the skull and crossbones, a motif which is prevalent on Masonic and Templar tombstones. The symbol is quite ancient, and several medieval stories use the device in tales that include a severed head. In addition, the story often includes a Templar. Antonio Sacci de Vercelli's version of these tales was told to a papal commission in 1311. A Templar Lord of Sidon, Matthew de Sarmage, was said to have lost his heart to an Armenian lady, who unfortunately died before he could consummate his love:

> . . . he secretly had intercourse with her when she was dead in her tomb, on the night of the day on which she had been buried. When he had done this, he heard a voice saying to him: 'Return when it is time for birth, because you will find a head, offspring to you.' And I

have heard that, when the time was passed, this same knight returned to the tomb, and found a human head between the legs of the dead woman. Again he heard a voice saying to him: 'Guard this head, because all good things will come to you from it.'[11]

This is a distinct echo of the Templar Baphomet, which was also said to be a provider of all good things.

Just as important, Templar burials mimic the manner in which, in Masonic lore, Hiram Abif was interred. According to tradition, Hiram Abif, builder of the Temple of Solomon, had died rather than reveal the deepest secrets of his Craft to three Masons not yet initiated into the mysteries. They murdered him and tried to bury the body to hide all evidence of their crime.[12] But I was able to discover a further part of the story, told only to Masonic initiates. In this, we are informed that, because the ground was stony, the murderers were forced to dismember the body so that it would fit a shallow grave. This is quite obviously a narrative twist designed to introduce the symbol of the severed head. The dismemberment was identical to that of the Templar burial rite, with head and legs removed, and strengthens the theory that the Templar interments were themselves a symbolic representation of the severed head. Moreover, Hiram Abif is known in Masonic circles as 'Son of the Widow' – and this same designation is also used for Jesus.[13]

To sum up, the Templars had dug beneath the Temple of Solomon for nine years in search of something that had lain hidden for over a millennium, a 'treasure' buried beneath the temple before its destruction in AD 70. It is clear that they did discover something: within a very short space of time the Order had become extremely rich in both gold and land. But they seem to have discovered something more than secular treasure, something that altered their world view and led them to change the way in which they prepared for death. Shortly after the excavations, high-ranking Templars began to be buried with their heads removed and placed on their chest. And they began to worship an embalmed severed head, long-haired and bearded, which they kept with great reverence and in the deepest secrecy. These facts were obviously related. It appeared that the best 'fit' for this constellation of events was that the Templars had discovered (along with secular treasure) a religious treasure of great worth, a relic in the form of an embalmed head. I believed this to be the head of Jesus, who we now knew was a Nazarite, a member of a sect that revered the head as holy, and whose own burial had been anything but orthodox. However, by the time of its discovery, the power of the Catholic Church and the inflexibility of its dogma of the physical resurrection of Jesus had made the head – the most important of all Christian relics – a liability. It was the Forbidden Relic, whose existence could only be hinted at, whose worship carried the risk of death, whose veneration could take place only in the strictest secrecy.

Heresy

In 1291 Acre, the last Christian fortress in the Holy Land, fell to the Mamluk Turks.[14] The disaster of this defeat, and the Christians' total expulsion from the Holy Land by the Saracens, was a colossal jolt to Christian self-esteem and confidence. The fight against the Turks had been seen as a simple fight of Christian 'good' against Saracen 'evil'. That God had allowed evil to triumph, had given to the infidel Turk every last inch of the Holy Land, was a heavy blow indeed, and many sought a scapegoat. They found it in the Templars, claiming that the Order had actively colluded with the Turks to bring about the downfall of the Christian cause. Such accusations were, of course, false. The accounts of the knights' stubborn resistance to the advance of the Turks, the countless tales of Templar heroism in the face of overwhelming Saracen numbers, all gave the lie to the accusations of treachery. But the disaster had lost the Templars their defining role as defenders of the *Terre Sancte*. By the late thirteenth century there was widespread resentment in most sections of the population against the Templars' continuing wealth and privileges.[15] That the Poor Knights remained exempt from tithes and taxes, that they still possessed vast holdings in land and property, and that they remained haughty and proud despite their failure to protect the Holy Land, all this fed the bitterness of the majority of Christendom and made the Order an easy target for attack.

Compounding these resentments were the rumours of the Order's heresy which, by 1300, were circulating widely throughout Europe. The Templar insistence on secrecy allowed imagination to run riot, and tales of necromancy, idol-worship and the conjuration of devils abounded.

All this played into the hands of the Order's detractors, and especially of one man, Philip le Bel, the king of France. Philip had his own reasons for wishing to see the demise of the Poor Knights. Although he had systematically despoiled both the Jews and the Lombards of his kingdom, confiscating all their wealth, ruinous wars had pushed his realm to the brink of bankruptcy.[16] The almost limitless wealth of the Templars was a tempting prize. Although he made show of friendship to the Order, by the beginning of the fourteenth century Philip was secretly planning to compass its destruction. And the weapon he chose as most effective against the Templar Knights was the Holy Inquisition, acting on a charge of heresy.

There is much reason to believe that these accusations were not simply fabrications of the French king and other enemies of the Order, but were at least partly based in fact. At least one informant had carried his story of Templar misdeeds to other royal ears before informing the French king.[17] On 24 August 1307 the incumbent Pope, Clement v, wrote to King Philip saying that, when he first heard the accusations, he simply would not allow himself to believe them. But since then he had 'heard many strange and unheard-of things', and he had determined to set up an enquiry into the Templar Order. But there was no hurry. The Pope pronounced himself unwell and let Philip know that he would be unable to receive messengers until 14 October.[18]

This information seems to have spurred Philip le Bel into action. The last thing he wanted was for the papacy itself to conduct an enquiry into Templar misdeeds. What Philip desperately needed was the wealth of the Order, and he could only get his hands on that if he alone had control over the proceedings. Unknown to Pope Clement, and less than a month after his letter to the French king, Philip le Bel sent sealed orders to his agents throughout France. They were not to be opened until 13 October, and their contents were then to be put into effect immediately. The orders contained instructions for the arrest and imprisonment of every Templar throughout the realm of France.

Perhaps because of the experience gained in the earlier arrests of Lombards and Jews, the putsch against the Templars worked perfectly. At first light on Friday 13 October, a date ever since regarded as synonymous with misfortune, the gates and doors of the Order's properties were broken down and all Templars, from the Grand Master Jacques de Molay to the lowliest probationer, were taken into custody. The arrests were made in the name of the Inquisition by the Chief Inquisitor of France, Guilliaume de Paris. But this was simply to perpetuate the convenient fiction that the arrests had the sanction of the Holy Father. In fact, Guilliaume de Paris was a creature of the king (he acted as the royal confessor) and was obeying Philip's commands.[19]

Accusations and Confessions

The charges the prisoners faced were extremely detailed. There were 120 Articles of Accusation lodged against the Order of the Temple. They included the standard litany of 'witchcraft charges': denial of Christ as God, spitting or urinating on the cross, obscene kisses, and worshipping a demonic apparition in the form of a cat. But more especially, they included accusations of head-worship, recounted in such detail that it is apparent that the accusations stem from definite evidence presented to the court before the arrests were made. No fewer than 15 items pertain to head-worship, the number attesting to the importance placed on this particular sin by the king and his minions. It is worth reviewing several of these:

> Item, that in each province they had idols, namely heads . . .
> Item, that they adored these idols, or that idol, and especially in their great chapters and assemblies.
> Item, that they venerated [them].
> Item, that [they venerated them] as God.
> Item, that [they venerated them] as their Saviour . . .
> Item, that they said the heads could save them.
> Item, that [it could] make riches.
> Item, that it gave them all the riches of the Order.
> Item, that it made the trees flower.
> Item, that [it made] that land germinate.
> Item, that they surrounded or touched each head of the aforesaid idols with small cords, which they wore around themselves next to the shirt or the flesh.[20]

Several points follow from this. The cords mentioned are characteristic of many gnostic dualist sects, such as the followers of Zoroaster and the Cathar Christians (contemporaries of the Templars and themselves suppressed with hideous cruelty). This would point to the Templars actually being 'heretics', at least as far as the orthodox Church of the time was concerned. In addition, the 'magical' attributes of the head echo with great precision the stories of severed holy heads from long before the time of Christ. Finally, the mention of the head being worshipped '. . . in their great chapters and assemblies' points to the fact that (as in all initiatory groups) the central secrets were known only to an elite, to those who had proved themselves worthy of being admitted to the mysteries. This is confirmed in Philip le Bel's orders for the attack on the Templars. The 'idol' was:

> a man head with a large beard, which head they kiss and worship at all their provincial chapters, but this not all the brothers know, save only the grand Master and the old ones.[21]

This description of this head, the Baphomet, was added to by the many statements made by the captives to the Inquisition. The Templar Etienne de Troyes has given perhaps the most detailed description of the relic and the ritual attending it:

. . . and at the prime of night they brought a head, a priest carrying it, preceded by two brothers with two large wax candles upon a silver candelabra, and he (the priest) put it upon the altar upon two cushions on a certain tapestry of silk, and the head was, as it seemed to him, flesh from the crown to the shape of the neck with the hairs of a dog without any gold or silver covering, indeed a face of flesh, and it seemed to him very bluish in colour and stained, with a beard having a mixture of white and black hairs similar to the beards of some Templars. And the Visitor (Hugues de Piraud) stood up, saying to all, 'We must proceed, adore it and make homage to it, which helps us and does not abandon us', and then all went with great reverence and made homage to it and adored that head.[22]

Of great interest is the fact that almost all the brothers confirm the head as being long-haired and bearded. Templar researcher Noel Currer-Briggs has shown that, like most medieval men, the Knights abhorred long hair as effeminate, 'so the length of the idol's hair was remarkable for this, if for no other reason'.[23] Had the idol been a contemporary fake, it would undoubtedly have mirrored the Templars' own preconceptions. This is good evidence for its antiquity, and for it having come into the Knights' possession by some means other than forgery. That the relic's long hair did not result in its rejection by the Order reveals that the identity of the head was regarded as extremely important to the Poor Knights. And their position as Milice de Christ, as Soldiers of Christ, makes it likely that this importance was connected in some way with Jesus himself.

The number and detail of the confessions (many extracted under torture) made some papal response inevitable. It was slow to arrive, but at the Council of Vienne in October 1311 Pope Clement finally called for the suppression of the Order, backed by the attendance of Philip le Bel and an armed contingent of his soldiery. Despite this, the decision was by no means unanimous, and Pope Clement was forced to take the almost unprecedented step of threatening excommunication on any members of the council who voiced dissent.[24]

Ordeal by Fire

The wheels of papal justice ground slowly on, and it was not until another three years had passed that the final act of the drama of the Templars was staged. On 14 March the Grand Master of the Temple,

Jacques de Molay, and three of the Order's high officials were led forth to hear their fate.

It was in the nature of a show trial: the authorities confidently expected the prisoners to confirm the guilt of the Order and meekly to accept their sentence of 'harsh and perpetual imprisonment'. But to general consternation the Grand Master recanted his confession and proclaimed the innocence of the Order of the Temple. He had confessed:

> . . . only to save myself from terrible tortures by saying what my enemies wished me to say. Other knights who have retracted their confessions have been led to the stake; yet the thought of dying is not so awful that I shall confess to foul crimes which have never been committed. Life is offered to me but at the price of infamy. At such a price, life is not worth having. I do not grieve that I must die if life can be bought only by piling one lie upon another.[25]

Two of the remaining Templars refused to speak, but the third followed the Grand Master's lead, repudiating his own confession and endorsing Jacques de Molay's words. This man, the Preceptor of Normandy, knew that with his action his death by burning was now certain. Of his own volition he chose to brave death by fire. He was Geoffrey de Charnay, the uncle of the first known owner of the Shroud of Turin, the relic that Margaret de Charnay stated was 'conquis par feu'.

With the death of the two men the Templars disappear from history. All that remained was for the victors to divide the spoils. To King Philip's anger and surprise, the Pope decided that all the lands and property of the Temple should be handed over not to the French Crown but to another Order of warrior-monks, the Hospitallers. Nevertheless, Philip still managed to do quite well out of his treacherous adventure: he demanded and received from the Hospitallers 'compensation' totalling 310,000 *livres tournais* (medieval currency), an absolutely enormous sum for those times.[26]

This was very welcome to the French Treasury, but it did not compare to the vanished wealth of the Order of the Temple. Despite careful and sustained investigations, very little of the Templar treasure was ever discovered. The copious records and the rule of the Order likewise disappeared. Moreover, and notwithstanding the most detailed search, there was also no sign of the Baphomet, the severed head that had done so much to bring about the downfall of the Poor Knights. What had become of the Templar treasure, and what of the head of Christ? If it was not in France, where was it?

Escape from France

Given the Templars' deep involvement, for more than 200 years, in the intrigues of Levantine politics, it is certain that the Order would have had spies set among Philip le Bel's courtiers, and that certain brothers in the Order would have been forewarned of the impending attack. It appears that these men, the illuminati of the Order, had time to prepare an escape plan. Land and property could not be moved, nor was it possible to alert the mass of the Templar soldiery without betraying to King Philip that his plans were known. But the treasure, records and relics of the Order were portable. According to the testimony of Templar Jean de Châlons, they were moved out of Paris under cover of darkness in three heavily laden carts accompanied by a guard of 50 knights.[27] The carts were taken to the Templar naval base of La Rochelle, and their contents stowed on board a fleet of 18 galleys, which set sail immediately into the dark reaches of the Atlantic.

This fleet seems to have acted on a prearranged plan. A small number of the galleys headed south for the Templar headquarters at Tomar in Portugal. The remainder turned their prows towards the Pole Star and sailed north.[28] Their destination was Scotland, and for a very good reason. The Pope's men, the Holy Inquisition, were on the Templars' trail, and the whole of Christendom (in theory at least) owed allegiance to the Holy Father at Rome. No matter how powerful, Christian rulers would find it hard not to accede to demands that the Knights of the Temple and all their possessions be given up to the papal authorities. Scotland was the exception. Because of his part in a murder committed before the high altar of Dumfries Church, the king of Scotland, Robert the Bruce, had been declared excommunicated. Scotland was the only nation in Christendom where the Pope's writ did not run, where the Templars could, at least for a while, find a safe haven.[29]

They would not arrive in Scotland empty-handed. Apart from the treasure they carried, the Templars possessed something of far greater worth to the Scottish king – skill in arms. Robert the Bruce had only recently declared Scotland's independence, and he was being hard pressed by the superior forces of England, led by King Edward II, who was intent on re-establishing his suzerainty. What Bruce needed more than gold and silver was men, men trained to war. And with the Templars he received an influx of the most formidable fighting men in Europe, a chivalry scornful of death, whose bravery was renowned throughout the civilised world. And it wasn't long before he found a use for them.

Bannockburn

In a brilliant series of small campaigns, Bruce had reduced the English presence in the central lowlands of Scotland to a single fortification – Stirling Castle. This was a disaster for the English. If Stirling fell, their attempt to reconquer the Scots might be set back for decades, or even lost for ever. Edward II led an army northwards, and the Scots did not impede his advance until he was almost within sight of Stirling Castle. Bruce drew up his forces in schiltrons (hollow circles of pikemen) across the road to Stirling at a ford on the River Bannock. With forest on one side and marsh on the other, there was no way for Edward to reach Stirling except through the Scottish forces. Battle was joined on 24 June 1314. The first English mounted attacks were beaten off, the fighting continuing until nightfall, when both forces withdrew to their camps. At sunrise the following day the English were astounded to see the Scottish pikes advancing on them – – until that time it was regarded as essential that troops of pikemen simply held their ground and awaited the onslaught of the heavy horse. When the Scots stopped their advance and knelt briefly in prayer, Edward is said to have cried out that they were kneeling for mercy. An English knight, more experienced that his king, answered: 'For mercy yes, but not from you; from God for their sins. These men will win all or die.'[30] Battle was joined, and the combat lasted most of the day, the advantage swaying from one side to the other. It was impossible to say who would emerge victorious.

It was at this point that tradition relates that a Templar contingent arrived and bore down on the English ranks.[31] The sight of the most feared warriors in Christendom, fresh for battle when they themselves had spent two days in the field, sent a shiver of terror through the English host. Edward, with 500 knights, was one of the first to turn tail. Seeing their king leave the battle, the English army wavered and then broke, fleeing for their lives. This one victory assured Scottish independence for generations to come.

Rosslyn

A hundred and twenty-six years after the Battle of Bannockburn, a Scottish noble began work on a chapel at Rosslyn, a small village to the south of Edinburgh.[32] By the time it was completed it was already notorious, known by many as a building not in keeping with any normal Christian chapel. Later, in 1589, it was denounced by the Calvinist William Knox as a 'house and monument of idolatrie . . .',[33] and in truth there was much to commend in this statement. The 'chapel' at Rosslyn was quite unlike anything that had been built in Scotland before. It was possibly unique in the history of Christian architecture. The man who conceived this mysterious building was Sir William Sinclair, a descendant of a family who provided three knights for Robert the Bruce at the Battle of Bannockburn. Some accounts claim that one of these knights, another Sir William, was Grand Master of the Temple and that he had had the honour of leading the Templar charge that routed the English. His descendant, Sir William, the builder of Rosslyn, was certainly a member of the Order, and a Grand Master of the masonic fraternity. He was a man steeped in esoteric learning, known to his contemporaries as 'Prodigus' for the depth and compass of his knowledge.

Although a rather small building, the interior of Rosslyn Chapel literally bristles with an almost countless number of carvings. Rosslyn's chroniclers emphasise that all these mysterious motifs were chosen by Sir William himself, who personally supervised the style of every carving.[34] Nothing was placed in Rosslyn by whimsy or chance; the carvings are a code in stone, spelling out a secret message to the cognoscenti. It is significant that very few of these carvings pertain to orthodox Christianity. Most are of Celtic, Templar or masonic provenance.

Most prominent among these is the Green Man, or rather the head of the Green Man. Over one hundred of these heads adorn the walls and roof of Rosslyn Chapel. This is a significant find. The Green Man is an ancient symbol representing the procreative powers of nature, the force that makes the trees flower and the land germinate.[35] These were precisely the powers that the Inquisition accused the Templars of conferring on the mysterious head, the Baphomet. Given Sir William's deep occult knowledge, it is hard not to believe that he was indicating the presence of the Baphomet and the Cult of the Head with the Green Man carvings. Even more intriguing, I found evidence that the Aten of Akhenaten is represented at Rosslyn. High in the chapel roof, hidden away and difficult to see, a representation of the sun-disc has been carved, its vivifying rays bursting forth in all directions. Below this, astonishingly, is a head of Jesus, bearded and long-haired, and beside it the manus dei, the 'hand of God'. To find such images in close proximity, and set in a spot so difficult to observe, made me believe that I was on the right track in my quest for the whereabouts of the head of Christ.

Close examination of the plans of Rosslyn has revealed that the chapel itself has been built to conform to the principles of sacred geometry. In cross-section it conceals three symbols used by the Templars: the foliated rose, the pattée cross and the Seal of Solomon. The plan view reveals even

45

more intriguing designs: the columns of the chapel mark out the sign of the triple tau, one of whose meanings is 'the Temple of Jerusalem' (figure 1a). And, indeed, many other symbols in Rosslyn point to the building

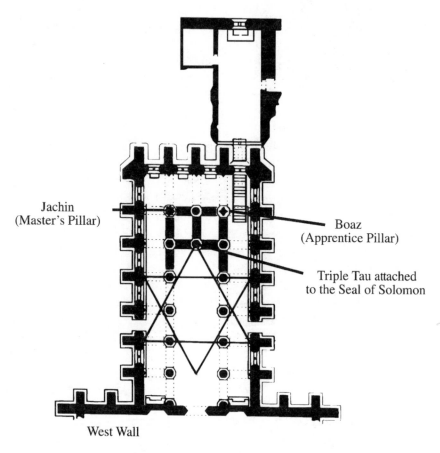

Jachin
(Master's Pillar)

Boaz
(Apprentice Pillar)

Triple Tau attached
to the Seal of Solomon

West Wall

Figure 1a: Plan of Rosslyn (after Knight and Lomas, 1996)

having been conceived as a new Temple of Solomon (figure 1b). The Templars had sworn to protect and rebuild the Jerusalem Temple, but time and circumstances had conspired to prevent the Order from fulfilling their sacred promise. Instead, here in Scotland, Sir William Sinclair, Grand Master of the Temple, had constructed a substitute Temple of Solomon as a means of fulfilling that ancient vow.

If the head of Jesus had been discovered by the Templars beneath the Temple in Jerusalem, then what more fitting place could there be for the

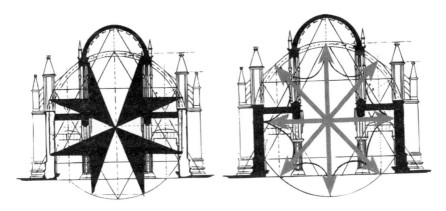

Figure 1b: Templar Geometry of Rosslyn Chapel (after Sinclair, 1992)

relic than here, in the 'new temple' at Rosslyn? The other meanings of the triple tau pointed to this same conclusion: the sign could also signify 'a key to a treasure' or 'a place where a precious thing is hidden'.[36]

The symbolism seemed perfect, and I discovered that even the name Rosslyn had its secret link to my quest. Rosslyn is the modern spelling, but for long centuries earlier the name had been spelled Roslin. According to the Sinclair family, this in turn derives from Rose-line, or Roseline, which is itself a symbolic representation of the blood or bloodline of Jesus.[37] In addition, a past Grand Master of the Priory of Sion had indicated that the secret known to that group resided on the 'Rose-line'.[38] Did he, I wondered, mean Rosslyn?

The Sancto Claros

The very name of the Sinclairs turned out to be linked to a holy head. They were known originally as Møre but had changed their name on gaining further lands in France. Their new title derived from Saint William Sancto Claros, a Scottish hermit who had ended his days in France. Saint William had been martyred, but it was the manner of his death that made me sit up and pay attention. The hermit had been beheaded. And he is usually shown as a headless figure, holding out his severed head in both hands.[39] Given the Templar connection, it seemed more than coincidence that the Møre family had deliberately taken their name from a man of great sanctity who had been beheaded. Might it be that the family were intimating their occult knowledge of another holy teacher, Jesus? Moreover, Catherine

Saint-Claire (an old spelling of the name) had married Hugues de Payens, the founder of the Templars, a knight whose coat of arms was three severed heads. Catherine had allowed the building of the first Templar preceptory outside Palestine, on lands near Rosslyn. A later Sinclair, Sir William, had been named by King Malcolm III as the Guardian of the Holy Relics of Scotland, a position which continued as a hereditary right in the Sinclairs. Such a family seemed tailor-made for the task of guarding the most precious relic of all Christendom, the head of Christ.

The Templars Disappear

Within a few years of Bannockburn, Robert the Bruce had begun to find the Templars an embarrassment. He wished to normalise relationships with other European states and especially with the papacy. But this was all but impossible while he harboured within his borders an Order of warrior-monks who had been formally suppressed by the Pope. And yet the Scottish king owed the Templars everything – at Bannockburn they had been vital to securing both his Crown and Scottish independence.[40] There was only one answer: the Templars had to disappear, to go underground. This they duly did, at the same time spawning another brotherhood of initiates, a group that in time became known as the Freemasons. The builder of Rosslyn Chapel, Sir William, is known to have been a hereditary Grand Master of the Masons, and he was reputed to hold the same title in the underground Order of the Temple.

So, we had Sir William Sinclair, a Templar and Mason, a man steeped in occult lore, building a 'heretical' chapel in Scotland crammed to bursting with esoteric carvings, many of which pointed to a knowledge of the Cult of the Head and the teachings of Akhenaten. The edifice itself was built to conform to the principles of sacred geometry, and the symbols formed by components of the building declared that this was a place of hidden secrets. The builder belonged to a family that owed its name to a headless hermit, and the chapel itself was dedicated to a saint who had been beheaded. Added to this, the Sinclair family were the hereditary guardians of the Holy Relics of Scotland. And the name of the chapel itself, Rosslyn, was in fact a corruption of an older name Roslin, or Roseline, which connected the building to the very bloodline of Jesus.

It was obvious that I needed to study Rosslyn Chapel in far more detail, and I made numerous visits to the site. Old Sir William Sinclair had been addicted to wordplay and symbolism. If the embalmed head of Jesus truly was at Rosslyn, I felt sure that he would have been unable to resist the temptation to allude to this momentous fact in some way.

My first break came very quickly. And it was so obvious, so blatant, it made me realise that those who held the hidden knowledge today were very sure that the secret was secure. It seemed unreal when I first saw it, something from a dream, and it did in fact fulfil my wildest dreams as far as proof of my theory was concerned. It was on one of the small stone shelves that function as altars on the east wall of the chapel: a crucifix unlike any I had seen. Instead of the body of Jesus, hanging crucified upon the cross, there was just the head of the Saviour, set in the centre of the cross. Jesus' disembodied head at the centre of a cross! Research at the Victoria and Albert Museum and other centres of art history confirmed what I had suspected: the cross was unique. I was unable to find even a single example of a crucifix carrying only Jesus' head. In the whole history of Christian iconography, the only place such a crucifix could be found was at the very location my researches had pinpointed as the resting-place of the embalmed head of Jesus. It was uncanny.

This gave my morale an enormous boost, but I was still faced with the problem of locating the symbols that would break the code and pinpoint the site of the relic. It was the scale and profusion of the carvings at Rosslyn that made the job so difficult. Which of the innumerable symbols was the symbol, the carving that was the hidden key to unlocking the location of the head of Christ? It would take a score of years to follow up the symbolic significance of each carving. The task seemed hopeless. I was badly in need of a helping hand. I needed a break.

It came from the most unlikely quarter. Like every other visitor to Rosslyn, I had been told that one of the columns holding up the roof of the chapel was 'the glory of Rosslyn'. Attached to the pillar was a story of an apprentice mason who, unknown to his master, had constructed a pillar of such grace and beauty that it far surpassed in skill anything his master was capable of. In a fit of rage and jealousy, the master had struck his apprentice on the forehead with a maul, killing him. In memory of this, the column carved by the murdered man had for ever since been known as the Apprentice Pillar.

I had accepted this tale uncritically until a chance remark by a visitor made me realise that the Apprentice Pillar was not, in reality, so special. It is a little more ornate than most of the columns, but certainly no more so than the Master's Pillar which stands close by. Why, then, I wondered, was the Apprentice Pillar so very special? What really made it the 'glory' of Rosslyn?

The Apprentice Pillar, like all the columns at Rosslyn, stands eight feet tall. Around its base are carvings of eight identical serpents; the capital is ornate and between the two extremities four spirals of stone leaves circle the grooved body of the pillar. The spiral itself is symbolic: in the architectural language of Freemasonry a spiral column denotes the Temple of Solomon.[41] So, the Apprentice Pillar is in effect a sanctum sanctorum, a symbolic Temple of Solomon within a substitute Temple of Solomon. It was the holy of holies. If any sacred relic was buried at Rosslyn, then this doubly sacred spot must be the most likely location. What I needed now was a sign that the object pertained to Jesus and to the sacred head.

On closer examination, the clues were everywhere, layer upon layer of visual metaphor that repeated the same message again and again.

But before I began to peel back the layers of this symbolism, I was given another confirmation of my theory. To my utter astonishment, the most prominent carving at the top of the Apprentice Pillar was one I could never have expected to see – a representation of Abraham and Isaac. The very beginning of the tale I had uncovered! And more: the head of Abraham had been destroyed by hands unknown. Mr Robert Brydon, the Templar archivist who had given invaluable help to my research, informed me that the damage within the chapel 'was very specific, not done by accident [but] for a reason'.[42] I suspected that the figure of 'Abraham' in the carving carried a clue that pointed to Egypt, and this had been the reason for its destruction. If my theory was correct, then the symbolism was very apt: Isaac, the beginning, the root of the Hebrew-Egyptian dynasty, was at the top of the column, and at its base would be the culmination of the story, a sacred relic of Jesus.

The Apprentice legend attached to the pillar was also more than it seemed. The Encyclopaedia of Freemasonry explicitly admits that it 'referred to that of the Third Degree' (that is, to the death of Hiram Abif, the builder of the Temple of Solomon, at the hands of the three conspirators).[43] But, as we have seen, the Hiram legend is itself simply a vehicle used to carry occult information on the cult of the severed head. In addition, Hiram Abif is known in masonic lore as the Son of the Widow, an appellation used for another individual – Jesus. So by attaching the Apprentice legend to this particular column, Sir William Sinclair was indicating a link to the Cult of the Head. And a connection with Jesus.

There was more. High up in the south angle of the chapel is a carving of the head of the murdered apprentice, complete with marks of the killing blow to his forehead. But such is the profundity of Rosslyn that even this carving conceals more than it reveals. Robert Brydon showed me how a careful examination of the face reveals that it has been very skilfully altered; stone has been removed to make the face clean-shaven when, in the original, it possessed a beard. As Mr Brydon pointed out, in medieval times apprentices were not allowed to wear beards, this being the sole prerogative of master masons. Therefore, the apprentice is in reality the master. And the Master is of course a synonym for Jesus.

In addition, the whole column is carved as a tree of life. And we have it on no less an authority than Saint Augustine that 'Jesus is the Tree of Life'. On another level, the serpent carvings around the base (admitted by the Earl of Rosslyn to derive from Nordic mythology) indicate that this tree of life is also the world ash, Yggdrassil.[44] It was on the world ash that, in an intriguing echo of Christian tradition, the god Odin was crucified. Once again, the carvings mutely point towards a connection between the Apprentice Pillar and the story of Christ.

But the most compelling evidence was yet to reveal itself. After many hours of study I realised that the Nordic serpent, whose name was Nidhogg, was concealing additional information. Nidhogg dwelled beneath the earth, constantly gnawing at the roots of Yggdrassil. It seemed clear that, by using this symbol, Sir William Sinclair was indicating that whatever secret the Apprentice Pillar concealed was to be found below ground. But I was wrong – the symbol meant far more than that. It indicated the identity of the treasure with surpassing skill and accuracy.

As I delved into the world of Norse mythology and the tales of Yggdrassil, I was shocked to discover that Nidhogg shared its home among the roots of the world ash with another astonishing object: an embalmed severed head.

It was the head of Mimir, embalmed by Odin after he was killed by his enemies.[45] The head became Odin's most prized possession, as it could see the future and help guard Odin from harm. Mimir's fame was such that many Nordic people regarded him as a god. But he was merely a man who great skills had gained him this reputation. The parallels with the Templar Baphomet and the Gnostic ideas of Jesus were uncanny.

But there was a final twist, a further symbolic correspondence that Sir William had woven into the web of motifs that made up the Apprentice Pillar. Unbelievably, the head of Mimir was known as the Father of Wisdom. This was the exact translation of the word Baphomet, the very title by which the head the Templars had worshipped was known.

So, it was all there: the links to the Cult of the Head, the link to Jesus, and now the connection between the Baphomet and the relic buried beneath the pillar. The 'glory' of Rosslyn was the most precious of all Christian relics – the embalmed head of Jesus. It had been held in trust by its discoverers, the Templars, for almost a thousand years. They venerated the head as, among other things, the relic of a holy king, a man who had represented God on earth, but who was not himself God. In essence, Jesus was regarded by the Templars as a divine king, an embodiment of God on earth, who had been sacrificed for the good of humanity.

But Jesus was not alone in this designation. As I was to discover, the concept of the divine king is deeply rooted in the human psyche.

CHAPTER THREE

THE DIVINE KING

The Blood Sacrifice

AT THE CENTRE of most ancient cultures lies the concept of the 'blood sacrifice', the shedding of blood in order to propitiate or please the gods and thereby ensure the continuation of the blessings the various deities were believed to bestow on humanity. From the sacrifice of children by Semitic tribes in time of war,[1] through the destruction of human captives in Mexico to the annual immolation of thousands of animals on the altar of the Jerusalem temple at the time of Jesus,[2] the blood sacrifice was universal among our forefathers.

While the practice is abhorrent to modern minds, it is important to understand how the ancients viewed such rituals. They saw the act of shedding blood not so much as one that *took* life as one that *gave* life to the universe. Blood was the essence of existence, shared by both animal and man; it signified a common bond, a spiritual link, between the two. The magical properties of this life-giving liquid could, it was believed, be transferred from one creature to another, or from one creature to the cosmos, for the benefit of the whole of creation. 'The outpouring of the vital fluid . . . is the act whereby life is given to promote and preserve life, and to establish thereby a bond of union with the supernatural order. This seems to have been the primitive conception out of which ritual and belief has emerged, involving notions of the reanimation of human gods by the immolation of animal and human quasi-divine victims . . .'[3]

In this conception, man was the steward of the cosmos, set at the fulcrum of existence, a special being whose actions made a difference to the wellbeing of the universe. His rituals, or his neglect of them, could make or mar the whole of creation.

The Divine King

One of the most important of all blood sacrifices was the ritual immolation of the divine king. The ancient conception of kingship differs radically from our modern-day secular view, which sees kings as men who, by guile and the strength of their sword-arms, have hewed a path to the throne. In earlier times the king held a far more exalted position: he embodied the psychic whole of the community; he was the divine source of all life.[4] The king was the point of contact between on the one hand his nation or tribe, and on the other the supernal regions with their gods and goddesses, any of whom might favour or frown upon the land. This laid on the king a great responsibility. As god on earth he must mirror the perfection of the gods – he must perforce be flawless. Any blemish, any imperfection would, it was believed, upset the balance between the natural and supernatural worlds and result in calamities such as disease, drought or loss of fertility in crops, herds or humankind. This is the initial reasoning that lies behind the ritual of the killing of the divine king.

In many cultures no man, no matter how wise or brave, could ascend the throne if he was marked by a defect. In Sparta an oracle warned against a lame king; in Ireland no warrior could be king at Tara if he showed the least sign of disfigurement. In similar fashion, neither the Sultan of Wadai nor the King of Angoy could take the reins of power if either revealed any physical flaw. With such a prohibition, it followed that a king who developed a defect or deformity during his reign could no longer be allowed to hold the royal sceptre. To permit his reign to continue was to risk celestial displeasure, with its resultant plagues and pestilence. In Ireland disfigured kings could abdicate, and we are told that Cormac MacArt, a great leader, immediately relinquished the throne when he lost an eye. In other lands, more extreme measures were considered necessary. The Sofala and Zulu tribes (in common with many others) put their kings to death at the first sign of imperfection or deformity.[5]

But even if a king was perfectly formed and remained free from disease and accident, no ritual or magic could for ever delay the passage of time. Old age would inevitably sap his strength, waste his sinews and turn his hair and beard grey. When the weal of the community, or even the whole world, was thought to be bound to the king's health and vigour, such a decline could not be countenanced, and we find in many ancient (and some not so ancient) cultures a tradition of killing the divine king at the first sign of his enfeeblement.

Some peoples took a more circumspect view, and (so as to ensure that there should never be any danger of his weakening) allowed the king to reign for only a set period of years. During this time he was normally worshipped as a god, and his authority was unchallenged. But at the end of his term of office he was ritually slain and another incumbent assumed the regal dignity until he, in turn, was put to death. In some cultures the body of the king was eaten as a sacramental meal, and as a way of distributing the power of the god among his followers.

The priest-king of the sacred grove of Diana at Nemi in ancient Rome was granted his title on slaying the previous incumbent. This 'King of the Woods' (rex nemorensis) retained the royal honours only as long as he could defeat all challengers to his position. He was 'the slayer who slew and would himself be slain.' Anyone, at any time of the day or night, might attempt to kill him, either in combat or by stealth. If the challenger succeeded, he became king – until he in turn became too slow-witted or weak to defeat the next aspirant to the title. According to James Frazer, this priest-king was regarded by his contemporaries as Virbius, the god of the sacred grove, and his death was seen as the death of the god, who presumably revivified in the person of the victorious challenger.[6]

At other times the king was expected to immolate himself. Perhaps the most horrific of these rituals occurred in Qilacare province in southern India. The king, at the end of 12 years, calls a great festival, at which he orders a huge scaffolding to be constructed, hung with silk, and before which all the people gather. The king:

> goes to bathe at a tank with great ceremonies and sound of music. After that he comes to the idol and prays to it, and mounts on to the scaffolding, and there before all the people he takes some very sharp knives, and begins to cut off his nose, and then his ears, and his lips, and all his members, and as much flesh off himself as he can; and he throws it away very hurriedly until so much of his blood is spilled that he begins to faint, and then he cuts his throat himself. And he performs this sacrifice to the idol, and whoever decides to reign (an)other twelve years . . . has to be present looking on at this: and from that place they raise him up as king.[7]

Similar rites appear to have existed in many parts of the world. The Khazars of southern Russia killed their kings after the expiry of a set number of years, or when a famine, drought or catastrophe in battle seemed to show that such a mighty sacrifice was demanded by the gods. Later 'divine kings' instituted the tradition of killing a substitute, in some cases allowing their proxies to take over all the royal prerogatives – including access to the harem – for a short period before being immolated. As I was later to discover, the practice of slaying the divine king in Western Europe lasted well into the Middle Ages, and at least one king of England disdained the use of a substitute and offered himself for death in this ancient ritual.

The Dying God

Such sacrifices mirrored in many ways the myths of the gods themselves. Unlike the more elevated concepts of deity (which postulate an eternal, unchanging essence at the heart of the cosmos), many early cultures believed that their gods were born, grew to maturity, aged and died, only to be reborn again in a continuous cycle. Tammuz was just such a dying god, whose religion was widespread throughout the Middle East and whose death was annually mourned, even in Jerusalem. He seems originally to have been a god of vegetation and to have symbolised the yearly growth and decay of plant life. Gradually, as agriculture became more and more important to the survival of the tribes and clans inhabiting the fertile crescent, Tammuz was increasingly identified with the staple diet of the region – corn. In Babylon a 'king' was sacrificed annually at the Festival of Sacaea in the Babylonian month of Tammuz, and it seems likely that the man immolated died in the guise of the god himself in order to ensure the fertility of the crops.[8] The Greeks also took to the worship of Tammuz, but, hearing him addressed as Adonis (a title identical to the Jewish Adonai and therefore derived from the Egyptian god Aten), used this title as his proper name. In Cyprus, this religion gave rise to a line of god-kings who claimed to be imbued with the spirit of the god, and even to take upon themselves the task of embracing Adonis's lover, Aphrodite (or rather Astarte, one name for the mother-goddess of the Middle East). The story of Pygmalion (who fell in love with a statue of the goddess) seems to mask a ritual where the king and the image of the goddess underwent a sacred marriage in which the king played the role of (and no doubt considered himself to be) the god Adonis. The king's sons were likewise considered as 'human gods', and 'Any one of these might probably succeed his father on the throne or be sacrificed in his stead whenever stress of war or other grave junctures called, as they sometimes did, for the death of a royal victim'.[9] In Egypt the god Osiris was also identified as the god of the corn; an ancient myth describes an annual human sacrifice to ensure a good harvest, and it

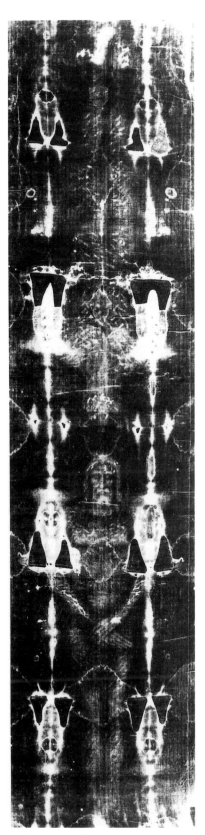

1. The back and front of the Shroud of Turin, as it appears in photographic negative.

2. The head on the Shroud, in photographic negative. Note the 'figure 3' blood-flow on the forehead, corresponding to the brow lines produced during stress or torment.

3. The Apprentice Pillar at Rosslyn Chapel. Note the spirals of leaves, Masonic and Templar symbolism for the Temple of Solomon. The leaves also denote the Tree of Life (a synonym for Jesus). The Nidhogg serpent at the base of the column points to an underground location for the sacred Templar treasure.

4. The 'Veronica' carving at Rosslyn Chapel, or a representation of the sacred embalmed head? According to a Templar informant, the identity of the person holding the object has been destroyed 'for a reason'.

is known that red-haired men (indicating a solar symbolism also) were sacrificed at his supposed grave, then burned and their ashes spread across the fields by means of winnowing fans.[10]

In Mesopotamia, and especially in Egypt, the concept of the divine king was also linked to the sun. Here, the connection between those aspects of human culture that we have been studying was made very clear. The Pharaoh, the sun-god incarnate, was hailed with the words: 'Life! Blood! Health! Pharaoh! Pharaoh! Pharaoh!' The nativity of the sun, the sun-god's rebirth, was celebrated, like Christmas, on the winter solstice (reckoned as 25 December by early Christians). Jesus' birthday is therefore also the day of the sun's rebirth. But the parallels do not end there: in Egypt, at the very moment of the sun's birth, the celebrants sent up the cry: 'The virgin has brought forth!' Moreover, the newly born sun was even figured as a young child (Harpocrates, the child-god of the winter solstice).[11] The virgin who 'brought forth' was the Great Mother, who was known in Egypt as Isis. There are many Egyptian representations of Isis with a child in her arms, the so-called Black Madonnas, several of whom have made their way into European churches and cathedrals in the guise of Mary and the infant Jesus.[12] Here again (as in the Jewish Talmud's Jesus ben Pandira stories) the person of Jesus is specifically linked to the divine king, to the sun-god himself.

Crucified Gods

One special set of dying god myths deserves our close attention: antiquity's gods and man-gods who suffered death by crucifixion. Incredibly, and contrary to the understanding of most Christians, this motif did not originate with the execution of Jesus. Over a hundred years ago Kersey Graves proved the great antiquity of the myth when he brought the story of 16 crucified gods or man-gods, all of whom predated Christianity, to the attention of Western scholarship.[13] Unfortunately, his writings are so vehemently anti-Christian (or rather, anti-clerical) in tone that he was for the most part ignored, and this vital information was passed over and forgotten. While some of the 16 crucified gods are included in the list on very slim grounds indeed (the crucifixion of Quirinius of Rome is very doubtful, for example), others are on a much firmer historical/ mythological footing.

The Greek myth of Prometheus is one example. Most people know how Prometheus was fastened to a rock by the angry Zeus and left there to suffer while an eagle fed continuously on his liver. This, however, is not the original version of the myth, which dates from around 500 BC. According to both Seneca and Hesiod, Prometheus was a demigod who voluntarily chose to die for mankind's sins. He was crucified on a wooden upright, to which were added 'arms' of wood. When, after suffering great agonies, he finally died of this torture, we are told that the earth was convulsed, that the graves gave up their dead, and the whole world was covered in darkness. The similarities with the Christian Crucifixion story are obvious and dramatic. In Syria the god Tammuz is said to have been crucified as a sin-atoning sacrifice. Again, the Tibetan Indra was put to death by crucifixion – he is depicted, like Christ, with five wounds, one in each hand and foot, and with his side pierced. Such representations of Indra are said to have been made several hundred years before Jesus was born. Closer to home, the life of the great sage and healer Apollonius of Tyana (in Cappadocia) is acknowledged as containing remarkable parallels with the story of Christ. What is seldom mentioned, however, is that this man is again said to have died by crucifixion.

There is a definite pattern here of gods and demigods who are used as atonement offerings. Their deaths appease an angry god and turn aside a terrible judgement on the sins of mankind. Many of these gods are born of a virgin; they are crucified, die to the accompaniment of earthly convulsions, are buried and rise again. Intriguingly, the Lexicon of Freemasonry states that the brotherhood secretly taught that the doctrine of crucifixion, atonement and resurrection preceded the Christian era. The same book also informs us that similar teachings were prevalent in all ancient mystery schools. This must have included the Templars from whom, as we have seen, Freemasonry derived many, if not all, of its doctrines. There is no way to escape the conclusion that, contrary to orthodox Christian teachings, Jesus' role and the manner of his death are not unique in the history of the world. Quite the contrary – this motif of a crucified god is very ancient.

The Crucified Sun

Tellingly, many of the crucified gods are linked in some way to the sun. Apollonius of Tyana was named after the Greek sun-god Apollo, which he presumably revered. The god Indra, like Apollo, drove a chariot of the sun, and Ixion, yet another crucified god, was put to death by being fastened to a wheel, again a solar symbol. The reason for this linkage is the sun's own 'astrological crucifixion' in the heavens, which is in turn symbolic of its cyclical movement across the sky, and the crossing of the equinoctial and solstitial lines. Here, the lower half of the sun's yearly course represents decline and death, while the upper half symbolises life and rebirth (see figure 2). Throughout those regions where civilisation first arose, in

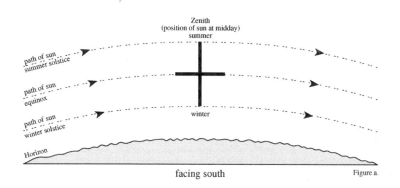

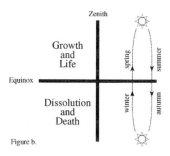

Figure 2a and b: The Cross of the Sun

Mesopotamia and Egypt, the sun was a prominent, insistent fact of life, whose superiority in the heavens was unchallenged and whose existence had to be incorporated into the religious world view. Even as early as the Fourth Dynasty of Egypt (approximately 5,000 years ago) there was already a line of divine sun-kings, reigning as the manifestation of the sun on earth and ruling from Heliopolis, the City of the Sun. The Pharaoh was regarded as god on earth and returned to his father the sun at the end of his earthly life.

To the ancients, the sun was born each morning, rose to maturity at noontide, and then declined to its 'death' at sunset. Superimposed on this was the cyclical yearly 'life' of the solar disc, waxing in power to its highest point in midsummer, then declining to death and rebirth at the winter solstice. One of the most important of the sun's 'rites of passage' in this yearly life was the spring equinox, marking its movement over the midpoint of the solstitial line into the season of fertility and growth. This 'solar crucifixion' (when the line of movement of the sun crossed the line between the winter and summer solstices exactly at its midpoint) was an event of enormous import to our ancestors. To a far greater extent than today, people's lives and wellbeing were literally dependent upon this Cross of the Sun, for without the solar heat and light nothing would grow, animals would die and mankind itself must perish. So, in a symbolic yet very real sense, the crucifixion of the sun was the cause of humanity's salvation. It seems that it was such a world view that originated and perpetuated the doctrine of one aspect of the divine victim: the crucified solar god.

The Dying God, Jesus and the Gnostics

As we've seen, this motif was repeated on many occasions up to Jesus' time. As well as his death by crucifixion, Jesus fulfilled all the criteria of a divine victim. He was 'god on earth', and he was regarded as a son of the sun (as we have seen, the Talmud names him 'Jesus ben Pandira', an Egyptian term signifying 'son of the sun-god'). He established a sacramental meal of his own flesh and blood, and he regarded himself, and was regarded by his followers, as an atonement offering, taking the sins of the people on himself, and thereby shielding them from God's wrath. Just as important, he was a willing participant in the sacrifice, which had a much more ritualistic aspect than orthodox Christianity is prepared to admit. However, although much of the Bible story of Jesus has been deleted and worked over by the apologists of orthodoxy, some clues have slipped past their careful editing. They show the occult 'mystery school' facets of the Saviour's life, and they reveal a deeply Gnostic flavour to Christ's ministry on earth.

Weeping for Tammuz

In Ezekiel's time the Daughters of Jerusalem are described as followers of the dying/crucified god Tammuz and are depicted as weeping for their dying god at the north gate of the Temple of Jerusalem (Ezekiel viii, 14). In Luke Chapter 23 a great company of women is said to have accompanied Jesus as he made his way with his cross out of Jerusalem towards Golgotha, weeping and lamenting as they followed behind the condemned man. Jesus turns on them and rebukes them for their wailing, pointedly using Ezekiel's phrase for the weeping followers of Tammuz, 'Daughters of

Jerusalem'. Archbishop Söderblom's comment on this episode is very apt: 'How strangely Christ fulfils even the idolatrous rites of weeping for Tammuz.'[14] Or perhaps, knowing what we know now, the episode is not so very strange after all.

'Paradise'

When Jesus is crucified, two thieves are condemned to die with him. One robber rebukes the Saviour, demanding: 'If thou be Christ, save thyself and us.' However, the other thief believes in the Saviour, saying that while they are robbers and are receiving due punishment for their crimes, Jesus himself is wrongly accused and has done nothing amiss. 'And he said unto Jesus, Lord remember me when thou comest into thy kingdom.'

Jesus' answer is well known: 'Verily I say unto thee, Today thou shalt be with me in Paradise' (Luke xxiii, 43). Nowadays this is taken as a simple promise to the condemned man that he will go to heaven with Jesus rather than to hell. However, we moderns fail to realise the full import of those words on Jesus' contemporaries, and the conclusions they would have drawn from his statement. For them, 'Paradise' was not a simple synonym for heaven but was instead a very specific place. 'Paradise' was the name given to the Fourth Heaven, known also as the House of the Sun. To people in the first century AD, and especially for those with Gnostic leanings, Jesus the son of the sun is promising rest in his own mansion.

Seamless Robe

The Gospel narratives show very little interest in describing any detail of Jesus' garments, or indeed those of any other character. Only in the most Gnostic of the four Gospels, that of John, do we have a description of the robe that is stripped from the captive Jesus before he is scourged. This robe, the same garment that the Roman soldiers later cast lots for beneath the cross, is expressly described as 'seamless'. The Synoptic Gospels know nothing of this seamless quality of the Saviour's robe and are content to concentrate on the drama of the narrative and not on the garment. Why, then, is the cloth in the Gospel of John emphasised as being 'without seam'? This question becomes even more pertinent when it is realised that, in the entire Bible, this one occasion is quite literally the only time that the word 'seam' or 'seamless' is mentioned.

The reason becomes clear when we look at Gnostic traditions and discover that the sacred robe of the sun cult (which was worn by most Gnostic sects: the Manichees and Cathars, for example) had specifically to be made of two pieces. This was an absolute requirement: the Gnostic robe had to be seamed. The seamed nature of the cloth was significant and was probably a symbolic reference to the dualistic philosophy of these sects. This appears to have been the reason for the Gospel's insistence on the 'seamless robe'. It is a veiled reaction, a counterattack, rebutting Gnostic Christianity's assertion that Jesus' robe was made of two pieces. In other words, very early in the Christian story, before the dead hand of orthodoxy imposed its own rigid interpretation on Christendom, the Gnostic Christians were claiming that Jesus was of their number and that he wore the 'uniform' of a sun-cult initiate when he was given up to be crucified.[15]

Lord of the Dance

In the Apocryphal Acts of John (written in the first century AD) Jesus is portrayed as singing a hymn, and dancing, with the 12 disciples also dancing in a ring around him, in the final hours before he goes out to be crucified. The dance he performs is secret ('seeing what I do, keep silent about my mysteries'), and the hymn's content is strongly Gnostic. Only part of this hymn was known before 1899, when M. R. James published a hitherto unknown and important fragment discovered in a fourteenth-century manuscript in the Vienna Imperial Library.[16] The Acts of John was one of a quintet of books used by the Manichaean 'heretics', and was used in place of the canonical Acts of the Apostles. It purports to be written by a disciple of Jesus, John the Beloved, and in it there is an account of what is said to have taken place at the Last Supper just prior to Jesus leaving for the Mount of Olives and his betrayal by Judas:

> Now before He was taken by the lawless Jews – by them who are under the law of the lawless Serpent – He gathered us all together and said: Before I am delivered up to them, let us sing an hymn to the Father and so go forth to that which lieth before [us]. He made us therefore make as it were a ring, holding one another's hands, and Himself standing in the midst He said: Answer 'Amen' unto Me. He then began to sing an hymn and to say:
> *Glory to thee, O Father.* (And we, going about Him in a ring, answered Him): Amen!
> *Glory to thee, Word [Logos].* Amen!
> *Glory to thee, Grace [Charis].* Amen!
> *Glory to thee, Spirit! Glory to thee, Holy One! Glory to thy Glory!* Amen!
> *We Praise thee, O Father; We give thanks to thee, O Light; In whom Darkness dwells not!* Amen!
> *For what we give thanks to the Word:*
> *I would be saved and I would save.* Amen!
> *I would be loosed and I would loose.* Amen!

I would be wounded and I would wound. Amen!
I would be begotten and I would beget. Amen!
I would eat and I would be eaten. Amen!
I would hear and I would be heard. Amen!
I would be thought, being wholly thought. Amen!
I would be washed and I would wash. Amen!
Grace danceth. I would pipe. Dance ye all. Amen!
I would play a dirge. Lament ye all. Amen!
The Ogdoad singeth praise with us. Amen!
The twelfth number above leadeth the dance. Amen!
The whole on high hath part in our dancing. Amen!
Who danceth not, knows not what is being done. Amen!
I would flee, and I would stay. Amen!
I would adorn and I would be adorned [clauses reversed by scribal error?]. Amen!
I would be at-oned and I would at-one. Amen!
I have no dwelling and I have dwellings. Amen!
I have no place and I have places. Amen!
I have no temple and I have temples. Amen!
I am a lamp to thee who beholdest Me. Amen!
I am a mirror to thee who understandeth Me. Amen!
I am a door to thee who knockest at Me. Amen!
I am a way to thee a wayfarer. Amen!

Now answer unto My dancing! Beholdest thyself in Me who speak; and seeing what I do, keep silence about my mysteries.

Understand, by dancing, what I do; for thine is the Passion of Man that I am about to suffer. Thou couldst not at all have understood what thou sufferest were I not sent as thy Word by the Father.

Seeing what I suffer, thou sawest Me as suffering; and seeing, thou didst not stand, but was wholly moved, moved to be wise.

Thou hast me for a couch; rest upon me. Who I am thou shalt know when I depart. What now I am seen to be, that I am not. [But what I am] thou shalt see when thou comest. If thou hadst known how to suffer, thou wouldst have power not to suffer. Know how to suffer and thou hast power not to suffer. That which thou knowest not, I Myself will teach thee. I am thy God, not the God of the Betrayer. I would keep in time with holy souls. In Me know thou the Word of Wisdom.

Say thou to me again: Glory to thee, Father! Glory to thee, Word! Glory to thee, Holy Spirit!

But as for Me, if thou wouldst know what I was: in a word I am the Word who did dance all things, and was not shamed [or deceived] at all. It was I who leaped. But do

thou understand all, and understanding, say: Glory to thee, Father! Amen!
Now having danced these things with us, Beloved, the Lord went
forth. And we, as though beside ourselves, or wakened out of sleep,
fled each our several ways.

The Gospels agree that a hymn was sung before Christ went out to
degradation and death (Mark xiv, 26; Matthew xxvi, 31), but they know
nothing, or will say nothing, of a dance. However, the Essene community,
according to Philo of Alexandria, celebrated a sacred meal, a hymn and a
dance in their rituals which correspond very closely to the Last Supper
(though without the wine) and its aftermath, as described by the Acts of
John. Philo records that in Essene communities a table was brought in by
the deacons and a solemn prayer offered to God 'that the feast shall be
agreeable to him'. On the table was bread, salt, hyssop and (instead of
wine and echoing the Nazarite prohibition) also water, 'the most sacred of
all elements in holiness'. After this holy feast had been consumed, the
community danced a sacred dance together, the exercise sometimes
continuing until dawn.[17] In similar fashion the Egyptian Therapeuts
(which seems merely to have been a different name for the same sect) also
had their mystical hymns and dances. In Philo's *On the Contemplative Life* we
learn that after a ceremonial meal: 'the chorus of men and women
Therapeuts . . . by means of melodies in parts and harmony . . . produces a
harmonious and most musical symphony. The ideas are of the most
beautiful, the expressions of the most beautiful, and the dancers reverent:
while the goal of the ideas, expressions and dances is piety.' Intriguingly,
when the dance was done 'they take their stand at dawn, when catching
sight of the rising sun, they raise their hands to heaven, praying for
Sunlight and Truth, and keenness of Spiritual Vision'. Such solar worship
also suggests a link with the Nazarites (whose philosophy was, indeed,
almost identical to that of the Therapeuts') and, through them, with the
religion of the Egyptian Heretic Pharaoh, Akhenaten.

'Amen'

Perhaps one of the more peculiar aspects of the 'Hymns of Jesus' is the
emphasis on the repetition of the word 'amen'. In contemporary Christian
usage this word signifies 'let it be', and usually, though not invariably,
appears at the very end of a prayer or invocation to the godhead. The
orthodox view of its derivation is that 'amen' was originally a Hebrew
word, an adjective that denoted 'certainty' or 'stability'. It is thought to

have evolved in normal secular conversation as an interjection, a word that emphasised the rightness or correctness of whatever had just been said, just as today we might say 'absolutely' or 'exactly'. Gradually, the use of the word became more and more restricted, until it was used only in religious ritual, normally as a positive response by the congregation to the statements of the priest.

However, the number and repetition of 'amen' in the Hymn of Jesus suggest that it may have been used in the first century in a somewhat different manner, and to have been derived from an extremely suggestive source. One researcher, pointing out that both Aramaic and Hebrew are rich in loan-words from other languages, has suggested that 'amen' has an Egyptian origin.[18] Plutarch, in his On Isis and Osiris (ix, 4), tells us that:

> ... the majority think that the proper name of Zeus with the Egyptian is Amoun ... Hacaetus of Abdera, however, says that the Egyptians use this word to one another when they call one to them, for that its sound has got the power of 'calling to'.
>
> Wherefore, when they call to the First God – who they think is the same for every man – as unto the Unmanifest and Hidden, invoking Him to make Him manifest, they say Amoun.

The hieroglyphic for Amoun or Ammon is normally transliterated from the Egyptian as Amen. 'We thus learn that in Egypt Amen was a "word of power", indeed the chief "word of power" in general theurgic use [and] used as a word of magic, for evoking the ka [spiritual essence] of a person, or as the chiefest of all invocations to the Invisible Deity.'[19] Given Jesus' connections with the Black Land, and the way in which 'amen' is used in the hymn, it is reasonable to suppose that the word functioned in this case as a power-word, to bring the deity into closer contact with the participants in the dance.

Dance or Initiation?

But was this simply a dance? The content of the hymn is extremely complex, and much of the text, taken at face value, is paradoxical. This is especially true of the 'double-clauses', such as 'I have no temple and I have temples' or 'I have no dwelling and I have dwellings'. Several interpretations have been advanced to explain these, but perhaps the most convincing is a scholarly argument, put forward by G. R. S. Mead, for the hymn being an early-Christian initiation document and not simply a paeon of praise to the Almighty. In this interpretation, at one point in the ceremony there would be two people in the ring (master and neophyte), and the chain of seemingly paradoxical phrases is construed as a dialogue between the initiate and the master along the lines of: Initiate: 'I would be saved'; Master: 'and I would save', etc.

Whatever the merits of this, there is absolutely no doubt of the hymn's occult nature and its overwhelmingly Gnostic content. When Jesus says that 'seeing what I do, keep silence about my mysteries' it is plain that this dance was not for the uninitiated. That the subject of this mystery concerned, at least in part, suffering and how to alleviate or neutralise such suffering is evident by the statement: 'If thou hadst known how to suffer, thou wouldst have power not to suffer', and by a comment later in the narrative: 'That suffering which I also showed unto thee and the rest in the dance, I will that it be called a mystery'. It seems that part of the teaching involved techniques that allowed the initiate to withstand physical pain, techniques that (from the manner in which they bore torture and the terrors of the auto-da-fé) many 'heretics' (and later witches) appeared to have mastered.

The Witch Connection

There are over a score of Gnostic words and phrases in the hymn. To take just one example: 'lawless Serpent' points directly to a Gnostic world view and signifies those men and women who are of this world, who are under the rule of Generation (reproduction and carnal birth) as opposed to the Gnostic way of Regeneration (or spiritual birth). Mankind was conceived as being a 'soul' entombed in a prison of flesh; the body was part of the material world created not by God but by the Demiurge, a lower god whom the Gnostics equated with Jehovah of the Old Testament. Pandering to the delights of the flesh, having children, being physically 'in love' – all these were believed to tie the soul down in the realms of matter and prevent it from returning through the regions of the Seven Powers to its home in the Ogdoad, the Eighth Heaven. The Church father Epiphanius quotes a Gnostic formula designed to free the soul after death from these malign influences:

> The Lord hath revealed to me the words the soul must use as it ascendeth up into Heaven, and how it must make answer to each one of the Celestial Virtues: 'I have known myself, I have collected myself from all parts, neither have I begotten sons to the Ruler of the World

[the Demiurge]. I know thee who thou art, for thou art one from above.[20]

Without such formulas, it was believed that the soul would be swallowed up by the great dragon of this world and 'excreted', reborn into the material world.

As described in the Acts of John, this ring 'dance' of Jesus and the disciples, of 12 initiates with the master in the centre, immediately and irresistibly calls to mind the European 'witch' ring-dance of the Middle Ages. Here, 12 coven members performed a ring-dance around the 'devil', representing God on earth.[21] This in turn links to the far older dance around a phallic central stone, or around a representation of a god. The Gnostic form of the dance is imbued with additional deeper meaning. The 12 in a circle signified the zodiac. With the master at its centre, the ring also represented a circle and point, a mathematical device of occult significance. In addition, the outer movement of the 12 introduces a solar meaning, with the coven (of 12) dancing around the master, who represents the god (or as the adherents of medieval Christian orthodoxy would have it, the 'devil'). I was greatly interested to discover that, in the witch-dance, there is evidence that the individual occupying the place that the Acts of John gives to Jesus (the 'god' in the centre of the coven) was on certain occasions sacrificed.[22]

From all this it appeared to me that the death of Jesus, far from being a unique event, was instead a link in a chain of ritual that led back to the time of the Egyptians and to other ancient cultures. That it was an important link was evident by the manner of his death – crucifixion. It seems that only the greatest and most worthy of such gods on earth could atone for the sins of mankind by undergoing the death on the cross, and such events were extremely rare. Other, lesser gods died by cleaner, faster and more 'humane' means. Nevertheless, they were still put to death as an essential part of the ritual. And if the trail of this ritual extended from Jesus back to the time of the Pharaohs, I discovered that it also moved forward past the first century into at least the Middle Ages. A king and a beatified prelate both chose to die by this ritual, and to fall either by the arrow or by the sword.

CHAPTER FOUR

BY ARROW AND BY SWORD

A S 'ORTHODOX' Christianity slowly gained the ascendancy, the numerous variations of the sun-cult 'heresy' were gradually driven underground. This included Gnostic Christianity, of which I believed certain sects carried as a central tenet a knowledge of the Cult of the Head. The clandestine existence they were forced to adopt was relatively easy for a mystery religion, in which initiation and secrecy were necessary parts of its world view. But periodically, over the centuries, the teachings resurfaced in wave after wave of heterodox thought, in the Bogomils, in the followers of Mani, in Massalians and Paulicians and latterly in the Cathar heresy of the twelfth and thirteenth centuries.[1] This latter movement commanded the loyalty of many adherents, especially in southern France, and it came close to toppling the overarching power of the Catholic Church in that region.

These diversions from orthodoxy were put down with increasingly Draconian measures. Although still regarded as 'sins' by the Church, in the first millennium many 'pagan' beliefs were treated simply as 'superstitions'; they sometimes required quite severe penances but were rarely regarded as capital offences. Not until the end of the thirteenth century did pagan rites begin to merit the death penalty as a matter of course. When this harsh ecclesiastical stance was taken, the most prominent Gnostic sect of the period, the Cathars, was put down with terrible ferocity in the Albigensian Crusade, a war of extermination that continued for the best part of 35 years and reduced much of southern France to a wasteland.[2] It was the same story with the adherents of the pagan cult of Diana, or the 'Craft of the Wise', as witchcraft was known. Its disciples were rooted out, tortured and consigned to the flames, a process that was continued and accelerated in the monstrous hysteria of the sixteenth- and seventeenth-century witch-hunts.[3]

This was sad indeed, for to a very great extent the competing religions all shared the same desire to worship the Most High. Where they differed was in the identity of the one true god. Orthodox Christians equated this deity with the Jewish Jehovah of the Old Testament. By contrast, the Gnostics believed that Jehovah was a lesser god, the Demiurge who had created this world of matter from which they wished to escape. The distinction seemed important to both sides, and neither would give ground. In similar fashion, the Church authorities could see no point of correspondence between a ring-dance with Jesus in the centre and a similar dance with the master of a witches' coven centre-stage representing the god. Or if they did, it was to see this ritual as a hellish perversion of their own beliefs, a diabolic charade set up to snare the unwary and lead them to damnation. So the 'god' of the witch-dance became transmuted in Christian philosophy into the 'devil'; and the witch's 'Lucifer', the light-bearer, was transformed by their bigoted world view into the principle of evil. This was, of course, a complete travesty of the facts. Except for possible rare exceptions, witchcraft never worshipped evil but instead the principle of light or truth. However, in the course of time many of the followers of the old religion began to use the term 'devil' as a form of shorthand, to differentiate their concept of God and his presence as 'God on earth' from that of the orthodox Church. The man at the centre of the ring-dance thus became the 'devil' for both religions, though what was meant by the two faiths' use of this same word was diametrically opposed. For Churchmen he was the evil spirit; for the witches' coven he was the divine king, the earthly representative of God – an exalted figure who, at certain times and on certain occasions, was put to death for the good of the people and the wellbeing of the world.

Despite the best efforts of the Church, these beliefs persisted long after Europe became nominally Christian. It proved to be easier to destroy villages and to burn individuals than to eradicate the Gnostic teachings of the Cathars, or the knowledge of the witches. And whenever persecution became too severe, the anti-Church simply went underground and awaited an opportune movement to reappear.

Not that it was ever far from the surface. This is especially true in Britain, and particularly for the 'pagan' old religion of the peasantry. Except for an area of western England and parts of Wales (which, as we'll see in Chapter Eight, were both early converted to the original 'Nazarite Christianity' of the disciples), most of the British Isles remained loyal to the old religion until long after the arrival of Augustine in the late sixth century AD. Augustine was sent by Pope Gregory I and is normally credited (wrongly, as it turns out) with the conversion of all Britain. Even in those areas in which Augustine did bring the word of Christ (or at least the Roman version of it), analysis of his strategy reveals that the rich and influential were the exclusive target of his sermons. As researcher M. Murray comments:

> The people who brought [Christianity] in on the east coast were foreigners who never amalgamated with the natives. Augustine was Italian, and for more than a century no native Britons were advanced to high places in the Church . . . Italians and other aliens held the high offices. The Augustine mission and their successors concentrated on the rulers and through them forced their exotic religion on a stubborn and unwilling people . . . The country, therefore, must have been Pagan, with Christian rulers and a Christian aristocracy.[4]

The truth of this can be seen from an appraisal of the ancient books of Penitence and Confession. The earliest book of English ecclesiastical law, the Liber Poenitentialis, written in the latter half of the seventh century, has a section devoted solely to penances to be imposed on those found practising the rites of the old religion. These included 'celebrating feasts in the abominable places of the heathen and offering food there, but also consuming it: serving this hidden idolatry, having relinquished Christ: [and] if anyone at the kalends of January goes about as a stag or bull – that is, making himself into a wild animal, and putting on the heads of beasts – those who in such wise transform themselves into the appearance of a wild animal, penance for three years, because this is devilish'.[5] Century after century we find the ecclesiastics railing against these 'heathen practices'. A ninth-century decree makes mention of 'certain wicked women . . . [who] believe and profess that they ride at night with Diana on certain beasts, with an innumerable multitude of women, passing over immense distances, obeying her commands as mistress'. The Ecclesiastical Canons of King Edgar, written in 959, requires:

> . . . that every priest zealously promote Christianity and totally extin-guish every heathenism; and forbid well-worshipping and the vain practices which are carried on with various spells and with 'frith-spots' [holy sites], and with elders and also with various other trees, and with stones and with many various delusions, with which men

do much of what they should not . . . And we enjoin that on feast days heathen songs and devil's games be abstained from.[6]

A hundred years later the situation was no better, when the Laws of King Cnut 'earnestly forbid every heathenism: heathenism is that men worship idols; that is, they worship the heathen gods, and the sun or the moon, fire or rivers, water-wells or stones, or forest trees of any kind; or love witchcraft'.

From this we can see that, among the common people, old habits died hard, and there was a regular and persistent flouting of Christian religious practices. Indeed, ecclesiastics themselves were often secret believers. Even as late as 1282 a priest at Inverkeithing was disciplined (but not dismissed) for leading an Easter ring-dance around a phallic representation of a god.[7]

So, the mass of the people retained their allegiance to the old ways, while the majority of the nobility apparently converted to the doctrines of Rome. But even here echoes of the old beliefs must have been retained, even if only on a subconscious level. Pagan traditions still held a strong hold on both nobles and commons. That dark currents of heterodoxy swirled silently below the tale that we are given by orthodox history is evident from the story of the Red King, William Rufus.

The Red King

Along with the date of the battle of Hastings, one of the few 'historical facts' that we carry with us into adulthood from our schooldays is the knowledge that William Rufus, third son of William the Conqueror, was a 'bad king' and that he died accidentally, but not undeservedly, shot by an arrow intended for a stag he was hunting with his courtiers. Strangely enough, it is this very notoriety, this place in history as an evil monarch, that has managed to obscure for centuries the important part that Rufus played in the history of England, and the curious, and suspicious, manner of his death.

It is obvious why the Churchmen (who alone wrote 'history' in the eleventh century) regarded Rufus as a 'bad king': he was most certainly not Christian in any orthodox sense of the word. He seemed to delight in persecuting the Church, stealing its lands and showing no respect for its precepts. He ridiculed the intercession of saints, and, when laying plans or discussing the future, would not allow the normally obligatory phrase 'if it be God's will' to be used in his presence. It was as if he were arrogating to himself some of the authority of the deity, and his actions were construed by many as a belief in his own divine nature. Indeed, in many ways he acted the part of a divine king.[8] Just as reprehensible to the ecclesiastical writers, Rufus's court was rife with homosexual practices. The chroniclers describe a close circle of Rufus's friends as 'effeminati', long-haired and close-shaven '. . . so that their beards should not chafe their friends when they kissed'. While the Church seems regularly to have ascribed the sin of sodomy to non-believers, there is reason to believe that in this case, and in the case of certain Gnostic sects, this accusation may not simply have been an example of ecclesiastical character assassination.

The belief of many Gnostic sects that the material world was evil, and that procreation in particular was the most heinous of sins, made a proscription of sexual intercourse between the sexes inevitable. 'If convicted of having left any offspring upon earth, the soul is destined there until it shall have collected all and attracted these unto itself . . .' This "Self-Collection" was to be effected only through the observance of perpetual chastity, or rather (inevitable compromise) the practice of the various unnatural vices that regularly spring from such an article of faith . . .' The Church father Epiphanius is very plain-spoken in this regard and gives a graphic (though probably biased) account '. . . of the mode in which the faithful observed in one sense their vow of perpetual chastity without renouncing the joys of Venus'.[9] He claims that the rites included sodomy and masturbation with the semen eaten as a sacrament. This latter was practised by both sexes:

> . . . the woman and man receive the male emission on their own hands. And they stand with their eyes raised heavenward but the filth on their hands, and pray, if you please . . . and offer that stuff on their hands to the actual Father of all, and say: 'We offer thee this gift, the body of Christ.' And then they eat it . . . And so with the women's emission when she happens to be having her period – they likewise take the unclean menstrual blood they gather from her, and eat it in common. And 'This', they say, 'is the blood of Christ.'[10]

Why the 'Red' King?

In the Middle Ages is was traditional for any great man (and many lesser men) to be given a nickname. This is apparent from even a brief trawl through British history: Edward the Confessor, Ethelred the Unready, William the Conqueror, Alfred the Great, etc. The list is almost endless. But, as the foremost biographer of William Rufus acknowledges, with the

Red King this nicknaming is transformed into something quite other than a simple sobriquet: '. . . the second William is yet more emphatically the Red King than his father is either the Bastard or the Conqueror.' And again: '. . . unlike most other names of the kind, his surname is not only used by contemporary writers, but it is used by them almost as a proper name.'[11]

The standard explanation of the title – that Rufus was so named because of his ruddy complexion – obviously lacks conviction. If true, it would be the first time that skin pigmentation has had so profound an effect on the owner's contemporaries that they used it 'almost as a proper name'. Hugh Ross Williamson, a parish priest who made a lengthy study of the problem of the divine king and Rufus, and on whose research much of this chapter is based, has suggested a much more likely hypothesis. According to this, '. . . red – the colour of blood – is and always has been all over the world pre-eminently the witch colour'. In addition, from the time of the Egyptian Pharaohs it was also linked to the worship of the sun. For King William to be known as Rufus is an immediate and obvious indication of a link to both the witch coven and to solar worship of the divine king. 'There is no need to labour a point so well attested or a symbolism so obvious; and there can be no reasonable doubt that the mere phrase "the Red King" would bear this inference to thousands of his subjects.'[12] In brief, William's title, the Red King, proclaimed to the followers of the old religion that Rufus was their 'devil', the divine king on earth, and that he would, in the fullness of time, sacrifice himself for their benefit.

The King's Companions

The identity and character of the most notable of the king's companions also points to his close affiliation to the Gnostic sects and witchcraft. During Rufus's wars in France, William IX of Aquitaine was his confederate and confidante. But this noble's other title was Count of Poitou, and it is under this title that he is well known to students of poetry. His is the first troubadour poetry that we have, and it is in troubadour verse that the doctrine of the Gnostic Cathari, the 'Pure', was preserved.[13] In the twelfth century Catharism spread through Europe like a flame, its influence reaching high into both the Church and the aristocracy. According to one specialist, during the twelfth century no fewer than 13 of the reigning heads of Europe were members of the sect.[14] The Cathar success lay partly in its secrecy and partly in its ability to interpret ostensibly orthodox writings and teachings in an esoteric, Gnostic way. The Prologue to the Gospel of John is one obvious example, with its dualistic undertones of light and darkness, and it was long used by the Pure in their services. In addition, the sect chose to promulgate its own teachings in an altogether novel manner, in the form of songs of 'love' sung by wandering jongleurs, better known as the troubadours. That the troubadours' poems carried an esoteric meaning is not seriously disputed by any scholar. In the same manner in which a tale of the Holy Grail could be enjoyed as an adventure story, and at the same time appreciated by an initiate for the secret teachings it contained, so the troubadour love poems could be understood on two levels, both exoteric and esoteric. Many lines of their poems read to us like nonsense verse, but this is not surprising. As we lack the key to the teachings, they are bound to be incomprehensible. But then, as Hugh Ross Williamson has pointed out, without a basic understanding of Christian symbolism, many of its sacred songs are equally impenetrable. Consider how this verse would sound to a Buddhist lama of Tibet:

> Life-imparting heavenly Manna,
> Stricken rock with streaming side
> Heaven and earth with loud hosanna
> Worship Thee, the Lamb who Died.

It is extremely unlikely that Rufus would have been ignorant either of his comrades-in-arm's poetic accomplishments or the heretical beliefs that underpinned them. Given his own antagonism to the established Church, the suspicion must be that he was at very least a sympathiser of the Cathar religion, if not a member of the cult himself.

The Red King's anti-Church attitude was displayed most notably in his choice of candidate for the Bishopric of Durham. This was one of the most important positions in the whole of England. It was given only to the most trusted of the king's followers, and with good reason. Durham was a buffer zone, a first line of defence against the depredations of the Scots. The area was a palatinate, with royal privileges devolved upon the ecclesiastical authority, so that the incumbent was, in effect, a prince-bishop. The ruler of the palatinate had power and wealth far beyond that of lands further south, and for nearly 900 years these prince-bishops held court in regal splendour.[15] Rufus's choice for this hugely powerful position was the man to whom he had earlier entrusted the financial health of the realm – Ranulf Flambard. Although he was a cleric, and at times acted as the king's personal chaplain, Flambard was no ordinary

Christian. Of lowly birth, he personified the religious ambiguity of the time. He was the son of a priest and of a witch who (like the Norse god Odin) was said to have lost an eye as a result of her dealings with the minions of the 'devil'. Although ordained, Flambard seems to have imbibed more of his mother's pagan traditions than those of orthodox Christianity. No less than Rufus, he acted as, and considered himself, a 'devil', an identification emphasised by his fiery surname, which carried the same solar implications as did William's own sobriquet, 'the Red'.

If King William's friendship with Ranulf Flambard links him to the witch cult, another of his close associates – the Welsh noble Bledri, son of Cadivor – connects him to the legends of the Holy Grail. This same Bledri has been identified by Grail researcher Dr J. L. Weston as Bleheris, one of the first authors of the original Grail romances that so fired men's minds in medieval Christendom. My own researchers had led me to believe that the Grail stories are a form of code, carrying (yet covering from profane view) a knowledge of the sacred head. Dr Weston wrote more than seven decades before I published my own conclusions and was not aware of the Grail's connection to the head of Christ. Yet her comments are as apt now as then; she believed that the Grail romances were a record 'of an ancient ritual, having for its ultimate object the initiation into the secret of the sources of Life, physical and spiritual . . . In its esoteric "Mystery" form it was freely utilised for the imparting of high spiritual teaching concerning the relation of Man to the Divine Source of his being and the possibility of a sensible union between Man and God.'[16] This was, and is, the goal of all Gnostic teaching and places yet another of Rufus's friends (and by implication himself also) firmly in the Gnostic camp.

William Rufus's association with Helias of Maine also points to Gnostic involvement. Helias, whose very name (= Helios = Apollo, the sun-god) suggests a link to the sun cult, was both a friend of Rufus and also almost constantly at war with the English king. Helias was also known as the White Bachelor on account of an enigmatic Essene-like white robe that he wore, which seems to have identified him as somehow 'special' and to have bestowed on him a passport among certain of his enemies. On one notable occasion the robe enabled him to enter freely into a tower that was being held by Rufus's men.[17] When Rufus finally captured Helias he inexplicably allowed him his freedom, without the customary ransom or promise of submission, with the words: 'I give you leave to do all you can, and, per vultum de Luca [by the face of Lucca], if you ever conquer me I will not ask for any grace in return for my favour today.'

The Face of Lucca

The use of the vow *per vultum de Luca*, or occasionally *per vultum dei* (by God's face), is remarkable. Many oaths were current at this time: men swore by God's blood, by God's eyes, God's bones, even by God's feet. But, so far as can be determined, *per vultum de Luca* is an oath unique to Rufus. It was Rufus's most holy pledge, and once the monarch had made any promise using this formula then (unlike many another promise he made) he always held true to his word. The king is never known to have been foresworn. This is very important. Given his apparently wayward and irreverent character, the phrase was obviously a most solemn vow and pertained to something that Rufus held especially sacred. And this raised a serious difficulty. Why should an avowed pagan, a man who despised the Church, have given such weight to an oath that, at first sight, is of definite Christian origin? Might it be, as one researcher has suggested, 'that Rufus's invariable oath, though apparently sworn on a crucifix, was in reality taken in quite another sense'?[18]

Some older writers took the oath to mean 'by the face of St Luke', but its true meaning has been shown conclusively by Ducange to refer to an object that had been the subject of my studies for many years.[19] The *vultus Lucanus* might be styled the face of Lucca, but it was Rufus's alternative name for the same object, the *vultus Deus*, the face of God, that gave the secret away. Both these titles refer to the same sacred object – to the head of Jesus, the same head that Nicodemus was said to have 'carved', and which was in his possession the day after the Crucifixion (see Chapter Two). What had happened to this relic is a mystery. I believe that it was most probably buried beneath the Temple of Solomon in Jerusalem and discovered a thousand years later by the excavations of the first of the Knights Templar, whose codename for the head of Christ was Baphomet. However, there was an alternative route. The head may have been spirited out of Israel, either just after the Crucifixion or at the time of the destruction of Jerusalem in AD 70, and to have come into the possession of the Templars via the Cathars or another Gnostic sect during the periodic suppression of such 'heresies' by the Roman Church. Many Cathars are known to have sought refuge in the Order, especially during the Albigensian Crusade.[20]

One account of the origin of the face of Lucca has Nicodemus, surrounded by enemies, fastening the head of Jesus to the mast of a ship in the port of Joppa. The boat put out to sea without rudder or crew and was said to have drifted across the Mediterranean until it reached the shores of Tuscany, when it miraculously sailed up the river Sérchio to the town of Lucca. Lucca was known as a city sympathetic towards heresies of many kinds. The remains of the earliest patron saint of Lucca, St Frediano, lay in a heathen sarcophagus carved with motifs of the pagan mysteries.[21] Sculptures depicting the legend of St Frediano's altar being brought into the city by two 'wild cows' reveals them to be, in reality, bulls of the god Mithras. So in the story of Nicodemus's 'carved' head of Jesus and the crewless boat we may have a mythologised historical account of the transport of the head of Christ from Israel to the European mainland.

The head of Jesus, and the reverence he paid to it, despite his rejection of orthodox Christianity is clearly the origin of the Red King's personal oath. Like many Gnostic believers, Rufus probably did not believe in the story of Jesus' bodily resurrection into heaven, but he may still, like them, have revered Jesus as a manifestation of a 'god on earth', a god of such esteem that he had died the death of solar crucifixion. Rufus's unique choice of vow reveals him to have been in possession of covert knowledge of the existence of the severed embalmed head of Jesus (knowledge he seems to have shared with the founders of the Knights Templar). Astonishingly, when the 'pagan' King William Rufus swore *per vultum de Luca* he was swearing by the most secret and most precious of all Christian Gnostic relics – by the head of Christ.

The King's Death

In trawling through the reports of the death of Rufus and its aftermath, it is necessary to be aware of the interests and motives of the monkish writers, of their duty (as they saw it) to do their best to uphold the values of the Church. The massaging of the truth is evident in the tales we have of William's repentance, or his calling for absolution, or for a mass wafer, just before he dies. Such deathbed conversion tales are very likely to be false, interpolated as exemplars to show the faithful that even so evil a king as Rufus finally understood the truth of the Church's teachings and returned belatedly to the Christian fold. Moreover, as one chronicler, William of Malmesbury, is candid enough to admit, the clerics who wrote these tales were dealing with contemporary or near-contemporary events: sometimes they were writing for patrons who were themselves near-relatives of Rufus. They could not afford to offend such powerful individuals. Short of actually lying, they put the best possible gloss they could on Rufus's character. As one biographer of the Red King put it, the chroniclers 'would forbid any *suggestio falsi* but would allow a good deal of *suppressio veri*'.[22]

The year of William's death and the day on which it occurred are very suggestive of a ritual sacrifice within the compass of the witch cult. There is no doubt that the year 1100 was seen by many as of almost equal importance as the end of the first millennium (about which there was as much, or more, apocalyptic dread than we moderns experienced concerning the advent of the year 2000). A feeling of foreboding hung over Christendom, and it may be no coincidence that the death of a true divine king – and not that of a substitute – was believed necessary at this time.

Portents and omens are said to have presaged the death of Rufus. A foretelling dream was vouchsafed, in some versions to a monk, in others to the king himself. In it, Rufus is figured as approaching and entering a chapel or a minster located, in some versions, in a forest:

> Its walls were robed with velvet and purple . . .Here were goodly books, here were the shrines of saints, gleaming with gold and gems and ivory . . . At a second glance all this bravery passed away; the walls and the altar itself stood bare. At the third glance he saw the form of a man lying bare upon the altar. A cannibal desire came on him; he ate, or strove to eat, of the body that lay before him. His victim endured for a while in patience; then his face, hitherto goodly and gentle as of an angel, became stern beyond words, and he spoke: 'Is it not enough that thou hast thus far grieved me with so many wrongs? Wilt thou gnaw my very flesh and bones?'[23]

In another account the words are stark and menacing: 'Henceforth thou shalt eat of me no more.'

The Witch Connection

We can see in these dream-accounts yet another attempt by monkish propagandists to enhance their own point of view. The body is obviously that of Christ in the form of his Church on earth. Rufus had stolen land and extorted huge sums from this 'body of Christ', and the tale's author is indicating that even God's patience has a limit. The Lord had quite simply had enough, and had decided to do away with the miscreant king.

However, some tales are not so easily dismissed. Insofar as they show that God wreaks vengeance on evildoers they are 'on message' and follow the Church line. But some are also shot through with details that do the Church no service, and as such they form important clues in the puzzle of Rufus's death – or at very least to the contemporary view of the reasons lying behind his death. At the same hour that the Red King went forth to meet his death, Count William of Mortain was abroad in the forests of

Cornwall, hunting deer. Parted from his comrades, he suddenly saw a huge shaggy goat, as black as night, emerge from the trees. On its back was a naked man, Rufus, bleeding from a wound in his chest. 'I bear your king,' declared the beast, 'or rather your tyrant, William the Red, to his doom. For I am the evil spirit, the avenger of the wickedness with which he raged against the Church of Christ . . .' And so saying the beast carried the unfortunate king off to a no doubt hellish fate.[24]

The story is interesting on account of the identity of the animal that carries the king. It is the 'evil spirit', in other words the 'devil', the god of the witches. That it is a goat points to the same conclusion. Along with the bull and the stag, the goat was a sacred animal of the witch cult, personifying the 'horned god', the same god that we saw impersonated by the man who on 'the kalends of January goes about as a stag or bull – that is, making himself into a wild animal, and putting on the heads of beasts . . .'. We have here, in this story of the king and the goat, an implicit assumption that the Red King was linked to the old religion, to witchcraft – to the very religion that, on rare occasions, required that the divine king, the 'devil', the personification of god on earth, should be immolated for the good of the world in general and of his subjects in particular.

Despite the wilder imaginings of such tales, there is no doubt that Rufus's death was anticipated in many quarters. He himself is said to have known that his end was nigh, and to have passed a sleepless, troubled night before venturing out to meet his death in the New Forest. There is more than just a passing resemblance here to Jesus' own agonised watch before the Crucifixion, and the parallel is maintained with Rufus partaking of a last meal just prior to his fatal 'hunting expedition'. Whatever the truth of this, that the death was expected, and even awaited, is undeniable. Three days before William's death, Abbott Hugh of Cluny informed Archbishop Anselm (with whom the Red King was bitterly at odds and who had been forced to live in exile in Italy) that in a dream he had seen the English king brought before the final judgement of God and condemned to eternal damnation. Moreover, accounts of the time stress that knowledge of Rufus's demise was known in several foreign locations far sooner than news could have been carried by any earthly messenger. The day before the death, on 1 August, a youth arrived at Anselm's door in Italy and informed the gatekeeper that the strife between his lord and the king was at an end. Again, at matins on the morning of Rufus's ill-fated hunt, one of Anselm's clerks was praying when he felt a piece of paper pressed into his hands. Opening his eyes, he found himself alone, with the message 'King William is dead' written on the paper in his hand. According to another account, in Devon just before the fatal hour, Peter de Melvis met a rustic carrying a

BY ARROW AND BY SWORD

dart who told him 'with this your king was killed today'. And on the night of the killing, the news was already current in Belgium, far faster than any boat could cross the Channel.[25]

The Sacrifice

Such foreknowledge points to one of two conclusions: either a planned sacrificial murder or an equally carefully executed act of treason. If regicide was the reason, then one would expect that those present at the death would have attempted to seize control of the nation following Rufus's death, or at very least to have benefited from their treachery in terms of rank or lands. But, in fact, the exact opposite is true. The presumed principal in the murder, the king's favourite, Walter Tirel, fled the land. And one of the first acts of the new king, Henry I, was to put an end to the 'degeneracy' of Rufus's court. The effeminati, with their silks and shaved faces, were broken and scattered, and Henry quickly settled down into the more 'normal' social life of European kings, keeping scores of mistresses and siring innumerable bastards. In many ways those present at the death of Rufus lost almost as much as the Red King himself. The treason motive must therefore be put aside, leaving us with the remaining hypothesis: a sacrificial murder. And, indeed, many parts of the story of the killing of the king point strongly to this conclusion.

The orthodox account of his death is that, while hunting with his friends in the New Forest, Rufus and Walter Tirel came upon an enormous stag. Tirel fired at the beast and missed, the arrow either striking the king directly or ricocheting off a branch to impale itself deep in Rufus's chest. Rufus fell to the ground, cried out for absolution, and then expired. Walter Tirel fled, as did most of the hunting band, and Rufus's body was left to lie where it had fallen, until carried back to Winchester in a cart by peasants who had taken pity on the dead man. However, contemporary accounts are replete with details and symbols which, to any initiate, would indicate that the king's death was anything but the accident that it has since been made out to be.

For the followers of the old religion, four dates were paramount: 1 May, 1 August, 1 November and 2 February.[26] These were 'Christianised' by the Church missionaries as Roodmass, Lammas, All Hallows and Candlemas. Strangely, this quarterly division of the year follows neither the cycle of the sun nor of vegetation. Its original importance seems to lie even further back in mankind's history, and to be linked to the breeding season of herd animals – goats, deer and cattle – just those species which figured so

81

prominently as symbolic substitutes for the 'horned god'. Testimony of cult members indicates that the sacrifice of the 'god', 'devil' or divine king took place on or around these dates, although in later times, in the sixteenth and seventeenth centuries, an animal (usually a goat) was substituted for the human 'god'. However, in earlier ages it is clear that the divine king had to die, and while a substitute was sometimes allowed, when the times demanded it the king himself was the only acceptable offering. That Rufus, the Red King, was killed 'on the morrow of Lammas' is surely no coincidence, especially when the other exceptional circumstances of his death are also considered.

If the time was carefully chosen, then so, it seems, was the place. The 'accident' occurred in a forest, a habitual meeting place of members of the old religion. It took place on the site of an ancient church, and, as early churches were invariably built on the site of a pagan holy temple or grove, we can safely assume that this site was also regarded as sacred by the followers of the cult.[27] When the time for the sacrifice came, at sunset, the specific place was chosen with much ceremony. In an apparently unimportant detail, we are told that the king's killer stood under an elder tree, with the aspen or white poplar behind him. But this seemingly random location would have been laden with symbolism to the initiates of the cult. The elder is the witch-tree *par excellence*. In Ireland, sticks of elder were used by witches for their magic rides. 'In English folklore to burn logs of elder "brings the devil into the house".'[28] It is the 'tree of doom', the thirteenth tree in the ancient 'woodland alphabet', for ever regarded as unlucky. The choice of the second tree, the aspen, is just as significant. This species was one of the three trees of resurrection. In it nested the crows sacred to the god Bran (whose severed head was kept as a talisman and protected London from invasion). 'In ancient Ireland, the fe or measuring rod used by coffin-makers on corpses was of aspen, presumably as a reminder to the souls of the dead that this was not the end.'[29] So, in this apparently insignificant detail we have a summation of much of the old religion's beliefs. The king was doomed; he must die, but only to experience resurrection and the return of new life.

The king was killed by those closest to him, individuals whose association with the cult is almost beyond cavil. In the accounts, the man who was to kill the king, Walter Tirel, is spoken of rather euphemistically as his 'familiar'. Given that Rufus's court was notorious for its homosexuality, that the king never married or sired an heir, nor was his name ever attached to any mistress, it is more than likely that he was done to death by his lover. Early that fatal morning Rufus had given Tirel two of six specially made arrows for his crossbow. Rufus handed them over with strangely prophetic words: "'Tis right,' he is reported as saying, 'that the sharpest arrows should be given to him who knows how to deal deadly strokes with them.'[30] Yet despite the apparent premeditation and preparation involved in the act, at the moment of truth the chosen executioner quailed before the task, half-lowering his weapon. Rufus is said to have ordered Tirel: 'Shoot, you devil!', or perhaps 'Shoot your devil!' In some versions he cries out angrily: 'Shoot in the devil's name or it will be the worse for you.' Whatever his exact words, the command had the desired effect. The arrow was loosed and Rufus fell to the ground, the shaft deep in his chest. As he lay dying, his friends clustered round and he was given a sacrament, not of the mass wafer but of a concoction of forest herbs. The gloss that the Christian chroniclers put on this is that the stricken king called out for absolution, and in the absence of a priest and the host his friends substituted flowers and leaves. However, as the old religion was primarily concerned with the vitality and fruitfulness of the earth, it is plain that this last repast of the dying king was more likely a nature sacrament, a ritual holy meal of the old religion.

That the common folk understood the importance of the ritual is attested to by the reverence with which they bore the body back to Winchester. All through the chronicles, Rufus is described as a tyrant, a puffed-up savage and an oppressor of the people. If this was truly the case, then the peasantry (who, in the nature of feudal society, would always suffer most from tyranny) should have had the greatest reason to hate the Red King. Why, then, did they treat the body of William Rufus with such reverence? Again, why was he so readily accepted as king when his father, William the Conqueror, was so universally loathed by the Saxon serf? Why should a newly conquered people, enslaved by another nation, their lands stolen, have taken the son of their persecutor to their hearts? Given the common people's continuing attachment to the old religion, the answer can only be that they perceived him in terms of their ancient traditions and regarded him as their 'devil', as 'god on earth', the foredoomed divine king, who would accept death for their sakes, and whose sacrifice would ensure the fertility of their crops, herds and indeed all nature. King William's title of the Red King proclaimed this and was confirmed by a legend that almost immediately grew up concerning his dead body. It was said that as he was carried from the New Forest to Winchester Cathedral, his corpse shed blood continuously from the cart, leaving a crimson trail along the ground. So strong was the tradition that, up until at least the middle of this century, this tale was still current, and the path of the cart across the fields continued to be known as Kingsway. It is, of course, impossible for a long-dead corpse to bleed so profusely, but it attests to the connection between the Red King and the old religion. The blood, the life essence of the divine victim, must be shed upon the soil to revivify and restore the fertility of the earth.[31]

Pagan Rites

The burial of William Rufus gave rise to two diametrically opposed traditions. According to one account, because of Rufus's undoubted status as an anointed king, when the cart carrying the king's corpse arrived at Winchester the body was allowed entrance to the grounds of the cathedral. However, the chroniclers insist that Christian charity ended there: they claim that the Red King was consigned to his grave without benefit of mass, bell or candle. Yet despite this, they are forced to admit that an enormous number of people attended the burial. Contemporary poems oppose this version of events. They agree that a huge multitude was present but insist that the funeral was a magnificent affair, that flowers covered the corpse, and that there was 'such saying of masses as no man had heard before or would hear again until the day of doom'. It would seem that these two accounts preserve the memory of the Church's refusal of burial rites to so ostentatiously pagan a king, to a king whose manner of death so obviously fulfilled the requirements of the old religion and Gnostic beliefs that they were fighting so hard to suppress. And that it was priests of this secret faith who instead undertook the interment of the divine king's body, to the accompaniment of solemn rites, perhaps a heretical Gnostic mass. It was a ritual that the multitude of common people – who well understood the importance of the death of their 'devil' – would expect and demand.

I sat back to consider what I had learned so far. That there was an ancient tradition of blood sacrifice seemed undeniable. That it involved a series of (solar) divine kings and, in the most rare and sacred instances, death by crucifixion was also clear. As has been pointed out by many scholars, the life of Jesus follows the required path of just such a divine king. The case for William Rufus, the Red King, being a divine victim within this constellation of beliefs is extremely strong. Rufus was slain in a sacred wood at sunset on the morrow of Lammas, shot by his companion as he stood looking west, a solar divine victim sacrificed as he stared towards the rays of the dying sun-god. Nor was he the only post-Jesus sacrifice on record. Saint Thomas à Becket has also been named, on the basis of equally strong evidence, as a substitute divine king, for Henry II, the Angevin king whose House was a known supporter of Catharism.[32] Dagobert II, a Merovingian king (whose own bloodline is intimately linked with that of

Christ's), was 'murdered' in a sacred wood on 23 December 679 on the very day of the rebirth of the sun. While still a prince of the royal line, Dagobert was credited with the discovery of the tomb of Saint Denys, a divine who, like Saint William Sancto Claros of the Sinclair family, is invariably pictured carrying a severed head.[33] Following his own sacrificial death, Dagobert's head was removed from his body and preserved as a relic, and his skull can still be seen in the convent of the Black Sisters at Mons.

But how did this relate to the image on the Shroud? If the Turin Shroud really was the gravecloth of Christ, imprinted with his image, then I began to wonder if it might show evidence of this cult. Even if it was a Templar fake, it was possible that important clues were to be found on the relic, perhaps even definite evidence of the removal of the head. It seemed like a vain hope at that time, but, astonishingly, such evidence was exactly what I did later discover. For the moment, however, it was enough that my theory of Jesus' links to the divine sacrifice and the Cult of the Head were holding together. There was a definite thread here, a line passing back through Becket and Rufus to Dagobert, to Jesus, and beyond. A thread in which the sacredness of the head, and blood sacrifice, formed a rare, but nevertheless vital, part of the belief system. If this was accepted, it was obvious that the Christianity that has come down to us today must be considerably at variance with the original teachings of Christ. But apart from the sacrificial elements of the doctrines, what exactly were those original teachings? Was it possible to determine the origin of Jesus' doctrines, and to discover just how he himself was regarded by those who knew him and lived alongside him during the time of his ministry?

CHAPTER FIVE

ORIGINAL CHRISTIANITY

Christianity before Christ

HE INFORMATION laid out in earlier chapters points to the fact that Jesus was regarded by certain of his contemporaries as one of a series of solar divine kings, whose immolation was part of a ritual that had existed long before Jesus and persisted after his 'execution'. Jesus had died the required death of such a king, a death both sacred and terrible – crucifixion – his sacrifice an atonement offering to appease the just anger of God at the sins of mankind. In addition, the evidence I had uncovered in *The Head of God* both reinforced and added to this view. It indicated that Jesus was a true lineal descendant of a sun-king of Egypt, the Pharaoh Tutmosis, and that, as the leader of the Nazarite sect, he had held to the secret teachings of a descendant of Tutmosis, the Heretic Pharaoh Akhenaten. These teachings had included a reverence of the solar disc as a manifestation of the one true god, the Aten, and the worship of the severed head (itself a solar symbol of some importance).

Curiously enough, the ancient existence of the religion that Jesus professed is confirmed by the Druids. I had discovered that ancient accounts told of the arrival of one of Akhenaten's daughters (named Scota in most versions) in Ireland. The time of this seaborne immigration is given as the same as that of the Exodus of the Jews from Egypt, around 1350 BC, at exactly the time that Akhenaten (as Moses) had been forced to flee Egypt by land.[1] The race founded in Ireland by Scota and her followers became the Scoti, or Scots, who eventually conquered and settled that area now known as Scotland. Scota had brought with her the teachings of her father, Akhenaten, including the Cult of the Head, and they had found expression in the Druid religion, which held sway over most of Britain until the coming of the Romans. And strangely, we find the great Welsh bard and Druid, Taliesin, confessing to an identity of religious beliefs between Druidism and primitive Christianity, stating clearly that:

> Christ, the Word from the beginning, was from the beginning our teacher, and we never lost his teaching. Christianity was a new thing in Asia [the Levant] but there was never a time when the Druids of Britain held not its doctrines.[2]

Druidism existed long before Christ's birth. Druidism's origin, philosophy and Cult of the Severed Head all link the religion strongly to the hidden teachings of Akhenaten.[3] And we have here, in Taliesin's strange statement, not only confirmation of the correspondence between Christianity and Druidism but a declaration that 'Christianity' is an ancient religion, predating the time of Jesus.

This claim is, astonishingly, confirmed by one of the greatest of the Church Fathers, Saint Augustine. It is not generally known that this pillar of the Church was a confirmed heretic between the ages of 19 and 31. He was a Manichaean (a Gnostic sect) and during his 12 years as a sect member he must have been initiated into a great many occult secrets. One of Saint Augustine's sayings has long resisted an 'orthodox' explanation, yet it is set out in very plain words:

> That which is called the Christian Religion existed among the Ancients, and never did not exist, from the beginning of the human race until Christ came in the flesh, at which time the true religion which already existed began to be called Christianity.[4]

It would be difficult to be more obvious or more explicit. Saint Augustine is saying quite literally that Jesus was a member of an *already existing religion*, one of very ancient provenance. In former times it had gone by other names, but when Jesus was chosen to preach the message (and to die the traditional and sacred death of the divine victim) it was his name that was attached to the teachings, which is why it is presently called Christianity.

This supports the belief that Jesus was one of a royal line of teachers who expounded the ancient doctrines enshrined in Akhenaten's teachings. These teachings were held in great reverence by the Nazarites, whose leader at the time of the Crucifixion was Jesus (Christ was crucified as

'Jesus the Nazarite, King of the Jews', an accurate and succinct statement of his status). It is the story of this forgotten group which forms the true history of the early Christians, the primitive Church. It also reveals the true Jesus – how his family and those who knew him personally perceived the status of this enigmatic preacher and prophet. A man who, through the agency of the 'Apostle' Paul and without in any way aspiring to the distinction, was later to attain not simply deification but *identity* with the Most High God.

Christianity – A Partial History

When reading the Christian scriptures, it is easy to forget that they were written around 50 years after Jesus' death,[5] and at a time and place when 'historical facts', as we define them, were very often of little account. Histories were structured and modified according to what has been aptly termed 'the fitness of things'. If, according to some individual scribe, a great individual *should* have said or done something, then very little compunction was shown in putting those words into the hero's or heroine's mouth, or in changing the story to suit the current politically correct view. Equally, if it was felt that an event or quote embarrassed the currently fashionable line, it was almost invariably omitted. As even a cursory study of the results of scriptural scholarship will confirm, the New Testament is riddled with such inconsistencies and omissions.

One example germane to our own study concerns the expansion of Christianity out of Palestine. The Acts of the Apostles purport to be a history of the early spread of Christianity through the then-known world. However, it treats exclusively the northward and westward expansion of the new faith into Asia Minor and then west into Europe. No mention is made of its eastward movement, or its southward extension, despite the fact that we know that Christianity was planted as far east as India or that there was a thriving Christian community in several Egyptian cities, especially Alexandria. I was later to find that there was a definite and very telling reason for the deliberate exclusion of Alexandria from orthodox Church 'histories'.

The letters of Paul, which form a large part of the New Testament, provide another example. Where are there so many of this individual's letters and so few by the other Apostles? It is not as if Paul's status was consistently high in the early Church. As I later discovered, he was regarded as a renegade by most of the disciples and by Jesus' own family. Scholars agree that the patchiness of the *corpus paulinum* reveals that Paul's

89

philosophy of Jesus was for the most part rejected, and during this early period many of his letters were lost and the rest packed away and virtually forgotten. When Paul's reputation was rehabilitated and his conception of Jesus gained the ascendancy, those missives that had survived were carefully collected and preserved, forming the bulk of those letters contained in the New Testament. However, there is ample evidence that the Mother Church at Jerusalem kept up just as voluminous a correspondence as Paul, and by no means all of the disciples were illiterate. Yet not a single epistle from these sources is extant.[6] And this despite the fact that, as we will see, the Jerusalem Church was in the early years regarded with as much respect among the faithful as Rome is by Catholics today. It is useless to say that the records were destroyed in the general conflagration caused by the Roman destruction of Jerusalem in AD 70. The letters had been sent not to Jerusalem but from Jerusalem to areas outside Israel. There is only one explanation for the total absence of this correspondence: it was suppressed and destroyed by those of the 'faithful' who wished to exalt Paul and his conception of Jesus Christ as God.

The truth of this can be gleaned by a careful reading of the New Testament itself. Here we find strong evidence that Paul's teachings were rejected by the Jerusalem Church, whose members, in contrast to Paul, had actually known Jesus and heard him preach (something the self-appointed 'Apostle to the Gentiles' had never done). Unfortunately, the writer of Acts, and indeed most of the Gospel writers, are all strongly Pauline in their world view and, true to the tradition of their time, they either modify or omit anything that they deem contrary to what they see as the 'truth'. To discover the authentic beliefs of Jesus' friends and associates concerning the Master, I was forced to carefully research the New Testament works of scholarship, and to collate all the information that has managed to escape the diligent and uncompromising eyes of the many Pauline editors and revisionists.

Christianity – The First 30 Years

The Israel of Jesus' time was a hotbed of political intrigue, factional infighting and shifting alliances. A foreign king, Herod, ruled over the country, acting in concert with the Roman authorities. Anti-mystical Israel held the reins of power in the form of a Sadducee High Priest whose party was in alliance with the majority of the Pharisee sect. Mystical Israel – including both the Nazarites and Essenes – were sidelined but increasingly resentful at what they saw as the straying from the Law by the priestly establishment. Such transgressions included winking at Herodian 'incest' (for example, Herod of Chalcis married his niece Bernice, an infamous young woman who was said to have 'fornicated' with her own brother[7]) and 'polluting the temple' by accepting gifts for the Jerusalem temple from Herodians and later from the hated Romans.[8] These were not simply religious questions. Just as in Iran and several other Muslim countries today, in ancient Israel it was impossible to separate religion from politics. Temple and state were one. It could hardly have been otherwise – the whole of Jewish society and the rule of law were based on their holy books. Religion was politics, and politics religion.

The breach between anti-mystical and mystical Israel was deep and bitter. Feelings ran so high that the Sadducee priestly elite enjoined its followers to execrate mystical Israel three times each day with the formula: 'Oh God, send thy curse upon the Nazarites.'

It is becoming increasingly clear that the 'Church' that survived the execution of Jesus had been and remained deeply involved with the political intrigues of the time. That it was a Nazarite Church, both in action and in name, is undeniable. Even in the Acts of the Apostles, Nazarite is the only term used by the writers when referring to the post-Crucifixion followers of Jesus. Jesus was executed as a Nazarite. And of equal importance is the identity of the leader who followed Jesus as head of the sect. This was James, the brother of Jesus. That he was a Nazarite is undoubted; his character and actions conform exactly to those of a member of the sect. Eusebius, quoting Hegessipus, states that James:

> Was holy from his mother's womb; drank no wine or strong drink, nor ate animal food; no razor came upon his head; he neither oiled himself or used the bath; he alone was permitted to use the holy places, for he never wore wool, but linen . . . Indeed, on account of his exceeding great righteousness he was called 'the righteous' and 'Olbias', which means in Greek 'defence of the people' and 'righteousness'.[9]

In addition, when Paul fell out of favour and decided to travel back to Jerusalem to face James and the remaining disciples, he was commanded to prove his innocence of a charge of 'preaching against the Laws of Moses' by a very telling ceremony. Paul was required to visit the temple and retake his Nazarite vows there. That he, too, had been previously inducted into the sect is admitted even by Acts. When Paul is brought before the Roman procurator, Felix, he is described as a known 'ringleader of the sect of Nazoraei'.

The Importance of the Bloodline

Not only was the sect of the Nazarites political, but its leadership seems to have been hereditary. James succeeded Jesus when Jesus was put to death for a political crime – sedition. And on James's own politically inspired death, it was a cousin of Jesus who assumed control. There seems no reason to doubt that, in the original 'Church', a bloodline and hereditary accession to the leadership was paramount. At the time of the Emperor Domitian, two great-nephews of Jesus (grandsons of his brother Jude) were head of the Nazarite sect, and, according to M. Martin, the Desposyni (descendants of the bloodline to which Jesus himself belonged) still possessed high positions until at least AD 318, when they had discussion with the Bishop of Rome in an attempt to re-establish their authority.[10] This hereditary principle is acknowledged by Eduard Meyer, the eminent authority in his monumental study of Christian origins. He agrees that James's rise to power was due to the supreme fact of his blood relationship to Jesus. He further suggests that, in the beginnings of the Christian Church, there were the seeds of a caliphate or imamate, based on the bloodline of the 'prophet' Jesus, such as was later to arise in mature form in Islam.[11] However, knowing what we now know concerning Jesus' ancestral links, it seems more likely that the succession was based on both his and his brother James's connection to a far earlier and exalted bloodline, that of the Pharaoh Akhenaten, known in Jewish history as Moses.

Virgin Birth

If a hereditary principle was involved, and the bloodline was of such great importance, then this negates to a very great degree the necessity of the Virgin Birth. Along with the concomitant 'perpetual virginity' of Mary (an untenable proposition, given the brothers and sisters of Jesus), this piece of dogma has a relatively late date, being made a required article of faith only in the nineteenth century. The early Christians apparently knew nothing of a Virgin Birth, and once again it seems it is to Saint Paul that we owe this doctrinal add-on. Paul was born in Tarsus, a city in Asia Minor whose atmosphere was suffused with many and various pagan cults and religions. The majority of such beliefs centred around a dying/resurrecting god (for example, Adonis, Tammuz and Attis) and in almost every case the god had miraculously been born from a virgin goddess. It appears that, either subconsciously or because he felt that the cult of 'Jesus as God' that he established would be disadvantaged in competition with these other beliefs, a similarly fabulous myth was appended to the birth of the historical Jesus. And this was done despite the ignorance of such an event among both his family and those who had known Jesus while he was alive.

Jewish Christians

There is overwhelming evidence that James the Just, Jesus' brother, his family and the whole of the Nazarite Church regarded themselves as Jews. They kept the Jewish dietary laws and feast days, they maintained the ritual of circumcision, and they continued to regard Jerusalem as the spiritual centre of the world, and their own race in particular as set apart from the ordinary run of mankind and privy to a special relationship with God. Josephus, the Jewish patriot turned Roman historian of the Jews, while specifically rejecting the Messiahship of Jesus, speaks of James in glowing terms as a man of righteousness. He even goes so far as to suggest that the destruction of Jerusalem by the Romans was God's retribution on the Jews for the murder of James, a man who so studiously upheld the tenets of their religion. This outraged the early Church Fathers, who believed that Josephus should have said that Christ's death was the reason for such divine retribution.[12]

So, like other Jewish sects and sub-cults, the Nazarites remained Jews, with a Judaic theology of strict monotheism. In fact, as spiritual and actual inheritors of Akhenaten's religious vision, they were more bound than most to this view. And this presents enormous problems for the orthodox view of the early Church as a body that considered Jesus as the divine Messiah; who actively believed in the divinity of Jesus, and in his equality with the Most High God of the Jews.

Such a concept is totally alien to Judaism of whatever colour. To begin with, Christian theology has corrupted the very meaning of the term 'Messiah'. It has conditioned us to a belief that the Messiah refers solely and uniquely to the divine son of God who came to earth to save mankind in general from our sins. However, the Jewish conception was of a much more secular and far more nationalistic champion of the faith. There could indeed be several Messiahs, and several Qur'an texts, including the Damascus Document, point to a priestly Messiah (the Messiah of Aaron) and to a Messiah of Israel, a form of hero-king.[13] This latter was to be a rightful king of the House of David, and his function in God's plan was to restore the independence and supremacy of Israel. The Talmud, and Jewish writings in general, give no indication that the Messiah was to be a divine being. Accordingly, we must be careful, when reading that the Nazarite Church regarded Jesus as Messiah, to understand the term in the strictly Jewish, as opposed to the later Christian, sense of the word.

The Suffering Servant

While the Nazarites were firm believers in the Jewish concept of the Messiah, this was, of course, only the public face of the sect, the aspect of the teachings that could be openly acknowledged. The inner mysteries of the Nazarites, including the ritual meaning of Jesus' death, and the removal of the head as a sacred relic, would perforce have remained secret, confined to the higher initiates of their sect. However, the 'Church' headed by James aspired to politico-religious power in Israel: they believed that they alone possessed the 'way', the manner of living which would reconcile the people of Israel to God. To implement this policy, they required political power and that demanded the support of the people. But acquiring that support posed a difficult problem, as the masses could never be made privy to the deeper secrets of the sect. The covert truth of the life and death of Jesus had to be supplemented by another account, an overt analysis that would satisfy and appeal to the people.

This was no easy task. The most that could be revealed was that they considered Jesus as a Messiah, but even this relatively simple statement faced immense difficulties. Jesus had been crucified by Rome, but he had also been arrested and condemned to death for blasphemy at a Jewish hearing, and the leaders of the Jewish religious-political establishment had played a decisive part in his demise. Had Jesus died by the hand of Rome alone, then he could easily have been proclaimed a hero and martyr for his people. But 'How could they reasonably proclaim Jesus as the long-hoped-for Messiah if he had been condemned to death on a charge of blasphemy by the High Priest and the Sanhedrin?'[14] The Nazarite hierarchy might know and believe that the orthodox High Priest was more in league with the devil than with the Most High, but such a statement would serve only to alienate a large segment of the populace, who still held the religious establishment in high esteem. But even if the Imperial forces had acted alone, without Jewish connivance, there were still immense theological problems to face: '. . . the mode of his death was particularly offensive to Jewish religious scruples, for the Law explicitly stated: "he that is hanged [on a tree] is accursed of God".'[15]

ORIGINAL CHRISTIANITY

To present their case to the Jewish people with any hope of success, at least one important factor had to be satisfied. The Jewish faith was to a very great extent a religion of the Law and Scripture: all acts and ritual had to be sanctioned by appeal to the Holy Writings. The Nazarite position on their 'Messiah Jesus' therefore needed a scriptural warranty. This was apparently found in the concept of the 'suffering servant' in Isaiah:

> Who hath believed our report? And to whom hath the arm of the Lord been revealed? . . . He was despised and rejected of men, a man of sorrows and acquainted with grief: and as one from whom men hide their face he was despised, and we esteemed him not. Surely he hath borne our griefs and carried our sorrows: yet we esteem him stricken, smitten of God, and afflicted. But he was wounded for our transgressions, he was bruised for our iniquities; the chastisement of our peace was upon him; and with his stripes we are healed (Isaiah liii, 1–5).

This was a passage in the Jewish scriptures that had held little interest to Jewish theologians before now. But for Jesus, rejected by many of his co-religionists, and accursed of God from his hanging on a tree, the text was remarkably apposite, and it ameliorated to some extent the terrible humiliation and curse of the Crucifixion. However, it is notable that although Jesus was regarded as a prophet and, in a strictly Jewish sense, Messiah (albeit a suffering Messiah), never at any point is there an attempt at identifying him as the Most High God that the Jews worshipped. This was, quite simply, impossible according to the Judaic world view.

The Impossibility of Deification

The essential fact of Jewish monotheism served as an unbridgeable chasm between man and God. As the biblical scholar S. G. F. Brandon noted, it proscribed the bestowing of any characteristics 'which would have changed the human status of an individual, no matter how highly honoured, to that of divinity. Already Hebrew history contained the record of great heroes who were deeply reverenced and proudly remembered by their descendants, but even though, as Abraham, they were named "the friend of God" . . . or, as Elijah, had been miraculously assumed into heaven, the absolute gulf which marked off human from divine was never transgressed . . . It may accordingly be fairly concluded that those Jews

95

who had learned to reverence Jesus of Nazareth but who also continued faithful to their national religion would have instinctively preserved that essential demarcation between human and divine in the conscious formulation of their belief about their Master's true vocation, and more especially in their exposition of that belief to their countrymen'.[16] In short, it is inconceivable that the Nazarite Church regarded Jesus as God.

Other evidence confirms this. It appears that the Nazarite Church eventually came to enjoy friendly relations with a number of influential Pharisees. The Pharisees are known to have believed in the resurrection of the dead, a tenet that subsequently became incorporated in Christian orthodoxy. But they remained Jews, monotheistic to the bone. It is therefore hardly likely that they would have associated themselves with a group that proclaimed the deeply heretical view that the crucified Jesus was God.

A further indication that the 'Messiah' explanation given to the masses was not the whole story is evident from the Nazarite Church's subsequent treatment of the logical repercussions of their theory. Quite simply, they ignored them. Although theological speculation was an integral part of Jewish culture, and despite the fact that the concept of the crucified Jesus as suffering Messiah opened a rich field for speculation, once they had formulated the concept the Nazarite Church made no attempt to investigate its theological consequences. We are therefore justified in suspecting that the overt 'Jesus equals suffering Messiah' concept was actually of far less importance to the Illuminati of the sect than the esoteric teachings of the divine king and the sacred head.

So, the original concept of Jesus, held by his brother and his disciples, appears to have been that of a great king and prophet (this latter is the title Jesus himself prefers in the Bible). For the masses, his death was explained in terms of the 'suffering servant' ideal. Those belonging to the inner circle, while believing in the spiritual mission of Jesus, nevertheless regarded him as mortal, born of a union between Joseph and Mary, and as a link in a continuing hereditary chain. It was this original Christianity (adhering most closely to Jesus' own teachings, and carrying with it the Nazarite reverence for the head) which lost the battle against Saint Paul's version of a deified Jesus, and which, as we will see in Chapter Seven, was eventually extirpated from the Holy Land.

But this original Christianity did not completely die out. It was transplanted to Egypt, and to another most unlikely location: to Britain. According to several ancient accounts, less than four years after Christ's death his followers, led by Jesus' uncle Joseph of Arimathea, had established their 'Church' in Somerset. The facts of the case were for centuries acknowledged by the Catholic Church, which accorded the British Church precedence above all others for this very reason. This is not as improbable as it sounds. There is much evidence that the Jews were great travellers long before the time of Christ.

CHAPTER SIX

THE MYTH OF ISRAEL

Tribal Migrations

ODERN HUMANS (*Homo sapiens sapiens*) are believed to have evolved somewhere between 60,000 and 80,000 years ago, and by 12,000 years BP they had spread themselves over the whole of the globe.[1] Technological advances enhanced human reproductive success and at the same time increased the level and speed of migration. Animal domestication evolved around 8,000 years ago, while mankind was still in the Stone Age, and was followed shortly after by settled agriculture.[2] This 'Neolithic Revolution', and hard on its heels the discovery of metalworking, produced a surplus of food which allowed for a spectacular 16-fold increase in human numbers between 8000 and 4000 BC.[3] City-states arose, and with them the development of a form of politics which, to all intents and purposes, is identical to present-day practices, with sovereign and independent states vying for supremacy and striving by whatever means to extend their territory at the expense of others.

The effects of population explosion and political adventurism combined effectively to increase the level of migration, especially across the Eurasian continent. To read the ancient records is to realise the reality and constancy of migration in antiquity. And the distances covered are truly vast, even by the standards of today. As early as 6000 BC migrants from Anatolia (one of the original centres of the agricultural revolution) sailed across the Aegean to Thessaly and Crete. From here they moved north and west, some even reaching the British Isles around 4000 BC. About 2,500 years later, certain

Celtic tribes were to make much the same journey across Europe, from the steppes north of the Caucasus Mountains as far as Ireland in the west. In the fourth century AD, the Huns travelled clear across the Eurasian continent from China to France (a distance of over 5,000 miles) and were repulsed only after their defeat at the Battle of Catalaunian Fields in 451 and the death of their leader, Attila, two years later. This invasion of mongoloid people forced a huge involuntary movement (to the west and south) of the 'Germanic peoples' who for several centuries had been settled on the northern border of the Roman Empire. This was the immediate reason behind the invasion of the Visigoths, who sacked Rome in 410. Wave after wave of migrant tribes followed: Alans, Vandals (who sacked Rome in 455), Sueves, Alemans and finally the Ostrogoths, who took over most of Italy by 493.[4]

The list of human migrations could be extended, page after page after page. It is, almost literally, endless. It is easy to feel swamped by the monumental nature of these migrations, by the terrible sufferings of those who made the long journeys and the misery they in turn inflicted on those whose homelands they invaded and whose patrimony they stole. But for the purposes of my investigation, two points stood out like beacons: travel and migration in what we regard as 'primitive' cultures has been commonplace in the ancient history of the human race. And the movement of large numbers of people across enormous distances was by no means a rare event.

The Myth of Israel

So, it is not surprising that the history of the Jewish race begins with the migration of the patriarch Abraham with his people and his flocks. Abraham moved north from Ur (close to modern-day Baghdad) to Haran, then westwards into Palestine. From here he and his entourage travelled to Egypt, and then finally back to Palestine, where he settled. Abraham's 'grandson', Jacob (later known as Israel), led his people south again to Egypt at the behest of Joseph (who has been identified as Yuya, the Vizier of Pharaoh Amenhotep III).[5] The Children of Israel settled in Goshen, around the Nile Delta, for between 12 and 14 generations, before the Exodus forced them north once again into Palestine.

This migratory pattern of the Hebrew nation is accepted as correct by most authorities. It is with Israel's subsequent story that problems begin. Orthodox history, if it considers the subject at all, relates that Israel's travels ended with the Exodus. Alone of all the nations of the earth, we have been taught to believe that, between the Exodus of around 1350 BC and their dispersion at the time of the fall of Jerusalem in AD 70, the Hebrews were an entirely sedentary and settled people – that they were somehow frozen in time and space. This is another example of the tendency to mythologise Jewish history, to make the Jewish nation 'special'; or rather, two-dimensional. As God's chosen people, we do not like the idea that the Jews could have been riven by the same factional infighting, religious wars, intolerance, expulsions and ethnic cleansings that have constantly plagued the rest of humanity throughout our species' troubled existence on this planet. Unfortunately, this myth – with the Israelites rooted to the Holy Land, worshipping a single god, and never migrating – is almost diametrically opposed to the true history of the Hebrew people.

Schism in Israel

Following the conquest of Canaan in around 1300 BC, the Children of Israel divided up the land between the 12 tribes. Or rather between the 11 tribes – the House of Levi was distributed as a priestly caste between the other tribes, and the House of Joseph (perhaps because of his earlier exalted position in Egypt) was given double portions in the half-tribes of Joseph's sons Ephraim and Manessah (see figure 3).

But this happy situation did not last very long. The high point of Jewish fortunes came with the tribal King David and reached its apotheosis in his son, Solomon, a monarch whose wealth was legendary, and whose name has become a byword for wisdom. It was Solomon who constructed the first Temple of Jerusalem, though the religious practices of those days were far less Yahweh-centred than the orthodox scribes of the Old Testament would have us believe. Sun-worship also formed a major part of the Temple of Jerusalem's cultus, with the temple itself being orientated to face the rising sun.[6]

This eclectic attitude to religion obviously angered those Israelites who adhered solely to the god Yahweh. It seems that there were great divisions within Israel, and only Solomon's enormous reputation and strong personality kept things from boiling over. However, as soon as he was dead, matters rapidly came to a head. The story given in the Bible is that when the Children of Israel gathered at Shechem in order to confirm Solomon's son Rehoboam as the dead king's successor, they complained formally to the heir apparent of his father's stern rule and asked that he promise to make their lot easier (1 Kings xii, 4). Rehoboam replied: 'My father made your yoke heavy, and I will add to your yoke: my father hath chastised you

The Tribes of Israel divided between the southern Kingdom of Judah and the northern Kingdom of Israel

DAN

NAPHTALI

ASHER

MANASSEH

ZEBULUN

ISSACHAR

ISRAEL

MANASSEH

Samaria

EPHRAIM

Jordan River

GAD

Mediterranean Sea

DAN

BENJAMIN

Jerusalem

REUBEN

Dead Sea

Arabian Desert

JUDAH

SIMEON

JUDAH

EGYPT

Figure 3: The Divided Kingdom of Israel (after Capt, 1996)

with whips, but I will chastise you with scorpions.' Faced with such arrogant boasting, a full ten of the tribes left to form their own kingdom, leaving this son of Solomon with the single tribe of Judah, and a portion of Benjamin, to rule over from Jerusalem. From that time, the Hebrews were divided into two separate kingdoms, Israel in the north, and the kingdom of Judah in the south.

On a closer reading, this Bible account, with kingly arrogance the sole reason for the schism, appears to be only half the story. Having rejected Rehoboam, the kingdom of Israel immediately chose Jeroboam as king. Intriguingly, he is a descendant of Joseph, who ruled in Egypt and was therefore a descendant of the Egyptian Pharaoh Tutmosis III. Was this, I wondered, Joseph's descendants reclaiming their birthright? And Jeroboam's first act is to set up as 'gods' two golden calves. The Bible makes out that these golden calves are Jeroboam's own invention, but they are obviously the symbols of the old cult that had followed the Israelites out of Egypt, the golden calf which was set up by Aaron below Mount Sinai, while Moses conversed with Yahweh among the cloud and thunder of the peak. The golden calf is one of the sacred symbols of the mother-goddess, known as Belial in the Levant and as Isis in Egypt. It is clear from this that at least part of the problem surrounding the schism was the religious direction of Israel. The majority of the Hebrews rejected Yahweh and wished instead to follow the religion of the Egyptian Great Goddess. And they chose as king a man whose right to rule depended on his association with the Egyptian royal family.

The Captives

Superimposed on this domestic crisis were problems generated by the region's unique strategic position. Around the time of the schism, and the division of the Hebrews into Judah and Israel, the hegemony of the known world was being contested by the powerful empires of Egypt and Assyria. With the easiest route between the two warring power blocs lying through Canaan, it was inevitable that the region would be drawn into the conflict. In the eighth century BC the Assyrian Empire was ruled by Tiglath-pileser III, a warlike monarch who initiated a policy of deportation of conquered or rebellious subject nations to new lands, usually on the more vulnerable borders of his empire. The territory made empty by such forced emigrations was not left fallow but was filled by further deportations of other conquered nations into the area.[7] Soon, it was Israel's turn to feel the full force of this innovative foreign policy.

In around 750 BC Tiglath-pileser moved his forces south, easily conquering the northern kingdom of Israel and taking many captives:

> . . . he carried them away, even the Reubenites, and the Gadites, and the half tribe of Manasseh, and brought them into Halah, and Habor, and Hara, and to the river Gozan, unto this day (1 Chronicles v, 25–26).

This attack degraded the strength of the kingdom of Israel, with three tribes forcibly settled in and around the area we now call Kurdistan.

Around 23 years later Assyria invaded again. For the most northern of the two Jewish states it was quite literally a deathblow:

> This conquest proved wholly destructive of the kingdom of Israel, Hoshea [the king] being made prisoner, and his subjects being transported to Media, in Persia, and replaced by people whom Shalmaneser caused to remove from the borders of Chuthah, a river in Persia, for the purpose of settling in the land of Samaria (Josephus, *Antiquities* ix, 13–14).

So all the Children of Israel, except the tribe of Judah (and a remnant of Benjamin) were moved beyond the Euphrates by the Assyrians. And a Persian people were settled in their place in Samaria. The ten tribes never returned and were either assimilated, or (a more likely occurrence) took on a new identity and way of life, and slowly forgot their original provenance. Their eventual fate is still a subject of heated conjecture among specialists, but the fact of their migration to Persia is not seriously doubted.

As if this were not enough, just 150 years later a Babylonian army under Nebuchadnezzar conquered the southern kingdom of Judah, whose king, Zedekiah, had rebelled against his authority. In imitation of the Assyrian custom, Nebuchadnezzar carried off the better part of the population of the kingdom of Judah to Babylon. The captives (numbering over 100,000 individuals) seem to have adapted well to their new lifestyle, and within a generation or two began to feel that Babylon was their home. When Cyrus of Persia destroyed Babylon in 538 BC and allowed the Israelites free passage to their homeland, fewer than 50,000 souls accepted his offer. The remainder chose to continue their new life in Babylon. It is this tiny 'remnant of Judah' (with admixture from the races surrounding Jerusalem) that gave rise to the nation we know today as the Jews.

The Tribe of Benjamin

It was not always foreign conquerors who forced such national migrations; civil war could be just as effective. Before the attacks of the Assyrians and Babylonians, the biblical Book of Judges tells the story of the conflict of one tribe, Benjamin, with the rest of the Children of Israel (Judges xix–xxi). According to the tale given in the Bible, the Benjamites refused to hand over certain 'sons of Belial' (Isis) who had committed rape and murder on the concubine of a Levite travelling through their territory. Why the Benjamites took this stance is not known, but it seems to suggest a sympathy with the sons of Belial, and to imply that many Benjamites were Jewish 'heretics' who had rejected Yahweh and were themselves adherents of the goddess Isis. Whatever the truth of this, a merciless civil war ensued, in which the Benjamites were at first victorious. However, numbers gradually told on the beleaguered 'heretic tribe', and they were finally routed.

An account in the *Dossier Secrets* of the Priory of Sion[8] indicates that, as a result of this defeat, many Benjamites crossed from Palestine to Greece, landing in the region known as Arcadia.[9] The account states that the Benjamites eventually left Arcadia and followed the Danube west into Europe, intermarrying with non-Jewish tribes as they migrated, and appeared in Western Europe in what is now Germany under a new name, the Sicambrians, led by an enigmatic line of priest-kings, the Merovingians, whose descent from the Benjamites is strongly implied. Intriguingly, certain sections of Salic law (used extensively by Merovingian monarchs) have been shown to include strong elements of Judaic law taken from the Talmud, an inclusion that is inconceivable without a close association with a Judaic element at some time in their history.[10] Even more telling, and in an echo of the Nazarite sect and the sacred head, the Merovingian monarchs were known as the Long-Haired Kings and were forbidden to cut their hair, which was held to be sacred.[11]

The Tribe of Dan

There is even stronger evidence for believing that another part of Israel, the tribe of Dan also emigrated to Europe. But while the 'captivities' were all forced migrations, and the Benjamites fled because of defeat in war, the Danites appear to have been willing travellers.

The Danites were descended from Dan, a son of Jacob by one of the patriarch's concubines, Bilhah. They became a powerful tribe, and even shortly after the Exodus were able to field some 62,700 fighting men. As their portion of conquered Palestine, the tribe of Dan were given the coastal cities to the north of Phoenicia, from Askelon to Joppa. However, this area was not considered large enough for so powerful a tribe, and the Danites cast covetous eyes on the Canaanite region of Leshem: '. . . therefore the Children of Dan went up to fight against Leshem, and took it, and smote it with the edge of the sword, and possessed it . . . and [they] dwelt therein, and called Leshem, Dan, after the name of Dan their father' (Joshua xix, 47). This commemoration of their ancestral title, in placenames and geographical locations, was continued by the Danites wherever they colonised or conquered, and it has allowed researchers to follow in some detail the tribe's migrations across the Mediterranean and beyond.

As a coastal tribe, living near the seafaring Phoenicians, it would have been entirely natural for the Danites to have acquired an interest, and a skill, in maritime enterprises. And so we find (Judges v, 17) that within a hundred years of the Exodus the Danites possessed a considerable number of their own ships, a fleet large enough to accommodate most of their number, who fled aboard when an invasion of their land was threatened.

Even before the time of Solomon, this fleet seems to have acted in conjunction with the Phoenician traders, and especially with the city of Tyre. In contrast to many Jews, and testifying to their more cosmopolitan attitude, Danites and the Tyrians often intermarried. Hiram Abif, the architect who supervised the building of King Solomon's temple (the edifice that looms so large in the legends of both the Templars and the Freemasons), was the offspring of a daughter of Dan and a man of Tyre (2 Chronicles ii, 14). King Solomon certainly had an oceangoing fleet that sailed at least as far as western Spain (Tarshish): 'For the king [Solomon] had at sea a navy of Tarshish with the navy of Hiram [king of Tyre]: once in three years came the navy of Tarshish bringing gold and silver, ivory and apes and peacocks' (1 Kings x, 22). That the Danites and men of Tyre were trading partners is confirmed by Ezekiel, in his fulminations against the 'infidel' city. Pronouncing the imminent destruction of Tyre, he says: '. . . Dan also and Javan [Greeks] going to and fro occupied thy fairs.'[12] It follows from this that the Danite ships had reached at least as far as Greece.

The Colonies of Dan

But it seems that the Danites wandered much further afield, 'because we find Grecian, Irish, Scandinavian and English histories teeming with notices of a certain race called Danai, Danaans, or Dannonii, who are either called Phoenicians, or mentioned in company with Phoenicians and almost wherever Phoenicians are said to have traded, there we either hear of these Danai, or we find a river or district stamped with the name of Dan . . .'.[13]

Strangely, by the time of the writing of the Old Testament Chronicles, the tribe of Dan vanishes entirely from the Bible records. In 1 Chronicles iv–vi, Dan is entirely omitted from the genealogies. The chronicler Grotius records the story that the Danites in Israel were reduced to just a single family, surnamed Huss, whose line was eventually extinguished. However, the tribe of Dan did not die out completely, as the later writings of Ezekiel indicate that in the future division of land the Danites are included, and in fact head the list of beneficiaries. But how could this be? If the Danites were extinguished from Israel, where else could they be? The answer seems to be that they, too, emigrated from the Levant and flourished in colonies far afield.

A ninth-century Jewish writer known to historians as Eldad makes a very telling comment on the fate of the Danites at this critical time in Jewish history. Writing to his co-religionists in Spain, he relates that 'in Jeroboam's time [when the ten tribes split from Judah and Benjamin, and the prospect of civil war was imminent] the tribe of Dan, being unwilling to shed their brethren's blood, took a resolution of leaving their country'.[14]

The Greek Danai

So, around 1000 BC, the Danites took ship en masse and left their homeland for ever. They were undoubtedly absorbed by existing colonies of their kinsfolk that we know were already thriving in such places as Greece, the Black Sea and even perhaps as far afield as Ireland. In addition, there is very good evidence that the Danite diaspora included the nation known to antiquity as the Danai. This famous Greek tribe is mentioned in many ancient writings (Pindar, Euripides and Strabo, for example) and their Judaic antecedents have long been a matter of controversy.

The Danai were said to have originated in Egypt, as, of course, did the Jews. The Egyptian priest Apion, writing at around the time of Christ, names the Children of Israel as renegade Egyptians; and Diodorus Siculus, writing in the first century BC, relates that the Egyptians 'expelled all the aliens gathered together in Egypt. The most distinguished of the expelled foreigners followed Danaus and Cadmus into Greece: but the greater number were led by Moses into Judaea.'[15] According to the Greek histories, it was King Danaus who arrived in Argos with his followers and who gave his name to the people and the land. Robert Graves is in no doubt that this is a folk-memory of the arrival of the tribe of Dan.[16] In similar fashion, Professor Latham believes that Danites were undoubtedly the Danai of Homer's Greece. He states firmly that:

> The Argive Danai were no other than that of the Israelite tribe of Dan, only we are so used to confine ourselves to the soil of Palestine in our consideration of the Israelites, that we treat them as if they were

adscripti glebae [tied to the soil] and ignore the share they may have taken in the ordinary history of the world.[17]

It is therefore very likely that those members of the House of Dan that left to avoid shedding 'their brethren's blood' made landfall among the Danai, or other areas previously settled by the descendants of Dan.

The Spartans

Those Danai calling themselves the Heraclidae, or Sons of Heracles, were traders (Hebrew: Heracleem = trader). From these Heraclidae descended the Lacedaemonians, or Spartans. Intriguingly, I discovered that the Spartans had the same taboo on cutting the hair as both the Nazarites and the future Merovingian monarchs. Moreover, at least one Spartan king had in his possession an oracular embalmed head, which he regarded as his most treasured possession and which (like the Templar Baphomet) was the source of all his good fortune.[18]

The Spartans are known to have claimed kinship with the Jews. Their letter to this effect, brought by two envoys, Demoteles and Araeus, was acknowledged by the Onias, High Priest of Jerusalem, with the following words:

> We joyfully received the epistle and were well pleased with Demoteles and Araeus, although we did not need such a demonstration, because we were well satisfied about it from the sacred writings (Josephus, *Antiquities* xiii, 8).

Just what this 'demonstration' consisted of is not recorded, but of vital interest is the seal which was set upon the Spartan letter to the Jews: 'This letter was four-square, and the seal is an eagle with a dragon in its claws' (Josephus xiii). This is a vital piece of information. In biblical times, the tribe of Dan had two symbols. The tribal sign was a serpent, but as the leader of one of the four 'camps' into which the twelve tribes were divided, Dan had a second symbol, the eagle, one of the four symbols of the cherubim. In the course of time both signs were combined: 'Ancient Hebrew and Caldee authorities say that Dan bore on his standard a crowned serpent or basilisk held in the claws of an eagle' (Mazzaroth 41); and again: 'Ancient Jewish authorities unanimously assert that Dan bore scorpio under an eagle' (Mazaroth 39).

The Spartan seal was likewise an eagle with a dragon in its claws. In other words, it was identical to the ancient standard of the Israelite tribe of Dan.

Tuatha de Danaan

Ireland's most ancient manuscripts tell of the coming of a race known as the Tuatha de Danaan, the people or tribe of Danaan, who arrived in Ireland sometime between 1200 and 1000 BC:

> The colony called the Tuatha de Danaan . . . became masters of Ireland. It appears that the Danaans were a highly civilised people, far more skilled in arts and sciences than any of the other colonies that settled in Ireland. They ruled in Ireland about two centuries, or 197 years according to the Psalter of Cashel, and were highly skilled in architecture and other arts from their long residence in Greece and intercourse with the Phoenicians.[19]

This long sojourn in Greece and close relations with Phoenicia correspond exactly to what we have learned so far concerning the history of the tribe of Dan. Moreover, additional Danaan colonists (together with Milesians – said to be of the same race) are described as arriving in small groups from Greece, Gothland on the Euxine and from 'near the Euxine and Caspian Seas'. These are all areas of known Danite colonisation. Later histories confirm the fact of a Danite presence in Ireland. When Israel was invaded by Nebuchadnezzar in 586 BC and King Zedekiah was blinded and taken in chains to Babylon, an ancient account tells that one of his daughters, Tamar Tephi, accompanied by the prophet Jeremiah, fled first to Egypt and then by sea to Ireland, carrying with them the sacred stone that had formed the pillow of the Patriarch Jacob. In Ireland, Tamar Tephi, as a princess of the royal line of David, married Eochaid the Heremon, the Ardath, or High King, of Ireland. Astonishingly, the chronicles record that Tamar Tephi's new husband was himself of Israelite descent, being closely allied to one of the Jewish tribes – the tribe of Dan.[20]

I sat back to consider what I had learned. The evidence was clear enough: most of the Children of Israel had been forcibly relocated beyond the Euphrates. Prior to this, the Benjamites had fled to Europe. And the Greek Danaans, the Spartans, and the Irish tribe of Danaan were all descended from the same stock, the Hebrew tribe of Dan, which had spread itself throughout Asia Minor and Europe. Long before the time of Christ, there were colonies of Jewish descent scattered all over the known world, in Media, Babylon, around the Black Sea, along the shores of the Mediterranean, and as far west as Ireland. Far from being the quiet, stay-at-home race of orthodox accounts, this information showed the Hebrews to have taken an active role in mainstream history, revealing them as one of the foremost pioneering nations in the millennium preceding Christ. And as I was soon to discover, this adventuring, colonising spirit did not perish in the century following Jesus' birth.

CHAPTER SEVEN

THE PAULINE HERESY

The Unique Status of the Jerusalem Church

WE HAVE SEEN in Chapter Five that the Jerusalem Church, headed by Jesus' brother James, enjoyed a unique status among early Christians. The brother of the Lord and the disciples were regarded, quite rightly, as the fount of all knowledge concerning Jesus. They were, after all, in the absolutely unique position of having seen the Master in the flesh, heard him speak, and imbibed his teachings at first hand. This was especially true of James, the brother of the Lord. He took over the running of the Nazarite Church following the Crucifixion, and it could quite truthfully be said that he excelled Jesus in his religious observances and ritual acts.[1] This behaviour set the seal on his reputation for sanctity: he was named James the Just and was held in high esteem by many Jews, including certain Pharisees who were not formally attached to his sect. To the Jewish Christians of Palestine and beyond, the position of the Jerusalem Church in the first century AD corresponded in many ways to that of Rome in its days of Christian hegemony. And the status of James the Just was somewhat analogous to that of the Pope: in questions of doctrine, all early-Christian roads led to Jerusalem and to James the Just. His word was law.

Despite the importance of the Jerusalem Church, we have absolutely no original documents concerning the Mother Church of Christianity and the major participants in its affairs. And while we have the letters of Paul in abundance, those of the Mother Church of Christianity have been completely lost, or more likely destroyed. For the most part, we are forced to rely on the New Testament for what little we know of the earliest history of the 'Church'. Unfortunately, such information turns out to be more than a little suspect. When subject to careful analysis, many biblical 'facts' concerning the organisation of which Jesus was leader are found to be contradictory. An example of this is the 'chain of command' inherent in the Jerusalem Church. According to the Gospels, immediately below Jesus was a band of 12 men, the disciples, of which either Cephas or Peter is represented as being the leader. In one Gospel Peter is singled out and given unique spiritual authority, a commission that became the religious underpinning of the Church of Rome. In these accounts, James, the Lord's brother, is nowhere to be seen, or if he does appear he is represented as, at very least, unsympathetic to Jesus' cause.

By contrast, the New Testament letters of Paul reveal that the Church was set up with a triumvirate of James, Cephas and John, with James (notwithstanding the Gospels' depiction of him as unsympathetic) the obvious leader of the whole Church.[2]

Why such discrepancies? The answer is to be found in the deep schism that split the 'Church' that Jesus had founded (or, more probably, continued). Its cause was the 'heretical' teachings of the Jew, Saul of Tarsus, better known as Saint Paul. 'Schism' is perhaps too strong a word – when it came to Paul's new interpretation of Jesus, and his role in man's redemption, Paul was in a minority of one. His interpretation of Jesus as God, and as God for the circumcised and the uncircumcised alike, was strongly opposed by every member of the Mother Church. It was, on the face of it, a wholly unequal fight: one man born outside Palestine against a Judaean community that could claim direct continuity with the Master's traditions and who had known Jesus personally. With its great reputation and power, there is little doubt that the original Jewish doctrine of Jesus would have triumphed over Paul's hellenised God. Paul was in fact all but ordered to return to Jerusalem and perform vows that amounted to an acknowledgement of the Mother Church's supremacy. But by a quirk of fate, it was the doctrine of the mighty Jerusalem Church which perished, and that of the upstart Paul which triumphed. The story of this controversy throws a strong light on the original conception of Jesus and the nature of the Church he founded, and its existence has long been suppressed in orthodox Christian teaching.

Paul's New Interpretation

Apart from the blasphemy of overt deification of a man they regarded as a mortal prophet, Paul brought a new interpretation of the meaning of Jesus' life that greatly upset the Jewish-centred Jerusalem Church. Paul was convinced that in his experience on the road to Damascus, God had singled him out for a special mission – the conversion of the Gentiles. This was a revolutionary concept. While they were prepared to accept the occasional Gentile into their ranks (more especially if that Gentile were of a high social caste), the Jerusalem Church believed that the message of Jesus was essentially for the Jewish race alone. They had good reason for believing this. Jesus himself had sanctioned such an attitude. In the story of the Syro-Phoenician woman, the teachings are likened to bread, the Jews to children and the Gentiles to dogs: 'Let the children first be filled: for it is not meet to take the children's bread and cast it to the dogs' (Mark vii, 24–30; Matthew xv, 21–28). Similarly, the parable of casting pearls before swine has an anti-Gentile focus. 'Pearls' refers to the law,[3] and 'swine' was a rabbinical term for the non-Jewish world, especially Rome.[4] Indeed, when Jesus sends the Apostles on their mission he admonishes them: 'Go not into any way of the Gentiles, and enter not into any city of the Samaritans.' Given such statements (which must preserve a very early tradition, as it is inconceivable that they would have been made up by later Gentile converts), the attitude of the Jerusalem Church (and presumably of Jesus himself) would seem to be one of national superiority and religious exclusiveness.

Paul completely repudiated this Jewish-centred view. He is at pains to insist to his followers that his conversion to Christianity was completely independent of the Mother Church, and that it was some three years after his conversion that he made contact with James the Just.[5] During this time, it appears that Paul developed his ideas of Jesus in relative independence. Paul does not seem to believe that this lack of contact with those who had known Jesus in the flesh was a hindrance to his spiritual development. All was revealed to Paul through personal visions which, of course, are completely beyond the analysis of anyone save Paul himself. As the passage in 2 Corinthians shows, Paul conceives of Christ as a supernatural being, rejecting any knowledge of the Christ of the flesh (2 Corinthians, v: 14–17). While the Jerusalem Christians saw the death of Jesus in terms of Isaiaic prophecy and the suffering Messiah, Paul conceived '. . . in the Death and Resurrection of Jesus a Divine Mystery of Cosmic significance'.[6] It transcended all demarcations of race, culture, religion or geography. Christ had died for all. It followed therefore that faith in Christ was the only requirement: 'there cannot be Greek and Jew, circumcision and uncircumcision, barbarian, Scythian, bondman, freedman: but Christ is all, and in all.' It was this conception that underpinned Paul's belief that Christ had told him to take this 'gospel of uncircumcision' to the Gentiles.

'A Different Gospel', 'Another Jesus'

This was, of course, anathema to the Jewish Christians of the Jerusalem Church led by James the Just. Paul was preaching that faith in Jesus was sufficient, circumcision was unnecessary, dietary laws were redundant. Jesus had never said these things, but Paul was claiming that the risen Jesus had appeared to him in visions and given him this 'Gospel' to preach to Jew and Gentile alike. It was intolerable, and there is much evidence throughout the Epistles of Paul that the Jerusalem Church sent emissaries to the 'churches' Paul had set up among the Gentiles to instruct them in the true way. Saint Paul himself is witness to the existence of two rival 'Gospels', writing to the Galatian Christians that he is surprised that they have not remained faithful to his teachings and have taken on another Gospel (Galatians i, 6,7), while in his Second Epistle to the Corinthians he suspects that his converts have been led from Paul's own teachings by someone preaching 'another Jesus whom we did not preach' from a 'different gospel' (2 Corinthians xi, 4).

Paul was at a distinct disadvantage when faced with the rival Gospel and 'other Jesus' of the Mother Church. It should be remembered that Paul had never met Jesus while he was alive. Paul could not even claim to have heard Jesus' 'populist' message as part of the general multitude that listened to the Master. His understanding of Jesus' words was therefore always second-hand and based on the memory of others. He was never part of the innermost circle of disciples, and, although he seems to have taken the Nazarite vow, there is no way that he could have been privy to the secret teachings of the sect, of the worship of the Aten, and the true reason that lay behind the sanctity of the hair. Paul was therefore unaware that the sacred head had been embalmed, that it was still possible to look upon the Holy Face of the man he regarded as God. He was 'outside the loop' in a big way, preaching a Jesus whom the inner circle knew was totally erroneous. And the evidence shows that all the prestige of the Jerusalem Church, of those who had actually lived with Jesus and who had watched him die, was directed against Paul's teaching.

The biblical scholar Robert Eisenman has argued persuasively that the Habbakuk Pesher, a scroll from the Essene community, tells the story of the power struggle between James the Just, known in the scroll as the Teacher of Righteousness, and on the one hand the Wicked Priest (identified as the Sadducean High Priest of the Jerusalem Temple) and on the other a 'traitor' from their own community, which Eisenman identifies as the 'heretic' Paul.[7] Significantly, in this manuscript one of Paul's main titles is 'Spouter of Lies'. It is obvious from this that Paul's new interpretation of Jesus was given short shrift by the Essene/Nazarite community.

Faced with such an overwhelmingly logical rejection of his Jesus, based on a knowledge of the Master when he was alive, Paul used the only defence left open to him. He rejected utterly the relevance of the historical Jesus and claimed that he was basing his teaching on the spirit-mediated revelation vouchsafed to him by God on the road to Damascus. 'In his great apologia to the Galatians he boldly claims that the Gospel that he preached had no human source . . . he had received it by the special revelation of Jesus Christ (Galatians i, 11, 12). Any suggestion that some vital part of his knowledge had been derived by him from the Apostles of the Jerusalem community is significantly repudiated at length.'[8]

It is important to be clear what is happening here. Paul is saying that everything that Jesus had done on earth, all the teachings the Master had imparted to his disciples, every word he had spoken to the masses was of no importance whatever. It was quite literally irrelevant. It must all be swept away when set against the divinely inspired vision that he, Paul, had experienced. The disciples, Jesus' brother, everyone who had known the Master – they were well-meaning, but they were all deluded. Paul alone knew the true Jesus.

The arrogance of this assertion is breathtaking, and it is little wonder that it was rejected in its entirety by the Jerusalem Church. It was put about by some that Paul was mad, an accusation he refutes angrily in his Second Epistle to the Christians of Corinth. Paul adds that even if he is, it is because he and his companions have minds orientated towards God (2 Corinthians v, 12–19). With such freedom to believe only what he felt was true, Paul preached that faith alone was sufficient to bring people to the Way: dietary laws, circumcision, all were irrelevant provided the followers believed. And as a hellenised Jew, it seems Paul sought to deify Jesus and to foist upon him all the attributes of a pagan god – Virgin Birth, resurrection after three days (cf. Adonis, Tammuz, etc.). This was rank heresy to James the Just and many of Jesus' contemporaries and led to a deep split in the 'Christian' ranks, with Paul and his Gentile converts on one side and the Jewish Christians of the Jerusalem Church on the other.

Paul in Jerusalem

But while Paul insisted vehemently on the right of Gentiles to the redemption that Jesus had brought to earth, as a Jew he was loath to reject completely the God of his fathers. In addition, he had to find some way of retaining his Gentile converts by reconciling his position with that of the

Jerusalem Church, whose authority was unchallenged and unchallenge-able, even outside Judaea. His own position was untenable without such a reconciliation, and, knowing that a meeting with the unsympathetic leaders of the Jerusalem Church was inevitable, Paul attempts to allay their suspicions and dislike by seizing the initiative and visiting Jerusalem himself. And in order to make the meeting more amicable, he plans to bring with him what in modern-day parlance would be termed 'a sweetener'. In his Corinthian writings he shows great concern for the success of the collection of alms from the churches he has instituted, making it plain that he hopes the offering will make the Church at Jerusalem favourably disposed towards him.[9] This is hardly the action of a man sure of his position. In Acts, Paul (with a number of his Gentile converts) is depicted as undertaking the journey to Jerusalem full of doubt and with considerable misgivings.

Paul's forebodings were well founded. Although the visit was a bold move, designed to take the fight to those who controlled the Mother Church, it misfired horribly. James the Just was far too astute a politician to be fazed by Paul's bold gambit. When Paul arrived in the Holy City, the 'heretic' was accused of disloyalty to Judaism, of being an apostate. This was an extremely serious charge, one to which Paul had to respond. To prove his fealty, James devised a public test for Paul which placed him in a literal no-win situation, and, in passing, again gave evidence of the true nature of the Mother Church.

Paul was required to visit the temple and to perform the purificatory rites of the Nazarite vow. This is important. No other test, vow or sacrifice (and there were many such rites in the Jerusalem Temple) would do. Only the vow of the Nazarite, with its hallowing of the head, would, it seems, allay the fears of James and his compatriots. This speaks volumes, and goes far by itself to prove the Nazarite orientation of the Mother Church, with all this entails with regard to the sect's reverence for the head and worship of the sun as a symbol of the One God. Taken together with the other evidence reviewed in Chapters 1 and 5, it clearly made the case for a Nazarite origin of Christianity unassailable.

But there was more to the vow than this. It

... put Paul in a fatal dilemma. If he refused to give this proof of his orthodoxy, then he was in effect declaring himself an apostate of Judaism and thus would merit excommunication. On the other hand, he had come to Jerusalem, with a delegation of his converts, as the champion of the Gentile right to full participation in the new faith [he had developed]; if, therefore, he submitted to the order of James and provided evidence of his orthodoxy, his position in the eyes of his Gentile followers would be gravely compromised, for they would know that he, their champion, recognised his subordination to the Jerusalem authorities . . . For Paul the dilemma was inescapable. For all his gospel of the sufficiency of faith in Christ, he had illogically continued to recognise the claims of Judaism upon a Jew. And now that he was faced with the consequences of this fatal weakness in his logic, he obviously felt that he could not repudiate his national faith and accordingly submitted to his opponent's astute demand.[10]

Worse was to follow. Before he could complete the Nazarite ritual, a great multitude of the Jews rioted, accusing him of preaching against the law and the temple and of breaking a temple taboo by bringing a Greek into the temple precincts. Paul narrowly escaped being put to death and was arrested by the Roman guard just outside the temple, where he had been dragged by the mob. For the self-styled 'Apostles of the Gentiles' it was a complete disaster. He was imprisoned, and his followers were left with the memory of his subordination to the Mother Church without Paul being able, afterwards, to engage in damage limitation and attempt an apologia or to rationalise his actions. He was eventually placed on a boat for Rome where, as a Roman citizen, he was permitted to plead his case before Caesar. We do not know the outcome of this appeal, but it was almost certainly not favourable. Had he been vindicated at his Roman hearing, it is hardly likely that the writer of Acts would have failed to mention such a triumph. As it is, we hear no more of Paul after his embarkation for Rome, and it is presumed that shortly after his arrival in the Imperial capital he was put to death.

This left James the Just firmly in control of the Mother Church, with its Jewish rituals and barely disguised intolerance for Gentile converts. The champion of the Gentile cause was either imprisoned or dead. To any contemporary, it must have looked as if the cause of Pauline Christianity was irretrievably lost. But fate decreed otherwise, and two accidents of history combined to alter utterly the apparent triumph of the Jerusalem Church over the 'Spouter of Lies'.

Death of James the Just

That James the Just was a figure of some importance in Jerusalem society is undeniable. And whereas the author of Acts attempts to give the impression that the Judaean Christian community pursued its life in serene immunity from the fierce Jewish nationalism with which it was surrounded, other evidence suggests the opposite. In the Slavonic Josephus (believed by many scholars to be far closer to an unexpurgated version of the original work of Flavius Josephus), the author claims that Christianity was primarily a revolutionary movement against the Roman occupation of Palestine. This is probably overstating the case, but a political element was inevitably involved in any Jewish religious party of the time. The death of Jesus was certainly steeped in political intrigue. Jesus was arrested by a cohort of Roman soldiers – at least 500 – hardly the number of men anyone would send to pick up a pacifist preacher.[11] And as all Christian scripture attests, Jesus was tried, sentenced and executed by the Roman authorities as a rebel against the rule of Rome. The Nazarites were a politico-religious party and, both during and after Jesus' death, were deeply involved in the politics of the time. They appear to have been allied, at least loosely, with the Pharisees against the Sadducee priestly aristocracy, who were generally despised by the Jewish populace for their pro-Roman stance. Jesus was executed with the active connivance of the Saducean High Priest, and it is significant that in the accounts of the death of his brother James the Sadducees also play a leading part.

According to Josephus (*Antiquities* xx, 9), the death of James the Just was judicial murder, engineered by Ananus, the High Priest of the Temple of Jerusalem. During a hiatus in Roman rule occasioned by the death of the Procurator Festus, Ananus illegally convened a Sanhedrin, arrested James 'and some others' and charged them with breaking the law (that is, Mosaic Law). From what we know of the Nazarite secret teachings, such a charge was very probably correct, as the Nazarites held that there was a secret Mosaic Law unknown to the sacerdotal authorities. Unfortunately, Josephus does not record either how the trial was conducted or the specific charges levied against the accused, contenting himself with the statement that Ananus sentenced James and his co-accused to be stoned to death. He follows this with the significant remark that other men zealous for the law (but not of the Sadducean elite) were outraged by these executions, which has led many researchers to conclude that both the trial and the death of James were politically motivated. This, of course, agrees with the evidence showing the highly political nature of the Nazarite cause.[12]

The Fall of Jerusalem

The extant evidence reveals both that the Nazarites were a highly politi-cised sect and that they identified closely with the cause of Jewish nationalism. What, then, would be their reaction to the popular uprising against Rome that erupted in AD 66, just a few years after the death of James the Just? It is clear that the sect of Jewish Christians, who regarded themselves as Jewish (albeit with a new interpretation of the Messianic aspect of Judaism), and who were politically orientated and fiercely nationalistic, would have had but one option: they would have risen with the general population and stood shoulder to shoulder with their country-men against the might of Rome. Moreover, it is hardly likely that the Nazarite Church, based as it was in Jerusalem, would have neglected to defend the Holy City and its temple from the 'pagan' legions of Vespasian and his son Titus.

The insurrection was doomed to failure. Vespasian gradually ate away at the Jewish forces; he destroyed city after city until the only major metropolis remaining in Jewish hands was Jerusalem. And in the siege that followed, the final fall of the Holy City and the destruction of its temple, the Jewish Christians would have shown the same obdurate courage as the rest of Jewry. And they would have shared the same fate. Annihilation. By their identification with the nationalist cause, the Mother Church of Jerusalem, like the temple, and the Jewish nation itself, was utterly destroyed.

The West Goes Its Own Way

With the Jerusalem Church obliterated, the force and authority behind 'orthodox' Jewish Christianity disappeared. The seeds that Paul had planted in the Gentile churches he had established in Asia Minor before his arrest began to germinate. Power lay with Rome, and Paul's hellenised Jesus was far more acceptable to the Roman world. So, against all the odds, it was Paul's version of Jesus that triumphed, and that later (helped by the power of the Roman Emperor Constantine) gained suzerainty over most of the Western civilised world, leading in course of time to the hegemony of the Roman Church. In 325 it was finally decided by vote that Jesus was a god and not a mortal prophet (a vote that, in itself, proves that until that time there was a countervailing view that the Saviour was mortal).

It was the followers of this 'Jesus as God' doctrine who stamped their authority on all aspects of Christian belief. This faction alone decided the content of the canonical Bible and (as we have seen) edited and amended it to suit their own beliefs. Competing 'Gospels' (of which at least 45 are known, and most of which regarded Jesus as a mortal man filled with the spirit of God) were ordered destroyed. The Gospel of Barnabus, for

119

example, was accepted by the Church of Alexandria until AD 325 when the Council of Nicea ordered that all copies be destroyed, and anyone found in possession of one put to death.[13]

Small wonder, then, that the story of those disciples and relatives of Jesus who adhered to the original belief pattern has been blotted out. While the New Testament is happy to record the life and travels of Saint Paul in great detail and to give a far less meticulous account of the exploits of a few other saints, there is a deafening silence on the fate of most of the rest of the Apostles. What became of them, and of the outer circle, the 'Seventy' that Christ elected and sent out into the world? What of Joseph of Arimathea, who had succoured Christ's body from the Romans, and of Mary, Jesus' mother? What became of James the Just, successor and brother to Jesus? The Bible is strangely (perhaps one should say suspiciously) silent about these central characters from Jesus' life.

However, secular traditions, long ignored, give us a wealth of detail on the fate of these lost disciples, and at the same time reveal further confirmation of the Cult of the Head among the early followers of Jesus. And while the Pauline doctrine struggled for supremacy at Rome and elsewhere, these same traditions relate that a far older Church was already in existence, one that adhered to the original beliefs, and one that had been established (as the Catholic Church itself admits) within four years of Christ's death. This was the Culdee Church of Britain, founded by Jesus' close relative, Joseph of Arimathea.

10. The Crucifixion of Mansur al-Hallaj, a Medieval Islamic painting. Note the striking similarities to the death of Jesus and the note of realism introduced by the wedges supporting the upright of the cross.

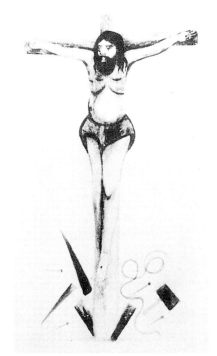

11. Professor Zugibe and the 'crucifixion' volunteer. The bowed posture of the volunteer is typical to all those tested in this way. It throws serious doubt on the validity of the 'crown of thorns' blood-flows seen on the back of the head of the man on the Shroud.

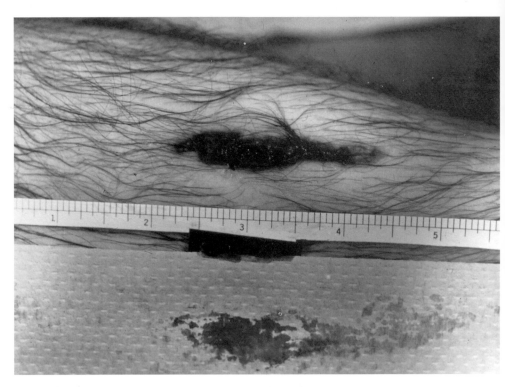

12. Blood seepage into the wound of a cadaver, with (below) the impression made on cloth when the material was gently touched against the wound.

13. The sixth century Christ Pantocrator Icon from St Catherine's Monastery, Sinai Peninsula, Egypt. Dr Alan Whanger claims over 175 points of correspondence between this image and the face on the Shroud. But was the artist copying the Shroud, or do both images derive from a single object, the embalmed head of Christ?

14. One of the many flower images found on the Shroud by Dr Whanger. It has been identified as *Chrysanthemum coronarium*, a species native to Palestine and the Jerusalem area.

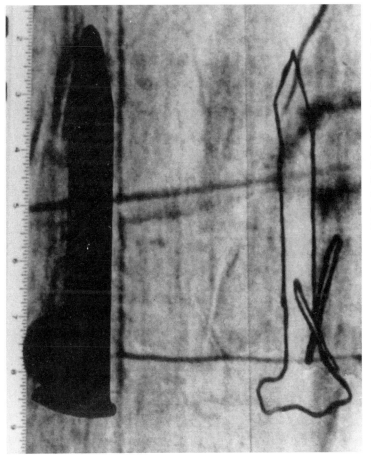

15. The faint image of a 6½ inch spike and two smaller crossed nails was found on the back of the Shroud near the right thigh of the man on the Shroud. The image has been placed between a modern-day railroad spike on the left, and on the right, an outline drawing of the image.

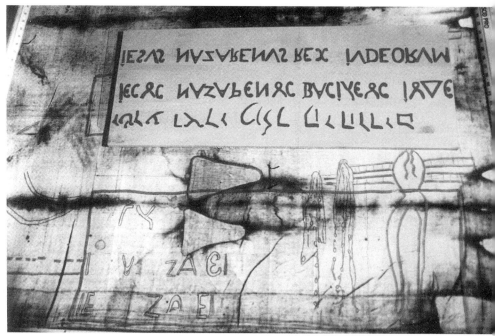

16. The Shroud image (as seen by the naked eye), with the letters discovered by Dr Alan Whanger outlined for clarity. At the top right of the photograph is the 'duplicate headboard' made by Dr Whanger. Note that the letters making up the duplicate headboard are reversed.

17. The Shroud image of the head overlaid with the darker bloodstains of the Sudarium demonstrates the marked degree of correspondence between the two relics, especially around the beard and nose region.

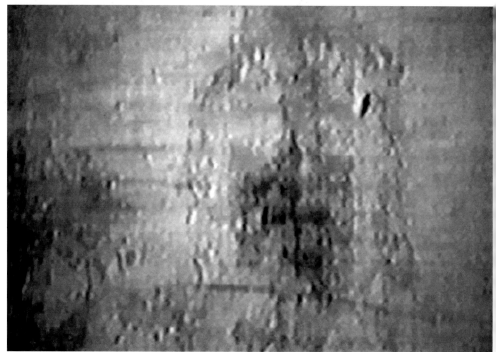

CHAPTER EIGHT

THE LOST DISCIPLES AND THE SACRED HEAD

The Lost Disciples

SECULAR HISTORIES take up the suppressed story of the 'lost disciples', the tale of the friends and family of Jesus whose beliefs did not conform to the doctrines promoted by Paul on the sole basis of his personal revelation. These histories cannot claim to be as ancient as the text of the Acts, or the Gospels; for the most part they date from the seventh, eighth and ninth centuries AD, but they are said to draw on far earlier records, now destroyed. This is not unlikely. We know such records existed, and, given the vicious repression visited on 'heretics', and the wilful destruction of all books and records that did not conform with orthodox teachings, it is a wonder that any trace of these events survived at all. What is impressive about these tales and legends, and what speaks strongly for their veracity, is the manner in which they support one another and combine to form a harmonious whole, quite in keeping with what we know of the historical situation of that time.

Briefly, the histories state that within four years of the Crucifixion, Joseph of Arimathea travelled to Britain with twelve followers (note the 12 + 1 symbolism again) and, at Glastonbury in Somerset, set up the first Christian Church outside Judaea. Mary Magdalene, Mary Cleopas, Lazarus and a number of the 70, the outer circle of Jesus' followers, also left

121

Palestine at the same time and made landfall in France, establishing churches and remaining in that country until their deaths.

Saint Joseph in Britain

Throughout the first millennium and beyond, this story of Joseph's mission to Britain was never questioned. The Roman Church itself acknowledged the truth of these events, according precedence to the British Church by virtue of its status as the first Church established outside the Holy Land.[1] Though disputed on several occasions, the primacy of the British Church was always upheld by Vatican authority. In *Disputoilis super Dignitatem Anglis it Gallioe in Concilio Constantiano* it is stated that 'Three times the antiquity of the British Church was affirmed in Ecclesiastical Concilia . . . It was stated that the British Church took precedence of all other churches, being founded by Joseph of Arimathea, immediately after the passion of Christ'.[2]

The evidence reveals that the story of Joseph's mission is extremely plausible. We have already seen the pioneering spirit of the early Hebrew traders, and it seems that Joseph of Arimathea was of their number. In both the Latin Vulgate of Saint Mark's Gospel (xv, 43) and in Saint Luke (xxv, 30), Joseph of Arimathea is named as 'Decurio'. This title is Roman, and was conferred on officials in charge of metal mines. In Saint Jerome's translation, he is titled 'Nobilis Decurio' which would indicate that he held a prominent position in the Roman administration, most likely as a 'minister of mines'. The traditions confirm this, and more specifically relate that Joseph was in the tin trade, buying and selling the metal between Britain and the Mediterranean world.[3]

This, too, sounds eminently plausible. Tin was found in abundance in only one specific area of the known world: the Cassiterides, the Tin Islands, as Britain was then known. That Semitic traders had reached these islands in the first millennium BC is beyond question. The Bible and other ancient documents state that long before Jesus' time the Phoenician/Hebrew navy and traders had travelled far past the Pillars of Heracles. In the Old Testament we read that '. . . the king [Solomon] had at sea a navy of Tarshish with the navy of Hiram: once in three years came the navy of Tarshish bringing gold and silver, ivory and apes and peacocks,' (1 Kings x, 22). Professor Rawlinson, in his book *History of Phoenicia*, describes how Phoenician and Hebrew settlements were found '. . . on all the coasts of the Mediterranean' and how in Spain these peoples 'had numerous colonies, and at Gades [modern Cadiz] had established a great centre of maritime traffic which is said to have included not only the coasts of Britain, but also those of north Germany and the Baltic'.[4] The tin trade between Britain and the Levant is an accepted historical fact, attested to by numerous ancient authors, including Herodotus, Phytheas and Polybius.[5] Diodorus Siculus (Book v) gives us the most detailed account of the trade, describing how the tin was smelted close to the mines, beaten into squares and transported to an island named Ictis, thought by some to be Saint Michael's Mount in Cornwall, by others Falmouth, known in Roman times as Vectis. From here it was shipped to Vannes or Morlaix in France, then transported on a 30-day journey by packhorse across country, arriving at Arles on the Rhône by way of Limoges. Following this, the metal was carried down the Rhône to Marseilles, whence it was again placed on board ship for the final stage of its journey to the ports of the Levant. This route of the tin trade was to prove vital to the story of the lost disciples.

Cornish miners as late as this century chanted 'Joseph was in the tin trade', as a 'charm' when tin was being 'flashed'.[6] And almost without exception the oldest tin workings, especially in Cornwall, are named 'Jews' houses'. The tradition is that the mines were 'wrought by the Jews with pickaxes of holm, box and hartshorn' from the earliest times.[7] Again, 'upon whichever spot the old miner had worked there we are told the Phoenician has been or the Jew has mined. The existence of the term "Jews' houses", "Jews' tin", "Jews' leavings", "attall" and "attall Saracen" prove the connection of these strangers with the Cornish mines.'[8] While some of these remembrances may possibly be of Jewish workers in early medieval times (Jews are known to have owned tin mines in the days of King John), the mention of pickaxes of holm, box and hartshorn undoubtedly points to a presence from the Levant in much earlier times.

What is impressive about the legends of Joseph of Arimathea's arrival in Britain is that the tales are localised legends, centred in precisely those areas in which the trade in tin and other metals flourished (see figure 4). The tales are found in Cornwall and Somerset, both of which had mining traditions. Devon, midway between Cornwall and Somerset but with no history of metalworking, has no Joseph legends.

Jesus in Britain?

These West Country traditions also claim that Jesus, as a boy, visited Britain. On the face of it, this is a far more preposterous claim than the Joseph legends. Had Cyprus or Greece claimed Jesus as a visitor to its shores, then fewer eyebrows would be raised. But Britain? Thousands of miles from

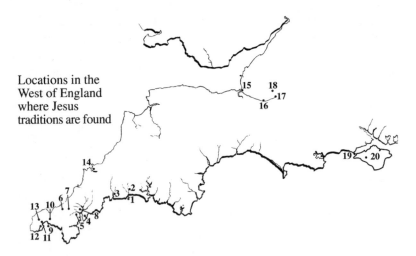

Locations in the
West of England
where Jesus
traditions are found

Figure 4: Location of 'Joseph of Arimathea and Jesus' Legends in West Country
(after Dobson, 1993)

KEY TO THE ABOVE MAP

(1) Lammana or Looe Island.
(2) Looe.
(3) Polruan by Fowey.
(4) Saint Just-in-Roseland.
(5) Falmouth.
(6) and (7) Redruth and Saint Day.
(8) Carnon Downs. A mining
district.
(9) Saint Michael's Mount.
(10) Nancledra.
(11) Penzance.
(12) Mousehole.
(13) Ding Dong, an ancient mine.
(14) Jesus Well.
(15) Burnham.
(16) Glastonbury.
(17) Pilton.
(18) Priddy.
(19) Hurst Castle.
(20) The Isle of Wight.

Palestine and situated at the very rim of the known world? And yet no
other country in Western Europe except Britain has such a tradition. It is
the very extravagance of the story that invites closer scrutiny, and on
investigation the matter turns out to be far less cut and dried than it first
appears. As we have seen, emigrants of Hebrew/Egyptian descent under
Akhenaten's daughter Scota arrived in the British Isles from Egypt at the
time of the Exodus. From these immigrants evolved the Druidic religion
with its emphasis on the Cult of the Head. The Hebrew/Egyptian settlers
were reinforced later by pioneers from the Israelite tribe of Dan, and later
by the arrival of Jeremiah and Tamar Tephi, escaping to their kinfolk after
the death of her father King Zedekiah and the fall of Jerusalem in 586 BC.
Tamar Tephi married the High King of Ireland, Eochaid the Heremon, a

descendant of the Hebrew tribe of Dan. So, there had been a Hebrew presence in these islands for at least 1300 years before Jesus was born. In addition, it seems that Britain was in many ways just as well known to some Hebrew traders as Cyprus or the isles of Greece. Trading fleets of Phoenician/Hebrew ships were regular visitors to British shores, where colonies of Jewish miners worked the mines, collecting tin and other metals for trade in the Mediterranean world. Joseph of Arimathea was a minister of mines and had made his fortune in the tin trade with Britain. He was also known as Joseph of Marmorica, indicating that he owned land in Egypt as well as Palestine, and revealing a continuing link with the Black Land. Joseph was Jesus' uncle or great-uncle. He would have taken over the guardianship of Jesus when, as seems to have occurred, Jesus' father Joseph died while he was still young. And it is in the company of Joseph that Jesus is said to have visited Britain.

There are, in fact, at least three separate traditions, apparently independent of one another, concerning the visit of the boy Jesus to the West Country. The Cornish tradition says only that the Lord visited Cornwall, where Joseph instructed him in the art of tin smelting. In Somerset there is a story of Jesus and Joseph arriving on a ship of Tarshish and staying for a while at a place called Paradise while trading for metals. Priddy, a small village in the Mendips, makes a similar claim. Strangely enough, the story of Jesus' sojourn in Britain receives confirmation from a most unlikely and apparently independent source. Traditions among the Maronite and Catleui villages of Upper Galilee agree with the British tales of Joseph taking Jesus with him into Britain. The Maronite story adds a further detail, claiming that bad weather kept Jesus and his uncle stormbound on the west coast of the Tin Islands throughout the winter before the pair managed to reboard a ship and sail back to the Levant.[9]

It seems that Jesus kept in regular touch with Britain, because the most famous of the British legends links Jesus with Glastonbury, claiming that, in the years just prior to his Passion, he stayed at the Crystal Isle (ie Glastonbury). Here, with his own hands, he is said to have built a small place of worship dedicated to his mother, Mary, which later became known as the Domus Dei, the House of the Lord.[10]

The Stranger Tax

The Bible is mysteriously silent on the subject of the Saviour's whereabouts between the age of 12 to 30 years. That Jesus was absent from Palestine for at least some of these 'missing years' is indicated in two Bible passages.

125

John the Baptist was a cousin of Jesus, and his father was Zacharias, a priest of the Jerusalem Temple. Mosaic Law enjoined that a family gather for the three great feasts of the Jewish year. If the two young men were both resident in Palestine, then, being cousins, it is inconceivable that John and Jesus would not have met at these feasts, the more so as they were both of the Nazarite sect. Yet, as described in Luke vii, verse 19, John sends two messengers to Jesus, asking 'Art Thou He that should come or look we for another?' This is hardly the question one close cousin would ask of another, and it suggests that, at the very least, they had not seen one another for some time, and that one or the other had been absent from Palestine for an extended period.

This supposition receives support in Matthew xvii. Jesus arrives at Capernaum, and a tax-gatherer asks his disciple, Peter, if Jesus pays the 'tribute'. Jesus replies by asking from whom custom or tribute is taken, from the children or strangers. Peter answers that strangers are obliged to pay, to which Jesus replies: 'Then are the children free.' Notwithstanding this response, he then declares to Peter: 'lest we should offend them, go thou to the sea and cast a hook, and take up the fish that first cometh up; and when thou hast opened his mouth thou shalt find a piece of money; take that, and give unto them for thee and me.'

Several commentators have stated their belief that the tax required of Jesus was the temple tax. However, this is unlikely. All Jews were required to pay this tax, so either the tax-collector was questioning Jesus' identity as a Jew – a most improbable and, to Jesus, an insulting suggestion – or we must look elsewhere for the true nature of the tax. The first question to be answered is: why did Jesus decide to pay the tax – whatever it was – when he himself had shown that it was not required of him? (This in itself shows that it could not have been the temple tax that was being referred to.)

Note that Jesus answers the tax-collector's question by speaking not of a religious tax but of government taxes, the Roman poll tax, and especially the 'custom' paid on the import and export of goods by traders. Merchants and traders at Capernaum were all taxed as strangers. It seems, then, that Jesus was being asked if he paid the stranger tax, which implies his absence from the country. Although still one of the 'children' (of Israel) and 'officially' a resident of Judaea, he appears to have been absent from the country for so long a time that he could almost be considered a stranger. He therefore decided to pay the tax 'lest we should offend them'. The conclusion is reinforced by the coin that was in the mouth of the fish Peter was sent to catch: a Greek stater. This is significant, as the temple tax had to be paid in shekels, and the Greek coin would therefore have been useless for this purpose. If Jesus had the power to cause a coin to miraculously appear in the fish's mouth, then he would certainly have had the ability to ensure that the coin could be used for the purpose he intended. By contrast, the 'stranger tax' was not paid in shekels; any coinage was sufficient.

The Secret of the Lord

When, in 597, Saint Augustine was sent to England by Pope Gregory to convert the populace to Roman Christianity, the saint reported on the existence of the 'temple' built by Jesus himself in Glastonbury, the same place of worship that he had dedicated to his mother, Mary. Saint Augustine describes the building with great reverence (although not without, untruthfully, claiming its discovery for Catholicism):

> In the Western confines of Britain there is a certain Royal Island of large extent, surrounded by water ... In it the first Neophites of Catholic Law, God before acquainting them, found a church constructed by no human art (or by the hands of Christ himself), for the salvation of his people (*Epistolae ad Gregorium Papam*).

This was the temple, or church, known as the Domus Dei, the House of the Lord. Intriguingly, its other title was Secretum Domini, the Secret of the Lord. Just what this secret was, and how it related to Jesus (who presumably was the 'Lord' referred to), has never been satisfactorily explained. From the first, this small church or temple was regarded with great reverence. For almost 2,000 years, the orientation and dimensions of the Domus Dei have been faithfully preserved, first by Joseph of Arimathea, then with the building encased in a protective sheath of lead by Saint David, and finally as that part of Glastonbury Cathedral known today as the Joseph Chapel.[11]

Significantly, this holy place, built by Jesus' own hands, conforms in its size and shape to that of the tabernacle devised in the Sinai by Moses/Akhenaten. The Mosaic tabernacle was, in turn, a representation of the sun-temples of Heliopolis. And the orientation of the Secret of the Lord confirms this. It faces east, towards the rising sun, just as did the tabernacle and the Heliopolitan temples (which, according to Apion, were set up in the city by Moses himself).[12] Such correspondences cannot be coincidental, and they point up, yet again, a definite solar dimension in the religion of Christ.

That these ancient accounts should place Jesus at Glastonbury is important. It had long been a Druidic holy place, and the land itself was to all intents and purposes controlled by the Druidic priesthood, in much the same way as the sacerdotal authorities in Jerusalem held sway in the land of Judah. That we should be told that Jesus 'retreated' to a Druidic centre just prior to his ministry is absolutely staggering. For what purpose? In what way could the Druidic priesthood help this Divine King, unless, as my earlier researches had revealed, their philosophies were essentially at one? Despite the initial strangeness of the tale, it did chime perfectly with my own belief in the Hebrew/Egyptian origins of Druidism, and with the evidence of continuing close links between Britain and Palestine. It also accords with Taliesin's enigmatic quote: 'Christ, the Word from the beginning, was from the beginning our teacher, and we never lost his teaching. Christianity was a new thing in Asia, but there was never a time when the Druids of Britain held not its doctrines.' And in addition it helps to explain the otherwise inexplicable accounts of what is said to have occurred after the death of Jesus on the cross. These accounts tell of an exodus of Jesus' friends from Palestine into Europe, and have Joseph of Arimathea returning once again to Glastonbury, this time for good.

The Exiles

The Bible tells us that after the death of the martyr Saint Stephen 'there was a great persecution against the Church which was at Jerusalem, and they were all scattered abroad throughout the regions of Judaea and Samaria' and '. . . they that were scattered abroad went everywhere preaching the word' (Acts viii, 1, 4). Biblical scholars are divided about the historical truth of so general a persecution, especially as, during and after this 'oppression', James the Just and many of the disciples continued to worship peacefully alongside other Jewish sects in the temple. Some scholars even consider Saint Stephen's martyrdom as 'unhistorical'.[13] Whatever the truth of this, there was certainly a very nasty undercurrent flowing through the body politic of Judaism at this time. The judicial murders of both Jesus and his brother James indicate a powerful faction ranged against the royal bloodline of which Jesus was a part. This animosity seems to have extended to other members of the royal line. John the Baptist, Jesus' cousin, was also put to death. Mary Magdalene was said to have also been of the blood royal, as was her brother Lazarus.[14] If, as many believe, the Magdalene was the wife of Jesus, then Lazarus was Jesus' brother-in-law, which would most certainly have made him a 'target'. And in the Gospel of Saint John we read that 'the chief priests consulted that they might put Lazarus to death' (John xii, 10). It was this same priesthood who successfully conspired to murder both Jesus and James the Just.

So it seems from this that the cabal lined up against the bloodline was the pro-Roman Sadducean aristocracy, who supplied the High Priest of the temple, who to the rage of the Essene/Nazarite community took gifts and offerings from the hated Romans, and who continued to hold the reins of power until just before the fall of Jerusalem. Given this powerful foe, it would make sense if James the Just, as head of the bloodline, decided to remove some of the more vulnerable members of his family, and any close friends and retainers, far from the clutches of their political enemies in Jerusalem. It would also be politic if they were to undertake their exile in locations where Jewish colonies existed, in order to promote and strengthen the claims of the bloodline in these regions. And this is just what the secular histories describe. The younger male members of the bloodline remain behind in the Holy City to continue their religious-political machinations against the ruling clique, while Mary Magdalene, Mary, wife of Cleopas, Mary Salome, Martha, Lazarus, Nicodemus and at least eight others of Jesus' inner circle, under the leadership of Joseph of Arimathea, left Palestine for Europe.

The Culdee Church

Joseph of Arimathea's wandering brought him eventually back to Glastonbury with a following of 12 disciples. Here, it is said that he found the remains of the Domus Dei, built by Jesus, and refurbished it. Tellingly, King Arviragus of the Silures or West Britons, gave the strangers temporary hospitality at a Druidic college before donating to them twelve hides of land. As a mark of his respect he declared that this land should never be subject to tax, an exemption that is recorded in the Domesday Book as continuing up until at least that time.[15]

Strangely, and uniquely, we are told in the *Ecclesiastical Antiquities* of the Cymry that when Joseph of Arimathea taught the news of Christ's ministry to the Druids of King Arviragus's realm, his words were well received: '. . . the Silurian Druids embraced Christianity on its first promulgation in these islands, and that in right of their office they were exclusively elected as Christian ministers.'[16] In essence, we are told that the Druid caste there converted en masse to the new religion: 'And those Druids that formerly had dominion of the Briton's faith become now to be helpers of their joy . . . which through God's mercy hath continued in this Island ever

129

since.'[17] This is one of the very few occasions in world history when a religion (and especially so powerful a religion) has allowed itself to be absorbed by another – if, of course, it was considered as another religion by the Druid devotees and not simply as a natural development of the faith they shared with the Hebrew immigrants. As Taliesin had said, the 'new religion' was already long known to them.

This amalgamation gave birth to the Culdee Christian Church. The meaning of the word 'Culdee' or 'Culdich' has excited much debate, but the two most likely interpretations are 'certain strangers' or (from 'Ceile De') 'Servant of the Lord'. In either case the translation appears appropriate to Joseph and his band of followers. That the word does refer to Jewish Christians is evident from the fact that in the Welsh Triads, the ancient records of the Britons, 'Joseph and his 12 companions are all referred to as Culdees, as are Paul, Peter, Lazarus, Simon Zelotes, Aristobolus and others'. All these individuals are said by tradition to have visited the shores of Britain.[18] The Culdee priests were therefore at first Hebrew 'strangers' and later Christianised Druids. The adherents of the 'new' faith kept the Druidic tonsure and refused to alter this style to that of the Roman 'Friar Tuck' hairstyle. Again, Druid colleges were converted to monasteries with the minimum of fuss, and small wonder:

> There are circumstances connected with the Culdees to show that if they practised a species of Christianity their doctrine still retained a large measure of the Druidic philosophy, and that indeed they were the direct descendants of the Druid caste . . . The Druids who dwelt on Iona and professed the rule of Columba were Christianised Druids, mingling with their faith a large element of the ancient Druidic cultus.

Saint Columba himself said 'Christ is my Druid'. Such an amalgamation of beliefs points to the close parallels between the Druid religion and the version of Christianity promulgated by the Jerusalem Church and taught to them by Joseph of Arimathea.

The Druid Cult of the Head, which I believed was also practised by Joseph and by the elite of the Nazarite sect in Palestine, was not blotted out by this amalgamation. When the coffin of one northern saint, Cuthbert, was opened, it was discovered that he had been buried with the head of King Oswald of Northumberland lying on his chest. Even 700 years after the arrival of Saint Joseph, Irish crucifixes still showed a crucified Jesus in which the head is abnormally enlarged. Such stressing of the head is believed by scholars to signify a surviving tradition of the ancient Druidic (and one could also say Nazarite) Cult of the Head.[19]

But if the Culdee Church contained much that was Druidic, what, exactly, were the uniquely Christian tenets of this branch of original Christianity? That they remained in accord with those of original Judaean Christianity (viewing Jesus as priest-king and great prophet but rejecting the Virgin Birth, resurrection in the body and Jesus' apotheosis) is evident. James the Just is credited with visiting Joseph in Britain, a gesture of support which suggests they were doctrinally at one. Saint Philip, the Apostle, is said to have been the greatest friend of Joseph of Arimathea. They would also, therefore, have been substantially in agreement doctrinally. And the Gospel of Philip says there is no resurrection after death, only a spiritual one before it.[20] It follows, then, that Joseph of Arimathea believed this same philosophy, as did the Christianised Druids/Culdees. This can be shown from their rituals and from the prominence given to a Druidic Cult of the Head. After his death, the tomb of Joseph in Glastonbury was said to have carried a most revealing epitaph: 'Ad Britannos veni post Christum sepelivi. Docui. Quievi.' The Latin translates as: 'To Britain I came after I buried Christ. I taught. I rest.'[21] This is a most startling admission, with a terrible ring of finality to it. Had Joseph of Arimathea believed in the bodily resurrection of Jesus, it is inconceivable that he would have been content simply to record that he 'buried Christ' without any mention of the momentous event that followed the burial, Jesus' resurrection. The Welsh bard and historian Melchinus confirms this conclusion. Speaking of the death of Joseph of Arimathea at Glastonbury, he states that buried with him were 'two silver white vessels filled with the blood and sweat of the great prophet Jesus'. Note the wording: not the 'god Jesus' but the 'great prophet'.

This accorded with what I had discovered concerning the beliefs of the early, pre-Pauline Christians. Jesus was known to at least certain Britons (whose Druidic religion was essentially at one with his own) as a prophet, one of a line of priest-kings. This line descended from the 'House of David', whose genealogical and religious origins lay with Tutmosis III, with the Heretic Pharaoh, Akhenaten, and with the occult worship of the sacred head.

The Sacred Head

But I had learned that Joseph was not the only one of Jesus' friends and family to escape to the West. Intriguingly, under the leadership of Joseph of Arimathea, the path of their flight can be seen to follow a very definite direction: *the exact route of the tin trade*. The *Life of Rabanus* (who was a seventh-century Archbishop of Mayence) and other accounts has them leaving Palestine and sailing to Marseilles.[22] From there, they moved up the Rhône Valley, north-west across Gaul to the coast, and then by ship to Cornwall and Somerset. And we find that at each major city along the route the group left one of its number to spread the news of their teachings. 'We can trace Saint Joseph, sent by Jewish persecution from Palestine, with his companions of the boat at Marseilles, evangelising there, and founding primitive bishoprics all along the Rhône Valley, the old traders' route to Britain, and leaving holy sites which exist to this day.'[23]

It is important to realise that, contrary to most writers' assumptions, the group was not evangelising in the name of Pauline Christianity; they were promoting the doctrine of the Jerusalem Church of James the Just which, as we have seen, spoke of a far different Jesus. If this is true, we should expect to find traces of the Nazarite sect and its reverence for the severed head among this group of Jesus' family and followers.

The association of the Cult of the Head with these exiles is demonstrated most emphatically in their remains. In Spain, the body of James the Just gave rise to the great pilgrimage centre of Santiago de Compostela. Here, there is an enigmatic statue named the 'Head of the Master', a carved bearded face, much worn and set atop a stone column, which is traditionally kissed by all pilgrims. The origin of this title and the ritual that surrounds it has been lost (or suppressed), but the head corresponds to the 'Head of the Master' at Rosslyn Chapel, which I have shown to be a symbolic representation of the head of Jesus. In addition, actual heads of the followers of Jesus are preserved all over France. The head of Mary Magdalene was preserved, and her skull can still be seen at the Church of Saint Maximin. The head (and body) of Saint Martha is at Tarascan, the head of Trophimus at Autum, and the head of Saint Lazarus at Ansbach, carried there from France. The relics of several other Jewish Christians were destroyed during the excesses of the French Revolution.

Continuing the head-cult association, Joseph of Arimathea is said to have brought the Holy Grail with him into England. This was a significant finding. In *The Head of God* I had discovered that the original Grail romances contained numerous references to severed heads, references that earlier literary researchers had chosen to ignore, or to conclude were a 'macabre obsession' and 'another symptom of an abnormal mentality'.[24] I was able to show, however, that far from being a psychotic preoccupation, the subtext of the Grail stories was concerned with the Cult of the Head, especially 'the head of the cousin', which I concluded was the head of Jesus. The Holy Grail was a covert title, a codeword for this relic, and perhaps for other, older heads of revered masters of the cult. That Joseph of Arimathea brought the Holy Grail to England could mean only that at least one such relic had accompanied him to these shores. A second tradition pointed to the same conclusion. It makes Joseph the man who brings Bran Vendigaeth (Bran the Blessed) to Britain. And it is Bran the Blessed whose head was cut off and continued to prophesy and speak.[25] Bran's oracular head is said to have been buried under the White Hill outside London (on which now stands the Bloody Tower) to protect the city from its enemies. This story refers to the legendary ability of Bran's head to make the land germinate and to protect its keeper from harm. These attributes are identical to those of both the Holy Grail and the mysterious severed head of the Templars, the Baphomet, which I have identified as the embalmed head of Jesus.

That this head-tradition was brought with the group from Palestine can be seen from the first church they consecrated in France, in the presence of Mary Magdalene, Lazarus, and many others. This is the old church of Les Saintes Maries, in the Camargue region of France. According to the Otia Imperialia, written by Gervais of Tilbury in 1212, beneath this church, from the time of its consecration, 'under the altar, formed by them of earth and covered by a slab of Paros marble, six heads of certain holy saints have been placed in the form of a square'.[26] As the exiles had only recently arrived in the Camargue from Palestine, it is impossible that all of these six heads are of French provenance. If this is so, then this tale is a clear and direct reference to a series of relics associated with the Cult of the Head, and brought by Nazarite refugees from the Holy Land to France.

But not only to France. There was another escape route from Palestine, just as time-honoured and certainly easier. This was the Way of Horus, the ancient road that led south to Egypt. And here again the association of early Christianity with the sacred head proved to be inescapable.

CHAPTER NINE

EGYPTIAN CHRISTIANITY

A S W E S A W in Chapter Seven, during much of the first century AD the Jewish Christian Church in Jerusalem, led by Jesus' brother James, held sway over the 'orthodox' interpretation of Jesus' life. This group considered Jesus as a Nazarite prophet and a priest-king, a suffering Messiah in the Jewish construction of that term: a king, sent by God, who had suffered for the sins of his people. There was no deification of the dead 'prophet and king', but due reverence and worship of his memory and, as my researches had shown, of his relics.

For a space of over 30 years after the Crucifixion, this view of Jesus was dominant. The Nazarite Church worked actively against the 'heresy' of Paul's view of Jesus, finally compassing the arrest of the 'Spouter of Lies', which led directly to his transport in chains to Rome and his eventual presumed execution by Roman authorities. With the apparent eclipse of the Pauline heresy, it appeared certain that the 'orthodox' Nazarite view of Jesus would prevail. But then came the Jewish revolt against Rome, the fall of Jerusalem, and the utter disappearance of all records of the Mother Church. With the destruction of the Jewish state, the history of Christian origins enters a black hole, re-emerging as a corpus of Christian writings that shows a total unconcern for the fate of the Holy City, its inhabitants and the Mother Church of their religion. The Acts of the Apostles and the rest of the New Testament are concerned exclusively with the spread of Pauline Christianity to the north and north-west, with the development of the new faith in the Graeco-Roman world. There is a deafening silence (and a suspicious lack of records) concerning the history of the Mother

135

Church in Jerusalem, and its subsequent fate during the convulsions of the Jewish revolt against Rome which resulted in the destruction of the Jewish nation. It has rightly been said that:

> Among all the documents which comprise the New Testament canon, and indeed among the other extant writings of the sub-apostolic age, there is no description of the terrible events which attended the defeat of Israel's cause against Rome or of the fortunes of the Palestinian Christians amid the convulsion and overthrow of their nation's life . . . Indeed, so complete a silence is maintained in these primitive documents that on their testimony alone nothing would be known of the disaster which overwhelmed Israel in AD 70.[1]

I had been able to trace the survival of this original concept of Jesus the Nazarite in the exile of Joseph of Arimathea and his party to Europe, and especially to Britain. But Egypt, too, had long been a haven for oppressed Hebrews. Abraham had travelled into Egypt, and his 'grandson' Jacob had also led his family there in time of famine. Rehoboam had sought exile in the Black Land, Jeremiah and the daughters of King Zedekiah had fled there, and Jesus himself as a child is said to have escaped the wrath of Herod by fleeing south. Given the tradition of flight into Egypt, it would have been most unlikely if some members of the Nazarite Christians had not also fled south to the land from which their religion ultimately derived. Indeed, Josephus reports that defeated Judaic fighters made their way to Alexandria in substantial numbers after the fall of Jerusalem.[2] This is not to be doubted: for Jews, Egypt was no foreign land full of strangers. Long before the time of Christ there were thriving Jewish communities in several Egyptian cities, more especially in Alexandria, that huge cosmopolitan port in which so many religions met, mixed and blended. In fact, it appears that a substantial Nazarite Christian community had established itself in Egypt even before the fall of Jerusalem. That this community believed in a Jesus very different from that of Pauline thought is supported by the New Testament itself. Despite the attempt to erase Egyptian Christianity from Church history, one interesting, and extremely significant, piece of information has escaped the Pauline editors.

Apollos

Apollos, in the Acts of the Apostles, is a Jew of Alexandria, a man obviously of great renown, highly knowledgeable in the sacred writings. In Paul's first Corinthian Epistle he is an important personage in the primitive Church and, at least at Corinth, he is placed on a level with two of the leading lights of the Jerusalem Church, Cephas and Paul (1 Corinthians i, 12). The Bible makes plain that the much-travelled Apollos was the leader of a faction in the Corinthian Church, and that this faction was opposed doctrinally to the Jesus preached by Paul. In stark contrast to the teachings of Paul, there is no indication that Apollos's views were considered antithetical to those of the Jerusalem Church, and we can assume that they were doctrinally at one. It is therefore reasonable to believe that the Alexandrine Church agreed in its essentials with the Jerusalem Church and that both opposed Paul's teaching.

But what exactly were the doctrines that Apollos preached? The answer is astonishing and illuminates the true beliefs of early non-Pauline Christians. The Acts recounts that Apollos enters Paul's sphere of influence at Ephesus and here he teaches 'diligently the things of the Lord'. He is said to be 'mighty in the scriptures . . . instructed in the way of the Lord, and . . . fervent in the spirit' (Acts, xviii, 24–25). The central phrase, 'way of the Lord', indicates that Apollos was a full initiate into 'the way', a characteristic phrase used throughout Acts to summarise the full Christian faith and practice. In sum, then, we have a man of great repute, high in the Nazarite Church hierarchy, who was travelling in Asia Minor to spread the doctrines of the Jerusalem Church.

And yet, astoundingly, we are told that this paragon of the faith knew 'only the baptism of John'. That is, it seems he knew nothing of the theory (or story) of the Holy Ghost and its descent on the Apostles at Pentecost. Nor did Apollos feel such a knowledge was necessary for a full exposition of the 'Christian' way. As one researcher has commented: '. . . it is a matter of legitimate astonishment that a man could carefully teach "the things concerning Jesus" and yet only know the baptism of John.' He continues: 'The amazing conclusion, therefore, follows that Apollos, despite his careful teaching of the "things concerning Jesus", did not even know or teach that John had borne witness to the unique vocation of Jesus.'[3] Once again, we find that a contemporary of Jesus, while regarding him as a fitting exemplar around which to build a religious teaching, did not accord to Jesus the unique status he was given in Pauline thought.

There was another aspect of Apollos that I found amazing, one that seemed to have escaped the notice of biblical scholars but which I felt was of great significance to the true nature of the first Christians – the name of this man who was 'instructed in the way of the Lord'. Apollos is quite obviously and literally derived from the Greek name for the

137

sun-god, Apollo. The choice of this title was no mere whim; in the first century AD names were not, as in our day, chosen at random, or bestowed on a child (or an adult) because they 'sounded nice'. Words were considered things of power, and a personal name was the most important, the essential attribute of a person, or a god (as witness the deep secrecy surrounding the forbidden name of the Jewish god Yahweh).[4] To know a god's name was to have power over that god. Equally, a person's name almost invariably gave a clear indication of his religious stance. To discover that an important initiate in the Alexandrian Church (doctrinally at one with the Jerusalem Church) had chosen the name of the sun-god was nothing less than astounding; it was perhaps even more astonishing than that he should know nothing of the baptism of Jesus. The name Apollos pointed once again to the Nazarite connection to solar worship, to the philosophy of Akhenaten, and to the Cult of the Head.

Jesus 'the Head'

Alexandria was a magnet to many sects and a melting-pot of doctrines. It is here that the great sage Ormus is said to have founded the Rose-Cross, from an amalgamation of Christian and Egyptian mysteries, not too difficult a task considering their common origins.[5] Here, sects of Nazarite and Gnostic Christianity flourished and intertwined, preaching their own very different version of Jesus. Scrolls found in 1945 near the town of Nag Hammadi in eastern central Egypt have thrown great light on the teachings of the Gnostic Christians, long suppressed and vilified by the Pauline Church Fathers.[6] They revealed the reality of the sacred head, and they proved to be of immense importance to the search for the true nature of the Shroud of Turin.

The manuscripts, in Coptic, date from the fourth century AD but are copied from much earlier texts, of at least the second century AD and possibly much older. The corpus includes manuscripts attributed to several of those Apostles of Jesus about whom the New Testament has very little to say, as well as documents such as the Gospel of the Ebionites, the sect known as the Poor, who are believed to have been closely affiliated to Jesus and his work. What these 'Apocryphal Gospels' have to say is extremely illuminating.[7] They are decidedly Gnostic in content, with detailed accounts of the spiritual construction of the universe and psychic roads to salvation. Several fulminate against other (unnamed) groups who are claiming to be Christian but who do not possess the inner mysteries of the

Saviour.[8] Interestingly, many of the manuscripts have Crucifixion scenarios at variance with the orthodox view of events. Equally, the Virgin Birth is denied in both the Gospel of Thomas and the Gospel of the Ebionites, who believed that Jesus was the son of Joseph and Mary, conceived and born in a normal human manner.

But it was a little-known and little-researched tract within the Nag Hammadi corpus that really made me sit up and take notice, a manuscript known as the *Interpretation of Knowledge*. It pointed unequivocally towards a knowledge of the Cult of the Head, and to Jesus' unique position within the cult, among at least some of the Gnostic community in Egypt. The *Interpretation of Knowledge* is concerned primarily, outwardly at least, with the escape of human souls from the prison of the flesh.[9] However, it was the name by which Jesus was referred to in the text that pointed clearly to Nazarite head-worship. Out of 19 other Nag Hammadi texts I examined, 18 named Jesus in relatively conventional ways – he is called 'Son of Man', 'Son of Light', the 'Good Shepherd' – together with some that were less conventional, such as 'Sun of Life' (Teachings of Silvanus, 98.23), the 'Hidden Mystery' (Gospel of Truth 18.15) and 'Wisdom' (of God) (Teachings of Silvanus, 106. 22–23). However, the *Interpretation of Knowledge* proved to be very different. While Jesus was called 'Son of God', 'Christ', 'Teacher' on single occasions in the body of the text, one title predominated over the rest. Nine times in the manuscript, Jesus is given the title 'the Head'. There is no explanation for this title. The author makes no attempt to use the word 'head' in allegorical phrases such as 'head of the Church' or 'head of the spiritual hierarchy'. Nor is there any 'Jesus is the head and we are the body' analogy. Jesus is named quite literally as 'the Head'.

Sophia

Nor was this all. I discovered that other early-Christian documents (for example, the early Christian source 'Q' – Quelle – from which many of the Synoptic sayings of Jesus derive) also identify Jesus as the Jewish principle of wisdom, 'Sophia'.[10] In early-Jewish philosophy, Sophia was regarded as the principle of wisdom, a feminine manifestation of the deity. To link Jesus to a feminine principle appears odd, but it is not so strange to those versed in the inner mysteries. In the Jewish mystical work the Sohar, or 'Book of Splendour', one of the titles of the first principle, the En Soph, is the Ancient of Days. And the Ancient of Days is also known (at times and in part) as Sophia. In the Sohar, the Ancient of Days is conceived of as an enormous head, containing within it a series of 'skulls'.

This was news indeed. Doubts had been cast on my identification of the Templar head Baphomet with the head of Jesus on the grounds that, at one level, the word 'Baphomet' was undoubtedly a form of code. While working on the Dead Sea Scroll manuscripts, Dr Hugh Schonfield discovered that several names had been hidden by the use of a code he termed the 'Athbash Cipher'.[11] When he applied this formula to the Templar head 'Baphomet', he found that the word 'Baphomet', when written 'BPWMTh' is transposed by the Athbash Cipher to 'ShWPIA', or 'Sophia', the Greek word for 'wisdom'.[12] Therefore, it was argued, Baphomet was simply a nonsense word, its connection to the Moorish Bufihimat, Father of Wisdom, purely coincidental, the word being used to cover the worship by the Templars of the principle of wisdom.[13]

But the identification of Jesus with Sophia provided the answer. It reconciled the two views and at the same time gave additional impetus to the head of Christ thesis. The elite of the Order of the Temple is known to have been deeply immersed in Gnostic thought (its possession of the Athbash Cipher alone reveals a connection with the Essene/Nazarite sects of first-century Palestine, who also used this means of concealing their messages).[14] They were also steeped in the intricacies of symbol and wordplay, as witness the Gothic cathedrals and the profusion of symbolic carvings at Rosslyn Chapel. If, like many Gnostics, they identified Jesus with Sophia, and connected Sophia to the 'head' of the Ancient of Days, then they would have taken great delight in naming the sacred head 'Baphomet', a title whose 'overt' translation, 'Father of Wisdom', pointed to Jesus, and at the same time meshed perfectly with the covert translation of 'Sophia', which was itself a code for Jesus and also indicated the 'head' of the Ancient of Days.

In short, I had shown in The Head of God that:

the embalmed head = Baphomet = Father of Wisdom = Mimir (the Norse head of God) = Jesus

Now it could also be demonstrated that:

the embalmed head = Baphomet = Sophia = Jesus = Head (of the Ancient of Days)

The symbolism was complex and multi-layered, but each layer pointed unmistakably in the same direction. The Baphomet of the Templars was being identified as the head of Jesus.

140

The Knights Templar and the Holy Face

Reviewing all the evidence, I now felt even more certain that Jesus had been a renowned leader of a Jewish sect that revered the head and that his own head had been removed and embalmed as a relic after the Crucifixion. Those closest to him in the Nazarite community had seen him as a great prophet, but he had never been conceived by them as synonymous with the Most High God of the Jewish faith, of which they remained a part. His death, at least on one level, was envisaged as an atonement offering by a Divine King, to mitigate the wrath of God on the king's people and to ensure their continuing fertility and good fortune in this life and the next. I was equally sure that this original concept of Jesus as great prophet and Divine King was carried out of Palestine to both Britain and Egypt, where, in both regions, I had found evidence for the survival of the 'primitive' Christian beliefs and the Cult of the Head. The heads of many of Jesus' contemporaries had been removed after their deaths and preserved as sacred relics. If such lesser lights of the cult were so honoured, it was inconceivable that the body and head of the 'great prophet' Jesus had not been treated in a similar fashion.

This was the cultus, the constellation of beliefs, into which the Knights of the Temple had tapped (or into which they had been initiated) at the end of the First Crusade. Their diggings at the Temple of Jerusalem in the twelfth century had opened them up to this new (in fact much older) version of Christianised Judaism – if indeed they were not already aware of a version of the doctrine. The Templars became the perpetuators of this original Christianity. They began the worship of heads, and in particular one head, the Baphomet, which I had conclusively identified as that of Jesus. They either found the head in Jerusalem as a result of their excavations beneath the ruins of the temple or it came into their possession later, possibly via the Cathars or some other Gnostic group.

By whatever means, the possession of this relic was both a great honour and at the same time a massive responsibility. There was, there could only ever be, one head of Christ, a relic of unique importance to the 'heretical' religion the Templars secretly professed. But given the vagaries of the time, the Templars (true pragmatists that they were) must have realised that an unforeseen reversal in their fortunes could mean the destruction of the relic. Such a disaster did, in fact, overwhelm the Order, and it came close to allowing the Baphomet to fall into the hands of the Roman Church, where it would either have been destroyed or consigned to the most inaccessible of the Vatican's many secret vaults.

Worshipping in secret, and faced with intimations of coming disaster,

141

the Templars would undoubtedly have cast about for some means of preserving a true likeness of the face of Jesus should disaster overtake them and the relic itself perish from the face of the earth. They had, after all, already used the art of architecture to preserve many ancient Gnostic secrets within the structure of Gothic cathedrals and other holy buildings.[15] They would certainly have lavished just as much thought and care on the task of preserving some image of this awesome relic, the head of Christ. The Templars were the ideal candidates for this unique task. As the freethinkers of their age, they were exposed to, and assimilated, many strands of knowledge, some Christian, but the majority 'pagan' and therefore beyond the pale to most of the rest of Christendom. Their open-mindedness was legendary, and they absorbed knowledge irrespective of its provenance. And for those who knew where to look, there was much knowledge available.

PART TWO

THE DIVINE DECEPTION

CHAPTER TEN

LOST PHOTOGRAPHIC TECHNIQUES

The Altamira Syndrome

O
NE AFTERNOON in 1879 Don Marcelino Sanz de Sautuola, an amateur archaeologist, was excavating the floor of a cave in the mountains of Altamira which had been used as a shelter by Stone Age hunters. With him was his daughter Maria, and she was bored. Looking up, Maria suddenly stiffened with excitement. Above her she could see multicoloured figures on the roof of the cave. The paintings were of European bison, a species that had died out in Spain more than 10,000 years before, and they had been executed with a verve and naturalism that would put most modern artists to shame. Don Marcelino was astounded by his daughter's discovery and soon became convinced that the paintings had been made by the Stone Age inhabitants of the cave. He quickly wrote to the doyen of Spanish archaeology, Professor Juan Vilanova y Piera, who visited the cave and was in turn convinced of the great antiquity of the bison paintings.[1]

However, persuading the scientific establishment was another matter altogether.

A year after the discovery, Professor Vilanova attended an international conference and presented his evidence on the Altamira paintings to the assembled savants. Their response was ridicule and rejection. While refusing outright to visit the site to view the paintings and other evidence at first hand, they declared the find a forgery and implied that Don Marcelino and the professor were either party to the plot or unwitting dupes, too obtuse to divine the 'true' nature of these fakes.

The 'experts' of that time were governed by a world view that restricted their ability to look at the facts dispassionately. It regarded evolution as a series of steps towards an ultimate perfection, a ladder up which humanity climbed, step by painful step, towards higher and better manifestations of art, religion and science. In this scheme of things, paintings of such grace and beauty as those found at Altamira – which rivalled in their own way the best that nineteenth-century art could offer – were simply impossible. They could not ever have been produced by a Stone Age savage. Rather than look at the subject objectively, they preferred to ignore any evidence that was prejudicial to their cherished theory.

The 'Altamira syndrome' is by no means an isolated occurrence. Unfortunately, it is an all-too-common example of what might be termed 'nunco-centrism', the tendency to believe that everything we have now must necessarily be bigger, faster, stronger and better than anything that has gone before. This concept of a straight line in human progress is a mirage. Advances in art, science and technology have been made, implemented and then lost on scores of occasions. Such knowledge is most easily forfeited when it is known only to a select few and passed on by word of mouth. But even when written down, history shows that its continued existence is by no means guaranteed.

Forgotten Knowledge

It is quite certain that most of the knowledge of the past has been lost to us. We know almost nothing of the secrets contained in the library of Alexandria, in the libraries of the Temple of Jerusalem or of the sanctuary of Phtah in Memphis. We are just as ignorant of the wisdom held in the 200,000 volumes burned in the library at Pergamo, or in the collections of Pisistratus at Athens. Ancient learning was quite literally prodigious, a huge towering edifice of which we now see at best but a few surviving stones. Nevertheless, a close study of what little does remain reveals that, in many instances, what we believe to be the 'first' discovery of a phenomenon is simply its rediscovery. Joubert's remark is apt here: 'Nothing makes men so imprudent or conceited as ignorance of the past and a scorn for old books.'[2]

The principles of empirical science were known to the ancients.

Contrary to most modern history books, Democritus did not formulate the atomic theory: according to Sextus Empiricus he learned it from Moschus the 'Phoenician', who may well have been of Jewish extraction. However, unlike Democritus, Moschus declared, correctly, that the atom was divisible, revealing that the more ancient theory of matter was, paradoxically, more in line with what we today conceive of as the true nature of the material world.

In the field of astronomy we are used to thinking of the ancients as primitive flat-earthers, who looked at the darkened sky and saw the stars as holes in the cloak of night. Nothing could be further from the truth: that the earth was a globe in space was known long before the birth of Christ. The circumference of the world was calculated as early as the third century BC by the Greek mathematician Eratosthenes. He estimated the figure at 24,700 miles, very close to the present-day figure of 24,902 miles. By contrast, the Egyptian astronomer and geographer Ptolomy (AD 100–170) was far wide of the mark – his estimate of the earth's circumference was 17,800 miles. Much other information was developed in ancient times only to disappear again into the abyss of ignorance: Thales and Anaximenes both regarded the Milky Way as composed of innumerable stars, each with planets surrounding it. Pythagoras formulated the inverse square law attributed to Newton, although in fairness to the great English scientist and hermeticist, he was modest enough to acknowledge that 'If I have seen farther, it is by standing on the shoulders of giants'. The Polish astronomer Nicolaus Copernicus admits explicitly that his theories on the earth's movements were inspired by the writings of the ancients. René Descartes, the father of rationalism, was less candid: he stole his quote 'He who seeks the truth must doubt everything' from Aristotle, and modified his famous 'Cogito ergo sum' ('I think, therefore I am') from the words of Saint Augustine.[3] On a more prosaic level, a statement attributed to a maid of Marie Antoinette best sums up this situation. Refurbishing an old hat, she is said to have exclaimed: 'There is nothing new except what has been forgotten.'

Practical Technologies

But this ancient learning was not simply theoretical. It worked on a practical level too, and sometimes on a monumental scale. In Jesus' time the great harbour at Caesarea Maritima, built by Herod the Great, is said by Josephus to have possessed a breakwater over 197 feet wide. It was generally agreed that the ancient writer was exaggerating, or boasting to exalt his former and his adopted nations, but recent underwater exploration in the area has proved the truth of his words. The coordinator of excavations at Caesarea Maritima is on record as stating that:

> This Herodian port is an example of a twenty-first-century harbour built 2,000 years ago. In fact, if the modern harbours of Ashdod and Haifa had employed such systems of design and engineering, they would not have had the problems they face today.[4]

There are innumerable examples of practical techniques and technologies that were invented, utilised (sometimes for centuries) and then, because of the vagaries of fate, forgotten, only to be discovered anew in later centuries. Heron of Alexandria's steam engine and the 2,000-year-old Baghdad battery are perhaps today's most famous examples.[5] Less well known are the techniques invented by Hindu doctors 2,000 years ago to rebuild lost noses and ears, techniques that were avidly assimilated by Western doctors and formed the basis of our present-day plastic surgery.[6] Vaccination was also practised in India, and was described in one of the Vedas (Books of Divine Knowledge) over two millennia ago: 'Collect the fluid from the pustules on the point of a lancet and insert it into the arm, so that the fluid mixes with the blood. This will produce fever, but the disease will be very mild and there will be no cause for alarm.'

Closer to home, the Romans used hardened glass for flooring and possessed the formula for a cement that would harden under water, something unknown to our civilisation until towards the end of the Middle Ages.[7] Again, in Celtic Gaul a reaping machine was invented in the first century AD but allowed to fall into disuse. The technology was not reinvented until 1,700 years later, and on the opposite side of the globe, in nineteenth-century Australia.[8]

Equally, other techniques were invented and have never been rediscovered. The Gauls produced, by an unknown process, a substance known as Pilema, wool treated with certain acids that rendered it fireproof and impenetrable to weapons. It was the Kevlar armour of its day and was used in the manufacture of breastplates.[9] Just as mysterious is the case of the Chinese aluminium belt ornaments. Found in 1956 inside the third-century tomb of a Chinese general, these artefacts were discovered to be almost pure aluminium (alloyed with up to five per cent manganese and ten per cent copper). This discovery created a sensation in archaeological circles – until the time of this find, it was thought that aluminium had first been isolated as a metal in 1827![10]

This last is a definite and irrefutable example of an 'out-of-time' technology. Because it oxidises rapidly, the separation of aluminium from its ores needs a great deal of energy, and in modern times the metal is extracted from bauxite using large amounts of electricity. As such, it is far more difficult to achieve than, for example, the subject of our quest, the capturing of an image on cloth. And yet these 1,700-year-old aluminium ornaments do exist and must be accounted for.

As with the cave paintings at Altamira, some archaeologists disbelieved the discoveries on principle, and true to form have suggested that the pieces were fraudulent. However, Professor Joseph Needham of Cambridge University, who until his death in 1995 had dedicated his life to the study of ancient Chinese technology, totally rejected the facile 'Altamira syndrome' solution. He had another answer, and one that is very pertinent to our investigation of the origin of the Turin Shroud. Professor Needham was aware of the high level of security surrounding the work of Chinese alchemists, and he knew that their deeper secrets were passed on (if they were transmitted at all) by word of mouth to a trusted circle of initiates. This is, of course, exactly the same system as was used by Western esoteric groups, such as the Druids, the Rosicrucians and the Templars. He also knew that these students of matter, like their European counterparts, had made practical discoveries of great benefit to mankind in the course of experiments made primarily to expand their own spiritual consciousness. Professor Needham concluded that the technique of aluminium production had been discovered in just this way, by chance, by a Chinese alchemist. Realising the advantages of the new process, he had kept this knowledge to himself, and either by accident or design he had taken this secret with him to the grave.[11]

The parallels with the Templars are very strong. Given their reputation as freethinkers and students of many esoteric subjects banned by the Catholic Church, and their study of forbidden knowledge, it is by no means impossible that a small group of initiates within the Order could have been privy to the secrets of primitive photography. If so, as the case of the Chinese aluminium reveals, such knowledge could easily have been lost for ever by a sudden catastrophe. And just such a catastrophe was visited on the Knights when the Order of the Temple was attacked and suppressed in 1307 and many of the Knights were put to death. But from whom might the Templars have learned this secret art of capturing an image by the manipulation of light?

Painting with Light

As with much other science, the principles of photography were known long before its 'discovery' by Daguerre in 1835. In fact, Daguerre was preceded by another Frenchman, Joseph Nicéphore Niepce, an amateur scientist who invented (or, as we will see, more likely reinvented) photography in the camera as early as 1816.[12] His first surviving photograph from nature is dated 1826, and he used as 'film' a pewter plate coated with light-sensitive bitumen. After exposure, the plate was washed with lavender oil and petroleum, removing those areas of bitumen not hardened by light, so leaving a negative image on the pewter. However, this is by no means the first description of photography. Almost a hundred years before, in the poem 'Giphantie' (1729), by Tiphaigne de la Roche, there is a description of both black and white and colour photography. Earlier Rosicrucian traditions also speak of instruments to record images, and during the early Renaissance Fabricius, in De rebus metallicis (1536), describes how certain metals are capable of capturing the true likeness of an object after light has been allowed to fall on them.[13]

However, for the origins of photography we must look further afield than Europe. It appears that at least 600 years before Fabricius, another race of men had advanced even further along this path. They were men whose civilisation was the most sophisticated of their time, men the Templars were to meet on the battlefield and whom they learned, eventually, to respect and to admire. The Arabs.

Our Debt to the Arabs

The West owes its knowledge of classical Greek and Roman authors almost entirely to the Muslim Arabs. With the foundation of Baghdad and the accession of the Abbasid Dynasty (AD 762), a Graeco-Arab translation movement began in Baghdad that lasted for over 200 years and resulted in virtually the entire corpus of classical literature being made available to the Islamic world.[14] Aristotle, Plato, Pythagoras and Galen were all but unknown during the Dark Ages of Western Europe, but they were studied diligently by scholars in the universities of the Near East. By the end of the first millennium, almost all scientific and philosophical Greek works had been translated into Arabic, including treatises on alchemy (itself an Arab word), astronomy, medicine, mathematics, physics and, most important for our purposes, optics. It was via the Arabic translations that most of the ancient learning eventually (and against the wishes of the Church) became available to the medieval Christian West.

The Arabs not only preserved the ancient lore of the classical period but also developed the theories they contained, advancing the old learning as well as preserving it. Baghdad:

. . . at the beginning of the ninth century, during the reign of Harun al-Rashid, was the world's richest and most powerful state, its capital the centre of the planet's most advanced civilisation. It had a thousand physicians, an enormous free hospital, a regular postal service, several banks (some of which had branches as far afield as China), an excellent water supply system, a comprehensive sewerage system, and a paper mill.[15]

Nor was science ignored. The caliphate of Baghdad employed two Iraqi scientists, the Banu Musa brothers, to check the circumference of the earth. By measuring the distance travelled to make the Pole Star's apparent position change by one degree, they used trigonometry to produce a figure of 24,000 miles. This was far closer to the true figure than that given by Ptolomy, but not, it should be noted, as accurate as the distance calculated by Eratosthenes in the third century BC.

Thanks to their close contact with the Arabs, and the emulation of many of their more civilised ways, the Templars came to have access to this knowledge long before most European scholars. The Order of the Temple is credited with the foundations of the banking system of Western Europe, but it is almost certain that they took this financial 'discovery', along with many others, from the more sophisticated Arab civilisation. They may well have taken a knowledge of optics and 'photography' too. Arab science in these fields was far in advance of the rest of the world.

Lost Photographic Techniques

The precursor of the modern camera was the *camera obscura*, literally 'the dark chamber'. This was originally a darkened room with a small aperture in one side, through which light entered and projected an inverted image on the opposite wall or on a screen set up in the chamber (see figure 5). The image formed in this way is neither very bright not very sharp. Enlarging the hole aids the brightness but decreases image definition. The way round this problem is to use a converging lens in place of the 'pinhole'. In this way the image can be focused sharply on to a screen.

The *camera obscura* was known to Arab scholars long before its advent in the West. A very clear description is given by the eleventh-century scholar Ibn al-Haytam (known in the West as Alhazen) in his book *Kitab al-manazir*, and it is known that knowledge of this device was widespread among educated Arabs. *Kitab al-manazir* deals extensively with the science of optics and was translated into Latin in the twelfth century.[16] Although firm data is

Figure 5: The Camera Obscura – knowledge of this technique of image formation was known to the Arabs before the end of the first millennium
© Science Museum/Science and Society Picture Library

lacking, it would undoubtedly have been known to the Templars. That there is no clear record of their openly implementing the *camera obscura* technique is not surprising. Experimentation of this sort was frowned on by the Church and was an extremely dangerous undertaking, as evidenced by the salutary tale of Giovanni Battista della Porta.

In the west, della Porta is usually credited with the first full description of the *camera obscura* which appeared in his book *Magia Naturalis sive de Miraculis Rerum Naturalium* in the year 1558.[17] It is obvious from the text of this tome that he regarded the technology as a covert technique that he had known for some time in secret and had finally decided to make public: 'Now I want to announce something about which I have kept silent until now and which I believed that I must keep a secret.' That his caution was justified and that this 'mystery' was regarded as unholy magic by the authorities became evident when he first demonstrated the *camera obscura* publicly. No sooner had the demonstration taken place than della Porta was arrested on a charge of sorcery.[18] And this was in the mid-sixteenth century, during the relatively enlightened Renaissance, a good 250 years after the suppression of the Knights Templar. Small wonder, then, that anyone in the fourteenth century with knowledge of the *camera obscura* would have avoided advertising the fact and kept his lips tightly sealed.

There is one other essential prerequisite for the production of a photographic image – the possession of an appropriate light-sensitive substance to capture and hold the image produced by the *camera obscura*. And here again the Arabs were far ahead of their time. Substances known for their photochemical activity had also been discovered by Arabian scientists, including silver nitrate and silver chloride (still used in photographic emulsions today). As early as the ninth century Jabir Ibn Hayaan had described how adding silver to *eau prime* (nitric acid) results in the production of silver nitrate.[19] Ibn Hayaan's writings were eventually translated into Latin as *De Inventione Ventatis*, but it is likely that the Templars, immersed in Arab ways, knew of such writings far in advance of most Western scholars.

All that was required now to produce a stable image was a fixative, the name given to a chemical that alters the light-sensitive substance (such as silver nitrate) so that – after the photograph has been taken – treatment with the fixative renders it unaffected by light. Such chemicals are simple to manufacture and are quite common in nature – in the case of silver nitrate, ammonium salts can act as a fixative. Urine, human or animal, will work very well in this regard.

There are hints in several Arab manuscripts that the authors may have put the two processes – *camera obscura* and light-sensitive chemicals – together to capture an image. Perhaps these Muslim scientists did manage to bring together all the necessary parts of the puzzle. Or it may be that it was their erstwhile enemies, and latter-day admirers, the Templars, who instead combined the two techniques and became the originators of the first primitive photographic process.

CHAPTER ELEVEN

COULD IT BE DONE?

The Leonardo Conspiracy

ROUND THE BEGINNING of 1990 a journalist who specialised in stories on unexplained phenomena, Lynn Picknett, began receiving information on the Turin Shroud, via letter, from a correspondent signing himself 'Giovanni' and claiming to be an agent of that shadowy group the Priory of Sion. In these letters, Giovanni informed Ms Picknett that the Priory had important information that they wished to share. The Turin Shroud was a fake. It was not Christ's gravecloth, nor had it been formed by a miracle, or contact with the body fluids of the dead Jesus, or any one of the myriad theories put forward to explain the relic. The Turin Shroud, said Giovanni, was nothing other than a photograph, the earliest photograph known to exist. It had been created using 'chemicals and light, a sort of alchemical imprinting', in the fifteenth century. According to the Priory of Sion agent, the author of this fabrication was none other than that renowned Renaissance artist and all-round genius, Leonardo da Vinci! Nor was this all. Giovanni further stated that the image of the body on the Shroud was that of a genuinely crucified man, which explained the anatomical correctness of the shroud's image and the exactness of the forensic evidence such as blood flows. But most astounding of all was his claim that the head was not that of the crucified man, but was instead the head of Leonardo himself, photographically superimposed on the decapitated corpse!

There was more to come, and all of it quite as unbelievable. Over a period of months, Giovanni provided Picknett and her partner Clive Prince with additional information in the form of thirteen letters and one personal meeting. The Shroud had been faked by Leonardo in the year 1492, and he had been commissioned to make the forgery by the Vatican, by Pope Innocent VIII, 'as a cynical publicity exercise'.[1] But Leonardo was said to have despised the Church hierarchy and its beliefs (he is claimed as a Grand Master by the Priory of Sion), and the use of his own head on the image was supposed to be the maestro's way of surreptitiously revealing his contempt for the whole mythos of the Roman Church.

The whole idea was, of course, ludicrous. How the maestro could possibly have foisted this counterfeit Shroud on a discerning populace when the first showing of the Shroud had taken place long before Leonardo had even been conceived was the first and obviously insurmountable problem. Even though it has proved impossible to trace the history of the Shroud back to first-century Palestine, there was nevertheless good records of the relic's existence from the present day until as far back as 1357. But Picknett and Prince were hooked by this 'revelation' from the Priory of Sion. It was, after all, a Fortean journalist's dream: to be chosen for contact by the most notorious secret society in the world, and given a scoop, an exclusive, on the origins of Christianity's most sacred relic. It was enough to turn the head of all but the most objective of writers.

So, despite the Priory of Sion's story being shot full of holes, Lynn Picknett and Clive Prince convinced themselves that the tale was true. They decided that the original Shroud had mysteriously disappeared just before Leonardo's supposed production of the fake Shroud and that a 'switch' had taken place. In support of this theory, they claimed to have the backing of the doyen of Shroud research, Ian Wilson, stating that Wilson had informed Lynn Picknett that the Shroud had indeed become temporarily lost around that time. This supposed statement has been strenuously denied in Wilson's latest book, *The Blood and the Shroud*, the author stating: 'I would never in my right senses have made this statement, as ought to be obvious from the chronologies of the Shroud set out both in my 1978 book and this present one.'[2] Moreover, the story of Innocent VIII's apparent involvement turned out to be simply that – a story with no proof to back it up, and a considerable body of countervailing evidence.

Picknett and Prince also chose to ignore the findings of the carbon dating researchers, or at least to bemuse their readers on the probability of a date of 1492 for the linen of the Shroud. Statistically, the carbon dating shows that there is a 99.9 per cent probability that the flax that provided the fibres for the Shroud was cut between the years AD 1000 and 1500. This splay of 500 years is itself subject to different probabilities, with the dates lying at the ends of the spectrum (that is, AD 1000 and 1500) being least likely. However, Picknett and Prince chose to gloss over this fact, and implied that as their date for the Shroud (1492) falls within this range, it is as likely as any other within the given 500 years.[3] What they omit to mention is that there is a further, much narrower date-range, 1260–1390, within which there is a 95 per cent probability that the Shroud fibres were cut. So rather than there being a very good chance that the 1492 date is correct, it in fact lies at the very margins of the possible dates. Fourteen ninety-two falls within eight years of the least possible date and, given the other evidence, this means that a 1492 origin for the Shroud can safely be rejected. As Ian Wilson commented on the 'Leonardo Conspiracy': 'intriguing idea, shame about the facts.'[4]

Nothing daunted, and notwithstanding the utter impossibility of the scenario as set out by the Priory of Sion agent, Picknett and Prince pressed ahead with their studies, and a book, *Turin Shroud: in whose image? The shocking truth unveiled*, duly appeared in 1994. Given the astonishing nature of the claim, it quickly received a considerable amount of publicity.

A Stalking-Horse

This, perhaps, was exactly what the Priory of Sion wanted. They had, without placing themselves centre stage, and with the minimum of fuss, created a frightful turmoil. They had cast doubts on the authenticity of the Shroud as the gravecloth of Christ, and they had smeared the reputation of the papacy, an establishment with which the Priory has fought a clandestine running battle for centuries.[5] And, despite the preposterousness of the claim, there was a certain twisted logic to the way in which this whole incredible story had been revealed, and why Lynn Picknett had been chosen as the recipient of the revelation.

Ms Picknett had been involved with the world of 'mysteries' for quite some time. She was a journalist and had been deputy editor of the publication *The Unexplained*. Shortly before the first mysterious Giovanni letter arrived, Lynn Picknett had helped organise an exhibition at the Royal Photographic Society in Bath under the title 'The Unexplained', which included a life-size negative of the man on the Shroud. In connection with this, she appeared on LBC and BBC World Service radio programmes, and during these interviews she had suggested that the Shroud was in some way linked with Leonardo, an idea she had apparently heard mooted (though without any substantiation) by one or two people during the exhibition of paranormal phenomena in Bath. It seems that the Priory of Sion became aware of the interviews, and learning of her interest in this area, and of her earlier romantic relationship with Ian Wilson, they decided to use this convenient web of circumstances for their own purposes. They manufactured a story that could be sent out as a stalking-horse, constructing a tale of Leonardo, the Shroud, the Vatican and a fraud, and then revealed it piece by tantalising piece in a manner calculated to whet the appetite and sustain the interest of Ms Picknett (and through her, as they later admitted, Ian Wilson). It was a story so bizarre that its more colourful aspects were sure to attract publicity. It would certainly harm the Priory's enemies. And under cover of this the Priory could perhaps disseminate valid information to a much wider audience.

It appears that Picknett and Prince proved to be just a little too trusting. They fell for the scam and swallowed the story whole, believing the Priory's obviously spurious statement that the photograph had been taken by Leonardo da Vinci (who was born over 90 years after the first confirmed exposition of the Shroud), using his own head as subject. And, given Ian Wilson's vigorous denial of his purported statement, and the verbal legerdemain used on the date probabilities, they seem to have been so enchanted with the Leonardo Conspiracy idea that they attempted to prise the facts into their own conceptual framework whether they fitted or not.

But we should be careful of throwing the baby out with the over-hyped bathwater. Faced with the Leonardo scenario, and its obvious impossibility, one's first reaction is simply to discard the whole story as a fabrication. However, revealing a seed of truth among a mass of disinformation is a well-established strategy of the Priory of Sion. I had discovered this myself in the Priory's statements that the 'secret' they held existed on the Roseline in France. This statement that turned out to be true only in respect of the Roseline component, which was a concealed reference to Rosslyn Chapel, whose title derives from its much older name of 'Roseline'.[6] What if the same was true of this particular Priory communiqué? What if only part of the tale had been fabricated?

I decided to look more closely at the various facets of this extraordinarily far-fetched story. Despite the spurious nature of the Priory *oeuvre*, I discovered that there were two nuggets embedded in this morass of misinformation that proved vital to my search for the origin of the face on the Shroud. Leaving aside its identity, there was no denying that the head on the Turin Shroud *did* appear to be completely separate from the body. And, equally, the image *did* have many photographic qualities. It was these two facts that I believe the Priory wished, in a roundabout way, to bring to the attention of researchers in the hope that they would follow the clues and finally come to a valid explanation of the Shroud's provenance, and a true appreciation of the image it contained. And, over a period of years, this is exactly what has happened.

Photography Without Film

While still trusting in the Leonardo Conspiracy hypothesis, Picknett and Prince were nevertheless spurred on by what they had learned to attempt a series of original and uniquely valuable experiments into the origins of photography. Their purpose was to determine if it was possible, as Giovanni had claimed, to produce a photographic image on a cloth and to have that image mimic all the essential characteristics of the figure on the Turin Shroud.[7] They began with a small, home-made *camera obscura*. Despite its simplicity, this set-up projects a perfect inverted image of any object placed in front of the *camera obscura* on the rear wall of the apparatus. Photographic lights (to mimic the sunlight of Italy) and a number of mannikin heads as models completed the equipment for the initial tests. The researchers discovered that forming a picture of these heads on the screen at the back of the *camera obscura* was child's play, and that the image formed had 'something of the ethereal, ghostly character of the Shroud image . . . there was indeed something impressive about the ability to create such an image so easily'. Progress was being made, but the major problem remained – how to fix the image on to the cloth.

Unfortunately, still blinded by the Leonardo hypothesis, and ignoring the carbon dating results for the age of the Shroud, they sought materials that would have been available to a Renaissance (as opposed to a medieval) forger. For several weeks they experimented with a number of chemicals. One intriguing possibility involved the use of bitumen, the same substance that had been used for Nicéphore de Niepce's original Provençal photograph way back in 1826. They reasoned that a cloth could have been coated with bitumen in just the same way as Niepce coated his pewter plate. When light fell on this cloth during 'filming' in the *camera obscura*, those parts of the bitumen exposed to light would harden to form an image. The forger could then wash away the unexposed areas using oil of lavender, leaving an intact image on the cloth. Keith Prince, the brother of Clive, proposed that the hardened and slightly raised image on the cloth could then have been used to print a second cloth with the image, so producing a passable Shroud imitation. For a while I was excited by this idea, especially as the light-sensitive bitumen Niepce had used turned out to have come from the Dead Sea. It was known as bitumen of Judaea, the very region where Jesus had lived and taught and where the Knights Templar had maintained a sizeable presence. Unfortunately, on looking more closely at Keith Prince's idea, I discovered that in his experiments Niepce had used lavender oil *and* petroleum as solvents, and the latter would certainly have proved difficult to find in Renaissance Italy! In addition, I realised that the negative image of the bitumen/cloth photograph, if used to 'block-print' a copy, would have resulted in a positive image on the second cloth, which would then have been passed off as the Holy Shroud. But the genuine Shroud of Turin is a negative, not a positive image. So the method was useless for duplicating the Shroud image and could not be regarded as a possible methodological contender.

Further research by Picknett and Prince turned up organic compounds, substances such as gum arabic, gelatine and egg-white, all of which had been used by Renaissance painters and which when mixed with certain sensitising chemicals (salts of chromium) would produce a light-sensitive solution. Unfortunately, the figure produced was indistinct and not at all like the highly detailed image on the Shroud. Once again, this seemed like a promising idea that had just failed to fulfil the hopes of the researchers. Adding pigment would enhance the image, but then traces of the pigment would have been left on the fibre, and no indication of such traces had been found on the Shroud during the scientific examinations that had been undertaken, notably by STURP in 1978.

It looked like a case of back to the drawing-board, until Clive Prince suddenly realised that simple, careful heating of the chrome/colloid-impregnated cloth should produce chemically induced 'scorch marks' on the cloth, but only in those areas sensitised by light. Moreover, the intensity of the scorching would be proportional to the amount of light that had been reflected from the model and fallen on the cloth. It was an easy, effective way of 'fixing' the image. In addition, washing would remove all traces of the chemicals involved, resulting in a 'scorched' image on only one side of the cloth, exactly as in the Shroud itself. Using chromium salts and egg-white Lynn Picknett and the Prince brothers painted a cotton cloth with the solution, left it to dry and then stretched it over a wooden frame to produce a screen for the back of the *camera obscura*. The subject was exposed for various lengths of time, and the cloth processed to produce an image.

It did not work. Exposure times, even those lasting several days, were too short to produce the required degree of chemical reaction. Exasperated, the researchers decided to take expert advice from Professor Michael Austin, a former president of the Royal Photographic Society and an expert in holography. Professor Austin noted that, despite having added a simple light-restricting mechanism to the opening of the instrument during some exposures, the aperture of the *camera obscura* was effectively still a simple hole. This, said Professor Austin, was the major problem: using this system, far too little light was hitting the light-sensitive cloth. The solution was simple: to greatly reduce exposure they must add a lens.

An 'Almost Shroud'

Several glass lenses were duly procured, and by trial and error one was eventually found that produced a reasonably undistorted image of the model. An eight-hour exposure finally proved the viability of the system, producing an image of the mannikin's head, 'slightly distorted but at long, long last . . . quite distinct'.[8] After washing out the chemicals from the unexposed areas, the final stage was to fix the image with heat. Sure enough, after heating, and washing to remove all trace of the chemicals involved, they had a negative image of their model scorched into only one side of the cloth. Further refinement of the light-sensitive solution (adding urine to reduce the heat required for scorching!) and the use of ultraviolet lights and a new, white-painted model gradually enhanced the final result. It even proved possible, after the initial exposure, to 'retouch' the picture, to refine the image by adding hair and beard to the model.

There were, of course, numerous shortcomings to this research. Picknett and Prince used chromium salts in their primitive 'film emulsion', salts whose first known discovery was in the late eighteenth century, over 300 years after Leonardo and more than 400 years after the first Shroud exposition in 1357. Artificial lighting was used, including specialist ultraviolet lamps that allowed sufficient UV radiation to penetrate the glass lens of the *camera obscura* and produce the required chemical reaction of the chromium/colloid film mixture. In addition, the model was small and inanimate, whereas it appears that an actual life-size body was used in the Shroud 'photograph'. Nevertheless, their research proved to be a true advance in the field of Shroud studies. What they had achieved was important in shattering the paradigm that had for so long circumscribed the thinking of Shroud researchers. Until 1993 the idea that the Shroud might be a photograph was an unproven fringe hypothesis, pooh-poohed by many 'experts' who wished to believe in the relic's authenticity. Picknett and Prince swept away this certainty, and established the principle that an image *could* be produced on cloth using technically unsophisticated equipment with chemicals that were not presently used for photographic purposes. They showed that the image they had formed reproduced the characteristics of the image on the Shroud to a remarkable degree, including anomalies that pointed towards a photographic origin. In short, they had proved that a photographic provenance for the Shroud was by no means unlikely.

The Templars Once Again

Unfortunately, Picknett and Prince continued to champion the Priory scenario, insisting that the face on the Shroud was that of Leonardo. It was an untenable position: leaving aside the chronological problems, careful scrutiny of the face on the Shroud reveals that it has a list of serious deformities, including a swollen right cheek and an apparent broken nose. The Leonardo Conspiracy would require that the maestro seriously damage himself before making the photograph of his own face, which, given his notorious vanity, must be considered extremely improbable.

There was, however, a far more likely candidate for the task of forger. The letters of Giovanni had revealed the photographic nature of the Shroud and the fact that the head and body were seemingly from different individuals. Such information, especially the latter detail, was completely novel, yet appeared to be correct. Even the choice of the Priory of Sion's agent, 'Giovanni', seems to have been carefully chosen to provide an additional pointer – the individual normally credited with the first full description of a *camera obscura*, della Porta, was also named Giovanni. It followed from all this that the Order knew more about the Shroud than most, that it did in truth possess secret information concerning the origin of the relic. The Priory of Sion is thought by many researchers to have been the parent Order from which the Order of the Temple was founded. Given this Priory–Templar link, plus the Priory's hidden knowledge concerning the Shroud, and the 'synchronicity' of important Shroud research dates coinciding with the date of the suppression of the Knights of the Temple, I felt that my theory of a Templar origin for the relic was becoming increasingly credible. It seemed that this Order of warrior-monks provided the best chance of solving the mystery of the origin of the Shroud image – and, perhaps more important, the identity of the head on the Shroud.

Apart from the Priory of Sion link, and the coincidence of shroud/ Templar dates, the other evidence I had amassed all seemed to point in the same direction. There were excellent reasons for believing that the Shroud image revealed a severed head on the linen cloth (and as my research progressed the evidence for a decapitated head became incontestable). At the same time, the original Christianity as practised by James the Just, Mary Magdalene and Joseph of Arimathea possessed an undoubted Cult of the

Head dimension. And it was universally acknowledged that the Templars had worshipped a severed head, the Baphomet. It was this relic that I had shown to be the embalmed head of Jesus. Moreover, as we've seen, the earliest known owner of the Shroud was a nephew of a high Templar official, Geoffrey de Charnay, a knight who was burned to death with the Grand Master of the Order for heresy. This same Geoffroi de Charnay was said to have owned the shroud 'conquis par feu'. And among all the organisations of medieval Christendom, it was the Templars who had the best access to those custodians of the secrets of early photography, the Arabs.

Could that be the answer? Could the Templars have used such techniques to preserve an image of their sacred embalmed head? It seemed to me the most probable solution to the mystery of the identity of the image on the Shroud, and the name of those that had made the image. However, there was a serious problem to contend with. Picknett and Prince had proved the possibility of producing a Shroud-like image, but not with medieval equipment or with chemicals of the Middle Ages. Without this, the photographic theory remained weak. So the question to be asked now was: Was the technology at the time of the Templars truly up to the task of producing a cloth-based photograph?

Another Approach to the Problem

Fortunately, at around the same time as Picknett and Prince were attempting to duplicate the Shroud in England, a lone postgraduate student at the University of Durban-Westville, South Africa, was also wrestling with the problem. However, unlike the English researchers, Nicholas Allen was not encumbered with the spurious claims of Giovanni concerning a Renaissance provenance for the Shroud. Working totally independently, he had decided that the Shroud possessed so many photographic qualities that it was reasonable to assume that it was indeed a photograph, produced by a technique that had somehow become lost during the ensuing centuries. He also believed that the carbon dating of the Shroud had to be accepted as genuine, and that it therefore behoved every bona fide researcher to examine the technology and equipment of the fourteenth century in order to determine if the necessary materials and equipment to produce the Shroud image were available to a putative photographer in the medieval period.

After careful consideration, Nick Allen decided to work within a far more restricted set of parameters than the experiments of Picknett and

Prince. His work would be overseen by a reputable university and would eventually form the basis of his D. Phil. Thesis.[9] He would attempt to produce a Shroud-like image using only techniques and apparatus that he could prove were available prior to 1350. In addition, his attempts to re-create the Shroud were to be made only by employing the sun, and known medieval chemicals which required no elaborate means of production. He also imposed on his work a further exacting requirement: the image produced must be life-size; it must be a true duplicate of the Shroud.[10]

It seemed an almost impossibly difficult task. Yet in practice, once the initial research was done, the procedure turned out to be simplicity itself.

The Shroud Duplicated

Only three simple substances were required: silver nitrate (a product of the medieval alchemist's *eau prime* [nitric acid] and silver); ammonia (for which human or animal urine was a perfectly acceptable substitute); and quartz. The silver nitrate and ammonia were used as the light-sensitive and fixing agents respectively. The quartz (optical-quality rock-crystal) took no part in the chemistry of image-formation; it was needed as a lens that would allow UV light to pass into the interior of the by-now-familiar *camera obscura*. It is UV light that reacts most strongly with the chemical to reduce exposure times (a glass lens filters out almost all UV radiation, slowing down the reaction). This trio of indispensable substances was not only well known in the Middle Ages, but all three can be proved to have been available to cultures that predated the medieval period.[11]

As a miniature *camera obscura* was obviously unequal to the task of producing a life-size photograph, Nicholas Allen was forced to construct a much larger version, measuring some 2,000 by 6,000 millimetres. He also constructed a life-size head and body cast of a long-haired and bearded model, which was painted white to increase reflectivity, and was used as the model in the tests. A large heavy wooden frame had to be built, from which the body cast was hung (see figure 6). The 'film' was a linen cloth of the same size as the Turin Shroud and soaked in the light-sensitive silver nitrate solution. A concentration of 0.5 per cent silver nitrate was found to give the best results. Silver sulphate, another easily obtained substance in the Middle Ages, also worked well, at a slightly higher (0.57 per cent) concentration.[12]

Subject–lens distance was arranged at 4.4 metres to produce a life-size image on the silver-nitrate-impregnated cloth inside the *camera obscura*. If the

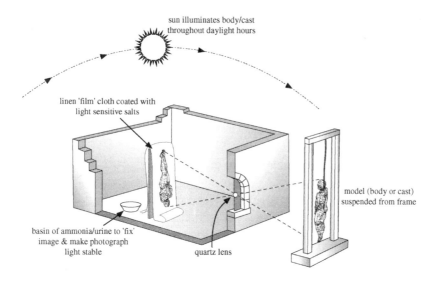

sun illuminates body/cast
throughout daylight hours

linen 'film' cloth coated with
light sensitive salts

model (body or cast)
suspended from frame

basin of ammonia/urine to 'fix'
image & make photograph
light stable

quartz lens

Figure 6: How the Shroud Photograph was Produced (after Allen, 1995)

subject was closer to the lens, the image on the cloth was smaller; if the distance was over 4.4 metres, the image expanded. This fact – that a small alteration in the subject–lens distance can produce notable differences in image size – proved to be of vital interest later in my own studies on the height of the man on the Shroud.

With such large distances involved, it proved essential to have as much light as possible enter the *camera obscura*, otherwise exposure times would have been increased past tolerable levels (it took at least four days to form an appropriate image). This meant that the simple, bi-convex quartz lens used had to be large, well over 60 millimetres in diameter.

It is important to emphasise here, that a pinhole and/or lens made from optical-quality glass will not suffice for this purpose. Indeed, only optical-quality quartz will permit the passage of UV radiation from the subject (corpse) to the specific silver salt which impregnates the linen material, and both silver nitrate and silver sulphate are particularly sensitive to the UV end of the light spectrum (particularly 195 to 240 nanometres). The image thus obtained is in the negative, and (surprising as it may seem) after immersion in ammonia becomes chemically stable . . . and the cloth together with its encoded

165

negative image may be brought out of the *camera obscura* into the light of day.[13]

Front and back 'exposures' were made separately, resulting in the production of two purplish-brown negative images where the light from the subject had struck the UV-sensitive silver salt on the cloth. Washing in a dilute 5 per cent solution of ammonia would fix the image, removing both exposed and unexposed silver salts and leaving behind two pale yellow negative images of the figure on the cloth, each of which had taken four or more days to complete. This long exposure time makes the image much more than a simple 'snapshot'. Modern-day photographs (because of the speed of today's film emulsions) capture a very small 'slice' of time, usually less than one-sixtieth of a second. By contrast, the image produced by Nicholas Allen's work had to be exposed to light over a period of several days and he says: 'For this . . . reason the visual record contains a negative encoding of the three-dimensional characteristics of the original subject according to the physical distance of a particular feature of the subject from the prepared organic support (for example, linen cloth). If a photographic negative is made of this cloth, then a highly detailed, positive image of the original subject will result.' This is *exactly* what we find in the image on the Turin Shroud.

Further analysis revealed that the images conform to other characteristics of the Turin Shroud. Like the Shroud they contain no pigment, powder, dye or stain; there is no directionality; the image is heat and water stable; the image is relatively chemically stable. In addition, they exhibit a straw-coloured discoloration (the 'scorch marks') of the upper fibrils of the linen which are identical to those which form the image on the Shroud.[14]

The reason for this discoloration in the image on the Shroud could now finally be elucidated. By analysing his own 'Shroud duplicate' Nicholas Allen has been able to show that the 'scorching' is produced by the action of free radicals on the molecular structure of the linen fibrils. In chemistry, a free radical is a molecule or atom that carries an unpaired electron, making it highly reactive. Although usually short-lived, they have been implicated in a variety of reactions, including human ageing, and in the destruction of the ozone layer. In the case of the Shroud, the action of ultraviolet light on the silver nitrate 'film emulsion' produces a free radical according to the following formula:

$$Ag^+ NO_3^- \xrightarrow{hv} AG + NO_3^\bullet$$

The linen fibres are composed mainly of cellulose, a complex carbohydrate that is in turn made up of long chains of a simple sugar, glucose (the same sugar that gives humans energy). The free radicals produced by UV light strike the cellulose and break the links between the glucose molecules at certain weak points (ketone, alcohol or acetal groups), producing oxidation of the molecule. This process of oxidation is indistinguishable from that produced by natural ageing of the fibres, or by scorching. The only difference is the rate at which such oxidation takes place, with the ageing process naturally taking longest, silver nitrate photography working over days and scorching being virtually instantaneous.

It is difficult to overemphasise the importance of this work. The manner in which the image on the Shroud of Turin was formed has always defied a scientific explanation. And in the eyes of some, that fact alone was sufficient to 'prove' its genuineness, or at least to leave open the file on a possible miraculous origin for the Shroud. As The Times commented shortly after the release of the carbon dating results: 'Modern science can discredit, but it cannot make its duplicate.' Such certainty is now impossible. The Turin Shroud image has been duplicated. It is a photograph (more strictly a solarograph) produced by the action of the sun on simple, light-sensitive chemicals that were available during the medieval period. The results of Nicholas Allen's work are incontrovertible and, like all good science, they are reproducible (several images have been made, including at least one with silver sulphate).

Covert Communal Action

So, contrary to popular belief, the technology for the production of just such an image could well have been available to the Templars, allowing them to produce a photograph of their most sacred relic. Might they have used this process to produce a true image of the head of Christ, a safeguard against any disaster that might have overtaken the Order? The answer had to be yes. It had become apparent from Nicholas Allen's work that the actual execution of the photograph could never have been completed by one man. The preparation of the corpse or body cast, its fixing to an appropriate framework for photography, the movement of the frame into position for the two exposures, all seemed to call for a group of men, dedicated and highly skilled, and working with a single end in view.

More important, taking the carbon dating of the relic into consideration, it required the involvement of men with esoteric knowledge, men who must have possessed a world view at odds with the narrow perceptions of most Church-dominated individuals of their time. It was only among the books and traditions of arcane lore that the necessary information to produce the Shroud photograph could be found. In addition, such an undertaking needed huge resources and an ability to perform the work in the deepest secrecy over an extended period of time. It was in a different league from the normal run of medieval relics that could be produced by an individual – it was emphatically not the work of a single medieval fraudster who might possess himself of a child's discarded tooth and proclaim it the milk tooth of Jesus, or of a village blacksmith surreptitiously knocking out an iron nail and claiming that it was one of the very nails that had pierced the feet of our Lord at Calvary. Such relics were easy to fabricate, but the Shroud was not. The Shroud was quite singular, altogether something else. A Shroud photograph called for collective, communal action. Its production was a major operation, requiring a large area of secure space, a considerable outlay in finance and plentiful time for experimentation. Knowledge of the technique presupposed a cabal of literate and learned men, initiates of a 'science' that was forbidden by the Church and condemned as heresy and sorcery. As we saw in the case of Giovanni della Porta and his *camera obscura* demonstration, such knowledge, if made public (and even without the 'heretical' purpose for which it was eventually used), would certainly have called down the wrath of the Church on the experimenters' heads.

In medieval times it can safely be said that only a nobleman or a religious Order would have possessed the worldly wherewithal to produce the Shroud photograph. Of the two, a religious Order must be deemed more likely, as a nobleman would have had to rely on the loyalty and secrecy of his retainers to perform the task and, as history proves, such underlings are just as likely to sell their lord's secrets as to keep them. Moreover, given the illiterate, untutored condition of many of the nobility during the Middle Ages, the requirement for men of learning in this enterprise must bring the balance of probability once again down on the side of a religious Order – an Order, moreover, that would have to be rich, to have been immune to Church and secular law, and to have concerned itself with heretical, forbidden lore, with knowledge proscribed by the Roman Church under pain of death. Of all the organisations of the Middle Ages, only one stood out as fulfilling all the requirements of a hypothetical Shroud maker: the Order of the Poor Knights of the Temple of Solomon.

The mystery of the Shroud maker's identity was at last becoming clearer. But other questions still remained to be answered, the solution of which would serve to confirm the photographic hypothesis and the existence of the head of Christ. Nicholas Allen's work had shown that a Shroud photograph in medieval times was certainly feasible. But was there any evidence that could conclusively show that the other Shroud theories were wrong, and demonstrate that the image on the Shroud was truly a photograph? And what of the head? What proof was there that the image was actually a composite of one man's head and another's body? It was one thing to say that the head didn't 'look right' on the body, but quite another to prove that the disparity was real. Obviously, the first requirement was to reappraise the other competing theories of the Shroud's origin and to see how they measured up to the photographic hypothesis. If the theory held up, I would then need to look at the head on the Shroud, and the body, in great detail, to settle once and for all whether the two were, indeed, from separate individuals.

CHAPTER TWELVE

THEORIES AND DISCREPANCIES

The 'How' and the 'What'

SINCE BISHOP D'ARCIS first claimed that the Shroud had been painted by human hands, there has been no dearth of theories purporting to explain away the mysterious figure on the Shroud. With the advent of the scientific method, explanations for the Shroud image have proliferated almost exponentially, impelled in large part by advances in human technology; many theories claim to prove the relic a fake, while just as many, if not more, assert that their thesis demonstrates the relic's authenticity. Some hypotheses (it must be said) are downright daft, while others deploy more subtle arguments in support of their own particular pet theory.

But we must be careful here. There are two major aspects to the image on the Shroud: how the image on the Shroud was produced and what data concerning the man on the Shroud can be extracted from the image. These are two entirely separate issues, and we must beware of the natural tendency (obvious in most Shroud debates) of conflating the two topics. In discussing the subject with other Shroud researchers I found that one line of evidence was often used to justify the other – when a problem concerning the Shroud's provenance was brought up, an appeal was made to the forensic evidence of the Shroud (and vice versa) in an attempt to bolster an otherwise untenable position. To my mind the two issues, the 'how' and the 'what' of the Shroud, had first to be discussed separately with the minimum of overlap. While it would be necessary at certain times to refer to the image while discussing how the Shroud was produced, insofar as it was possible, each issue must stand or fall alone. Only then could we see which theories were tenable, and only after that could we bring the two lines of evidence together and attempt to draw conclusions that were consistent with both sets of data. So I set myself the task of reviewing the theories of how the figure of a crucified man was imprinted in such detail on the linen fibres of the Shroud. I did not overly concern myself with what the image showed, with any of the apparently impressive 'forensic' evidence that revealed that the man on the Shroud had actually been crucified. Instead, I contented myself, at this stage, with looking at the different versions of how the image itself might have been produced.

Competing Shroud Theories

Apart from the photographic hypothesis, all the competing theories of image manufacture can be conveniently divided into four major sections.

1. The Shroud Image Is a Supernatural Manifestation
It is only in the past hundred years or so that those who accept the Shroud as genuine have felt the need to find a 'rational' explanation for its existence.[1] Until the end of the nineteenth century and the advent of Secundo Pia's photographs of the Shroud, the miraculous nature of the relic was accepted uncritically by believers in the Shroud's authenticity. And this earlier attitude is, in many senses, the more rational of the two. If Jesus truly died on the cross, if he was as fully dead as the Gospels would have us believe, then his coming back to life would be (as far as our narrow and restricted understanding of this vast universe is concerned) nothing short of miraculous in the true sense of the word – that is, an event which is beyond our rational understanding and which goes against the laws of nature as we conceive them. There is therefore no need to produce a logical explanation for the image's origin; in fact, such an explanation is impossible. 'With God, all things are possible,' says the believer, and holding such a perception of the universe it is perfectly reasonable to conceive that, should God will that an image of Jesus appear on the gravecloth of Christ, then such an image will simply appear.

It is obvious from this that, for such a person, the origin of the Shroud image requires no so-called rational explanation. It is a miraculous example of the will of God. And, indeed, who can gainsay this? We are in the realms of personal faith here, well beyond the pale of logical thought, and therefore beyond any rational argument. A person is at liberty to believe that God produced the image on the Shroud. But it must be pointed out that, once we pass beyond the portals of logical discussion, it is equally valid (and just as unprovable) to believe that leprechauns magically produced the Shroud image, or the god Seth, or the Wicked Witch of the West. When the only evidence of the truth of your statements is an appeal to 'faith', when the cry of 'miracle' precludes any argument pro or con, then there is really nothing else to say.

Thankfully, nowadays not many believers in the Shroud's veracity take this position. Immersed as we all are in a society based upon the precepts of science, upon a view that everything in the universe is ultimately knowable, those who believe that the Shroud is a 'silent witness' to the miracle of the resurrection seem, paradoxically, to feel a need to provide a rational explanation for this quintessentially miraculous event. In doing so, they have often tied themselves up in a knot of propositions which, when looked at carefully, need even greater suspension of belief than that required to accept that the image appeared on the cloth by God's will.

2. The Shroud Image Is a Painting

Over against the miracle theory stands what is certainly the oldest debunking explanation for the Shroud image – that it is painted. This is probably the least likely of all 'rational' explanations. Although scientific analysis of the Shroud, notably by the STURP team, found paint pigment on the linen, the distribution of the pigment in no way corresponded with the image. If the Shroud had been painted, one would expect to find more pigment on those fibres where the Shroud figure can be seen than on those areas devoid of any image. But, in fact, the density of paint fragments is random. The simplest explanation for these pigment traces seems to be the known tradition of holding painted icons and other religious images against the Shroud in order to transfer the odour of sanctity from the Shroud to the paintings. In the course of this procedure, minute traces of pigment from the paintings would have adhered to the linen of the Shroud, to be subsequently discovered by the STURP analysis.[2]

Others disagree with this assessment. The microanalyst Dr Walter McCrone is probably the champion of the 'painted Shroud' theory. He was asked to examine the Shroud samples taken by the 1978 STURP investigation, primarily because of his fame as the 'debunker' of the Vinland Map. This supposedly shows that Viking seafarers had sailed the North Atlantic and discovered America long before Columbus. Dr McCrone was asked to examine the ink used to draw the Vinland Map. After analysing samples, he announced that he had discovered relatively large quantities of titanium dioxide in the ink, a substance whose invention was dated to the 1920s. It was obvious, therefore, that the Vinland Map was a forgery.[3]

Ironically, this triumph of Dr McCrone's microanalytical technique – the basis for his involvement in Shroud studies – later proved to be incorrect. Further tests by researchers at the University of California revealed that the amount of titanium dioxide in the ink was far less than that reported in the microanalyst's research – the actual figure for the chemical was a thousand times less than Dr McCrone had claimed. Such minute levels were by no means unusual and fell well within the range of expected concentrations for medieval inks. On the basis of these, and other facts, the Vinland Map is now considered by most experts to be genuine, and its reputation has subsequently been restored.[4]

This embarrassing denouement was, however, still some time in the future. In the late 1970s Dr McCrone, flushed with the Vinland Map 'success', was asked to examine the Shroud samples by Ian Wilson. Within a few weeks he reported that he had discovered iron oxide samples on the linen plus traces of a protein medium (collagen) in which he believed the pigment had been held. He then boldly declared that the presence of these traces was due to the fact that the image had been painted, just as Bishop d'Arcis had claimed almost 600 years before. The problem with this theory was, and remains, that the concentration of iron oxide particles in the Shroud, like the microscopic paint fragments, bears no relation to the image. One would expect higher concentrations of iron oxide where (according to the paint theory) the artist had traced the outline of the negative image using the iron-impregnated paint. However, there is no detectable difference between image and non-image areas of the Shroud.[5] Moreover, Dr McCrone's test for the protein medium was shown subsequently to produce 'false positive' results on cellulose, a major component of the linen that makes up the Shroud. Dr Alan Adler re-examined the Shroud fibres using tests that were not affected by the cellulose component. He found no evidence of a protein medium on the material.[6]

Such results have generated endless bickering and bitter controversy, with Dr McCrone insisting on the accuracy of his analysis, and his detractors equally convinced that his results are invalid. On balance, it does seem that Dr McCrone got it wrong. And this conclusion is not based solely on the veracity or otherwise of the dispute over the pigment/collagen data. Other evidence of a much more general nature also militates against the 'paint theory's' veracity. We know that in 1532 the Shroud was damaged in the fire that swept through Sainte Chapelle, Chambéry, and that it was also doused with water during the course of the conflagration. There is no doubt at all that a painting would be changed by such treatment, yet the Shroud image has remained unaltered.

There are further objections. As Nicholas Allen has pointed out, if an artist had applied an iron-containing compound to the cloth of the Shroud, then the liquid would need to have soaked into the material. This means that the fibrils of the linen would be stained throughout; but in fact they are stained on one side of the cloth only. Nicholas Allen has other pertinent objections: 'One must also ask how an "artist" could possibly view what he/she were painting/staining since the image is so subtle that it can only be clearly discerned from some distance.' In addition, '. . . any answer to image formation on the Shroud of Turin which insisted on the employment of pigments, dyes and staining compounds would have to explain why the artist concerned would have wanted to produce an image (complete with anatomically accurate details) in the negative, such that its visual information was largely inaccessible to its proposed viewing audience at the time of this manufacture.[7] Faced with such a barrage of unanswerable queries, we can safely assume that, whatever its true nature, the Shroud of Turin is not a painting.

3. The Shroud Image Is a Contact Print

Essentially, this theory proposes that the image was produced when the Shroud, draped over Jesus' body, came in contact with bodily exudations and/or chemical products of the burial rites, which reacted with the linen fibres of the Shroud, leaving an imprint of the body on the cloth. Believers in the Shroud's authenticity have cited several substances or combination of substances as the possible catalyst behind the production of a true image of Jesus as he lay dead in the tomb. Soapwort or extract of the terebinth tree have been suggested, as has common salt, as well as the spices carried into Jesus' tomb by Nicodemus, aloes and myrrh. Paul Vignon was the first to suggest the aloes and myrrh theory in 1939.[8] He knew that the bodies or torture victims are suffused with perspiration as a result of their ordeal, and that this sweat contains very high levels of urea. Vignon proposed that ammonia, given off from the urea, reacted with the myrrh and aloes spread on the burial cloth and produced the discoloration on the fibres that resulted in the Shroud image.[9]

Unfortunately, despite the plausibility of the theory, Vignon was able to produce only vague human-shaped stains on his 'shrouds'. This result was not appreciably bettered in a later attempt, undertaken by two German researchers, Elmar Gruber and Holger Kersten. They introduced an added element to Vignon's theory, proposing that Jesus did not die during the

Crucifixion, and that he was in fact still alive when taken down from the cross. If this was true, they believed that the heat from his living body would have given an added impetus to the chemical reactions proposed by Paul Vignon, so enhancing image formation. Accordingly, Gruber and Kersten used a heated body in their experiments, hoping thereby to increase the clarity of the image. They did manage to produce images using this technique, but the quality was not much better than the original attempts by Paul Vignon. The image was by no means as detailed as that on the Turin Shroud and, once again, the *bête noire* of all shroud-draping theories – distortion of the figure – was a major problem, so much so that the two researchers are on record as stating that 'the original could not have been formed in this way'.[10]

Undeterred by these disappointing results, many Shroud believers have clung to this theory, justifying their belief by citing the one known example of a cadaver leaving an image on cloth. This is the case of a man known only by his given name, 'Les', who died of pancreatic cancer at a hospice in Thornton, Lancashire, in 1981. After his death, it was found that a partial image of his body had been imprinted on the mattress on which he had spent his last hours. The image was distorted, but some parts presented a tolerably recognisable picture, most notably the left hand. While the mattress-image reveals a superficial resemblance to the Turin Shroud, closer study by Professor James Cameron demonstrated that the phenomenon was due to the patient's incontinence and the abnormal, highly alkaline content of his urine. Enzymes present in the urine, which pooled in certain areas beneath the patient, reacted with the material of the mattress to produce the image.[11] The patient's body weight produced a bodily distortion which is reflected in the mattress-figure, and it should be noted that the image formed only in the areas where the body was immersed in the atypical urine.

Such an enzyme-urine scenario cannot be postulated for the corpse of the man on the Shroud. As far as can be determined, he died of crucifixion and did not suffer from the disease that caused the death of 'Les'. Even if this had been the case, then only the back image of the figure should have been produced (the upper image could never have been subjected to the required degree of immersion). And, of course, we would expect such an enzyme-formed back image itself to be distorted, whereas, like the frontal view of the man on the Shroud, it is, as everyone agrees, in perfect proportion.

Or not quite perfect proportion, as would become increasingly clear as my research progressed. This question of image distortion was later to prove critical in determining the veracity of the Shroud.

Other, similar theories, while not proposing painting, or bodily secretions, have suggested that the relic may have been faked by imprinting a human figure on the Shroud using a process analogous to brassrubbing. Here, a life-size body cast is carefully prepared and the linen Shroud, previously soaked in hot water, is placed over the body cast and made to conform closely to the contours of the figure. Once dry, red ochre, the iron-based pigment suggested by McCrone as a painting pigment, is rubbed over the cloth, depositing itself with greatest density on the high spots of the body cast and producing a negative image on the cloth. The resulting 'Shroud' does produce a full-size negative image of the body.[12] However, it is nowhere near as detailed as the original Shroud, and nor does it possess the original's three-dimensional quality.

In addition, there is again a serious problem of image distortion associated with this technique. A similar difficulty is also experienced with a related theory: that of using a body cast to scorch an image on to cloth. Here, the body cast is made of metal and is heated to a temperature that would produce a mild scorch on linen cloth. The Shroud is then wrapped around the body cast and an image of the statue burns itself into the cloth, the intensity of the scorch being proportional to the degree of pressure on the material, high spots such as the nose or cheekbones scorching more than low areas and so producing an image in negative. This method duplicates one important aspect of the Shroud: that the image is found on one side of the cloth only. Unfortunately, the figure produced is once again bloated and distorted.

4. The Shroud Image Was Formed by Gas or Radiation

A still-unexplained 'photographic effect' – Volkringer patterns – has been invoked to explain the Shroud. These are sepia-coloured negative images of leaves and flowers found on paper used to press plant specimens in botanical collections, and are named after Jean Volkringer, who first noted the effect in 1942.[13] Intriguingly, the images do not appear overnight, but instead take several years (and occasionally decades) to form. And as they show the leaf or plant in pristine condition, they cannot have formed over such lengthy periods of time, but must have been imprinted on the cloth during the first few days of the plant being processed for the collection. The unexplained nature of this image formation has proved attractive to Shroud believers, who use the theory to explain the otherwise embarrassing silence of the Bible on this subject – the Gospels make no mention of any marks being present on Jesus' gravecloths at the time of the resurrection.

One explanation for the Volkringer patterns has been named Free Radical

Catalysed Polymerisation by its inventor, Dr Alan Mills. He proposed that the cut plants give off free radicals, similar to those produced in Nicholas Allen's photographic process. These volatile molecules react with lignin present in the paper to produce the 'self-portrait' of the pressed plant. As lignin is also a component of linen, the idea is that the Shroud image was also formed by a similar process of free radical action on the cloth. There are problems with this, however, in that the theory calls for the hypothetical free radicals to rise vertically on stable currents of warm air in order to produce the distortion-free image we see on the Turin Shroud. This is a great weakness of the theory, and would be highly unlikely to have occurred in the atmospheric conditions of a tomb. As Dr Mills himself admits, the theory would lead to the production of an upper figure only, and could not account for the appearance of the ventral (back) view that we see with such clarity on the relic.[14] And, of course, image distortion would once again be present. All in all, despite the intriguing similarities between the Volkringer patterns and the Shroud figure, we can safely reject this concept as the precursor of the image on the Turin Shroud.

The Impossibility of a Draped Image

Whether the image resulted from contact printing, by bodily secretions, paint, scorching, or whatever, only a little thought is needed for one to realise that – no matter how plausible superficially – all theories that rely on an image produced when the Shroud is draped over a body contain one fatal flaw: gross distortions of the image would inevitably result. Paul Vignon proved this decades ago when he attempted a direct contact print of a model head he had painted. The negative imprint he obtained was much wider than the dimensions of the original head. This will always be the case no matter how many times such an experiment is performed. The truth of this can easily be proved at home with a simple experiment. Take an egg and sketch a face in pencil on the shell with a pencil. Use a small piece of plasticine or blu-tack to form a nose at the appropriate point on the face. Then outline the position of the eyes, nose, cheekbones and other prominent facial landmarks using paint, crayon or any other substance that will transfer easily and visibly to another object (lipstick works particularly well). Next, lie the egg on a flat surface, held to this base by plasticine, and cover it with a handkerchief. Allow the material to lie naturally over the 'face' and make sure that it picks up pigment from each of the marks on the egg. Remove the handkerchief and compare the position of the marks on the cloth with those on the egg. It will be found that the two bear very little relation to one another; there is certainly no exact correspondence of the copy to the original, the former being distorted and giving a bloated impression of the face on the egg. At best, the marks on the handkerchief give a representation of what might be called the contact topography of the face, but this is very different from the actual appearance of the face as we see it, or as it would appear if photographed using an appropriate lens.

Exactly the same principles apply when it comes to a consideration of producing a representation of a human body using 'contact printing'. The topography of the body over which the cloth is draped produces distortions in the contact image in exactly the same way in which such distortions occurred in the egg and handkerchief experiment. Those areas with the most prominent high spots (particularly the face, with the Shroudman's Semitic nose) would produce the greatest distortion. Having been blessed by fate with a proboscis of no small dimensions, I could experiment with various methods using my own face as a model. I was able to demonstrate the reality of the distortion quite easily. When I duplicated a contact print using my own head as subject, the effect was most marked.

In addition, high points on the body would mask, or rather 'shadow', surrounding lower areas. This can be seen most strongly in the region of the hands, which are laid one over the other. Common sense dictates that the cloth draping the topmost hand would fail to make contact with parts of the lower hand. This means that no contact printing could occur in the shaded parts of the lower hand; or if vapour or radiation were involved, then image distortion would inevitably result, as the cloth would be sloping. Again, if it is assumed that the cloth was patted down around both hands (though why this should be done is yet another unanswered question), then the distortion of the resulting image would be emphasised. But neither distortion nor loss of image can be seen on the hands of the Shroud image: every part is visible and in perfect proportion.[15]

The simple truth is that neither contact printing nor radiation could ever produce the distortion-free perfect image that we see on the Shroud. This may be an unpalatable truth to some, but it must be acknowledged as true by all bona fide researchers into the mystery of the Shroud. There is simply no way to get past this distortion problem. Consequently, we can safely reject all those many theories that call for the production of an image from contact of a draped linen shroud with a human body. It is quite impossible for any of them to have produced the image that we see on the Turin Shroud.

Resurrection Radiation

Perhaps the most favoured explanation among Shroud believers is that put forward by Dr John Jackson, a USAF physicist and co-founder of STURP. Like many others before him, Dr Jackson noted that the Shroud image seemed to have been formed by scorching the linen cloth, but with his background in physics he came up with a theory for the origin of these scorch marks which was highly original and, at first sight, extremely plausible.

The concept was that, at the moment of resurrection, the dead body of Jesus emitted a burst of high-energy radiation that flooded the tomb. Passing through the enshrouding linen cloth, this radiation burned into the fibres a permanent representation of Jesus at the very instant of his conquest of death.[16] If correct, it would mean that we had a snapshot of the most momentous event in human history, proof positive of the resurrection.

This is a heady thought indeed. The idea of actually possessing physical proof of the essence of the Christian story is extremely seductive. But we must be very cautious here: what is being proposed is that the Shroud is a physical artefact or by-product of an essentially miraculous event. This 'mix' of miracle and mundane makes any attempt to pin down the truth of the theory extremely difficult indeed. The first step in such an investigation would be to determine what type of radiation might produce such an effect, and whether the laws of the 'real' world admit the possibility of such a precise image being formed. But if the event itself was a miracle, then it could be argued that the theoretical resurrection-radiation might also be a one-off miraculous event, a unique phenomenon with no corresponding counterpart in the material world we mortals are forced to inhabit. This may indeed be so, but if such is the case then we must transfer this theory in its entirety to the 'supernatural/miraculous' category. And, as noted above under that section, there is really nothing else to say, and there is no point in discussing the matter further. There would be no physical proof that either the resurrection or the hypothetical radiation had occurred, or that it had formed the image on the Shroud. Belief in the theory would be entirely a matter of personal faith.

Fortunately, very few Shroud investigators will argue from this basis. For the believers, the attraction of Dr Jackson's theory is the very fact that it provides a material, concrete explanation for the Shroud image. As far as they are concerned, the miracle of the resurrection produced, as a by-product, a perturbation in material existence that manifested itself physically in the world we know. That is, the radiation that produced the scorch marks was 'real' radiation, with a frequency, intensity and amplitude which (had appropriate instrumentation been available in the first century AD) would have been perfectly amenable to recording and analysis. It can therefore be investigated by modern-day researchers.

This position does allow us some leeway: the resurrection itself might have been miraculous, but the resurrection-radiation was not. This permits researchers to examine the plausibility of the theory in relation to what we know of the physical laws of radiation. Unfortunately, as soon as I began to look at the theory in this way, I discovered enormous, and in truth insurmountable, problems with the nature of the resurrection-radiation.

Given that the Shroud reveals a full-length figure, we must assume that the radiation emanated from every part of the corpse, presumably as a result of the revivifying process that occurred in each of the cells of the dead man's body. Only with such 'whole-body' radiation could we reasonably expect to observe the sort of image we see on the Shroud. It is the direction of such radiation that constitutes a grave problem to this theory. In nature, radiation is normally incoherent: that is, it is emitted from its source in all directions. Radioactive substances do this, as do light and heat radiation. The hypothetical resurrection-radiation should, therefore, have been emitted in all directions equally. If this radiation was of a frequency and intensity to scorch the cloth of the Shroud, then it should have been scorched in all directions, producing, at best, an extremely vague human silhouette. This is emphatically not the case – the Shroud is a highly detailed image.

Several factors, each of them vital, must act in concert to produce such an image, but perhaps the most basic of these is that the radiation must be coherent: essentially, it must travel in parallel lines and, in this case, at 90 degrees to the horizontal body, both into the earth (to produce the rear image) and towards the sky (to produce the front image). No appreciable leak of radiation in other directions could have occurred, or the image we see on the Shroud would have looked considerably different. Therefore, we are forced to postulate either that some outside control ordered the radiation (for example, a strong magnetic field will alter the direction of most types of radiation) or that some supernatural power sensed or knew the orientation of the body in the tomb and arranged in some way for the radiation to be fired at 90 degrees to the horizontal.

Such a scenario is far-fetched enough, but even if all this occurred we would not obtain a detailed image such as is seen on the Shroud. All that would result is a human silhouette, much more sharply delineated than the silhouette produced by the incoherent source perhaps, but essentially a simple outline of a human figure. This is undoubtedly an improvement, but it brings us only a small step closer to producing a detailed Shroud

181

image. For this to occur, the parallel lines of radiation would need to be blocked differentially by some substance. This would lead to varying amounts of radiation reaching the Shroud, and only in those areas where enough radiation got through would scorching occur. In addition, scorching would have to be proportional to the amount of radiation getting through to the cloth, leading to a detailed graded image such as we see on the Turin Shroud. Given that the body is naked, and that there is nothing interposed between the cadaver and the Shroud, then the substance that differentially blocks the radiation must be the body of Jesus itself. And this conclusion, in turn, produces yet another stumbling block to the theory.

We have seen that the hypothetical radiation must have been a whole-body emission, emanating from every cell in the body, and to produce a detailed image it would have to be blocked differentially by the body itself. If this radiation was natural, as opposed to miraculous, we would expect it to be blocked most by the densest parts of the body – that is, the bones – and least by the soft tissues – muscle, skin and vital organs.[17] These three factors – whole-body radiation, differential blocking of radiation, and decreased transmission of radiation through the bones – lead to a surprising conclusion. The intensity of the radiation passing vertically downwards would hardly be diminished by the flesh and soft tissue, whereas the bones should appreciably decrease the strength of the radiation impinging on the lower half of the cloth. Equally, that radiation directed upwards would be reduced in intensity by its passage through the bones, but, where it travelled through the soft tissue, it would reach the upper half of the cloth with almost all its original energy. We should therefore expect to see an 'X-ray' of the body, with the bones of the skeleton revealed as relatively unscorched areas, surrounded by scorched areas outlining the soft tissue (this soft tissue image would, of course, remain a silhouette). The image would be, essentially, a skeleton within a human outline.

Once again, this is not what we see on the Shroud. We have on the relic a picture of the skin and hair of the man 'scorched' on to the linen cloth. It is obvious, therefore, that, unlike all other known radiation, this resurrection-radiation must travel unopposed through the densest tissue of the body, the skeleton, and yet be differentially blocked, with exquisite exactitude, by one of the finest and least dense of all the body's organs, the skin. This, quite simply, beggars belief.

The impossibility of this occurring is seen in one particular area of the Shroud image that depicts the hands of the deceased. Here, the hands of the dead man are placed one above the other, and both hands lie over the groin. Therefore, we have at this point five layers of skin between the innards of the body and the cloth of the Shroud: namely, the skin of the groin, the skin of the palm and back of the right hand, and the skin of the palm and back of the left hand. If it is true that the skin differentially blocks the transmission of the resurrection-radiation, then this five-layered area should produce a far different level of exposure compared with the rest of the Shroud. In fact, this area has exactly the same exposure level as the rest of the figure.

Even if all these enormous difficulties are pushed aside, the problem that besets all draped Shroud theories remains – the image produced would be grossly distorted. It cannot be emphasised enough that such radiation can only have reproduced a true likeness of a body if both the top and bottom halves of the cloth were at precisely 90 degrees to the vertical radiation burst: that is, if they were perfectly flat. So for the 'radiation' theory to work, we must imagine that, on top of everything else, the upper half of the Shroud miraculously lifted above the body and hovered, in a perfectly horizontal plane, parallel to and about a foot above the bottom half of the Shroud. Only then could the hypothetical 'radiation' have produced the image seen on the Shroud. There is no getting round this.[18]

It must be remembered also that all these peculiarities must also be compatible. The radiation must not only travel at right angles to the corpse, but it must be strong enough to scorch the linen and pass through bone without being appreciably diminished in strength and at the same time be weak enough to be differentially blocked by skin and hair. Such a radiation, such a phenomenon, is unknown in the material universe. There is quite simply no radiation that will pass through bone, be stopped by skin and yet be powerful enough to scorch cloth. The proposed resurrection-radiation is itself a marvel, and we are back once again in the realms of the supernatural. In short, to subscribe to the resurrection-radiation theory you must believe in miracles.

Further Problems

Even if it were possible to overcome all the above objections, further anomalies on the Shroud make the resurrection-radiation theory untenable, while at the same time being in perfect harmony with a photographic image.

The hands of the man on the Shroud are in an impossible posture for a horizontal cadaver. The sceptics claim that the hand position is just a little too convenient, in that it hides the genitals of the dead man. If the figure was purposely faked as an image of Jesus' corpse, then, so the argument goes, the forger would have realised that it would be indelicate to expose the private parts of God to the full view of the faithful and would have set up this awkward pose to obviate the problem. The believers reply that the body of Jesus was in 'cadaveric spasm' (a contraction of the voluntary muscles in the dead man which would hold the body rigid). If this was the case, the hands would certainly need to have been tied together. However, if the Shroud is authentic, it would not have been necessary to hide the bonds, in which case the thong or rope used to fasten the hands together should be visible. Unfortunately, no evidence of any bonds can be seen on the Shroud. Had the body been suspended for photography, the hands would also have had to be tied together, but in this case there would have been a motive for hiding the bonds (to give the impression of a body lying in the tomb and to mask the groin area). As most photographers know, careful positioning of hands or other body parts can hide a multitude of sins, and the hands could have been easily (and invisibly) fastened together for a photograph.

Moreover, while there has been much discussion as to whether 'hands crossed over groin' was an authentic (albeit rare) first century AD burial posture,[19] less attention has been given to medieval burial practices. According to Dr Tom Gledhill, an experienced field archaeologist who has researched the remains in several medieval cemeteries, 'hands over groin' was by far the most common burial posture in the twelfth and thirteenth century interments he has studied.[20] Such a finding must increase the suspicion that the image on the shroud derives from the medieval period.

The colour of the hair and beard are equally suspect. On the Shroud they are of approximately the same tone as the skin of the body; indeed, many parts of the hair and beard are darker than the body. Assuming that Jesus was white (though his face may have been tanned), this means that – as the Shroud image is a negative – in life the hair would have been lighter than the skin. Therefore, if this is an image of Jesus in the tomb, Jesus must have had very light brown or blond hair. While this is not impossible,[21] it is more likely that what we are seeing is an artificially lightened hair and beard. If a dark-haired subject is photographed against a dark background, then the subject's hair would be 'camouflaged' against the backdrop – it would merge into the background and virtually disappear. The image left would be of the facial features alone. I tested this by looking at a picture of the face on the Shroud and masking off the hair. One is left with a long rectangular 'box' of a face, which is not at all convincing and extremely unrealistic. Something would have to be done to rectify this, and increasing the reflectivity of both hair and beard is the obvious answer. So unless

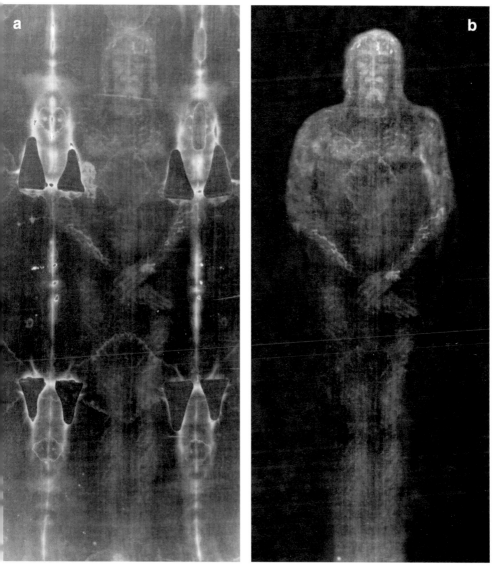

18. Mark Hardy's reconstruction of the figure on the Shroud (b), with the original image (a) for comparison.

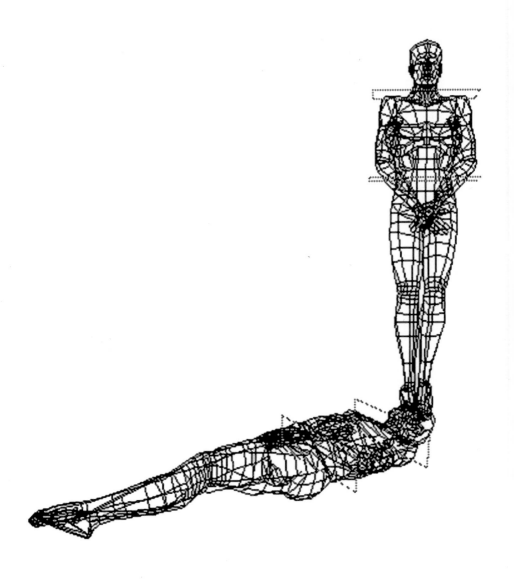

19. The computer-generated figure 'Mr Perfect', showing the body in a supine position duplicating the presumed posture of the Shroud image, and the identical posture transferred to a vertical position.

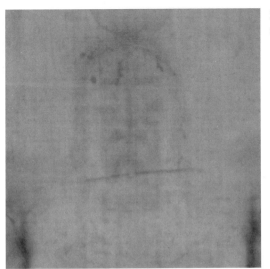

20. a) The Shroud head and neck as seen by the naked eye, in greyscale.

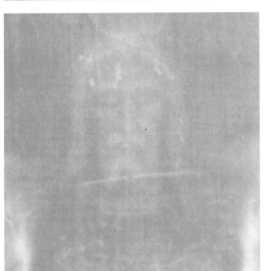

b) The image has been inverted (i.e. made negative) and the rectangular-shaped 'plinth' begins to gain prominence.

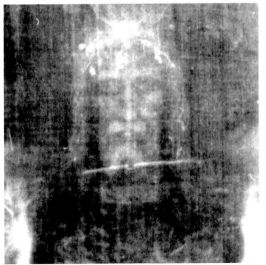

c) The red light component of (b), when posterised, gives the 'plinth' even greater significance.

21. Isabel Piczek at work in her studio, attempting to duplicate the posture of the figure on the Shroud using a life model.

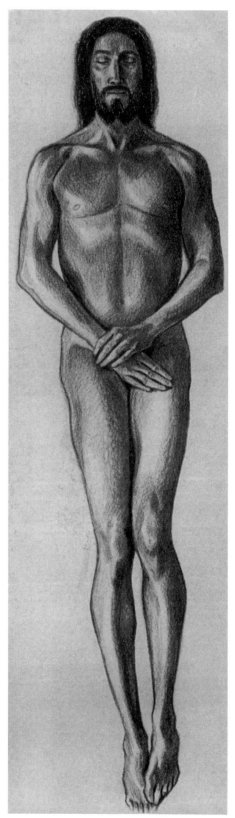

22. Isabel Piczek's reconstruction of the man on the Shroud, based on a life model.

Jesus was blond, what we have here is evidence that the hair was artificially lightened (probably with powdered chalk). And the only theory of Shroud production for which such powdering is essential is that which postulates a photographic provenance for the Shroud.

The hairline is that of a vertical figure, not a horizontal: that is, the locks of hair fall in line with the longitudinal axis of the body, duplicating the hairline of an individual standing upright, as envisaged by the *camera obscura* theory. The much-vaunted anatomical correctness of the figure speaks for this conclusion; if everything else about the body is correct, then the hairline must indicate that we are looking at a vertical figure. In addition, the forehead appears foreshortened, and, compounding this, the face is too narrow, with no ears and no temples. Intriguingly, exactly the same distortions have been shown to occur in some of the modern-day *camera obscura* images.

The Bottom of the Problem

All this is very suggestive, but it was another aspect of the Shroud image that really brought home to me the impossibility of it being a picture of a man lying in a tomb. Perhaps because of the delicacy of the problem, I had never seen it mentioned before in any book on the Shroud. I came to think of it, perhaps irreverently, as 'getting to the bottom of the problem'.

The Bible account states that, after death, the body of Jesus was laid in the tomb of Joseph of Arimathea. It is fairly safe to assume that he was laid out on his back, the normal practice in such rites, and one that appears to correspond to the image on the Shroud. But closer consideration of this position makes it obvious that the cadaver's own body weight would cause compression of the dorsal surface of the body, especially in the trunk region. In other words, the back and buttocks of the deceased would be squashed against the stone floor of the tomb. The effect of such compression on the back would be difficult to see; owing to the nearness of bony tissue (ribs, vertebrae and shoulder blades) to the surface of the body. However, the gluteus maximus of the buttocks is one of the largest muscles in the human body and would have shown a much greater degree of compression. Just such distortion-by-bodyweight was seen in the image of 'Les' described on page 176.

I knew the truth of this from personal experience. As a zoology student I was taken into an anatomy class by my 'medic' roommate, and I still remember the thrill of horror when he turned 'his' cadaver over and I saw with disgust how the gluteal muscles had flattened under the

185

pressure of the body – and how, unlike living tissue, this deformation was permanent. While I all but gagged at the sight, my friend flippantly remarked: 'Flat, isn't it? You could put your tea and a plate of sandwiches on it!'

Yet the rear image on the Shroud told a very different story from the body I had seen. The gluteal muscles of the man depicted there showed no sign of deformation. They were perfectly curved and, tellingly, they looked exactly as they should for a normal human male standing vertically. It was clear from this that the image cannot have been produced from a cadaver lying in a horizontal position, a posture that is *de rigueur* if the figure is to be accepted as an image of Christ in the tomb.

Computer Analysis

Using new computer software, I was able to confirm another remarkable discrepancy: *the front and the rear images are not the same.* My analysis has revealed that the image of the back of the head is wider than the front. Much more damning, the front view of the man on the Shroud is five centimetres shorter than the back view! This cannot be explained by the 'radiation' (or any other) theory, but it is an obvious and almost inevitable error in a life-size *camera obscura* photograph.

To understand why this is so, we must consider the dynamics of the *camera obscura* procedure in more detail. The subject would have been fastened to a heavy frame to allow the body to be positioned vertically in front of the *camera obscura*. After photographing the front of the body, it would be necessary to turn the life-sized subject a full 180 degrees in order to 'photograph' the rear view. This essential manoeuvre produces a very interesting and important alteration to the image. Unless the subject was repositioned with pinpoint accuracy, a fundamental law of optics predicts that the front and rear images would be a different size, *just as we see in the Shroud images.* Even a slight mis-positioning from the original position would lead to a noticeable increase (or decrease) in the apparent image on the cloth 'film' inside the *camera obscura*. Dr Andrew Campbell of the University of Teesside, an acknowledged expert in optics, commented that the discrepancy in sizes is exactly what you would expect even with far more modern equipment: 'To get it right within one or two per cent would be very difficult. You would need an optical bench and everything placed in exact registration to produce front and back images of identical size.'[22]

The reason for this lies in a very basic optical law, a fundamental rule

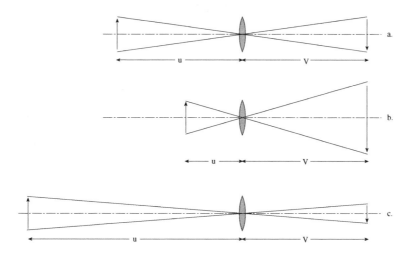

Figure 7: Relationship Between Object/Image Size, and Distance from the Lens
    u = object distance; v = image distance
    a. object and image distance equal, image is life-size.
    b. object closer to lens, image is enlarged.
    c. object further from lens, image is diminished.

that nevertheless requires only a simple mathematical equation to understand. In figure 7, U = the distance from the object to the lens of the *camera obscura*, V = the distance of the image inside the *camera obscura* to the same lens, and M = the magnification of this image. The formula states the magnification M is related to V and U in the following way:

$$M = \frac{V}{U}$$

That is, magnification is equal to the image-to-lens distance divided by object-to-lens distance.

When Nicholas Allen's figures (V and U both equal 4.4 metres) are put into this equation, we get:

$$M = \frac{4.4}{4.4} = 1$$

That is, the image is exactly the same height as the object. This is exactly

187

the result Nicholas Allen obtained in his photographs. The image is life-size.

But Nicholas Allen used an easily moved body cast for his experiments, hung by a chain fastened to the top of the model's head, and making the change from front to rear views simple to achieve. By contrast, moving a real body would prove far more complicated. As we have seen, after photographing the frontal view of the model, both the frame holding the corpse, and the frame carrying the Shroud, would need to be turned around, so that the rear view of the model could be exposed on to a new area of cloth. But, as Dr Campbell so cogently pointed out, to obtain exact registration (that is, to place the rear view of the model and the cloth 'film' in *exactly* the same position as the front view, relative to the lens) would require the services of an optical bench. This is a sophisticated piece of equipment, and it was quite certainly unavailable to any medieval 'photographer'. In the absence of an optical bench, Dr Campbell tells us that we must expect a misalignment, in either the subject-to-lens or the image-to-lens distance (or in both distances) relative to the distances in the original (frontal) photograph. And that this misalignment would produce different front and back image sizes. To put numbers into this: if we assume a 2 per cent difference in magnification (which, as we have seen, is within expected limits), then for a 2-metre Shroudman we would have a discrepancy of 4 centimetres between the height of the front and rear images. This is precisely what we see in the Turin Shroud images.

But what sort of misalignment of the model/frame or image/frame would this entail? Using the $M = \frac{V}{U}$ formula, we have an overall misalignment of 8.8 centimetres in a total length of 8,800 centimetres. That is, a 1 per cent increase or decrease in the total length from subject to image produces a 2 per cent discrepancy in the image height compared with that of the original model. In essence, the medieval photographers would have had to inadvertently reposition their equipment so as to misalign both subject and image by just 4.4 centimetres in order to produce the difference in height between the front and rear images that we see on the Shroud.

This was an extremely important finding. Without an optical bench, the chances of getting the two images precisely the same height are extremely remote (and especially so considering the crude technology used). If the two images on the Shroud had been identical, the photography hypothesis would have been considerably weakened, as the probability of an identical alignment of both front and rear images is almost nonexistent. But if the front and rear images are indeed primitive photographs, then a height discrepancy (an embarrassment to other theories) is precisely what we would expect to find. And such a height difference is present on the Shroud in exactly the amount the theory would predict. This difference in height gives the lie to all those theories of an image formed in a tomb.

It cannot be stressed too strongly that the photography hypothesis is the only theory that actually *predicts* a difference in height between the front and rear images. No other explanation can account satisfactorily for the discrepancy in the two views of the man on the Shroud. This makes the photographic hypothesis far and away the frontrunner in any plausible theory on the origin of the Shroud image. The logical conclusion from this is that the Shroud *is* a photograph.

CHAPTER THIRTEEN

A MEDIEVAL CRUCIFIXION

WITH THE QUESTION of how the Shroud was produced solved, the problem of exactly what details could be extracted from the image on the Shroud became paramount. First among these was the question of whether the figure really had been crucified, and, if so, did this necessarily prove a first-century date for the event? Could the execution have been performed at some other time, in the medieval period, for example? An answer to this query demanded a careful study of the history of crucifixion.

The Most Wretched of Deaths

The origins of crucifixion are lost to history, but it is certain that the practice was established in the Mediterranean world at least 500 years before the birth of Jesus. As we have seen, the cross symbolised the crucifixion of the sun and was the most hallowed means for the sacrifice of 'gods' and 'man-gods'. Paradoxically, it was also the punishment reserved for society's most heinous crimes, for sacrilege and, especially during the imperium of Rome, for acts of rebellion against the state. Apart from the death of Jesus, the fate of the rebellious slaves under Spartacus is probably the best-known tale of crucifixion. In 71 BC, at the end of a failed revolt that had lasted two years, destroyed five Roman armies and at one time seemed set fair to reduce the Eternal City to ruins, 6,000 captives were crucified along the Appian Way in celebration of the Roman victory. The choice of the Via Appia, the main thoroughfare to the capital, was deliberate. The location gave the suffering of the victims maximum exposure, for as Quintilian explained: 'Whenever we crucify the guilty, the most crowded roads are chosen, where most people can see and be moved by this fear. For penalties relate not so much to retribution as to their exemplary effect' (Quintilian, Declamations 274). The Greeks, too, used the cross to intimidate their enemies. After Alexander the Great's seven-month siege of the Phoenician city of Tyre in 332 BC, the survivors, some 2,000 souls, were crucified along the Levantine coast by his express command.[1] The method could also be used simply for revenge and amusement – during the reign of the Roman Emperor Caligula, many Jews were crucified in the Alexandrian amphitheatre purely for the edification of the Gentile inhabitants.

Nor were the Jews themselves immune from the practice; together with the Scythians and Persians they were using crucifixion long before the advent of the Roman Empire. In Sanhedrin 6.5 the story is told of 70 to 80 'sorceresses' (for which read 'priestesses' of another religion) who Simon bar Shetah condemned to be crucified in the city of Askelon. On another occasion, Josephus records that 800 Pharisees who had rebelled against the Maccabean King Jannai were crucified after being forced to watch the slaughter of their wives and children.[2] Josephus was himself a Jew and a rebel against Rome, but prudently changed sides after being captured by his foes. Because of his treachery he was spared what he called 'the most wretched of deaths' – crucifixion – a punishment he saw visited upon hundreds of his former comrades following the fall of Jerusalem.

This method of torture and execution has been used right up to the present day, most notably in the Far East. In the West, crucifixion continued to be the punishment for sedition and other crimes against the Pax Romana until the fourth century, when it was banned around the time of the 'Christian' Emperor Constantine. It is generally believed that the practice ended in the West at that time, and, apart from various anti-Semitic fictions of Jews crucifying Christian children, it does seem that this method of execution was successfully tabooed at around this time. However, my researches revealed that crucifixion remained a punishment in the Middle East, and was used by a religion with whom Christendom had a continued, and for many years a very bloody, association – Islam.[3] I was extremely interested to discover that crucifixion could sometimes be the required punishment demanded for crimes against Islam, and especially for blasphemy. At least one member of an Islamic sect was crucified for this crime towards the beginning of the Middle Ages. Intriguingly, the sect in question, the Sufis, professed mystical teachings that possessed many points of correspondence with the mysticism of the Nazarites, the Templars and other Gnostic orders of the West.

Sufism

Although Muslim mysticism has a long and intricate history, the Sufis are regarded as the mystics *par excellence* of Islam, and have been rightly likened to the Gnostics of Christianity.[4] There is no single creed or orthodox group in Sufism. Sufis agree with Muhammad's words that God is one, is infinite and present everywhere. However, they go further and, like the Gnostics, believe that we can identify with God and, by means of an elaborate path (*tariqa*) of spiritual grades (*maqamat*), that we can achieve a beatific vision by which we become absorbed in God. 'The mystic feels himself identified with the being, goodness, wisdom and enjoyment that are God's, or, rather, that are God.'[5] 'Love is the mood of the Sufi, gnosis his aim, ecstasy his supreme experience.'[6] Many Sufis also subscribe to the belief in a 'perfect man', a master who appears once every generation, who can perform miracles by virtue of his God-given authority and knowledge. Not everyone is aware of this master: only when a combination of gnosis (*marifa*), personal knowledge of the divine truth (*haqiqa*), obliteration of the ego (*fana*) and survival with God (*baqa*) is achieved is it possible to know his identity.

Much of this is familiar from our study of Gnosticism. Indeed, 'from what we know of the movement's lifestyle, doctrine and ritual, almost all of Sufism's salient features are remarkably similar, if not identical, to those older, non-Islamic ascetic and mystical movements such as Eastern Christianity (Nestorianism and Syriac), Gnosticism, Neoplatonism, Manichaeism and Buddhism'.[7] The word 'Sufi' is derived from the Arab word *suf*, a coarse woollen garment, and relates to their habit of wearing such clothing, a tradition they acquired from Nestorian monks. In addition, I discovered that the Sufis traced their movement back to Muhammad and the prophets who preceded him, which means ultimately to Moses, Jacob, Joseph and Abraham, the very figures who stand out so prominently in the story I had uncovered in *The Head of God*. Looked at in overview, it is clear that Sufism was one part of the great web of mystic knowledge that covered much of the ancient world and that passed on secret teachings derived from the mystery schools of even earlier times. Given that the Sufis ascribe the origins of their teachings at least in part to the Jewish patriarchs, much of this knowledge must derive ultimately from the forerunner of all monotheistic mystery religions, from the founder of the Great White Brotherhood, Akhenaten/Moses. While the Templars pursued their Gnostic rites under the cover of an ostensibly orthodox Christian military order, the Sufis may well have trod essentially the same path to *marifa* (gnosis) within Islam.

If the analysis of the respected Arabist Idries Shah is correct, there was indeed much in common between the two groups. Like the Templars and the Hospitallers, Sufi groups occasionally renounced their usual pacifism and founded their own military-religious Orders, zealously taking part in jihads against predominantly Christian foes. Yet this does not seem to have altered their essentially friendly relations with other Gnostic groups from the Christian West. Robert Graves, in his introduction to Shah's book, *The Sufis*, goes so far as to claim that Templar and Sufi warriors fought as comrades-in-arms in Muslim Spain.[8] The evidence that the two Orders acknowledged their religious affinities, and that they were derived from a common store of mystical beliefs – that of Akhenaten – is therefore very strong. I began to wonder if Sufis might possibly have been privy also to all such secrets, including the traditions of the sacred head?

Mysticism versus Orthodoxy

In common with the 'heretical' Christian Gnostics, at several points in history the Sufi movement met great resistance from orthodox Islam. Especially galling to the orthodox clerics was the Sufi mystic's assertion that he and God were one. Seen from the mystic's point of view, his statement is perfectly reasonable: he had experienced sensations of Oceanic Oneness, he felt himself blessed with a revelatory experience, a vision of the indivisibility of all creation, and of its identity with the creator. Unfortunately, while the statement 'God and I are one' was meant solely in a mystical sense, it was often interpreted literally, with disastrous consequences for the enlightened one. To the orthodox clergy, claims of oneness with God smacked strongly of blasphemy, of claiming to be God, and the charge, if proved, brought down the wrath of the religious establishment on the head of the unfortunate visionary. But few mystics were inclined to submit to the dead hand of orthodoxy, 'Since the experience of the identity of self with God was intuitive and sure, neither scriptural revelation, orthodox traditions, rational arguments, nor social sanctions were needed for the assurance of truth'.[9] The mystic's belief in his experience was so strong, so certain, that he often refused to bow to the authority of religious establishment and repudiate his statement. Nor were the literalists of orthodox Islam prepared to give way. Completely misunderstanding the mystic's meaning, they continued to demand that the Sufi recant and to insist on the supreme punishment for such persistent and impenitent blasphemy. As by its very nature Sufism rarely held the reins of power, terrible retribution was often wreaked on the unrepentant 'heretic'.

It was the story of one of these early Sufi visionaries that set my pulse racing – the martyrdom of Husayn ibn Mansur al-Hallaj. This tragic story furnished evidence not only of a link with the Cult of the Head; it also provided a key to the likely provenance of the body whose image appears on the Holy Shroud.

The Reader of Hearts – an Islamic Jesus?

The modern Western world owes its knowledge of Mansur al-Hallaj to one man, the orientalist Louis Massignon. In 1908, while working on a research project in Mesopotamia, Massignon was arrested by Turkish police as a spy. Although ill with malaria, he escaped his captors and fled to the town of Ctesiphon where, filled with despair, he tried to stab himself to death. But with the knife at his chest '. . . he was stopped by a sense of spiritual intervention on his behalf',[10] an experience that had the most profound religious effect on him, and he terminated his attempt at self-immolation. Massignon was eventually recaptured and, during his ensuing confinement in Baghdad, became acquainted with the tale of Sufi Mansur al-Hallaj. He was released eventually through French diplomatic pressure and thereafter took every opportunity to learn about the Arab mystic whose story had become his main obsession. In an early letter to his father he states his desire to work on 'a critical study of the martyrdom of a tenth-century mystic of Baghdad . . . His character was indeed very beautiful, and the account of his martyrdom has a very deep quality, a tragic appeal, which overwhelms me.' This study was to become the central passion of Massignon's life – on his deathbed in 1962 one of his last requests was that the story of Mansur al-Hallaj be made known to as wide an audience as possible.

According to oral accounts, Mansur al-Hallaj was born in al-Tur, in south-west Persia (Iran), in AD 858. The new Islamic civilisation was flowering at this time. The Arabs had discovered the Greek sciences and philosophies and, melding them with their own unique genius, had developed a new analytical method that brought rapid technological advance as well as heretofore inconceivable theological speculations and liberties.

Astronomy, mathematics, physiology, botany, to say nothing of alchemy, were growing preoccupations of the age. Natural scientists even developed the idea, though they lacked the technology, for the construction of a robot . . . Religious leaders haggled over theological fine points of Qur'anic exegesis and sacred law.'[11]

It was a world of experts, an age of pedantry over which, despite the mass of technological advances and theological speculations, Muslim religious orthodoxy held an implacable sway.

Mansur al-Hallaj erupted into this fabulously prosperous (and already corrupt) society with his doctrine of love. He had travelled widely in the East, exploring eastern Persia and India and on one occasion leaving his family for five years. A belletrist, knowledgeable in both law and religious tradition, his poetry is at times abstruse, more often a simple, clear evocation of the intimacy of God's love:

> The sum of everything I am
> You are. And everything I am
> Is Mystery. I have confused You
> With my little meaning
>
> It is You I have been in love with
> And been crushed, in moments
> When You let Yourself
> Become my prisoner.

* * *

> Though You are hidden
> To my eyes
> My heart perceives You
> In the distance.

He preached his doctrine openly, combining it with homilies against the injustice of the times, against corruption in government, private misuse of the public purse, and greed of gain among the elite. His targets ranged from high-placed palace guards to jurists, judges and viziers. Even the caliph of Baghdad was not immune to the stinging barbs of his sermons. Despite this, he attracted many followers and patrons at court, including the caliph's own mother, Shaghab. He was soon to need them.

As he progressed on his spiritual journey, al-Hallaj experienced the extinction of self, a total at-oneness with God, the ultimate mystical union. God was in him and he was in God. And in his usual outspoken manner, the visionary was not slow to proclaim this great truth to the masses. Such forthrightness made him many enemies among the Sufi brotherhood, who felt that such experiences were the province only of the initiated and must be held secret. They should never be made public to 'ordinary' people. This part of the tale has strong parallels with Jesus. In the Jewish Talmud one of the accusations levelled against Jesus is that he 'burned his food in public', which the biblical researcher G. R. S. Mead has interpreted as meaning that Jesus '. . . taught the wisdom to the unpurified people and so violated the ancient rule of the order'.[12] In addition, al-Hallaj was also accused of stealing God's words; similar stories (that he had stolen 'magic' words out of Egypt, or from the temple) were also current concerning Jesus.

If al-Hallaj was concerned by this loss of support from his fellow Sufis he did not show it, and he continued to preach his message. At one time, in trying to explain his belief in his union with the divine through the experience of mystical love, he declared: 'I am the truth.' To many Muslims, such a statement could mean only that al-Hallaj was equating himself with God; this was the worst kind of heresy. He would not retract his statement. His enemies at court and in the theological schools quickly moved against him, and he was arrested and interrogated.

However, he still had powerful friends in the upper reaches of Baghdad society, and he could count on the protection of Shaghab, the caliph's mother. Through their influence, no real action was taken against al-Hallaj for several years. But he remained under arrest and was held captive in a variety of places, including at one time rooms at the caliph's palace. It was not until eight years later (when Hamid al-Bakr, an anti-Hallaj vizier, had the ear of the caliph) that his enemies finally felt strong enough to demand that he be tried for heresy.

The Trial of Mansur al-Hallaj

Al-Hallaj welcomed the trial and seemed to regard the fate he knew awaited him with an almost Christ-like indifference. He answered all questioning boldly, truthfully and ultimately disastrously. Thanks to this forthrightness, and aided by the spite of the vizier Hamid and the scholarly pedantry of the prosecutor, Ibn Dawud, the conclusion of the tribunal was a foregone conclusion. In 922 judgement was finally handed down on Mansur al-Hallaj and his doctrines. He was found guilty of one form of heresy (*zandaqa*), for which the Qur'an prescribes the following punishment:

> Verily the reward of those who make war against God and his
> messenger and create corruption in this world will be that they will
> be killed or crucified or have their hands and feet cut off, or will be
> banished from Muslim lands. Such will be their degradation in this
> world, and in the hereafter theirs will be an awful punishment
> (Qur'an v, 33).

Largely through the hatred of Hamid the vizier, the original sentence of
flagellation, then beheading, was altered to include both crucifixion and
dismemberment. By all accounts, Mansur al-Hallaj acknowledged the
judgement as just and accepted his sentence without bitterness. He had
written:

> Murder me now, my faithful friends,
> For in my murder is my life,
> My death would be to go on living,
> And my life would be to die.

For al-Hallaj, the 'temple of his body' had to be smashed in order that life
everlasting might be achieved.

The Execution

On the morning of his death, he was taken from prison, bound with
chains and seated on a mule for his final journey to the place of execution.
A placard was placed round his neck, with the words 'An Agent of the
Carmathians'. This was a blatantly false attempt by Vizier Hamid to link
al-Hallaj with one of the most feared of all the groups in Islamic lands, a
group responsible for fomenting revolution among the disadvantaged
classes. By so doing, Hamid believed he could further excuse the death of
al-Hallaj and in addition present himself as the guardian of law and order.
The waiting crowd grew unruly, and the commissioner escorting the
prisoner was forced to deny his identity for fear that he would be killed
before the punishment demanded by law could be exacted. Al-Hallaj was
taken to the esplanade near Baghdad's Khurasani Gate, on the west bank of
the River Tigris, where a cross had been set up and the executioners
awaited him. By this time the crowd had swelled to enormous proportions:
thousands of local Baghdadians together with strangers who had travelled
to the City of Peace in order to see the final moments of this famous
teacher.

As soon as he was lifted from the mule and set down on the esplanade, the visionary (in a striking parallel to the Gnostic tale of Jesus' dance) began to caper about in his chains in a macabre dance-before-death. People laughed nervously at this prancing mystic – no one had seen the like before. For the authorities it was a disaster. The whole scenario had been stage-managed to create the utmost horror in the minds of the onlookers, and yet al-Hallaj appeared totally unconcerned about his imminent torture and death. Looking at the cross and the nails, he was seen to laugh so heartily that tears ran down his cheeks. He was quickly seized, his clothes were torn from his back and the scourging began.

The number of lashes demanded by the sentence varies in the different accounts between 600 and 1,000, but the number hardly matters: 500 lashes was the darbat al-mawt and regarded as fatal.[13] The executioners worked in shifts so as not to lessen the force of the blows because of tiredness. 'They beat him to the point that there was no more [skin] on his body, and he looked to me to be skinned alive. (May God destroy them all; their hearts and their eyes were blinded; none showed any pity or mercy; and so, may God punish them in this world and the next).'[14] Al-Hallaj was still alive at the six-hundredth stroke 'but it was feared he might die without undergoing the full prescribed punishment; and so the commissioner ordered the executioners to stop the flagellation, and the remainder of the thousand lashes was cancelled . . . Once the lashes had been administered, they cut off one of his hands, then a foot, then the other hand, followed by the other foot.'[15]

Then Hallaj, terribly mutilated but still alive, was lifted on high and nailed to the cross, facing the onlookers so that they might see that the prescribed sentence had been carried out. The air was filled with screams. He was left here until nightfall when 'someone came on behalf of the caliph to give the authorisation to behead him. But the officer of the Haras said: "It is late; let us postpone it until tomorrow." '[16] And so the still-living, broken shell of Mansur al-Hallaj was left to suffer on the cross until the following dawn. Several Sufis came to speak to him as he hung on the cross; one threw a rose at him, in apparent reproval of his making public the secrets of the sect. Al-Hallaj's friend, Abu Bakr Shibli, was a little more direct. He sent a message via a woman, Fatima Naysaburiya: 'God gave you access to one of His secrets, but because you made it public, He has made you taste the blade.' In this account, al-Hallaj is said to have admitted his rashness but then to have said: 'Go and find Shibli and tell him: by God, I did not divulge His secret.' How al-Hallaj could simultaneously have revealed and not revealed God's secret remains a mystery.

When morning came they lowered him from the cross, and brought him forth to cut off his head. He said then in a very high voice: 'Everything for the ecstatic is to be alone with his Only One.' He then recited a verse from the Qur'an. And it was said that this was the last utterance heard from him. After that they . . . beheaded him; then his body was rolled up in a mat made of reed strips that they soaked in oil and burned. Afterwards they carried his ashes to Ra's al-Manara for the wind to scatter them.[17]

A Sacred Head

Al-Hallaj's body was burned to ashes, but all the accounts agree that his head, for some reason, was saved from the flames. There are several differing accounts of what became of the head of the mystic. It was said by some to have been thrown unburned into the Tigris with his ashes. But if this is so, why keep the head intact; why was it not burned along with the rest of his body? The official version states that the head was hung on the wall of the New Prison in Baghdad, then kept for a year in the grotesquely named Museum of Heads, before being sent to Khurasan to convince the mystic's disciples that al-Hallaj was truly dead. (Like Jesus, stories arose that another had been crucified in place of al-Hallaj. It was also claimed that, although al-Hallaj had truly died, he would nevertheless return from the dead in his body after 40 days.) But the account that greatly interested me was that which averred that the head was kept in secret as a sacred memento of the Sufi saint. In this version, the caliph's mother Shaghab was said to have succoured the head and prevented its destruction. She had commanded it to be embalmed and had kept the head of al-Hallaj with her as a holy relic.[18]

The parallels with the story of Jesus were compelling. Al-Hallaj had taught a gospel of love; he had been accused of stealing secret knowledge, of sharing such knowledge with the uninitiated; he had been tried and sentenced to death for blasphemy (one of the accusations against Jesus); he had accepted his fate willingly; he had danced before his execution; and he had been crucified. After his death, stories arose that exactly reflected those of Jesus; that he had not died on the cross but that a substitute had been executed in his place; that he would return in the body; that he appeared to certain individuals in visions. It is little wonder that in Muslim countries and in Christendom, the two names were linked. A medieval Islamic miniature shows the degree to which the two holy men were identified. Al-Hallaj is shown in a typical Christ-Crucifixion pose, hanging from the cross with his hands and feet intact.[19]

I was totally taken aback by the narrative of Mansur al-Hallaj. So many threads from my research seemed to come together in this one man. His story revealed that, just before the time of the Crusades, Arab religious zealots regarded beating followed by crucifixion as an appropriate and fitting punishment for those who doubted and spoke out against the dogma of their own version of Islam. Indeed, the punishment was one of several considered appropriate for such crimes in the Qur'an. Did this mean, I wondered, that crucifixion had at times been commonplace in the Muslim world? And, if so, at what particular dates was the practice current?

Mamluk Crucifixion

One detail of the al-Hallaj crucifixion miniature proved extremely pertinent to the line of research I was pursuing. It was the presence of large wooden wedges around the foot of the cross and driven down on each side of the upright. This was very telling: in biblical epics and other dramatisations of the Crucifixion of Jesus, when the cross is raised it falls sickeningly but solidly into the prepared post-hole and thereafter remains perfectly upright. I had always accepted this, but seeing the wedges made me reflect carefully on the mechanics of the operation, and I realised that the post-hole would never be an exact fit for the upright. To hold the structure firm and vertical, the gap between the upright and the sides of the post-hole would have to be filled. And the easiest and most practical way to do this was to drive wedges down on all sides of the upright. In the miniature of the crucifixion of al-Hallaj, two wedges are already in place and two more lie waiting to be inserted. Such a detail is an unnecessary addition to the composition and would hardly have been the product of the artist's imagination. It was clear that the artist must have had some experience of the mechanics of crucifixion, that he must have been personally acquainted with the practice, or was at least advised by someone who had such knowledge. In other words, it appeared that crucifixion may not have been an uncommon means of execution in the Muslim world. But Islam has a long history. Was crucifixion practised at the time of the Templars?

As it turned out, the timescales of Muslim crucifixion and the Templars married perfectly. Thanks to the help of Dr Robert Irwin, one of the foremost authorities on the Mamluk sultans, I discovered that these Islamic warriors made something of a practice of crucifying people – 'crucifixion and the cutting off of limbs were familiar retribution in the Arab world'[20] – although, as Dr Irwin pointed out, 'they tended to crucify Muslims – either failed politicians or Islamic heretics'.[21] Even the sultan himself was not immune from the terrors of the cross – Tumanbay, the last Mamluk sultan, was crucified by Selim the Grim.[22]

These Mamluks were originally Turkish slaves held in Egypt, who came to form the royal bodyguard early in the thirteenth century. In a coup in 1250 they placed one of their own number on the Egyptian throne and proved themselves worthy rulers, extending their frontiers and becoming the terror of the Christian Holy Land. They were also the Templars' final foe. It was a Mamluk army that succeeded where Saladin had failed, destroying Christian Syria and settling the fate of the Levant for centuries to come. The final battles in this conflict were fearsome affairs, ferocious struggles with quarter neither asked nor given on both sides.[23] Atrocities, by both Christian and Muslim, were commonplace. Surely, I thought, given the barbaric nature of the times and their eager use of crucifixion, the Mamluks might have utilised this same punishment against non-Muslims? After all, in Arab eyes the enemy were 'infidels', unbelievers. And while the Christians did not repeat al-Hallaj's crime and identify themselves with the deity, nevertheless they did regard Jesus, a known Islamic prophet, as god. This, surely, was blasphemy and merited the approved punishment? Even without such a pretext, the Mamluks were certainly sufficiently bloody-minded to torture any of their foes in this way. In short, might the Arabs have crucified Christian Crusaders?

The Shroud figure provided mute support for this conjecture. The man on the Shroud was a powerful individual; he was well-knit, with a strong, muscular physique – certainly not the figure of an ascetic holy man, his body schooled in privation and self-denial. Such a strong build did not come without effort. It required regular training and constant exercise with heavy instruments. The most likely profession for such a man was obvious. He looked like a warrior.

The wounds from an Arab crucifixion would be no different from those we saw visited on the body of the man on the Shroud. Every study undertaken agrees that the figure on the Shroud is that of a man who has actually undergone the torments of beating, scourging and crucifixion. I began to wonder if this knowledge might not hold at least a partial solution to the origin of the image on the Shroud. While it is not beyond the realms of possibility that a medieval forger could have crucified some unfortunate victim in order to achieve the perfect fraud, the absence of crucifixion in the Christian West for over 800 years prior to the carbon date for the relic argued against such a hypothesis. But Arab crucifixion was a fact. It was enshrined in the Qur'an, and it was now established that during the time of the Order of the Temple crucifixion was freely used by the Mamluk Turks as punishment for 'crimes against the true religion' and for sundry other offences.

It was at this point that I discovered that I had not been alone in considering this possibility. Someone else had been reasoning along similar, if divergent, lines and had come up with a theory that purported to explain the medieval origin of the Shroud.

A Crucified Crusader?

Dr Michael Straiton is a general practitioner, now retired, who had become interested in the Holy Shroud after the carbon dating results had proved the relic to be a 'fraud'. Dr Straiton had realised that crucifixion did not die out at the time of Constantine. As he pointed out, 'Emiliano Zapata was dispatching landowners and opponents by crucifying them on telegraph poles in Mexico as late as 1910'.[24] In the Far East the Japanese crucified prisoners until the 1800s, and were reported to have used this form of execution on rare occasions during the Second World War. Similarly, Franciscan missionaries sent to China were put to death by crucifixion, in mockery of their beliefs. Dr Straiton was apparently unaware of the story of Mansur al-Hallaj, or the other Arab crucifixions, but he had wondered, as I had, if this punishment might not have been practised by the Arabs on Christian warriors in medieval times.

He also pointed up a statistic that is rarely mentioned in Shroud research: that while the carbon dating of the Shroud to between AD 1260 and 1390 has a 95 per cent confidence limit, 'there was a 68 per cent probability of a much narrower range – of between 1270 and 1290 – the exact period at which the Christians' two-century Crusade struggle to hold on to the Holy Land at last came to a violent end, with the sack of Acre in 1291'.[25] This was the period of the Mamluks and the death throes of Latin Syria, a time of almost unrelieved atrocity between Christian and Muslim forces. Dr Straiton suggested that, just as the Chinese had tortured the Franciscan monks with death on the cross, the Mamluk Turks may well have executed Christian captives by crucifixion. The prisoners would have been scourged and beaten before being nailed to the cross and left to die. Being well acquainted with the Christian 'heresy', the soldiers of Islam would have provided a crown of thorns, and completed the macabre pantomime by piercing the right side of the victim after death.

Later, possibly removed by sympathisers, [the body would be] interred, wrapped in a simple, locally made cloth, into one of the many long-plundered Roman tombs scattered in the area . . . The body or bodies would be discovered by peasants who recognised the value of the cloth to relic-hunters who would take it/them home to France with no idea of provenance. What would be more natural than that such a cloth, bearing details exactly conforming with the Gospel accounts of Christ's Crucifixion, would be thought to be the burial cloth of Christ himself?[26]

I had to commend Dr Straiton for putting together a theory that endeavoured to reconcile the carbon dating with the undoubted realism of the image on the relic. It was a bold attempt to explain the existence, on a medieval Shroud, of a forensically correct image of a crucified man. Unfortunately, I could not for a moment believe that the whole scenario was true. As detailed in Chapter Twelve, the failure of anyone to produce a detailed image from a combination of body exudations and chemically impregnated gravecloths spoke against the theory. Added to this was the problem of the swollen and deformed image that would inevitably result from a Shroud that was draped over a supine human figure. Quite simply, the theory in toto was a non-starter.

But the idea of Arab crucifying Christian, of a re-enactment of the Passion of Jesus as a means of mocking and ridiculing a hated religion, that part of the scenario was, I knew, a real possibility. I had already discovered that in Muslim lands crucifixion was thought of as an apt punishment for religious crimes and that the Mamluk Turks made a practice of removing their enemies by just this method. There is no doubt that the Islamic military regarded the Christian warriors as 'unbelievers', just as to Christendom the Muslim was an 'infidel'. At the same time, the Templars (who I believed were the instigators of the Shroud relic and who possessed also the embalmed head of Jesus) were intimately connected both to their Arab foes and to this disastrous page of Christian history. They played the foremost role in the defence of the Holy Land at this time, and, when only the city of Acre remained, it was the Poor Knights of the Temple of Solomon who were in the front ranks during its defence. Even when the Turks had breached Acre's walls and the city was doomed, it was the Templar citadel alone that had held the Muslim army at bay. My research had shown that it was only at this point, when defeat and expulsion from Palestine was certain, that the holy relics of the Order were finally dispatched from the Holy Land. After they had left, the remaining members of the Order had refused to surrender and had awaited the final onslaught of the Arab forces, fighting and dying to the last man.[27]

But long before the fall of Acre the writing had been on the wall for

Latin Syria. From the time Saladin recaptured Jerusalem from the Crusaders in 1187, the Arab war machine had gradually eaten away at the territory of the Christians. At times this process was reversed, but by the 1280s it was obvious to all that, barring a miracle or substantial reinforcements from Europe, it could only be a matter of time before the last fortress fell and the Christian presence was removed utterly from the Holy Land. It was during this period, I believed, that the Shroud had been produced by the Templars, 'photographed' using Arab technology, a *camera obscura*, quartz lens and simple chemicals, as had been so ably demonstrated by Professor Nicholas Allen. It had been done as a means of recording the very likeness of Jesus, a perfect image of their most sacred relic, the head of Christ. And now it appeared that, at the very time, and in the same area that I believed the Shroud image had been made, their foe, the Mamluk Turks, were in the habit of using crucifixion to dispose of Islamic, and possibly Christian, enemies. There was therefore no doubt that of all the centuries between the Emperor Constantine's banning of crucifixion and the present day, the thirteenth century was the only period in history when Western civilisation and crucifixion were closely associated, both politically and geographically. It was also the very moment of crisis for the Templar Order, when Latin Syria was about to collapse, when their most prized possession, the head of Christ, was under threat, and the need for a true likeness imperative. There is no doubt that crucified corpses were 'available' in the Holy Land. Could the Order of Poor Knights have availed itself of this 'resource'? Might the Knights have made use of a crucified body to produce an image that pointed unquestionably to Jesus?

CHAPTER FOURTEEN

THE CRUCIFIED MAN

Where to Now?

I
T WAS OBVIOUS that I now needed to look at the image on the Shroud much more closely. Armed with the new information on medieval crucifixions, the first question to be answered was whether there was any evidence to date the time when the man on the Shroud had been executed – was it a first-century or a medieval crucifixion, or might it be dated to some other time period? This would be no easy task, as I already knew that information on the mechanics of crucifixion was extremely scarce.

Once that analysis had been performed, I would have to examine the proportions of the figure on the Shroud. If the head was what I believed it to be – an embalmed relic of Jesus – and it had been 'photographed' with the body of another individual crucified at a much later date, then it was extremely unlikely that the two parts of the composite 'photograph' – head and body – would match perfectly. I had become rather tired of hearing personal opinions on this aspect of the Shroud image dressed up as evidence – I wanted some cold, hard facts, and I could not see why I should not be able to get them. It was not as if the Shroud was some transitory phenomenon like a vision or a ghostly apparition. The image was there permanently on the Shroud and excellent photographs were available. Given this, I decided that it simply would not do to say, for example, that 'the head looked wrong' on the body, or, equally, that it 'looked OK'. I wanted figures, numbers to back up any statement. It all came down to measurements; I needed a way of measuring the figure that other Shroud researchers could emulate easily.

I was fortunate in that part of my doctoral research had been in physical anthropology. I had spent long hours measuring the anatomical landmarks of a growing orang-utan, and relating these to similar measurements in humans.[1] So I was more aware than most that there are known correspondences between different parts of the human figure, ratios of body parts that varied only slightly between a whole range of individuals. I had to find a way to demonstrate these correspondences, to discover a means of measuring aspects of the Shroud figure so that it would be obvious to all whether the figure conformed to expected norms or whether the measurements of the man on the Shroud were idiosyncratic.

This would be the *experimentum crucis*. If head and body fitted seamlessly together, then they were from the same individual. And my theory was wrong and destined, quite rightly, for oblivion. But equally, if I found discrepancies that lay outside normal human limits, the onus would be on Shroud believers to come up with a theory that explained these results more plausibly than the head of Christ/photographic hypothesis.

That was the plan. But following it led me into a number of utterly fascinating byways that made me at first dismayed, then perplexed and puzzled, but which eventually left me even more convinced of the correctness of my theory. I did not know it at the time, but I was to discover that the images on the Shroud provide unassailable evidence that all previous theories cannot possibly be correct, and that photography was the only coherent and rational explanation for the origin of the relic.

The Physiology of Crucifixion

My first step was to discover just what bodily processes were disrupted by crucifixion and led to the death of an individual tortured in this way. And whether such trauma could be seen on the Shroud image. In earlier times, the Gospel account of water and blood flowing from the spear thrust into Jesus' chest led to the suggestion that crucifixion caused death by rupturing the heart, but this has long since been discounted.[2] Until very recently the consensus was that death on the cross is primarily due to asphyxiation. Most Shroud books follow this line uncritically, but the subject is, as ever, a little more complicated. It turns out that the cause of death depends predominantly on the position in which the crucified victim is fastened to the cross.

Crucifixion covers a very wide splay of postures. The body can face towards or away from the cross. A small seat, or a footrest, or both, may be provided. The feet can be nailed together, or separately, through the heels or the arch of the foot; the legs can be straight or bent at various angles. With the upper limbs, the method can vary from crucifixion on a post with the hands being fastened (either together or separately), directly above the head, to the 'traditional' posture of fully outstretched arms, individually nailed. Strangely enough, it is this latter, seemingly more awkward posture, that is associated with much longer survival times on the cross.

During the Second World War, torture of prisoners by the Nazi SS in Dachau concentration camp revealed that crucifixion with the arms fastened above the head led to rapid onset of death. This is because this position affects the efficient working of two important sets of respiratory muscles, the intercostal muscles between the ribs, which expand and contract the chest, and the diaphragm, the sheet of muscle between the chest and the abdomen, which when contracted causes inhalation by increasing chest volume. A person suspended with his hands above the head can inhale relatively easily, but exhalation in this position is all but impossible. The victim must pull his body up in order to breathe out, and fatigue of the arm muscles will eventually leave him unable to perform this life-saving manoeuvre. In Dachau, most victims died within an hour. If the legs were tied to prevent them raising themselves up towards the beam, death by asphyxiation occurred much faster, usually within ten minutes.

Most authors and researchers have believed that crucifixion with the arms outstretched produces similar breathing difficulties in the tortured victim.[3] However, recent research, the most detailed study on the physiology of crucifixion so far, has cast doubt on the asphyxiation theory.

Frederick T. Zugibe is both Adjunct Associate Professor of Pathology at Columbia University and Chief Medical Examiner of Rockland County in the state of New York. He used college student volunteers between 20 and 35 years of age to investigate the effects of crucifixion on the human body. They were fastened to a large wooden tau cross ninety-two inches tall and with a patibulum (crosspiece) approximately six and a half feet in length. Holes had been drilled into this crosspiece to allow for different arm lengths, the hands being fastened in position by means of special gauntlets that held the volunteer securely but did not compromise blood supply to the hands. Zugibe kept his volunteers on the cross for periods of up to 45 minutes and carefully monitored many aspects of their physiology, including pulse rate, blood pressure, oxygen tension, vital capacity (of the heart), arterial blood gases and the blood chemistry of the returning (venous) blood. A 12-lead electrocardiogram was also attached to the volunteer to monitor heart performance, and a 'crash cart' was available in case of emergencies. During suspension, the volunteer was requested to comment on his subjective feelings, anxiety, breathing problems and pain; at the same time, periodic observations of skin changes, sweating, chest exertions and muscle twitching were also made.[4]

Three experiments were performed. In the first the volunteers were suspended with their feet fastened to the stipe (the upright of the cross). They were requested not to push themselves up with their feet to aid breathing. The second group of volunteers were allowed to use their feet to help in respiration. The third group was suspended only by their arms to determine if foot support had any effect on respiration.

Much to the surprise of anyone familiar with the asphyxiation theory, tying the students to a cross in the manner normally depicted in Western Christian art produced no breathing difficulties. Even more surprising, those volunteers who had no leg support 'had no difficulty breathing and afforded identical clinical values as those who had their feet secured'. The individuals in the test unfailingly complained of muscle cramps in the shoulders and arms (this was the major reason for terminating the test). Those with their feet fastened to the stipe almost invariably arched their backs to relieve this pain, typically assuming a 'bow' position, with only the feet and the back of the head touching the cross (see plate 11). This pressing of the head against the upright turned out to have important consequences later in my research. But for the moment it was clear that for individuals crucified in the traditional manner, with arms outstretched, it was no longer possible to believe that death occurred due to asphyxiation. But if asphyxiation is rejected as a cause of death, just what is the reason for the victim's undoubted demise?

It turned out that death was brought about by a whole constellation of separate traumas to the victim's body. And although the victim suffered less in the initial stages of crucifixion, his agony was far more prolonged, and his eventual death just as sure. Professor Zugibe maintained that the traumatic shock induced by beating and scourging is exacerbated and increased by the nailing of the victim to the cross. Compounding this, sweating and pleural effusion (the accumulation of fluid around the lungs due to scourging) would lead to hypovolemic shock (an acute decrease in the amount of blood available to the tissues). In addition, injury to the chest may have produced 'traumatic wet lung', the accumulation of blood, fluid and mucous within the alveolar cavities of the lungs, which would hamper breathing and also increase the intensity of hypovolemic shock. Nailing to the cross would, of course, contribute to traumatic shock, with the nails to the hands damaging branches of the median nerve and eliciting 'one of the most exquisite pains ever experienced by people and known medically as causalgia'. The agony of hanging from the cross, plus the increased fluid loss from sweating both in pain and because of the heat of the sun, would all contribute to traumatic and hypovolemic shock.

Whether traumatic or hypovolemic, physiological shock results in '. . . low perfusion and circulatory insufficiency, leading to an imbalance between the metabolic needs of vital organs and the available blood flow'.[5] In essence, the circulatory system shuts down and cannot supply the body with nutrients or oxygen. Gradually, over perhaps a period of days, irreversible cell death occurs in the limbs, and the internal organs also begin to break down. Such a crucifixion is death by inches, a slow, agonising and terrible dissolution of the body, and it is small wonder that such executions struck terror into the hearts of all those who witnessed them. Josephus cites one occasion during the Jewish uprising against Rome when simply preparing to crucify a popular leader led to the surrender of a citadel and the rebels defending it.[6]

Conflicting Reports

From what I had discovered so far, it was apparent that crucifixion was a far from homogeneous event. It could, and often did, vary on the whim of the executioner or the caprice of the populace. The spectacle might last for days, or it could be over in minutes, depending on how the victim was fastened to the cross. When comparing this knowledge with the Gospel accounts, two contradictory aspects quickly became apparent. The Gospels note that Jesus spoke from the cross, and there is no mention of respiratory distress. It seems from this that he was indeed crucified in the 'traditional' manner, with arms outstretched. If it had been otherwise, his conversation from the cross would undoubtedly have been much shorter. In addition, had he been hung with his arms above his head, he would certainly have expired far earlier.

However, the Gospels also note that the executioners intended to break Jesus' legs in order to hasten his end (as they had already done with the two robbers crucified with him), and stopped only on discovering that he was already dead (John xix, 33). The reason advanced for such leg-breaking is that it prevented the crucified taking some of the weight on his lower limbs, which, while the legs remained intact, allowed him to raise his body and breathe more easily. Without the support of his lower limbs, so the story went, death by suffocation quickly followed. But, as Dr Zugibe's experiments have shown, outstretched-arm crucifixion involves no breathing difficulties. So this part of the account seems to be indicating that Jesus was crucified with his hands above his head (or in some posture approximating this position), presumably with his legs nailed in a bent position so that raising the body would have been possible.

There did not seem to be any way of reconciling these two pieces of information: one indicated an outstretched-arm execution, the other an above-head immolation. Compounding this confusion is Pilate's reaction to the knowledge that Jesus has died within four hours of the start of his torment – the Roman governor is said to be astonished that Jesus expired so soon. This can only mean that, as far as Pilate was concerned, Jesus was to have been crucified in the traditional manner, with arms outstretched, so as to prolong his agony.

All in all, this new information on the body's reaction to various forms of crucifixion only left me even more confused than before. It appeared impossible to reconcile the Gospel accounts with the conflicting physiological data, or to use the information from either to determine the exact date of death for the man on the Shroud. However, there was one ray of hope, a find that might possibly cast some light on the problem – the body of Jehohanan, the only remains so far discovered that show definite evidence of crucifixion.

A Unique Find

In 1968, at Giv'at Ha-Mivtar just to the north of old Jerusalem, building contractors discovered a first-century AD tomb containing a Jewish ossuary, a receptacle for the bones of the dead.[7] Such ossuaries are quite common, the orthodox Jewish burial practice being to leave the body of the deceased in a tomb for a year or so until all the soft tissue of the body had rotted away, and then to return and collect the bones, which were stored in the ossuary. But if finding the ossuary was a relatively normal occurrence, the contents of the box were anything but commonplace. Lying in the ossuary, bearing the inscription in Hebrew "Jehohanan, the son of HGQWL" was the skeleton of a man in his twenties who had been crucified. The nail of the crucifixion was still embedded in Jehohanan's right heel bone, bearing mute testimony to his awful death.

This was the first time in the history of the archaeology of Palestine that any remains of a crucified individual had been discovered. The find created a sensation – and not just among archaeologists. Ultra-orthodox Jewish groups descended on the site, demanding that the bones of the dead man be reinterred immediately. Their requests were complied with, but not before a rather hasty examination of Jehohanan's remains had been conducted by Dr Nicu Haas, of the Hebrew University-Hadassah Medical School's Anatomy Department.[8]

Most consideration was, of course, given to the right heel bone during the examination. It had been pierced by an iron nail, driven into the lateral surface (the right side) of the heel and emerging on its inner surface. The nail must have been hit with great force as its tip was bent, apparently a result of its having struck a knot in the upright of the cross to which the victim's feet had been spiked. In addition, a plate of olive wood was found between the head of the nail and the heel bone – the executioners had driven the nail through a wooden plaque before using it to pin the man's heel bone to the upright of the cross. This chillingly professional touch was apparently to increase the head of the nail, and so prevent the victim from freeing his legs from the upright.

Dr Haas believed that the nail had been some 17–18 centimetres long, and on the basis of this assessment he decided that a single nail had been used to pierce both of Jehohanan's heels and to fix them, one up on the other, to the upright of the cross. He concluded that the most likely position in which the victim had been crucified was seated on a narrow crosspiece, or sedile, legs together and bent to either the left or the right. Dr Haas also found a scratch at the wrist end of one of the forearm bones, and inferred that nails had also been used to hold the arms in place on the cross. Broken lower leg bones indicated that, just as in the Gospel story, this method had been used to hasten the death of the victim.

It seemed that, at last, we had a clear picture of how at least one crucifixion had been performed at around the time of Christ.

However, a reassessment of the material by Drs Joseph Zias and Eliezer Sekeles some 15 years later rejected almost all of Haas's findings.[9] The scratch on the arm bone was put down to the bone rubbing against the remaining bones while in the tomb (other parts of the skeleton also showed similar scratch marks). The broken leg bones were said to be due to mishandling of the skeleton. But most telling of all, the two scholars discovered that the nail found with the body was far shorter than the original assessment of 17–18 centimetres: according to Zias and Sekeles the nail was just 11.5 centimetres long. Nailing two heel bones together and securely fastening them both to the upright of the cross was therefore an anatomical impossibility – another method must have been used for Jehohanan's crucifixion. At the present time, it is believed that the victim's arms were bound to the cross using ropes, and that the right and left feet were nailed separately, through the heel bones, one to each side of the cross upright. One school of thought believes that this was done with the victim facing outwards from the cross: that is, in the traditional crucifixion pose. Another, equally plausibly, argues that the execution would have occurred with the crucified facing the cross.

The truth is that the actual physical evidence of crucifixion at the time of Christ comes down to a single, nail-transfixed heel bone. So we are certain of very little. We simply do not know if there was a preferred method, a standard procedure, which the Roman Army used to crucify its enemies. We do not know if tying or nailing the victim to the cross was the most favoured method, if the victim faced or backed the cross, or what parts of the body normally received the nails. The Jehohanan material is just one example of this method of execution, and for all we know his crucifixion may well have been idiosyncratic. We can draw no firm conclusions from it. In fact, from the little we can glean in the ancient writings, it appears that the position of the victim on the cross could vary at the whim of the executioner. During the siege and subsequent fall of Jerusalem (AD 70), Josephus reports that 'the [Roman] soldiers out of rage and hatred amused themselves by nailing their prisoners in different postures' (Jewish Wars, vii).

This was all very discouraging. Our present state of knowledge meant that, essentially, anything was possible. Whatever evidence I might uncover concerning how the man on the Shroud was crucified was to all intents and purposes meaningless; there were so many variations of this form of punishment that no matter what I found it could easily be passed off as a first-century execution – or as a medieval one for that matter. Was there any way around this impasse, some sign on the Shroud that might help, any clue on the body image that might betray the date of this execution, or define the cultural milieu in which the burial took place? Was I missing something?

The Crucified Man – A Ritual Washing?

It turned out I was. And the break I needed came during a study of the scourge marks that literally pepper the Shroudman's body and bespeak a whipping of terrible proportions. Each of the dumbbell-shaped wounds of the scourge are clearly visible, the marks corresponding to a Roman design called the Flagrum Taxolatum. Much has been made of this by believers in the Shroud's authenticity, but the facts are far less certain. Because the design of instruments of torment is remarkably conservative, many medieval scourges also conform to this pattern.

So, once again, there was no help to be had with dating from this particular quarter, and I was inclined to pass on to another facet of the research when I noticed a paper by the indefatigable Frederick Zugibe on the scourge wounds that are revealed on the Holy Shroud. It was the remarkable clarity of the scourge marks – which I, like everyone else, had accepted uncritically – that excited the attention of the Chief Medical Examiner of Rockland County. In his work as a forensic pathologist, Professor Zugibe had seen a great many bodies exhibiting a huge variation of wounds. And he knew that the wound marks he saw on the Shroud were extremely unusual. While I had naively imagined that the dumbbells of the scourge had impressed themselves into the victim's skin in much the same way as an impression of a key is taken in wax, Zugibe knew that such trauma would break the skin and produce a lot of bleeding. Adding to the severity of this haemorrhage, the torment that the crucified underwent on the cross would have produced an even greater degree of bleeding. The marked hypotension (low blood pressure) that would have preceded death would then have encouraged clot formation in these wounds. Each scourge wound would therefore have bled profusely before clotting, and 'the shape of the scourge wounds including the bloody areas around the wounds would be indistinct and extremely variable in size and shape depending on the depth of the wound, the angle of the wound, the amount of blood flow, the flow pattern and . . . only indistinct and variable impressions would result'.[10]

In other words, the body of the man on the Shroud, after scourging, crucifixion and death, would have been quite literally bathed in blood and covered with a mass of irregularly shaped bloody scabs, and not with the neat, precisely defined impressions of the scourge tips that had made the wounds. All of this should still be apparent on the body, but is not.

Did this mean, then, that the scourge marks had been faked? Professor Zugibe did not believe so. Again, drawing on his knowledge of postmortem blood flows, he realised that the precise delineation of the scourge marks could have come about only by the body being thoroughly washed of all its accumulated dried blood. This would have exposed the wounds once again to the light of day. The small amount of blood and serum that would seep into the wound after postmortem washing would, Professor Zugibe believed, have no effect on the clarity of the edges of the scourge wounds.

In his paper, the pathologist insists that the body we see on the Shroud has been thoroughly washed after death. He theorises that the postmortem seepages from each wound would have gently touched against the linen of the Shroud, adhering to the fibres and so producing the wound marks seen on the relic. While I could see no way of disputing Professor Zugibe's conclusions regarding the washing of the body (and several

215

professional pathologists have since confirmed the correctness of his statements on the bloodiness of a body after scourging and crucifixion), I could also see no way that postmortem seepage could have produced such an abundance of clear-cut wound images. It should be remembered that every scourge mark is revealed with a wonderful completeness on the Shroud, and for this to occur we would have to assume that the cloth of the Shroud touched each and every scourge wound in exactly the same way with exactly the same amount of pressure. As some of these wounds are on the front and others towards the side of the body, this is clearly impossible. The Shroud would need to have been pressed around the contours of the man on the Shroud with a degree of care and attention that boggles the imagination, and which, if this had been done, would have led to gross distortions of the total figure. In addition, it is by no means certain that postmortem seepage could ever produce such marks on the Shroud. Professor Zugibe illustrates his paper with photographs of wound seepage from a cadaver whose wounds were rinsed with water to mimic the washing of the body and against which pieces of linen were gently touched. Although he claims that 'This resulted in reasonably good impressions of the wounds', his own photographs reveal that these impressions in no way correspond to the well-defined images of the Holy Shroud (see plate 12).

The Chief Medical Examiner of Rockland County also extended the postmortem seepage theory to include other wounds seen on the body of the man on the Shroud. He is not convinced that the famous V-pattern on the back of the left wrist corresponds to the victim assuming two different postures on the cross. Instead, he feels that this is again the result of wound seepage after death, the blood bifurcating as it ran around both sides of the ulnar styoid protuberance (the bump on the back of the wrist on the little finger side). This seems a very reasonable explanation, as Professor Zugibe's other research on the physiological effects of crucifixion had shown that the wrist angle did not change when his 'crucified' volunteers attempted to raise their bodies. Such a change in wrist position is essential for the 'two-postures' theory to work.

The Head Wounds

While I was greatly impressed by the quality of Professor Zugibe's research, I could not help noticing one glaring omission from his fastidious account of blood flows on the Shroud image. Although the flows on the body are covered in impressive detail, nothing is said about the blood flows that can be seen on the head. And concerning the blood on the hair there is a deafening silence.

The reason was easy to discern. The blood flows across the hair are anomalous in the extreme. For a person in the terrible predicament of crucifixion, even the smallest wound will bleed copiously. Professor Zugibe gives his own example of a lady who cut 'a tiny vein' with a carving knife then went to bed believing that she would bleed to death. She did not, but overnight her whole body became 'literally covered with blood'. If this is true for a small cut and a night of relatively peaceful repose, how much more must it apply to a man who has suffered beating and scourging, followed by the torments of crucifixion? It is quite obvious, therefore, that the wounds from the crown of thorns (placed on Jesus' head long before his actual Crucifixion) would have bled profusely over the hours of torture, and would have turned the crucified's hair into a tangled mass of clotted blood. This is especially true of the back of the head. As Professor Zugibe had shown with his college volunteers, any individual hung from a cross with his feet fastened invariably pushes against the upright of the cross with his feet and the back of the head, assuming a 'bow' position, with the back arched away from the stipe. When this position is assumed, the blood flowing from wounds at the back of the head would perforce have been pressed and squeezed between the upright and the skull. It is at the back of the head that the hair and blood would have been most intimately mixed.

But when we look at the Shroud, what do we find? Instead of any indication of a bloody mass of hair, there are discrete blood flows at several points around the head, giving the general impression of the head being surrounded by a band of spikes (and, of course, irresistibly calling to mind the crown of thorns). These discrete blood flows well up from tiny pinpricks and trickle down the outside of the hair mass. It is as if each blood flow had formed a tunnel of small diameter and made its way through the hair without adhering to or being in any way mixed with the hair through which it passed. And it is, of course, totally unbelievable. This is best seen at the back of the head where the hair would have been a grotesque tangled mass. And yet even here we see the same fine discreet blood flows.

It was clear that while the blood flows on the body could be accounted for easily, forensic science had no theoretical explanation for the blood flows from the head, and more especially from the scalp. They looked artificial, and they very probably were. Once again, it appeared that, in yet another crucial aspect, the image of the man on the Shroud differed markedly between his body and his head.

Jewish Burial Customs

But all this was, at the moment, of lesser importance than the solid evidence this researcher had found of the body on the Shroud being washed. Although he admits no expertise in the area of Jewish burial customs, Professor Zugibe believes that taharah, the washing of the body, is fully in accord with the scriptures on this point, pointing to the statement by the University of Kent's Rabbi, Dan Chn Sherbok, that 'it was a legal obligation not only to enshroud the body but to wash it . . . even on the Sabbath'.[11] Despite the fact that the Gospels relate that Jesus' interment was hurried as the Sabbath approached, Professor Zugibe believes that washing the body and performing a shortened ritual could be accomplished 'in minutes'.

Unlike Professor Zugibe, Ian Wilson has studied the possible Jewish burial customs in detail. His researches uncovered a previously unknown fact concerning Jewish individuals who died a violent death (which crucifixion most certainly was). Such persons were not to undergo taharah.[12] This was because the blood was thought to represent a portion of the life-essence or soul of the deceased and had therefore to be allowed to remain on the body until, as the Pharisees of Jesus' time believed, the body would be physically resurrected during the Jewish version of the Christian Last Trump (the Day of Judgement). Wilson quotes from the Code of Jewish Law, an abridged version of the Shulchan Aruch, written in the sixteenth century but which 'modern-day Jewish scholars recognise as codifying laws and practices that go back to ancient times': 'One who fell and died instantly, if his body was bruised and blood flowed from the wound, and there is apprehension that the blood of the soul was absorbed in his clothes, he should not be cleansed.'[13] As Jesus died a violent death (though not dying instantly), Wilson believes that the body would not have been washed. Apparently unaware of Professor Zugibe's findings on the scourge wounds, Wilson is confident that the blood flows on the arms and head of the man on the Shroud, plus the postmortem flows from the lance wound in the side, and from the feet, prove that washing did not take place (by contrast, Professor Zugibe holds that all the blood flows seen on the Shroud are postmortem and post-washing).

But this trail of evidence leads to a rather unsatisfactory conclusion as far as the veracity of the Shroud is concerned. Professor Zugibe's data on the scourge marks seems unassailable, and we have to believe that the body on the Shroud was washed. But equally, if as seems to be the case, Wilson is right about the Jewish burial practice, then no taharah, no washing of the corpse, could have taken place within the context of an orthodox Jewish burial. We are therefore left with only one conclusion: we have on the Shroud the figure of a crucified man whose body was washed and who therefore cannot have been an orthodox Jew. Either an unorthodox burial took place or the body on the Shroud is not Jewish.

If this analysis is accepted, then a first-century date for the body on the Shroud becomes far less likely. The only reason such a date is advanced is because the image on the Shroud is thought accurately to reflect the Crucifixion of Jesus, who was a Jew and who, most researchers believe, was subject to an orthodox Jewish burial. But the body *was* washed, which is against Jewish burial practice, a fact that at a stroke negates the orthodox identification of this figure.

Might the man on the Shroud therefore be a Gentile? If the Shroud figure was not Jewish (and the washing of the body would indicate that he was not), then the balance of probabilities must shift to the alternative 'most likely' explanation – that the image is that of a man who died at the same time that the carbon dating suggests the Shroud was manufactured: that is, the image on the Shroud shows the body of a crucified medieval man.

The Necessary Body

Because the forensic evidence reveals that the man on the Shroud was actually crucified, and because the chances of a medieval European forger attempting a crucifixion were deemed so remote, the image on the Shroud has been used by believers as evidence of a genuine first-century crucifixion. However, my researches had shown that, owing to the many variations in execution 'style' (and the lack of any unequivocal first-century evidence from the image), it was actually impossible to say definitively that the man on the Shroud was crucified during the first century AD or the medieval period (or, indeed, at any other time). But the investigation had turned up a number of important clues that had made it easier to suggest the most probable date for the image.

I knew now that medieval Islamic culture, standing in opposition to the Christian Crusaders, did have crucifixion enshrined as one of their punishments in the Qur'an. I knew, too, that they had not been chary of using such a punishment, not least on a man belonging to a sect that traced its teachings to Moses, whose beliefs paralleled many Western Gnostic sects, and who at times had fought alongside the Templars as comrades in arms. Intriguingly, the disciples of this crucified 'Islamic Jesus' had preserved his head in much the same way as I had deduced Jesus' own head had been embalmed as a relic some 900 years before.

In addition, during the barbaric frenzy of the Crusades, Arab forces had crucified Islamic offenders and possibly Christian warriors on several occasions. And such executions were occurring at the exact point in time when the Crusader state in the Middle East was crumbling and in danger of imminent collapse. The very time, in fact, when it would have been most needful for the Order of the Temple to attempt to produce some form of 'true likeness' of the face of Jesus so that if events led to the destruction of the head of Christ, there would always remain a genuine duplicate, an authentic copy of this, the most sacred relic of Christendom.

And on top of this, the evidence of the scourge wounds had established that the body on the Shroud had been washed, in direct contravention of the appropriate orthodox Jewish burial practice which called for the blood of the deceased to be left on the body. This one fact made the cadaver's identity as a Jew almost impossible. The simplest reason for the washing was also the most logical, and it fitted well with the theory I had proposed: no Jewish burial rites were performed on the dead man because the body was that of a non-Jew. Forensic evidence had also strengthened another aspect of my scenario. While the blood flows seen on the image of the body could be easily explained in terms of what we know of the nature of postmortem bleeding, those from the head were inexplicable and appeared to be artificial. Once again, head and body appeared to have originated separately.

It seemed that Dr Straiton's, and my own, intuitions concerning the provenance of the body on the Shroud were not quite as far-fetched as at first appeared. It now appeared likely that, around the end of the thirteenth century, the Templars could have gained possession of the bloodstained crucified body of a Christian warrior, which they washed and used as the 'post-cranial' section of their photograph of the sacred head. In fact, the cadaver need not have been Christian at all – that of an Islamic 'failed politician' and/or blasphemer would have served them just as well, and may even have been easier to acquire. Such a body was essential for their purposes. Without it, the photograph of an isolated head on a linen cloth would be meaningless. To make the image they wished to produce understandable, to reveal the true identity of the head, a crucified body was indispensable. For medieval man, the marks of crucifixion on the body would have been a potent symbol of Christ's Passion.

But there was yet another argument against the relic being from the time of Christ. If this were a genuine first-century Shroud, then, even granting a miracle, a simple image of a crucified man is all that we might expect to find on the cloth. However, the latest image-enhancement techniques have revealed an absolute profusion of other images on the Shroud: faint signs of an abundance of mysterious additional objects.

CHAPTER FIFTEEN

A SURFEIT OF SYMBOLS

I T I S T H E image of the body on the Shroud that, not unnaturally, draws the attention of both researcher and public alike. The figure is so dramatic, so imposing and offers such opportunities for study that it is little wonder that virtually the whole of Shroud image research has been concerned with the figure of the man on the Shroud. Indeed, it could hardly be otherwise: there appears to be no other image on the Shroud but that of the crucified man.

But is this true? Might our belief in a single human image be an artefact of the way we view the Shroud? Two strands of information point to such a conclusion. Numerous cognitive studies have revealed that the human brain is not simply a passive receiver of the visual information gathered by our eyes. It actively processes and edits the information to construct its own picture of reality. The brain has a natural tendency to disregard any image whose edges are fuzzy, or of low contrast or which is simply much fainter than other competing images. We just don't see them. So there is a definite possibility that when we look at the Shroud, we are unconsciously discarding information that might prove crucial. Quite as important is the way in which the original photographs of the Shroud have been treated before being released for public inspection. We like to believe that the camera cannot lie, but without in any way suggesting a deliberate cover-up of data it is evident that some visual information could be lost in the processing of the image for public consumption. It is normal practice to increase the contrast between the figure on the Shroud and the background in order to make the former stand out with more clarity.[1] The whole body image may be lightened, so as to bring out fine detail in the shadow areas of the figure and to obscure any creases, wrinkles or stains on the linen, giving the 'background' to the body a cleaner, lighter, more attractive and uniform appearance. However, while it would undoubtedly enhance the image of the man on the Shroud, this same procedure would certainly have unfortunate consequences for any smaller, fainter images that might surround the body. They would effectively be burned out of the picture, and disappear into the background.

Alan and Mary Whanger have blazed their own trail in this area of Shroud research. Dr Whanger is Professor Emeritus at Duke University Medical Center, Durham, North Carolina, and his wife Mary holds a degree in religion. They began with an interest in the Holy Shroud by researching possible correspondences between the face on the Shroud and various icons (holy paintings of Christ) of the first millennium. They were interested in finding a means of comparing these images in an objective and reproducible way, one that could be repeated and checked for accuracy. This led them to devise a method known as Polarised Image Overlay Technique (PIOT), where two similar images, reduced to the same scale, are projected on to a lenticular screen and overlaid one on the other. They are then positioned precisely, using features such as eyebrows, end of nose and mouth, to achieve the correct alignment. One of the images is projected through a polarising filter that allows only light in the vertical plane to reach the screen, while the other image is projected through a second polarising filter that permits the passage of horizontal-plane light alone. The screen is then viewed through a third polarising filter held before the eyes, which, when rotated slowly, allows either the first or the second projected image to be viewed in turn, giving the researcher the ability to move quickly between the two images to assess their compatibility.[2]

Using this procedure, the Whangers note 'Points of Congruence' (PC) – specific areas where the two images showed the same feature, such as the end of the nose, a dot to one side of the mouth, etc. – recording the number and position of each. In order to decide when the number of PCs reached a significant level to allow the Whangers to conclude that the two images were the same (or, perhaps more accurately, that they may have derived from the same source), they decided 'to go with the forensic standard. In a court of law . . . for more complicated images such as a face, forty-five to sixty PCs are enough to declare the faces to be the same'.[3] When they used the PIOT system to compare the icons with the face on the Shroud, the Whangers claimed to have found several icons of Jesus with over 100 PCs, the most impressive being 175 PCs for an icon known as Christ Pantocrator from Saint Catherine's Monastery in the Sinai Peninsula, Egypt, made about AD 550.[4] This, of course, predates the thirteenth/fourteenth-century carbon dating for the Shroud by at least 700 years. As far as these researchers were concerned, their work proved that the carbon dating was wrong and that the Shroud was in existence long before the scientific community claimed it had been manufactured.

It has to be said from the outset that this branch of the Whangers' work has not been verified by independent observers. The technique is undoubtedly a very useful tool for such comparative work, but it is the choice of features that constitutes a significant similarity that is still open to a great deal of subjective representation. Looking at the Whangers' book, at photographs of icons that were said to show a huge number of Points of Congruence, I was aware of several other rather gross features that, while present on the icon, were not mirrored in the Shroud image. No comment was made on these 'Points of Incongruence', and, despite the apparent scientific qualities of the methodology, I was left wondering just how great was the subjective element in this research.

However, if we grant that the Polarised Image Overlay Technique is truly able to show that two images are related, then we must also admit that the evidence the Whangers have put together does blow a rather large hole in the carbon date of 1260–1390. If the Pantocrator icon derives from the image on the Shroud, then the Shroud must have been around during the sixth century: ergo the carbon dating is wrong and the probability that the Shroud is a genuine gravecloth of Jesus is greatly increased.

There are, nevertheless, two other, equally valid, possibilities. Although these researchers do not mention it, the 'Points of Congruence' methodology cuts both ways. There is, of course, the possibility that the Shroud image is actually a copy of the icon and not the other way round. A medieval forger may have viewed the icon, as famous in the Middle Ages as it is now, and simply copied the face for his forgery as the most acceptable and accepted image of Christ available.

The other possibility, and one that seems to me more likely, is that both images derive from a common exemplar – the head of Christ. We have seen that the embalmed head of Jesus was either buried under the Temple of Solomon in Jerusalem or carried into France, ultimately coming into the possession of the Templars via the heretic Cathars in the course of their near-extermination during the Albigensian Crusade. If Gnostic groups possessed the sacred relic during the first millennium, then it is likely that paintings or drawings of the head might have been made from time to time. This certainly seems to have happened in the case of the Templars – the painting of a disembodied, long-haired, bearded 'head' discovered on the site of a Templar preceptory at Templecombe, England, is clearly a representation of the Baphomet, the head worshipped by the Templars. And it bears a striking similarity to the face on the Shroud.[5] We know also that the head of Jesus that was in the possession of Nicodemus was held by him for a considerable length of time. It is possible that during this period a two-dimensional copy of the head was made before the sacred relic itself was consigned to the vaults below the temple. It is from such a copy that the Pantocrator icon may derive.

The head image we see on the Shroud would still be derived via the *camera obscura*/photography method described earlier. The reason for the high degree of congruence in the two images (always assuming that the methodology of the Whangers is accurate and the two images do not simply look similar because they are of two bearded Semitic-featured adult males) would then be explained by the fact that they are derived from the same model, from the head of Jesus.

Other Images on the Shroud

Spurred on by their findings with the Shroud face, the Whangers decided to use their expertise to see if there were other objects on the Shroud. They were fortunate in obtaining from Father Francis L. Filas second-generation copies of the negatives taken of the Shroud by Guiseppe Enrie in 1931. These black and white photographs were taken on large photographic plates and are of first-class quality. The Whangers claim that, in the search for faint images of other objects on the Shroud, such black and white photographs are superior to the more modern colour shots taken in 1978 by STURP photographers Vernon Miller and Barrie Schworz.

Using a number of different methods of photographic enhancement has revealed an astonishing number of faint secondary images surrounding and overlaying the figure of the man on the Shroud.[6] A total of 21 separate categories have been listed by the Whangers. Examining the photographs these researchers present, there are eight objects where, although there may be an image present, what exactly the object was that produced the image is highly speculative. The Whangers interpret these eight images as:

1. sandals
2. cloak
3. tunic

4. belt
5. head phylactery
6. arm phylactery
7. amulet
8. coins over the eyes.

There has been much argument over some of these interpretations, especially a long-running dispute on the presence or absence of coins over the eyes of the man on the Shroud.[7] There may be a head phylactery (a small pouch or box containing texts from the scriptures) at the very top of the forehead, and an arm phylactery on his left arm, but it is very difficult to be sure. As with all these suggested interpretations, the faintness of the image preludes any certainty. The jury is most certainly still out as far as this particular octet of Shroud objects is concerned.

With some of the other images the researchers are on much firmer ground. It is clear that at least 13 separate classes of objects (comprising 18 individual items) do seem to be sufficiently well defined to allow a fairly confident identification. And these comprise an astounding constellation of objects. They are:

1 *Flowers*   The Whangers have identified 28 species of plants on the Shroud. The identity of 22 of these has been confirmed by Avinoam Danin, Professor of Botany at the Hebrew University in Jerusalem. Twenty-three of the plants are flowers, three are bushes and two thorns. What is particularly impressive about these findings is that all 28 plants grow in Israel, 20 in Jerusalem itself and the remaining 8 close to the capital, in the Judaean Desert or close to the Dead Sea.[8] Whatever the true status of the Shroud of Turin – whether miraculous witness to the resurrection, fake or photograph – this evidence appears to show conclusively that the relic originated in the Holy Land.

2 *Crown of thorns*   One of the thorn species mentioned above, *Gundelia tournefortii*, makes an unusual circular pattern on the Shroud, a circlet of thorns lying near the man on the Shroud's right shoulder. This has been convincingly interpreted as the scriptural crown of thorns that Jesus was forced to wear during his humiliation just prior to the Crucifixion itself.

3 *Nails*   The faint image of a large nail was discovered lying next to the right thigh of the figure on the Shroud. The Whangers claim that the nail fits the wounds seen in the hands and feet of the body, but this is very speculative. Considering the obscurity of the wounds themselves, it is actually impossible to determine the exact size of nail that produced the puncture wounds. However, there is no doubt that the nail may well have been responsible for producing such trauma on the body. Close to this

large nail are two crossed smaller nails, which the Whangers surmise were used to attach the nameboard 'Jesus the Nazarite, King of the Jews' to the cross.

4 *Spear head*   On the back view of the Shroud, at the level of the man on the Shroud's head, and lying close to the left edge of the linen, there is a faint image of what appears to be the bottom half of a spear blade. The top half is not present on the cloth, seemingly obscured by a water stain caused during the fire of 1532.

5 and 6 *Hammer and pliers*   An odd-shaped hammer, the head in the form of a wedge, can be faintly discerned lying next to the right calf of the figure. In an almost identical position on the other side is a pair of long-handled pliers, lying at right angles to the longitudinal axis of the Shroud.

7 *Scourges*   Two of these instruments of torture, corresponding to the number apparently used to scourge the body seen on the Shroud, have been identified next to the man on the Shroud's left calf. They are three-thonged scourges, their ends tipped with bone, probably of sheep or goat.

8 *Sponge and stick*   At the right-hand side of the body, on a level with the top of the head, the Whangers have detected the image of a sponge attached to a long rod. The botanist Avinoam Danin subsequently identified the rod as the reed *Arundo donax*, a species found in Israel. After careful scrutiny, he believes he can also discern the string by which the sponge was fastened to the reed.

9 *Two brooms*   Of all the 13 'good' images, this interpretation is the most problematical. There are two cone-shaped light areas which merge into a series of twisted irregular lines. Each of these suggest, say the Whangers, a brush, broom or besom.

10 *Box and trowel or spoon*   At the right side of the body at ankle level is what appears to be a small, almost square box measuring five by five and a half inches. Tied to the box by a cloth strip is a trowel or spoon approximately 12 inches long.

11 *Dice*   Two square-shaped images, one of which seems to show six dots and the other five dots, have been discerned on the Shroud. The dots are arranged in the characteristic pattern of die numbers. There is the possibility that a third die is present, but a patch covering a burned region of the Shroud covers most of this area, making it impossible to say if this third die is actually present.

12 *Rope*   A length of rope has been found at the base of the Shroud figure, loosely coiled and laid next to the feet. There are also faint indications of other sections of rope.

13 *Board*   The presence of the two small nails, crossed next to the large nail image, suggested to Dr Whanger that they were used to support the board that was placed on the cross of Jesus. This prompted him to search for any indications that the board itself had been placed on the Shroud. After much scrutiny, he discovered the faint outline of such a board, approximately 24 by 13.5 inches. Of far greater interest was the writing on this board. Several letters are present, all of which conform to the lettering said to have been on the board of Jesus, 'Jesus the Nazarite, King of the Jews' written in Latin, Greek and Hebrew.

Evidence – But of What?

These findings have been trumpeted as positive evidence that the Shroud is genuine, for where else could these flowers have been collected but Jerusalem? And who but Jesus would have such a collection of objects surrounding him: crown of thorns, pliers, nail, sponge and spear? Most convincing of all is the image of the writing from the headboard that appears on the Shroud. This, above all, must surely be regarded as proof positive that the body on the Shroud is that of Jesus?

In fact, this surfeit of symbols proves exactly the opposite. And it is the board itself, the most solid proof of the Shroud's identity, which demonstrates undeniably that the Shroud cannot have been produced by any of the multitude of theories reviewed in Chapter Twelve. Only a photographic theory can account satisfactorily for the discrepancies I have discovered on the supposed headboard of Jesus.

A Surfeit of Symbols

Consider first the number of objects present on the Shroud. Even when the problematical eight images are discounted, and the large number of flower images is considered as a single 'object', there are still no fewer than eighteen Shroud objects in *toto*.

Next, consider the dynamics of the Crucifixion: Jesus is scourged by Roman soldiers, who crown him with thorns. They fasten him to the cross with nails and hammer, and nail above him a sign saying 'Jesus the Nazarite, King of the Jews'. They play dice for his 'seamless robe', and when he thirsts they torment and mock him with a sponge of vinegar. A soldier pierces his side with a spear. Finally, when his body is taken down, the nails are extracted by pliers.

At least eight separate actions, and for each we are asked to believe that a Jewish bystander has approached the Roman soldiery and requested the object of torture. Indeed, as we know that very few of Jesus' followers attended the Crucifixion (most, like Peter, having fled in fear of their lives), we must imagine that each remaining disciple carried more than one symbol of the Crucifixion with them when they left Golgotha. Even more incredible, we must believe that, on each occasion that the disciples requested a spear, hammer, nail or what have you, the legionnaires acquiesced and provided these objects to the despised Jews.

In the account of their research, Alan and Mary Whanger point out on several occasions that the indignities heaped upon Jesus by the Roman soldiery stemmed from a deep-rooted antipathy between the two nations.[9] That such enmity existed is accepted by all historians. Why, then, did the soldiers conducting the execution provide every single important object in the drama to a people whom they loathed, and to a group, moreover, whose leader was being crucified specifically for an act of rebellion against the very state and emperor they served?[10] They handed over pliers, hammer, sponge, and obligingly pulled down the headboard from the cross and made it available to the followers of the man on the cross, even supplying the two nails with which the board was fastened to the upright. And they handed over the dice they were gambling with? 'Unlikely' does not begin to cover it. It is quite simply an unbelievable scenario.

But there is more. The spear that pierced Christ's side also appears on the Shroud, and once again it, too, must have been turned over to the grieving Nazarite mourners. But in the Roman Army of the first century AD, it was a capital offence to lose this weapon – a legionnaire's life was forfeit if he gave away or otherwise mislaid his spear. That one of the imperial soldiery should have voluntarily handed over his weapon in such circumstances is inconceivable. And yet the image of a spear is present on the Shroud.

A Hurried Burial?

There are other objections to consider. The positioning of the articles and objects on the Shroud conforms to no known Jewish burial ritual. Indeed, it makes a nonsense of the provision of a Shroud for the dead man. The point of the Shroud was to wrap the body. There is some disagreement as to how exactly the Shroud was tied around the cadaver, but even the most 'minimalist' of Shroud researchers concedes that the Shroud would, in a normal ritual, be tied around the body at ankles, waist and neck. Given that the Shroud image could be formed only when the linen cloth was untied, this problem is either ignored by pro-Shroud advocates or we are told that the reason the Shroud was untied was that the Sabbath was approaching and there was not enough time to complete the ritual. Now this rite of enshroudment was, as we have seen, demanded by Jewish law; it was incumbent on all participants to perform this task. Yet despite this religious imperative, there was not enough time to complete the ceremony. But there *was* time to collect all the artefacts that we see on the Shroud and to place them with care and precision on the linen, and to take such pains that even a trowel was carefully tied to its box. Does this appear plausible? And the placement of the objects was done in the full knowledge that the disciples planned to return after the Sabbath to complete the ritual: that is, to bind the Shroud around the body. This would require them to remove all the articles they had so carefully placed on the Shroud. It does not seem likely that, with their time severely limited by the approach of the Sabbath, they would have preferred to have performed this essentially trivial act when one of far greater religious importance, enshrouding of the body, remained to be completed.

It should be noted that we are told in the Bible that the disciples did not know Jesus would resurrect, that they believed he was dead.[11] This fact compounds the implausibility of the scenario. We are asked to believe that the disciples, facing the imminent start of the Sabbath, chose to carefully position spear, sponge, crown of thorns and all the other objects we see on the Shroud, knowing they would be removed in just over a day's time, when the burial rites would be completed. And that they did this at the expense of performing a religious sacrament that benefited the dead man and was, moreover, required of them by Jewish law. It is simply not credible.

Why So Many Objects?

It is the sheer number of the objects that the Whangers have found on the Shroud that throws doubt on their interpretation of the events surrounding the Shroud's origins. Had they found only a single instrument or artefact on the relic, a nail or a hammer, or even two or three objects, then one might reasonably accept the story of devoted followers obtaining such instruments and placing them with the body. Even the time factor, the rapid approach of the Sabbath, would not pose a problem. Slipping one or two or even three objects under the Shroud just before hurrying from the tomb is at least plausible. But 18-plus objects, all neatly positioned? And why so many?

The explanation provided by the Whangers is one with which we are already familiar: that the blood of the dead was, according to Jewish law, of paramount importance; so precious is it that every drop spilled must be saved.[12] Hence, their explanation for the presence of the two phylacteries, the spear head, crown of thorns, nail, hammer, pliers, the paired scourges, paired brooms, the tunic, cloak, belt, amulet and sandals, is that they each contained at least a single drop of Jesus' blood.

This might be an acceptable analysis but for one critical factor – the body on the Shroud has been washed of its bloody covering. If the blood that quite literally covered the unfortunate victim has been removed, and Professor Zugibe's work has shown that this must be so, then it follows that in this particular instance the blood was not regarded as 'precious', that it had very little, if any, religious significance. This is a very important point – if the body is washed, there is no religious or ritual reason of which we are aware that makes it necessary to retain such objects of the Crucifixion 'because they would have been bloody' or because 'the lifeblood was so valued by the Jews'.[13]

One final point on this subject: the scourges are said to have been kept with the body because they contained the blood of the man on the Shroud. Yet the scourge tips do not correspond to the wounds on the body: they are made of bone, whereas the scourge wounds are dumbbell-shaped. There are no scourge wounds corresponding to the bone scourges. Therefore (even supposing the 'precious blood' theory to have been correct), the bone scourges could not have been bloody. The inescapable conclusion is that, in the absence of the actual scourges that performed the flagellation, these scourges were provided as 'props' for the photograph.

Symbolic Overkill

We have seen that none of the disciples expected Jesus to rise from the dead. They certainly would not have known that a 'burst of energy' would imprint the images of the flowers and objects on the linen of the Shroud. There are no religious reasons for retaining these objects because they had upon them the blood of the dead man. Why, then, were all these objects placed so carefully around the body? In the vast literature on Jewish burials, such a practice has never been seen. And in truth there is no possible reason for them, *except to reveal the identity of the figure on the Shroud.*

As any photographer knows, the background can add much, symbolically, to the main subject of the composition. This was known to medieval artists, whose religious paintings are crammed with a multitude of additional background symbols.[14] And this is exactly what we see in the Shroud. We should remember that in earlier centuries the images of these objects would have been more prominent, as the Shroud had aged less and the objects would not have faded so far into the background. Those who made the image were ensuring that no one could say 'Yes, this is an image of a crucified man. But how can you be sure it is Jesus?' The flowers of Jerusalem, and the surrounding objects (especially the spear, scourges, sponge/stick and crown of thorns) make the identification incontestable. But this is also its fatal weakness. It is symbolic overkill. The very number of symbols makes it inconceivable that they were actually present at the time of the burial of Christ. Instead, the image bears all the marks of a very well-thought-out and cleverly arranged photograph.[15]

At the time, this seemed to be about as far as I could go with the evidence from the Shroud. I did not know it then, but there was one further conclusion to be gleaned from the objects surrounding the body on the Shroud. One of these images held the key to proving just how the Shroud image came about. The evidence was plain for all to see, but at the time I missed it completely. Its discovery proved to be absolutely crucial to an understanding of the true nature of the Shroud. The image provided unassailable evidence that all theories advanced so far were seriously flawed, and that the Shroud truly was a primitive photograph.

CHAPTER SIXTEEN

THE SECRET IN THE HEADBOARD

I T W A S W H I L E looking through the photographs in the Whangers' book *The Turin Shroud — an adventure of discovery* that the breakthrough I had been hoping for finally seemed to appear. I was examining a picture in their book which showed the location of the headboard on the Shroud.[1] The photograph showed a life-size reproduction of the Shroud, dark stains on a white background, just as it is seen by thousands during the relic's rare expositions. Dr Whanger had outlined in black the letters he and his wife had discerned on the Shroud: they clearly corresponded to the words 'Jesus' and 'Nazarite', written in three languages, Hebrew, Greek and Latin. It was a fair surmise that the whole board had contained the words 'Jesus the Nazarite', and perhaps also 'King of the Jews', as described in the biblical accounts (other objects obscure part of the headboard where the latter phrase might be located).

Overlying the image of the Shroud, at the top of the photograph, was a replica, made by Dr Whanger, of the headboard of the Crucifixion. This was in accord with his helpful habit of producing copies of each artefact he discovered on the Shroud, in order to give aficionados a better understanding of his findings. According to Dr Whanger, this replica was identical to the headboard that had been fastened to the cross of Jesus during his execution, the one whose wording had been seen by the witnesses to Christ's torment and reported by the Gospel writers. This original, first-century board had produced the image of board and lettering discovered by these researchers on the shroud.

But there was something not quite right about the replica board. At first

I could not put my finger on it. Something was amiss, and it had to do with the lettering of the replica. I gnawed at the problem for a while, then suddenly it sprang into view and I realised what had been bothering me about the image. A trip to the hallway mirror confirmed it – the letters on the replica board were the wrong way round: it was mirror writing! But the writing Dr Whanger had found on the Shroud was normal and could be read easily without recourse to a mirror. What was going on?

At first I thought that the original image had been 'flipped' – that the photograph in the book had been printed using a negative that had been inadvertently turned so that the film emulsion was on the wrong side. This is quite a common mistake in publishing, and it is sometimes used deliberately, if the 'mirror-image' view is considered more artistic, or aesthetically pleasing. The replica headboard certainly showed reversed lettering, and I could think of no reason why it might have been purposely produced back to front, so 'flipping' seemed the obvious answer. But I realised with increasing excitement that if this was so, then the lettering on the Turin Shroud must be inverted! There was no getting round this – if the Whanger photograph was 'flipped', then the letters on the Shroud must be reversed.

This was an almost unbelievable breakthrough. I knew from my earlier researches that the image produced by a *camera obscura* was 'laterally inverted': not only is the image thrown on to the screen within the apparatus upside down, but it is also a mirror image of the scene it reproduces, the left side of the object appearing on the right side of the image. I had envisaged a photographic scenario where, to aid identification, the objects had been carefully placed around the main subject (the head and crucified body), before the 'cloth negative' within the *camera obscura* was exposed to light. If, as appeared to be the case, the photographers had included a board bearing the words 'Jesus the Nazarite' in three separate scripts, then these letters would have appeared reversed on the Shroud negative. And this, it seemed, was exactly what we did have on the Shroud. The lettering on the Turin Shroud was laterally inverted. That the letters were reversed on the relic was extremely strong evidence that a *camera obscura* had been used to produce the inverted image on the linen cloth of the relic.

I thought I had something very solid here. But further consideration of the problem destroyed all my earlier elation. With an awful sinking feeling I realised that there was nothing conclusive about the inverted letters: all those theories claiming that the Shroud image was produced by contact, by vapour or by radiation and/or corona discharge – each of them would have produced the same result. As the cloth lay upon (or just above) the letters, every one of these theories would predict the appearance of reversed lettering (see figure 8). It was true that most of these proposals were disqualified on the grounds of image distortion (with perhaps the theory of corona discharge during resurrection coming closest to overcoming this objection). But setting that aside, on the specific point of the lettering on the headboard, there was no doubt that I had been wrong. The mirror writing on the Shroud could never prove the use of a *camera obscura*. There was no way of deciding between the competing theories, or the genuineness of the relic itself, on the basis of the lettering on the Shroud. My theory had turned out to be, quite literally, a dead letter. As far as I was concerned, it was the end of that particular line of enquiry.

Figure 8: The Reversal of Letters on the Shroud

Light Dawns

A full seven days later, in another book I was studying, I came across a large full-length shot of the Shroud as it appears during its periodic expositions in public. I was skimming the book and had almost turned the page when suddenly I noticed something that set my pulse racing. I looked once more to be sure, then rushed off to consult the Whanger photograph one last time. I checked and double-checked, then checked again – I had been fooled and disappointed by this particular problem once before, and I had no intention of letting it happen again. But holding the two photographs side by side convinced me: I was certain that, at long last, I had it right. The hands on this Shroud photograph were folded right over left – exactly as they were in the Whanger photograph of the headboard!

It took me some moments to work through the implications of this discovery. If the hands in both photographs were just as they appear on the real-life Shroud, then the Whanger photograph had not been 'flipped'! What you saw on the Whanger picture was exactly what was on the Shroud. This meant that the lettering found on the Shroud was not reversed but was set down correctly and perfectly legibly. The letters on the Turin Shroud were normal. There was no need to view the writing through a mirror.

A second vital point followed from this one. The headboard replica that the Whangers had constructed had also not been flipped. It had been made in mirror writing by Dr Whanger himself; but he had not seen fit to draw his reader's attention to this strange aspect of the replica. Indeed, he makes no comment whatsoever on the inverted nature of the lettering. And I understood immediately the reason for his reticence, for the replica's strange mode of manufacture, and for the deep silence that surrounded it.

The fact that had destroyed my original theory (when I believed the photo had been flipped) was the realisation that every Shroud theory predicted and required that any lettering transferred on to the Shroud should be reversed. This is so important that it must be emphasised. Every single theory on the origin of the Shroud image has, as an absolute requirement, the supposition that writing on or surrounding the body must be reversed when transferred to the Shroud. As I had said, there was no getting round this fact.

And yet the letters on the Shroud are not reversed.

For those researchers who (like Alan and Mary Whanger) believed in the Shroud's veracity as the gravecloth of Christ, this was a terrible barrier to belief. There was only one solution by which they could continue to hold to their own theories on the Shroud's origin and at the same time come to terms with the letter-reversal problem. It was a solution that Dr Whanger had quietly implemented when he made his replica of the headboard. For the Shroud to be genuine, *the original headboard of the Crucifixion must have been made in mirror writing.*

I stared into space, trying to envisage what such theories now required of their believers. To hold to the 'Shroud is genuine' hypothesis, it is now necessary to believe that, as Jesus hung on the cross, above him was affixed a headboard of the most singular design. It was a notice written in Latin, Greek and Hebrew, and all three scripts were written in mirror writing. For reasons known only to themselves, the Roman soldiers conducting the execution had written out the headboard with all the letters reversed. It is difficult to believe that anyone can sincerely consider such a scenario as possible. Three separate scripts, each written in reversed form. It simply beggars belief.

There is no doubt at all that the letters are there on the Shroud, and the Whangers must be congratulated not only for the skill and dedication they had put into discovering such hidden objects on the relic but also for their honesty in revealing the hard fact that the lettering is not reversed. The Whangers are 'believers'; they are convinced that the Shroud is genuine and that it was formed by some type of electrical corona discharge at the time of the resurrection. It seems that they are so attached to their corona theory, so awed by the Shroud's appearance and the veneration in which the relic is held, that they cannot bring themselves to follow through their discovery to its logical conclusion. Instead of admitting that no radiation/ vapour/contact theory could ever explain how the Shroud exhibits non-reversed lettering, they have quietly proposed a preposterous theory, that at the actual crucifixion, Jesus' headboard was written in mirror writing in three separate scripts. It is a theory they cannot themselves believe in, and yet it seems that it would require too much of a paradigm-shift for them to admit it.

Alternative Answers

At first I felt that this discovery immediately invalidated all other theories. But, considered in isolation, this is not so. What it does prove is the utter impossibility of the Shroud image being produced at the time of the resurrection. In other words, the Shroud of Turin must be a fraud.

However, other fraud theories can also account for the presence of these letters on the relic. It is perfectly possible to envisage a medieval forger using mirror writing so that his counterfeit Shroud (produced by contact, rubbing, vapour or heat) would show the writing in its correct, non-reversed form. However, two points argue against such a schema. The presence of a multitude of additional objects on the Shroud raises enormous problems for all but the photographic hypothesis. The contact rubbing and heat/radiation theories envisage the production of a body cast, or of the image being produced by the interaction of spices and body fluids, or by some form of radiation from the body. But the body cast theorists must now postulate the casting not simply of a perfect human figure but of all the other objects, all of which must be heated to just the right temperature to produce the scorched image, or which must be rubbed carefully to give the same effect. Such an undertaking would involve enormous logistical problems and make the production of the Shroud a far more onerous undertaking.

By virtue of its reliance on the chemical interaction between a recently dead body and spices or other chemicals, the contact vapour theory effectively rules itself out of the discussion. The inanimate objects surrounding the body could never have produced the chemical reactions required for them to leave an image on the linen of the Shroud.

The resurrection radiation theory fails for the same reason: that the hammer, pliers, spear and headboard, etc. would never have experienced the surge of mystical power that returned life to the body of Jesus. The latest spin-off of this theory – corona discharge – overcomes this objection by suggesting that the discharge was conducted over the whole area of the Shroud, so forming the multitude of images. However, all radiation theories presuppose an actual resurrection, not a forgery, and as we have seen, unless one is prepared to accept a reversed-lettering headboard at the Crucifixion, the lettering on the Shroud rules these particular theories out of court.

Assessing the validity of the competing Shroud theories reminded me of a steeplechase. There are a number of hurdles between start and finish, and a theory must ride effortlessly over all hurdles if it is to be considered as a valid explanation for the origin of the Shroud. Some theories can clear some fences, but none, with the exception of the photographic hypothesis, seems capable of leaping all barriers. The corona discharge theory comes closest to finishing the course, but it falls at the two highest hurdles in this 'race': the reversed lettering (as described above) and the problem of image distortion.

The image on the Shroud is distortion-free, and it is this photographic exactness that convinces many people of its veracity as the Shroud of Christ. Yet ironically, the perfection of the image is the very property that invalidates any hypothesis relying on a cloth lying draped over a recumbent figure. As numerous experiments have shown, barring divine intervention such an arrangement will always result in a bloated and disfigured image.

The Eyes Have It?

There was another piece of data on the Shroud that, if confirmed, helped to prove the photographic origin of the Shroud: the coins that are claimed to lie over the eyes.[2] The images of these coins are said by Dr Whanger and others to show two lepta from the time of Pontius Pilate, the very period in which Jesus was crucified.[3] There is some evidence that coins were placed over the deceased's eyes in certain Jewish burials, so the presence of these coins on the eyes of the man on the Shroud is not impossible.[4] But what is extremely telling, in view of what has been said concerning the lettering of the headboard, is that, if they exist at all, on the original Shroud these coins have on them a series of letters – *and these letters are inverted.* This throws the impossibility of the headboard into stark relief. On the Shroud image, the lettering of the headboard is normal, but the lettering of the coins is reversed, both series of letters appearing on the same Shroud image! It is clear that either coins or headboard are counterfeit and, given the improbability of someone producing a tiny reversed-image coin for each of the eyes, the strong suspicion must be that it is indeed the headboard that has been faked. Failing that, like the Whangers, we must fall back on the thesis that the legionnaires prepared the headboard in mirror writing.

How It Was Done

How, then, does the photographic theory stand in all this? We saw in Chapter Eleven that image distortion is not a problem with this theory – but what about the reversed lettering? A photograph's 'lateral inversion' would unfailingly reverse any letters. Surely the fact that the letters are not reversed on the Shroud is a considerable problem for the photographic hypothesis? This would be true, but only if the original board had been written in normal, unreversed characters.

Unlike Shroud believers, I was not suggesting that the board that formed part of the photographic subject was genuine. It quite obviously was not. While a mirror-written headboard is inconceivable at the actual Crucifixion, its manufacture during the course of a 'forgery' is more than probable. We should remember that when it was first produced, the objects surrounding the man on the Shroud would have been rendered in a much clearer fashion. If the headboard was included among these objects and there was writing on the headboard, then we must assume that this writing was meant to be read. It was important, therefore, that it was reproduced in a legible form: that is, that the writing was not reversed on the finished Shroud.

The time involved in setting up a *camera obscura* for such photography would have given the principals in the drama ample opportunity to notice that a reversed-lettering error would occur in the finished 'photograph'. It would also allow them sufficient time to take steps to correct it. The *camera obscura* throws a perfect, full-colour image of the subject on to a screen within its darkened interior. Every detail is faithfully rendered on the screen, and it would have been immediately noticeable that the large letters on the headboard were reversed. If the purpose of the photographers was to include objects that unambiguously indicated the identity of the sacred head, it is clear that such reversed lettering simply would not do. But the problem was easily rectified. A new board would be constructed, in mirror writing, and the resultant image inside the *camera obscura* would then show the words 'Jesus' and 'Nazarite' in perfectly legible form.

An Unassailable Conclusion

This scenario appeared to me to be the best explanation for the origin of the Holy Cloth. Indeed, it was the only explanation that took into account all the information concerning the Shroud. I had started this part of my quest intending to discover if the relic contained evidence that would indicate either a first-century or a medieval date for the crucified body we see on the Shroud. While the result here had been equivocal (with either timescale being equally likely), other evidence I had turned up during the course of the investigation had revealed a definite bias towards the thirteenth-century date, and in addition, an overwhelming presumption in favour of the photographic hypothesis.

But it had revealed far, far more than the mechanism by which the Shroud was produced. Leaving that question aside, I realised that the conclusion that I had drawn from Dr Whanger's research had finally answered a question that had exercised the minds of thousands of people for the last 600 years. The secret in the headboard had at last been uncovered. It had produced a conclusion concerning the veracity of the Shroud that was unassailable. It is a conclusion that will disappoint many and will undoubtedly anger some. But unless one chooses to believe in a reversed-lettered headboard at the Crucifixion, it is a conclusion that simply cannot be evaded. It can be stated simply in three sentences, but its implications are enormous:

- Letters on the Shroud indicate the titles 'Jesus' and 'Nazarite' (or 'Nazareth').
- Any method of Shroud image production that occurred at the time of the burial of Jesus would produce inverted lettering on the Shroud.

- The letters on the shroud are not reversed.

Therefore, the Shroud cannot be the gravecloth of Jesus.

I did not feel that this conclusion invalidated the worth of the Shroud. Unlike many others, I was not prepared simply to write it off as an ingenious medieval fake. Too many aspects of the image pointed to the Shroud as a true relic of Christ, a photograph of the most revered relic of the Templars, the embalmed head of Jesus. I was now certain that the figure on the linen sheet was a medieval photograph. It remained to prove that the head and body on the Shroud were derived from two separate individuals.

CHAPTER SEVENTEEN

OVIEDO'S 'HOLY FACE'

T
HERE IS ANOTHER linen relic of Jesus' Crucifixion that has received much less publicity than the Shroud of Turin, yet it has a much greater claim to authenticity than its more famous cousin. This is the Sudarium (Facecloth) of Oviedo, known as the 'Holy Face', and supposedly the cloth that covered the head of Jesus after he was taken down from the cross.[1]

History

Historical records of the Sudarium can be traced back much further than those of the Shroud. While the latter can be dated with certainty only to 1357, the Oviedo relic's history goes back to the seventh century AD, when it was carried into Spain from Palestine. Pelagius (also known as Pelayo), a twelfth-century bishop of Oviedo, wrote down the history of the Sudarium in two works, the Book of Testaments of Oviedo and the Chronicon Regum Legionensum.[2]

If it is genuine, the Sudarium must have survived the Fall of Jerusalem for, according to bishop Pelagius, it remained in Palestine until 614. In this year Chosroes II, King of Persia, invaded the country and conquered Jerusalem. Philip the Presbyter is said to have brought the Sudarium and other relics of Christ safely out of the city and to have carried them to Alexandria in Egypt. When the Persian king continued his advance, marching into Egypt two years later to seize Alexandria, the relics were spirited out of the doomed city in a cedar chest. Carried through North Africa by Christian refugees, the chest eventually crossed into Spain at Cartagena. Saint Fulgentius, Bishop of Ecija, met the refugees and the precious relics on their arrival in Europe. He took possession of the Holy Chest and in due course surrendered it to his brother, Saint Leandro, Bishop of Seville. Here, the relics remained until, towards the beginning of the eighth century, the chest was moved to Toledo, the capital of the Spanish Visigoths, when Saint Ildefonso was appointed the city's bishop. The *Ecclesiastical Dictionary of Spain* confirms Pelagius's history at this point, attesting to the presence of the chest in Toledo in the early eighth century. But the relics were to find no rest here. In 711 a Berber Muslim army under the command of Tariq ibn Zayad crossed into Spain from North Africa, defeated Roderick, the last of the Visigothic kings, and began a war of conquest across the whole of the Iberian peninsula.[3] To avoid destruction at the hands of the Muslim invaders, the relics were again moved north, carried in a new chest made of oak, and hidden in a cave six miles from the city of Oviedo. Later, as the Christian situation in Spain improved, they were brought to the city and housed in a chapel specially built for the relics by King Alfonso II the Chaste. This chapel now forms part of the cathedral of San Salvador and is known as the Camara Santa (Holy Chamber) in honour of its oaken chest of relics.[4]

On 14 March 1075 the chest was officially opened in the presence of King Alfonso VI and Rodrigo Díaz de Vivar (known to history as El Cid) and an inventory made of the sacred contents. These were listed on the outside of the chest when, on the orders of Alfonso, the container was completely plated over with silver. Prominent among the relics was the Sudarium, the Holy Face of Jesus. An inscription in silver calls on all Christians to revere the relic, which it says contains the holy blood of Christ.

Since that time the Sudarium has never left Oviedo. During the Middle Ages the Camara Santa became an important pilgrimage centre, receiving thousands of devout visitors each year. But over the centuries the believers seem to have gradually lost interest in the silver chest of San Salvador Cathedral, and the Holy Face of Oviedo sank slowly into obscurity, all but forgotten by the world at large.

The Holy Face

The Sudarium of Oviedo presents a far less dramatic appearance than the Shroud of Turin. It is a piece of linen cloth some 85 centimetres long and

53 centimetres deep, and, like the Shroud of Turin, the linen fibres composing the threads are Z-twisted (that is, the spindle used to twist the yarn was spun in a clockwise direction – S-twisted yarns were spun anticlockwise). However, while the Shroud shows a herringbone weave, the Sudarium's weave is taffeta. Although originally white, the relic is now quite brown and creased with age, burned in places, and with a number of bloodstains on both sides of the cloth. In contrast to the Shroud, it is the very ordinariness of the Sudarium that excited my interest. The Sudarium's appearance is exactly what one might expect of a cloth that had bound the head of a man who died a violent death. It shows no evidence of supernatural radiation or any other mechanisms that produced the image on the Shroud – indeed, despite being called the Holy Face, there is absolutely no discernible human image on the cloth. Far from condemning the relic, for many its nondescript appearance speaks strongly for its authenticity. The relic has no monetary value or artistic merit whatsoever. Why, then, say its supporters, should it have been accorded such high veneration if it is not the genuine facecloth of Christ?

Of itself, such an argument is inconclusive. During the cult of relics of the Middle Ages, there were many examples of seemingly ordinary objects being accorded immense respect – to pick two among many, an ordinary pair of pliers was held in high esteem in Byzantium as one of the instruments used in Christ's Crucifixion, while several milk teeth were considered to be those of the Saviour and were accorded great reverence.[5] The desire to believe and to revere something is a basic imperative in Homo sapiens, and we must be wary of any argument whose sole basis is that an object is holy simply because it has been considered holy for a long time. Fortunately, there are other, stronger arguments in the Sudarium's favour. Its apparently nondescript nature belies a wealth of information hidden on and within its fibres.

Pollen Analysis

In 1969 the forensic scientist Dr Max Frei took an interest in the Holy Face of Oviedo. His work on pollen samples contained in the Shroud of Turin had produced strong evidence that the Shroud had spent time in Israel, Asia Minor and Europe. He now used similar techniques on the Sudarium, pressing adhesive tape on to the fabric of the relic to pick up any grains of pollen and other debris that might be held between the linen fibres. The samples he collected contained pollen of various species, which revealed a history of travel for the Sudarium that was far different from that of the Shroud. In contrast to the Turin relic, Dr Frei found no trace of pollen from Asia Minor, or from any area of Europe save the Iberian peninsula. What he did discover was pollen from plant species that grow in Palestine, and others from North African species. This, together with the Spanish pollen species, is, of course, just those areas through which tradition states that the Sudarium travelled when its guardians fled Jerusalem before the might of Chosroes II. Whatever the true identity of the Sudarium, the pollen evidence goes a long way to corroborating the story of the cloth's movements – the relic has spent time in Palestine and in North Africa prior to its finding a home in Oviedo during the eighth century.[6]

The Forensic Evidence

Following a series of photographic studies on the Sudarium in 1985 by Shroud researcher Dr Baima Bollone, the Spanish Centre for Sindonology (CES – Centro Español de Sindonologia) took an increasing interest in the Holy Face. One of its members, Guillermo Heras, suggested an interdisciplinary study of the relic and EDICES (Investigation Team of the CES) was eventually formed with Señor Heras as Head of Scientific Investigation. It is this research group that has conducted most of the investigations on the Sudarium.[7]

Forensic studies by EDICES members have provided striking evidence that the cloth covered a dead man's face, that it was put on after he had died, and that the individual concerned expired in a manner similar, if not identical, to that of Jesus at his execution. The analysis has also shown that the man whose face the Sudarium covered was bearded and moustached and had long hair tied at the base of his neck into a ponytail. The parallels here with the head image on the Shroud of Turin are striking and too obvious to labour.

EDICES' Dr José Villalain conducted other tests on the cloth, trying to determine the composition of the bloodstains on the cloth and exactly how they were formed. He noted first that the main bloodstain on the Sudarium is in duplicate, almost like a Rorschach test board. However, the duplicate stains were not completely identical – counting both sides of the cloth (blood had seeped through on to the front and back of the Sudarium), he observed a gradual fourfold decrease in the intensity of the stain. This only made sense if, when the cloth had been placed around the dead man's head, it had been positioned so that it was doubled over his

23. The image of the body of the man on the Shroud has been married to the body of Mr Perfect, reduced to the same scale. While the bodies match perfectly, the head of the Shroud figure can be seen to be bizarrely out of place.

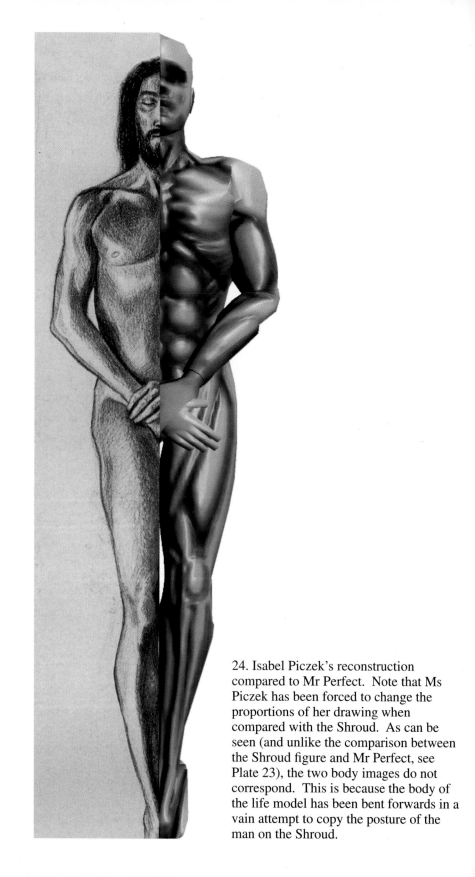

24. Isabel Piczek's reconstruction
compared to Mr Perfect. Note that Ms
Piczek has been forced to change the
proportions of her drawing when
compared with the Shroud. As can be
seen (and unlike the comparison between
the Shroud figure and Mr Perfect, see
Plate 23), the two body images do not
correspond. This is because the body of
the life model has been bent forwards in a
vain attempt to copy the posture of the
man on the Shroud.

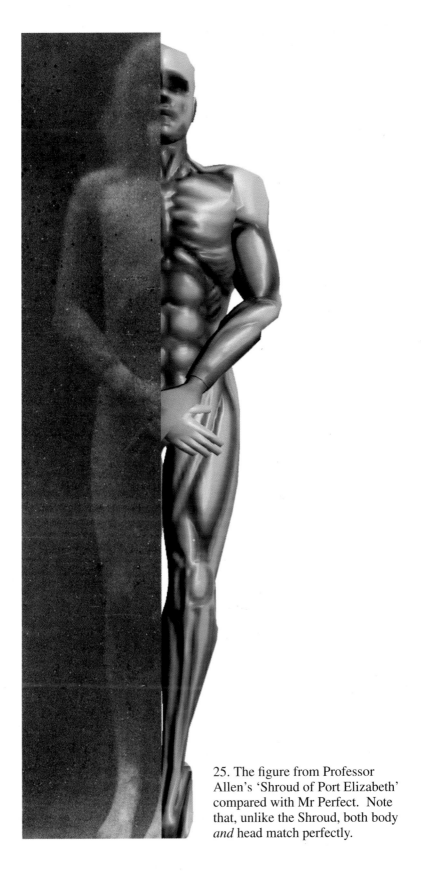

25. The figure from Professor Allen's 'Shroud of Port Elizabeth' compared with Mr Perfect. Note that, unlike the Shroud, both body *and* head match perfectly.

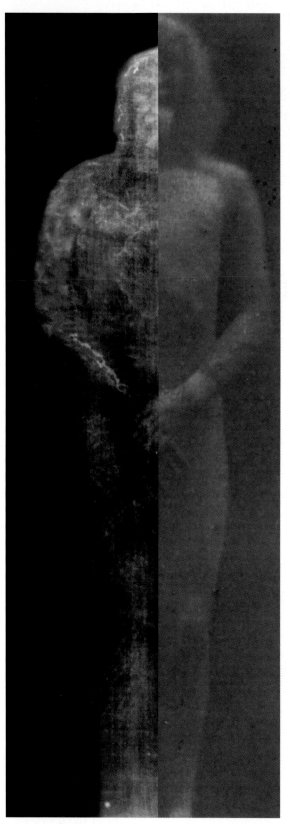

26. Professor Allen's shroud-figure compared with the Shroud. As with the computer-generated figure, while the two bodies make a good match, the head of the figure on the Shroud is unnaturally low, confirming the conclusion that it is in an impossibly incorrect position and has been artificially attached to the body on the Shroud.

face, forming two layers and tied in place with a strip of cloth. This 'doubling' was presumably to give additional material to absorb the copious bleeding which erupted from the nose and to a lesser extent from the mouth.

From the composition of the stains on the cloth, Dr Villalain decided that the Sudarium covered the face of an adult male who had died in an upright position, with his head lying forwards at an angle of 70 degrees to the vertical and 20 degrees to the right, so that it lay against the man's right shoulder.

This finding goes some way to explaining an odd fact about the Sudarium. Strangely, the facecloth was put on so that it covered only just over half the face. The right cheek appears to have been left bare. Knowing the position of the head at death, it seems that the right cheek lay hard against the right shoulder of the deceased and that whoever fitted the linen around the dead man's face was unable to raise the head in order to cover the face completely. This may have been due to cadaveric spasm of the body or simply to the fact that (in the Crucifixion scenario) manipulating the head was impossible due to time constraints and an awkward positioning of the ladder at the time of fitting the cloth. A further important finding emerged from this study: the right arm must have been held at a very high angle for cheek and shoulder to have been so closely aligned. This suggests that the crucified was not put to death in the traditional position of arms at 90 degrees to the body but with the upper limbs on a much shorter crosspiece, so that together the arms formed a deep V-shape on the cross.

This conclusion was corroborated by an analysis of the bloodstains, which indicated that they were composed not of venous or arterial blood but of a very dilute blood solution: one part blood and six parts body fluid from pleural oedema (fluid on the lungs). Such a condition gives a strong indication of the position in which the man would have died. Like the odd positioning of the facecloth, it suggests a nailing of the hands close to the vertical, as it is only in this position that asphyxiation and pleural oedema are likely to occur during crucifixion. It also explains the biblical account of the Roman executioners' intention to break Jesus' legs to hasten his end. If Jesus had been crucified in the manner suggested by the Sudarium, leg-breaking would certainly have induced a much quicker death from asphyxiation. Without such a *coup de grâce*, pleural oedema produces a gradually increasing amount of liquid which settles in the lungs. After death, if the corpse later suffers jolting movements, the blood and fluid mixture can be voided through the nostrils. This would explain why there is not simply one large bloodstain on the face and mouth area of the Sudarium. Several stains are superimposed one on the other in this region.

Such staining and restaining implies a series of bleedings, the first having already dried before a second flow of blood formed the second stain, and so on.

It occurred to Dr Villalain that it might be possible to discover just when, after death, each of these stains had been made. He could then compare this information with the Gospel post-Crucifixion accounts and see whether they tallied with one another.

To test this idea, Dr Villalain had a model head built through which he could release known quantities of blood-fluid solution on to a simulated Sudarium. He was able to alter the amount of solution that was released until the stain produced on the modern facecloth matched the first stain on the original Sudarium. He could also note the time each took to dry sufficiently so that, when a second quantity of the solution was released, the two did not merge with one another, so allowing him to produce a copy of the superimposed stains seen on the original Sudarium. After long hours of trial and error, he was able finally to manufacture a tolerable reproduction of the three main blood-fluid stains on the Holy Face – and, more, to know just what time had elapsed between the various bleeding events. The results made very interesting reading.[8]

Shortly after death, the Sudarium was wrapped around the face of the corpse, with the right cheek left uncovered. This produced the first main stain on the Sudarium. The man whose face was wrapped was quite definitely dead: 'The mechanism that produced the stains is not compatible with any kind of breathing movement.' The second stain formed about an hour later, after the body was taken down and (with no change in the position of its arms) laid on its right side, with the head still lying 20 degrees to the right against the right shoulder, and the top of the head approximately 115 degrees to the vertical. The corpse lay in this position for approximately 45 minutes before being carried briefly, face up. This movement and the fact that the feet were lifted above the level of the head caused bleeding from the nose, producing the third stain. There are signs that someone tried to stem the blood by using their fingers to squeeze both nostrils of the corpse. The body was then deposited for the last time, on its back, presumably in the tomb. Shortly thereafter, the Sudarium was removed from the head.

It is obvious that this forensic evidence mirrors the Gospel story of Jesus' Crucifixion to a quite remarkable degree. The vertical position of death and lung congestion (oedema) are exactly what one would expect from crucifixion. The timetable of movement also echoes the Crucifixion story, with the body removed and carried a short distance to Joseph of Arimathea's tomb, which 'was nigh at hand' (John xix, 42). The face-wrapping is in keeping with the cultural milieu (corresponding to the Jewish practice of covering the disfigured face of a corpse with a cloth). But, strangely, the final fate of this facecloth of Christ does not follow normal Jewish burial practice – quite the opposite. What happened to the Sudarium gives strong additional evidence that the burial of Jesus was anything but orthodox.

The Facecloth in Jewish Burial

A facecloth was an essential part of Jewish burial rites, as reported in the Bible and elsewhere. It was especially required when the person had died a violent or painful death, the cloth being bound around the head in order to preserve the dignity of the deceased and to remove so upsetting a sight from the view of the onlookers. We know that a facecloth was used in the burial of Jesus. Speaking of the interment, John xx mentions 'the napkin that was about his head'. Moreover, that the presence of the facecloth was not solely due to the violent nature of his death is shown in the story of Lazarus. When Jesus raises Lazarus from the dead, he is said to come from the tomb 'and his face was bound about with a napkin' (John xi, 44).

However, one important point is studiously overlooked by those who wish to use the Sudarium to verify the biblical story: the facecloth of Jesus was not left on his head. This is an extremely unusual, and perhaps a unique, occurrence. We know that in a Jewish burial the facecloth was not removed from the body at the time of burial. In the case of the burial rites of Jesus' closest followers, this is certainly true. The raising of Lazarus (who was probably Jesus' brother-in-law and was certainly within the inner circle of initiates) states this quite explicitly. Lazarus has been in the tomb for four days when Jesus returns to the town of Bethany, long enough for corruption of the body to have begun. Martha, the sister of Lazarus, protests when Jesus commands that the stone before the tomb be taken away, saying: 'Lord, by this time he stinketh.' This shows in no uncertain terms that whatever was in the tomb – including the facecloth – was to be left there until the full dissolution of the body had occurred. And yet when Jesus commands that Lazarus comes forth from the tomb, we are told: 'And he that was dead came forth, bound hand and foot with graveclothes: and his face was bound about with a napkin' (John xi, 44). There is no suggestion here of a temporary facecloth that was placed around the deceased for a short time and then removed. The facecloth was to be left on the body until it had rotted away and only bones remained for transfer to the ossuary, where they would spend eternity.

This is a very serious obstacle. There is no good reason in any of the orthodox accounts to explain the removal of the Sudarium. The Gospel of John finds the fact of the 'napkin's' separation from the other graveclothes unusual enough to merit a specific comment, stating that the disciples find 'the napkin that was about his head, not lying with the linen clothes, but wrapped together in a place by itself' (John xx, 7). In fact, as Ian Wilson has shown, Jewish law in this case (where a man has died a violent death) explicitly states that the body should be unwashed and the 'blood of the soul' kept with the body. This tradition has been used *ad nauseam* to excuse the enormous number of objects seen around the image of the man on the Shroud. In almost every instance, the explanation for the object's inclusion on the Shroud has been that it must have been besmirched with the blood of the crucified and therefore had to be placed next to the body. But in most cases the amount of blood involved can only have been minuscule, if indeed any blood was present at all – how much, for example, could there have been on the dice, or the reed that held the sponge, or the headboard for that matter? And yet the Sudarium, quite literally soaked in the blood of Jesus, is said to have been removed from the head of the deceased and placed outside the shroud! If any object was suffused with the precious blood of Christ, it was the Sudarium. If any object justified inclusion with the body, it was this facecloth of Jesus. Why, then, was it kept separate when all these other, lesser objects were apparently placed in close proximity to the corpse?

So there were no good reasons for removing the facecloth, and a great many incentives for keeping it on the body of the dead man. The believers' account simply does not stand up to scrutiny. Why, then, was the Sudarium removed?

The Ritual of the Head

If, as I had deduced from other sources, the head of Jesus had been ritually excised, then for such an undertaking the removal of the Sudarium would have been an absolute necessity. Only with the facecloth removed could the excision of the head take place, probably at the site of the fifth vertebra, as had been the case for other ritual decapitations noted in the Bible.[9] Removal of the facecloth would also have been necessary for the delicate and intricate process of preservation of the head, using the embalming spices brought in especially for this purpose. Nicodemus had brought almost 100 pounds of embalming spices to the tomb (John xix, 39), an enormous amount, and of use only if some form of embalming was envisaged. Nor could such a mass of spices be put together hurriedly. This prior preparation must indicate a scheme that had been well thought out and planned long before the Crucifixion. The removal of the head was no mere whim but a definite ritual beheading and preservation. This scenario is the only one that addresses the serious problems inherent in the removal of the facecloth, and which gives a credible motive for the mystery. It is only with such a theory that the otherwise inexplicable unfastening of the Sudarium is resolved.

And such a theory also explains another seemingly insoluble puzzle of Oviedo's Holy Face – the mysterious correspondences between the Sudarium's 'facial features' and those of the face on the Shroud.

Correspondences with the Shroud Face

The data that had been extracted from the Sudarium of Oviedo make a strong case for its being the actual cloth that wrapped the face of Christ. Just as impressive are the number of details in which both the Sudarium and the Shroud show marked correspondences:

Blood group The blood on both the Sudarium and the Shroud has been analysed. Intriguingly, each belongs to the same AB blood group, a fact that, at first sight, appears to be a remarkable coincidence, and good evidence that the two objects were in physical contact with the same human being.[10] Of the four major blood groups (A, B, AB and O), the AB group is the rarest. So it is surprising to find that the two relics share this trait. Among modern-day peoples inhabiting Palestine, the incidence of this blood group is slightly higher than in Western Europe; around 6 or 7 per cent of the population are AB.[11] However, according to Dr Malcolm Smith of Durham University's Anthropology Department, a world-renowned centre for studies on human blood types, this apparently small percentage of humanity with the AB blood type is quite sufficient to explain the correspondence between the Shroud and Sudarium. Dr Smith has studied blood from different populations for more than 25 years. He points out that in absolute terms, 7 per cent of a population such as existed in first-century Palestine is still a huge number of people. So in his opinion it is not too unexpected to find that the Sudarium and the Shroud blood type correspond. In conversation with Dr Smith, he was adamant that the coincidence was 'enough to be surprising, but not enough to be convincing'.[12]

Physiognomy Using the blood-fluid stains, calculations have been made to determine the length of the nose from which this bleeding came.

Utilising the stain that marks the ridge of the nose, a length of eight centimetres has been suggested, and this is in perfect harmony with the nose length of the man on the Shroud. The general shape of the face, deduced from the location of blood patterns on the Sudarium, is said by the Spanish forensic experts to conform to that of an adult male of Semitic racial origin. Moreover, when the stains of the Sudarium are placed over the face of the man on the Shroud, there is a marked correspondence between the stains and the lower portion of the face, especially the beard.[13]

In addition, Dr Whanger (whose research revealed the faint images of flower and other objects on the Shroud) has claimed that there are over 70 points of correspondence between the marks on the Sudarium and the face of the man on the Shroud, indicating that the head the Sudarium was wrapped around was that of the man on the Shroud, and proving, for Dr Whanger at least, that the Shroud is genuine.

Further Mysteries

The evidence of nose length and general Semitic features found on the Sudarium is intriguing, but as with the blood group data it is, once again, not incontrovertible. Nevertheless, if this data is taken together with Dr Whanger's research, it does point to the conclusion that the two objects derive from a common individual. However, as ever, things are not quite that simple. Dr Whanger finds points of identity on the two relics via two separate analytical routes: one using the actual physiognomy of the face as revealed on the Shroud and betrayed by the bloodstains on the Sudarium, the other by way of correspondences between discrete bloodspots and stains on both cloths.

While the evidence of the former seems to be clear-cut and to support the 'same individual' hypothesis, the bloodstain/spot correspondence are far more problematical. As with the data claiming to prove congruity between the Shroud and various icons (Chapter Fifteen), conclusions seem dependent on what the individual researcher regards as important. While Dr Whanger claims that certain stains on both cloths are positioned identically, it turns out that other bloodstains that ought to be there are not present at all. The marks from the crown of thorns are said to be present on both cloths for the back of the head but are not present anywhere else on the Sudarium. As the wounds from the crown were all made at the same time, it is logical to assume that, if blood from some of the head wounds could leave traces on the linen of the Sudarium, then all such wounds should do the same. That they do not casts doubt on this aspect of the analysis. Likewise, the famous 'figure 3' bloodstain running down the forehead in the Shroud image is nowhere present on the Sudarium. But the Sudarium was the first cloth to cover Christ's face, so why is there no evidence of this prominent blood flow on the facecloth while the same bloodflow is obvious on the Shroud? Such awkward questions have led to some rather extreme explanations, with the Whangers postulating that a thorn remained embedded in Jesus' forehead and held the facecloth away from the blood, so preventing it from staining the Sudarium.[14]

A more likely explanation is that this is evidence that the Shroud head bloodstains were forged. Indeed, if the photographic hypothesis is correct, faking of the bloodstains would have been absolutely essential.[15] But for those who, like Professor Nicholas Allen, believe that the Shroud is simply a medieval photographic fraud, the undoubted correspondence between the face on the Shroud and the Sudarium is far less easy to explain away. As we will see, it poses an insuperable barrier to an acceptance of their view.

However, even when Dr Whanger's work on the correspondence between bloodstains on both cloths is omitted, the rest of his research (added to that of the Spanish workers) provides strong evidence that the Sudarium covered a head that was very similar, perhaps identical, to that shown on the Shroud. The bloodspots may not match, but the face does. Believers will, and do, trumpet this as further 'proof' that the Shroud and the facecloth covered the same face and that therefore both are genuine. But this is only partially true. As we have already seen, barring a miracle (or a mirror-written headboard) there is simply no way in which the Shroud could have covered Jesus' body.

But if, as now appears certain, the Shroud really is a thirteenth-century photograph, we are left with a further mystery. How could the Sudarium – a relic that predated the Shroud by many centuries – possess evidence on its linen surface that the *same face* was responsible for both sets of impressions: for the bloodstains on the facecloth and the face on the Shroud?

An Alternative Explanation

There are only two ways to explain such a remarkable similarity: it is either due to an outrageous and frankly unbelievable coincidence, or both relics are, in different ways, portraying the same object. That is, they were formed, both in their separate ways, by the same head. In which case another startling conclusion is unavoidable. The head which acted as 'subject' for the photograph and which produced the bearded image on the thirteenth-century Shroud must be far more ancient than the Shroud itself. It must have existed in the seventh century at least, long before the Shroud was made.

There appears to be only one way to resolve this paradox. It is an alternative explanation for the extraordinary congruence between the face on the Shroud and the marks of the Sudarium, one that accounts in full for this remarkable 'fit' between the two relics. There is good evidence from the Sudarium of Oviedo to suggest that it is indeed the facecloth that covered Christ's head. That the facecloth, in defiance of normal Jewish burial custom, was taken off the dead man's head soon after he was placed in his tomb supports my theory of the ritual removal of Jesus' head for embalming as a holy relic, according to the traditions of the head-reverencing Nazarites. If this is accepted, it lends great weight to the theory that the face on the Shroud is the face of Jesus.

Three main points have been thrown up by these researches, and each must be reconciled with the others. First, we have seen that the Shroud, in its entirety, cannot be genuine. The other theories purporting to explain its origin are flawed; they cannot account for the relic's undistorted perfection, or the mirror-written headboard. The evidence that we have points ineluctably towards a photographic origin for the Shroud. Secondly, the Sudarium appears to be the true facecloth of Christ, the Gospel 'napkin' that covered the face of the dead Jesus. And finally, the face on the Shroud corresponds to that deduced from the stains on the Sudarium. How can this be? How can a true likeness of Jesus be preserved on a thirteenth-century cloth? There can be only one explanation. The head imaged on the Shroud is the same head that was covered by the Sudarium.

An astounding conclusion follows from this. If the head wrapped by the Sudarium was that of Jesus, then his head was in existence in the first century AD. If this head was available as a model for the Shroud photograph, produced in the thirteenth/fourteenth century, then this can only mean that the head of Jesus was also in existence during the Middle Ages. In other words, that the head had been embalmed and preserved for more than 1,200 years, from the first century to the time of the Templars. That the Templars are the most likely contenders for possession of a medieval photographic technology is undoubted. That they possessed a sacred head called the Baphomet, which I have identified as the embalmed head of Jesus, is based on even stronger evidence. It is this relic of Christ which was photographed by the Order. Given this conclusion, the extraordinary congruence between Shroud and Sudarium is explained. Indeed, it would be strange if these two relics did not show exactly the correspondences we see. The Sudarium covered the head of Jesus, and the Shroud is a photograph of this same head, embalmed, as it appeared towards the end of the thirteenth century.

CHAPTER EIGHTEEN

THE FACE OF CHRIST

THESE RESEARCHES into both the man on the Shroud's mode of crucifixion and the forensic details to be gleaned from the Sudarium of Oviedo had immeasurably strengthened my thesis that, while the Shroud of Turin had indeed been manufactured in the thirteenth or fourteenth centuries, it was much more than a simple fake. It was, in fact, an icon in the original sense of that word: a holy picture of God or his saints. But the Shroud was much, much more than this. As a photograph, the relic was the only image that revealed the actual features of Jesus. It was a unique portrait, the sole photographic likeness of the face of Christ in existence.

However, despite these advances, the *experimentum crucis* remained. Although the evidence pointed to the fact that the head on the Shroud had been in existence long before the Shroud image was manufactured, was it possible to prove beyond any doubt that the head and body on the Shroud were from different individuals? I had intended to work from Shroud photographs and to use physical measurement of the body parts of the man on the Shroud as a method of proving or disproving my belief that the head and body were separate. However, matters turned out otherwise, for it was at this critical point in my research that I was granted another of those occasional pieces of good fortune for which every author hopes and prays. It came in the form of the arrival in our village of Mark Hardy, an ex-Disney artist and a maestro of computer graphics. From our first meeting Mark showed incredible enthusiasm for the project. His knowledge and innovative skill brought out hidden aspects of the Shroud image and opened up for me a whole new vista of research possibilities. And, strangely, it was the head itself, for many the most impressive evidence for the Shroud's authenticity, that was to provide the strongest evidence against the veracity of the relic as the burial cloth of Christ.

Perhaps one of the more powerful features of the Shroud image is its undoubted 'presence'. Even a cursory examination produces an immediate presentiment that the figure is 'otherworldly'. It is this essential otherness that inspires such awe when the relic is first seen and which gives such a numinous quality to the figure on the Shroud, a quality that casts its spell over sceptic and believer alike. I believe that this is due, in large part, to the unnatural position of the head on the Shroud. The whole figure is so powerful, it looks so real, and yet at the same time there is a gut feeling that the image is somehow 'wrong'. There is a mismatch between the head and the rest of the figure, unconsciously perceived, which gives the image an odd, even eerie aura. Subconsciously, we realise that the head does not sit naturally on the rest of the body. And this intuitive response can be shown, quite unequivocally, to be correct.

The Neck

Close examination of the image reveals that the neck disappears completely just beneath the base of the head. This can be demonstrated electronically, and it is a definite phenomenon. Unlike other parts of the shroud figure, there is no gradual decline in the image, no falling off of shading (see plate 20). Instead, there is blackness, a definite gap between the base of the neck and the rest of the body. This has been put down to the linen of the Shroud not touching the body as it formed a 'bridge' over the gap between chin and chest. It is true that other shadowed areas do exist on the Shroud where such bridging might also be expected to occur: for example, along the forearms. But in these regions the image slowly merges with the blank areas, whereas in the case of the neck there is a very sudden and total loss of detail. Moreover, if draping was the reason for the cutoff at the neck, then we should see other 'blank spots': for example, in the area of the folded hands, where details of the fingers and palms should also be lost but are not. Again, if bridging was the reason for the lack of detail at the base of the neck, then, because the cloth would be furthest from the body where the chin or beard fell away into the neck, such loss of image should begin just below the beard, and no part of the neck should be visible. In fact, just the opposite is true. We have a very good image of the neck, and only after this is there a definite, complete and extremely abrupt termination of image detail.

The most plausible explanation for this phenomenon is the simplest – that there is an actual gap here, and that head and body are separate. But there is more to this section of the Shroud. Each colour photograph is made up of different wavelengths of light. It is known that one 'wavelength' of colour may contain information not found in the other wavelengths, but that such information may sometimes be masked by the other two colours in the final picture. Fortunately, the image can be manipulated electronically and viewed, in turn, in each of the three colour bands. When this was done, we discovered that further detail emerged in the red colour band of the picture. The neck itself appeared very unusual. If, indeed, it was actually a neck that we were looking at.

While almost all lines in nature are curved to some extent, in the single-colour image the neck of the man on the Shroud appears straight-edged. Both the right and left sides, and the lower horizontal region where the 'neck' terminates abruptly, are ruler-straight. This would not be the case for the neck of a natural corpse, and the conclusion we are left with is that we are actually not looking at a neck at all, but at some man-made artefact. To an unbiased viewer, the 'neck' appears suspiciously like a ring into which the real neck of the relic 'sits' to prevent it falling, or a plinth on which the head has been fastened (see plate 20(c)).

False Perceptions

Even if the neck had not shown such anomalous detail, the head itself gives grave cause for doubt. One aspect that has distorted researchers' perceptions of the size and shape of the head is the presence of a beard. It seems that, for many, the bottom of the beard is taken to be synonymous with the end of the chin. As a consequence, the whole visage is said to be extremely long and narrow. In addition, this misconception makes the top half of the face appear too short, and the forehead is then said to be foreshortened.

However, these conclusions are demonstrably false. There is a definite relationship between many aspects of the face, and in our case one ratio in particular is crucial. The distances between the base of the nose and the lip line, and between the lip line and the end of the chin, conform to a definite ratio. This ratio is normally 1:1.75 and rarely exceeds 1:2 (i.e. the distance from lip line to chin is twice the distance from the base of the nose to lip line). Fortunately, both nose and lip line can clearly be seen in the shroud figure and once this measurement is taken, the position of the

261

end of the chin can be determined by doubling the distance. This, it should be pointed out, is a rather extreme figure, on most people the chin would be slightly smaller. Even so, drawing in the chin line at this point, we are left with a face that is anything but long and narrow (see figure 9). This work throws up an additional fact: it is well known that the position of the line of the eyes is half-way down the face. As we now have the location of both the bottom of the face and of the eyes, it is possible to estimate where the top of the head ought to be. And despite all that has been written about the foreshortening of the forehead, it turns out that the top of the head is just where it should be. In brief, the head falls within normal height/ width limits and there is no foreshortening of the face of the man on the Shroud.

This points up another important fact. While the length of the beard had produced an illusion that the chin was much longer than it really is, the strange rectangular 'ring' or 'plinth' below the head could still reasonably be imagined as a part of the neck. However, when the true position of the chin is calculated, it turns out that the distance from chin to plinth-area is far greater than first imagined. The plinth is now seen to be much further away from the head proper; too far away for it to form any part of the throat of the man on the Shroud. Whatever this object is, it is most certainly not the neck.

A Diminutive Head

If the proportions of the head were normal, the head's relationship to the rest of the body proved embarrasingly awkward. Its size is wrong – it is quite simply too small for the body. I was able to prove the truth of this using a computer-generated 'ideal man' for comparison with the Shroud figure.

After his work on the neck anomalies, Mark had begun work in earnest. He started by cleaning up the image on the Shroud, shading out the distracting 'poker holes' and the patches sewn on to the Shroud to repair the damage caused by the 1532 fire. Next, he carefully reconstructed the most appropriate shape of the missing body outline, a job that consisted essentially of 'reconstructing' the shape of the upper arm. The final result allows a far neater and more accurate view of the true appearance of the man on the Shroud.

After a long search and much experimentation, Mark was able to provide a computer-generated figure whose bodily dimensions were drawn from a large database of medical information.[1] This computer-generated body is the average of many persons, a Mr Perfect if you will, and the data in the software can be further manipulated to produce an image of different body types: athletic, obese or ascetic, for example. Given the man on the Shroud's powerful physique, I settled for an athletic build for our Mr Perfect. We then reduced both Shroud and standard figures to the same scale.

When we compared the computer-generated image with that on the Shroud, a great many striking anomalies were apparent. Not least of these was the fact that while both bodies matched seamlessly, the size of the heads of the two figures was severely at odds. As can be seen in the plate section, although the two bodies are of equal size, the head of Mr Perfect is much larger than that of the man on the Shroud. Figure 9 shows the two heads side by side to the same scale, and it is immediately obvious that they are different. In fact, the Shroud head is 11 per cent shorter and 10 per cent thinner, compared with the head of the standard figure. Put another way, the area of the head of the figure on the Shroud should be more than 22 per cent larger in order to fit the body on the Shroud. This is a huge percentage, and well beyond any 'normal' bounds of human variation.

Professor Nicholas Allen, whose invaluable work on the photographic nature of the Shroud was reviewed in Chapter Eleven, has attempted to explain the small size of the head as an artefact of the photographic process. He is on record as stating that the apparent small size of the head is due to a spherical aberration of the lens used, which has made the head and (he claims) the feet smaller in relation to the centre of the image. However, as we have seen (and will consider in more detail later), a 50–50 comparison of Shroud and Mr Perfect (plate 23) demonstrates convincingly that the proportions of all body parts are perfect, with the exception of the head. In addition, and given the large percentage discrepancy in head sizes between the two figures, Professor Allen seriously undermines his line of argument when he admits later in his analysis that spherical aberration of the lens 'plays a very minor role in the whole visual effect'.[2]

As I was quickly to discover, the head played anything but a minor role in the elucidation of the Shroud mystery. But it was not only the head that yielded up its secrets to the power of computer analysis.

An Artistic Verdict

Several researchers (each assuming that the Shroud shows a crucified Jesus) have tried to use the image to establish the exact pose taken by the body in the tomb, how the legs were bent, how the head was positioned,

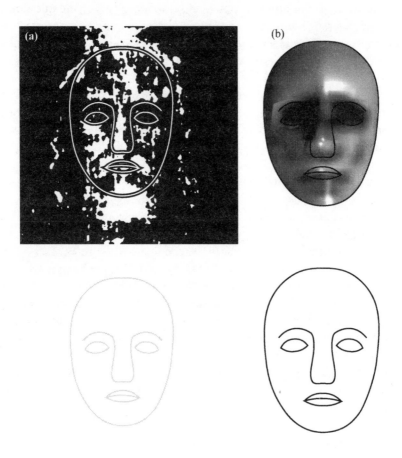

Figure 9: Facial masks of shroud figure (a) and Mr Perfect (b) when bodies of both are aligned. The outlines of the facial masks are given below each image for ease of comparison

etc. While leg and arm positions are relatively easy to emulate, the head has always proved to be the problem with such a reconstruction, and a number of workers have resorted to suggestions that the head was supported with pillows that pushed it up and forward. This in itself would have seriously distorted the image of the face, and in the opposite direction to that seen in the Shroud image. While the forehead of the man on the Shroud may be slightly foreshortened, positioning it with pillows would have brought the head forward and up, allowing more, not less, of the forehead and crown to be seen. Others have insisted that the whole upper torso and the head of the man was raised with pillows, which, as well as begging the question of why such a strange and certainly unique burial posture was necessary for the corpse, would only compound the foreshortening effect described above. None of these suggestions has any merit – put bluntly, the posture of the man on the Shroud has proved impossible to duplicate.

Perhaps the most careful study of this subject has been carried out by the renowned religious artist Isabel Piczek. At the age of 13, having recently 'defected' to the West from Moscow where she was in training as an artist, Ms Piczek won an open competition to paint a large mural for Rome's Pontifical Biblical Institute.[3] More commissions followed, and since emigrating to the United States she has worked on numerous religious murals for cathedrals and other religious buildings, some of her work covering an area as large as 3,000 square feet. She is an artist of great skill and high repute. Her assessment of the Shroud image must be treated with respect, the more so because of the time and effort she has expended in trying to produce a modern-day duplicate of the relic. Piczek has interviewed scores of professional life models, assessing their physique for its similarity to the figure of the man on the Shroud. She has constructed a 15-foot-tall ladder in her extensive studio and spent long hours perched on its rungs, attempting to position her carefully selected model in exactly the same posture as the man on the Shroud (plate 21). No one has done more to try to demonstrate empirically that such a posture can be achieved. And yet, despite a huge effort and expenditure of time and money, Piczek has been unable to find a human being who can duplicate the head and body image of the Shroud. Even when she used a large resting-block under the spine to raise the upper half of the model, the posture was impossible to duplicate. She was forced to the reluctant conclusion that 'the head appeared separated'.[4]

This is crucial. We have a professional artist, a woman used to working with nude models, who has tried diligently to reproduce the posture of the man on the Shroud, and has failed. But reproducing this pose is an absolutely basic prerequisite for establishing the relic's veracity. Despite all the theories, it is astonishing to discover that no one has yet been able to place a human volunteer in the body position shown on the Holy Shroud. This failure is a huge barrier to the acceptance of the relic, and yet it is one that the believers consistently ignore.

The only way to achieve the posture shown on the Shroud is by removing the head and placing it in the position shown on the relic, a position that is totally unnatural, a posture that no human body can accommodate itself to. This one point alone should give us all pause when we contemplate the figure on the Shroud. It is so important it deserves to be re-emphasised: *it is impossible for an intact human body to be placed in the posture taken by the man on the Shroud.*

Out of all Proportion

This is damning enough, but, using specially developed software and state-of-the-art graphics (technology that was not available to Isabel Piczek), I have been able to confirm and extend her findings.

Once again, this was due in no small measure to the expertise of Mark Hardy. Using a full-length model of our standard figure, reduced to the same scale as the Shroud image, Mark was able to overlay one figure on the other, both on a computer screen and with images printed out on acetate sheets. We knew already that the head was too small for the body, but this procedure revealed yet another, equally telling anomaly. It demonstrated immediately and convincingly that, as Piczek had intimated, the actual placement of the head relative to the body is, to put it mildly, far from normal. Even more dramatic was a side-by-side graphic, with the right side of the man on the Shroud married to the complementary half of the standard figure. On the computer-generated figure there are horizontal axes that lie through shoulder, hips and ankles. As can be seen in plate 23, these axes line up perfectly with the relevant anatomical landmarks of the figure on the Shroud, revealing that the two bodies are unquestionably correctly aligned, and validating in the process Mark's reconstruction of the Shroud image shoulder-line. This procedure also reveals that Isabel Piczek's artistic eye did not fail her when she noted that the body is perfectly proportioned.

But while all the rest of the body fits perfectly, the head itself is impossibly incorrect. It lies sunken into the upper chest in an astonishing and quite alarming manner. The anomalous head position is striking. When the Shroud figure is viewed in isolation, there is a natural tendency to compensate for the 'odd' positioning of the head, to make allowances and to accept the figure as a whole as a reasonable representation of a human being. We know that there is something strange about the figure, but most people put this down to the figure's presumed identity and to the numinous feeling one naturally experiences when viewing what is apparently the body of God Incarnate. It is only when a true 'normal' image is set side by side in direct comparison that the outlandish, and frankly bizarre, nature of the Shroud image is revealed. The head has been positioned on the body in an utterly unnatural way, making the overall height of the man on the Shroud far shorter than would be expected in a normal human being (we estimate a difference of some three inches). This explains why Isabel Piczek had been unable to make her life models assume the pose on the Shroud – her frustrated comment that the head appeared to be separate was more accurate than she knew.

When we turned the power of the computer program on to Ms Piczek's brilliant line drawing of her Jesus-model, additional disquieting facts emerged. Seen by itself, her attempt to mirror the pose of the man on the Shroud is convincingly natural, and at first sight bears a striking resemblance to the Shroud figure. But most tellingly, when Ms Piczek's 'Jesus' is placed 50–50 with Mr Perfect a number of problems immediately arise. It can be seen at once that the two bodies do not fit. Nor, as the bodies of the Shroudman and Mr Perfect are in perfect register, can the drawing coincide with the body on the Shroud. The artist has grossly altered the dimensions of the torso in her drawing, making it far too short in comparison with either image. This, of course, is the direct result of her hunching the model's body in a skilful, but ultimately vain attempt to get a human figure to fit the dimensions of the man on the Shroud (see plate 24).

But is the Shroud figure hunched? The answer must be an emphatic no. The body on the Shroud corresponds with a great degree of accuracy to that of our computer-generated figure only when this latter figure is lying (or standing) with its torso perfectly straight. Therefore, the torso of the man on the Shroud must also be unbent. This conclusion can be confirmed in another way. The body cast used in Professor Allen's research is of a normal human Caucasian male, again standing straight. When this image is placed 50–50 with Mr Perfect, then (just as with the Shroud figure) the trunk of both figures can be seen to correspond, demonstrating once again that the torso on the Shroud is not hunched: that is, it has emphatically not been propped up with pillows or other objects (see plate 25).

This discovery makes the problem of the head doubly difficult for anyone who believes that the head and body are intact. No one has ever duplicated the head and body position of the man on the Shroud. The only way in which even a weak approximation of the Shroud figure can be obtained is by curling the body of the model, hunching the spine into a grotesque posture, as was done in Isabel Piczek's drawing. But now we have conclusive proof that the body on the Shroud has no appreciable curvature of the spine. The back of the man on the Shroud is straight. The head position is therefore even more impossible than has been previously believed.

Once more, it is obvious that the overall shape of the man on the Shroud follows none of the rules of normal human proportion, and that it is impossible for any human being to assume the pose seen on the Shroud.

267

Hard Questions

It was only later, when I had the chance to assimilate the full importance of these findings, that I realised that, while they struck a deathblow to all but the photographic hypothesis, they also posed a number of hard questions for the orthodox version of this theory.

The anomalous head position is a very definite phenomenon, and it is not due to any blocking off of part of the head, as Professor Allen seems to be suggesting in one of his many papers on the subject. He believes that the man on the Shroud possesses a low forehead due to 'masking off' the top of the head with very dark material so that, in essence, the top of the man's head becomes invisible on the finished photograph. This, he says, was necessary to balance the unnaturally long and narrow appearance of the face of the man on the Shroud. Such a procedure would, of course, reduce the height of the head, and, if masking was not performed on the back view of the image, might explain some of the height difference between the front and rear images. However, no researcher has yet been able to detect such a masking off of the image, and, indeed, Professor Allen merely states that it has occurred, without adducing any proof as to the veracity of his statement.

Moreover, masking would affect only the appearance of the top of the head of the Shroud image. As we've seen, the proportions of the head are quite normal; it is the beard that induces a false perception that the lower half of the face is longer than it really is. In addition, if masking was truly responsible for the anomalous position of the head, then logically the rest of the head should continue to conform to the standard image. The forehead might be lower, but the chin, mouth, nose, eyes, eyebrows and other facial landmarks would all be in line with those of the standard figure. That this is not the case is obvious from the plate section. The whole head and neck of the Shroud image can be seen to be misaligned.

In addition, Professor Allen's excellent and original research serves to weaken his own arguments in this regard, and supports the separate head theory. As can be seen in illustrations of his own duplicate Shroud (see plate 9), this is an extremely detailed image of head and body in which the proportions of the head (despite a very slight degree of foreshortening) are perfectly acceptable without any masking being necessary. The relative perfection of Professor Allen's image compared with the Shroud, is emphasised when a 50–50 image is constructed of the two figures. The head of the man on the Shroud is once again seen to be bizarrely low, while that of Professor Allen's figure is identical to that of the standard model (see plate 26).

On this basis, we have to conclude that Professor Allen's analysis of the odd proportions of the man on the Shroud cannot explain the visual evidence. Neither spherical aberration nor masking of the head (nor both in combination) is adequate to account for the anomalous position of the head. Faced with this evidence, it is impossible for anyone to believe that the Shroud image portrays an intact human being. The conclusion to be drawn from this is obvious: head and body are separate.

But Why Bother?

Professor Allen believes the Shroud to be a put-up job, a simple fake. He sees its importance solely in terms of a technological discovery, a historical breakthrough, a photograph produced in the Middle Ages.[5] The image itself is of little account and in his view lies firmly in the tradition of the cult of relics. There was presumably only one motive for the Shroud's production – it was made to be sold for profit. According to Professor Allen, a body cast is the most plausible 'subject' for this medieval photograph, although he does not specifically rule out the use of a crucified cadaver.

However, as we have seen, this theory fails to take into account the anomalous position of the head in relation to the body. With this in mind, an important question arises: how did it come about that expert forgers, men who had shown such enormous skill in casting an anatomically perfect body, were unable to extend this perfection to the head? Why did they make such an elementary mistake in the positioning of the cast head when the execution of the remainder of the counterfeit image had been literally flawless?

The evidence makes sense only if a real body was used for this unique photograph. But if so, the orthodox photo-hypothesis is still in trouble. Much the same arguments apply as with the body cast: why is the head in so strange a position, set in a pose that an intact human body finds impossible to assume? The answer, inevitably, is that the head is separate. If this is accepted, why did the hypothetical forgers, who had dared to sacrifice another human being solely to produce their fake, remove the head and then put it back on to the body? And not only that: as the small size of the head has shown, why did they put a different head on to the body? There does not seem to be any good reason for such a procedure, unless it was this particular head that was the whole raison d'être for the production of the image – in which case the orthodox photo-theory has two other important questions to answer: to whom did this head belong? And why was it so important?

CHAPTER NINETEEN

EPILOGUE

EVEN WITH THE best will in the world, I now found it impossible to believe that anyone could cite physical evidence as proof of the Shroud's authenticity. As far as the origin of the Shroud image was concerned, the entire constellation of 'draped Shroud' theories had proved to be untenable, primarily because of the appallingly distorted image they inevitably produced. Equally, the 'radiation' theories (resurrection radiation and/or corona discharge) had been shown to be impossible, not only because of the distortion problem, but also in light of the mirror-written headboard. And this same headboard objection applied equally to the 'draped' theories that regarded the Shroud as a genuine relic of the resurrection. Just as damning, perhaps even more so, was the discovery that no intact human being could assume the pose of the man on the Shroud. If this posture was physically impossible to achieve, how could the original body, from which the image was derived, be considered anything other than abnormal?

Apart from these primary considerations, numerous other points of evidence weighed against the possibility that the Shroud recorded the image of Jesus as he lay dead in the tomb of Joseph of Arimathea. The front and rear heights of the man on the Shroud were different; the body was surrounded by a surfeit of symbols; the coins on the eyes showed reversed lettering while the headboard did not; the head was the wrong size; the neck looked unnatural and artificial. In addition, whatever the mechanism by which the Shroud image was impressed on the linen fibres, the image itself had been revealed as an impossible chimera – the torso, arms and legs of one man and the head of another. The figure on the Shroud is a composite, made up of the body parts of two separate individuals. And put

271

together in such a way that the whole ensemble does not really bear too close a scrutiny. Given such glaring anomalies, it is astounding that any critical person can continue to believe that the Shroud is the burial cloth of Jesus and that an image was imprinted thereon at the time of the Crucifixion.

By contrast, the lack of directionality, its three-dimensional quality, its top-lighting, the chemical alteration of its linen fibres and other lines of evidence supported the idea that the Shroud was in fact a medieval photograph. And Professor Allen's pioneering work had shown beyond doubt that the production of a 'solarograph' was indeed possible using only the technology available to medieval man. With the demise of competing theories, only the photographic hypothesis remained as a viable scenario.

If this is accepted, then it is obvious that, as Pope Clement VII had proclaimed over 600 years before, the Shroud is not the burial cloth of Jesus. Equally, it is clear that for the best part of a millennium, some form of deception has been practised on the whole of Christendom. But exactly what kind of deception? Was it simply that, as Professor Hall had stated at the carbon dating announcement, 'There was a multimillion pound business in making forgeries in the fourteenth century. Someone just got a piece of linen, faked it up and flogged it'?[1]

A simple medieval fraud, then, made purely for financial gain. Or was there much more to it? While he had rejected the Shroud as the burial cloth of Jesus, Pope Clement had been careful not to prohibit the Shroud's expositions as a likeness of Christ.[2] And he had intimidated those who threatened this 'reduced' status for the relic with the spectre of excommunication. Why did he overreact in this way for what was, after all, a very minor relic housed in a tiny, unimportant church? Why should he have taken such a stern line if there was not something about the relic that required a careful distinction between the Shroud itself and the image imprinted on it? What was so special about the Shroud image that he would hold the curse of excommunication over dissenters' heads? Was cash really the spur for the Shroud's manufacture? Or did a far higher motivation drive the production of this enigmatic 'relic'?

Secret Relic

It is important to remember that the evidence we have shows that Geoffrey I de Charnay, the noble who owned the Shroud just before its exposition, was apparently very careful not to publicise the existence of the relic. This must cast doubt on the idea that the Shroud was made solely for pecuniary gain. It appears more likely that Geoffrey de Charnay was aware that the Shroud had an importance that transcended the purely financial advantage to be gained by showing it off to a credulous public, and for that reason he held the image in secret. His wife, Jeanne de Vergy, seems at first to have been ignorant of the true relevance of the Shroud – perhaps because Templar ritual rigidly excluded females, or possibly the death of her husband left her with no alternative but to reveal the relic as a way of raising funds. Geoffrey had died a hero's death on the field at Poitiers. But the French had lost the battle, and the victorious English army had afterwards rampaged through the country: 'Arson, pillage, murders and rape, burning crops and mutilated cattle marked the progress of the proud island race and their continental levies.'[3] In short, the country was in ruins, and it seems that Jeanne de Vergy was pushed into revealing the Shroud's existence by force of circumstance. It was only after the death of her husband, when possession passed into her hands – and penury stared her in the face – that the public expositions began.

While it was still owned by Geoffrey I de Charnay, and despite its near-contemporary origin, the Shroud seems to have been regarded by him as somehow special, as a precious possession to be kept from the gaze of the common mass of humanity. It was an object that had to be held in secret and, presumably, shown only to a select few. Why? If it was simply a fraud of the true Shroud, why keep it secret? Counterfeit relics abounded in the Middle Ages; they were seldom denounced, and possession of one carried no irredeemable social stigma.[4] Equally, if it was the true Shroud (or a counterfeit which de Charnay considered genuine), why keep it secret? Other cloths purporting to be the true Shroud were extant at this time, and they brought down no doom on the head of their possessors.[5] Quite the contrary. The influx of pilgrims to view the relic often enriched their owner enormously. This was the time of the cult of relics, a period when any genuine relic or reasonable fraud stood every likelihood of being accepted.[6] True or false, there was precious little incentive to keep the Shroud secret, and much to be gained from following exactly the opposite route.

The evidence shows that the Shroud was almost certainly held in secret at first. But why hide something that would generate so great an income? If the body is not of a crucified Crusader or Muslim, then the victim must have been purposely chosen, and crucified, for the sole purpose of producing a counterfeit relic. But is this credible? What sense does it make to kill a man by hideous torture to produce a believable Shroud for monetary gain – and then to hide it away?

Unless the Shroud was something more. Unless it carried hidden information that was inimical to the interests of one section of the medieval establishment. And might make the possessor vulnerable to its wrath. As the Shroud seems to pose no secular threat, and was in any case quite obviously a religious icon of Christ, we must conclude that the unfavourable information pertained to the Christian religion and to the other major power of the medieval world, the Church.

The Hidden Information

The truth is that, as a religious fake, the Shroud is singularly disappointing. The image that forms the figure on the Shroud is profoundly undramatic – it is only in the negative that we are able to experience its detail and numinous quality. This would still be true even 600 years ago, when we might expect the marks on the cloth to have been more prominent. The whole problem with the Shroud is that the original negative image on the cloth is hardly conducive to an instant recognition of the figure as that of Christ. This, of course, explains the inclusion on the Shroud of the many symbols and objects that are identified with Jesus. If a 'normal' fake had been required, there were many other methods in the forger's armoury that would have produced a far more dramatic image, one that, given the credulity of the time, would have better served the counterfeiter, if his sole motive had been greed of gain. The other 'true shrouds' of medieval times had none of the Turin Shroud's film-negative qualities, yet each was accepted as genuine by a considerable proportion of the population. The simple forgery scenario is simply not credible. There had to be some additional motive for the production of the Shroud image.

Professor Allan reinforced his conclusion that the Shroud is a medieval photograph with the words:

> . . . any answer to image formation on the Shroud of Turin which insisted on the employment of pigments, dyes and staining compounds would have to explain why the artist concerned would have wanted to produce an image (complete with anatomically accurate details) in the negative, such that its visual information was largely inaccessible to its proposed viewing audience at the time of this manufacture.[7]

However, what Professor Allen appears to ignore is the fact that this same argument cuts both ways. It can equally be advanced for the photographic production of the Shroud image if it was manufactured purely as a fraud and solely for financial gain. Why would anyone bother to invest the enormous amount of time and resources necessary to make such a photographic fake if the visual information that so convinces modern-day believers was almost entirely unavailable to a medieval audience? Painting or other more orthodox methods of counterfeiting would have done a much more convincing job of fooling the punters if cash was the only reason for the relic's manufacture.

No, the *raison d'être* for the Shroud's photographic production must lie in some property of the photographic process that could not be found in any other method, and which was at the same time extremely important to the needs of those who originated the Shroud image. What, I wondered, was so unique about photographic imaging?

The answer is that photography produces a true copy, an exact visual re-creation of the subject to be photographed.

Because the final product of the primitive form of photography used in the Shroud is a vague sepia-toned negative image, it is natural to assume that this is what would also have appeared within the *camera obscura*. However, this is far from being the case. It is the choice of film that defines the quality of the final image – and the medieval photographers were stuck with very simple chemicals that could not do justice to the detailed image the rest of their equipment was able to produce. The *camera obscura* may invert the image, but it throws on to its screen a perfect, full-colour picture of the object under investigation. All aspects that can be seen on the original are present on the image down to the finest detail. Visually, the image is the object viewed.

The individuals who made this photograph in the late thirteenth century did not possess the technology to produce a film emulsion capable of capturing this image in anything other than a sepia tone. But they would have known, from the colour image inside the *camera obscura*, that the photograph they would take would be as close to perfection as they could possibly achieve. It would not be an artist's impression, whose work is limited by his skill, and inevitably altered and coloured by his own perceptions and preconceptions of the object under study. Instead, it would be a true, two-dimensional re-creation of the subject. More than any other medium, a photograph 'tells it like it is'; it gives a perfect likeness, an exact copy of the object, warts and all.

This, it is clear, was the specific feature that made photographic imaging the process of choice for those who made the Shroud. In short, the Shroud photograph was produced as an exact record of a particular precious object. And given the main subject matter, and the numerous secondary images placed around it, this object has to be a revered relic of Christ.

Head or Body?

What we have in the Shroud is most definitely a photograph. But more than that, it is a composite photograph, of two individuals, a body and a completely separate head. One or both of these body parts was regarded with sufficient reverence to require the production of an exact duplicate image. It is most unlikely that the headless trunk was revered. The pages of archaeology and anthropology hold many examples of head-worship, but trunk-worship is unknown. In addition, there is no doubt that the body is 'fresh'; there is no evidence that it has been preserved. However, when we look at the head this is certainly not the case. The features of the face are clearly distorted. It is therefore extremely unlikely that this is the face of a living man (as suggested by the Leonardo da Vinci hypothesis). The 'broken' nose, swollen cheek, 'bruised' chin and all the other facial deformations have been interpreted as the result of the beating given to Jesus just prior to the Crucifixion. There is, however, an alternative explanation. If this is the embalmed head of Jesus, then such trauma may indeed be present. But these facial 'injuries' also conform perfectly with the condition of a preserved head, which would necessarily have suffered deformation both during the embalming process and over the centuries of its existence as a relic.

If the Shroud image was a total counterfeit, why was there a need to employ two bodies? My analysis of the Shroud makes clear that there is absolutely no doubt that the head is separate from the body, and that head and body do not belong together. The body has certainly been crucified – why not leave the unfortunate victim's head on his shoulders and photograph the corpse complete? It makes no sense – unless the head itself is the important part of the image.

It is important to realise that, apart from the crucifixion wounds (which, as we have seen, are probably of medieval origin), all the evidence on the Shroud figure that points to a first-century Jewish provenance *are found on the head*. It is the face, with its definite Semitic features, first-century Jewish hairstyle and ponytail, that do most to convince an observer that it is a Jewish man from the time of Christ that is figured on the Shroud, and that the relic is therefore genuine. But as this evidence is restricted solely to the head, and this head has now been proven to be separate from the body, these facts say nothing about the body and prove only that the head is genuinely derived from the first century.

But a head alone signifies nothing; it could be anyone's. However, attached to a body of a crucified man, it becomes a potent symbol of Jesus, and the objects strewn around the Shroud (which bear no relation to any known burial rite) clinch the identification. It is impossible to see a crucified body, crown of thorns, scourges, reed and sponge, nail and hammer, and so on and not think of Jesus. And all these things, artefacts and body, are there to point up the significance of the head: the face on the Shroud is the Head of God, the embalmed head of Jesus.

Historical Alignment

Not only does the visual evidence prove the truth of this, but the historical evidence confirms it also, and points to the perpetrators. We must ask ourselves: who had the resources and the motivation to accomplish this astonishing achievement? Such an undertaking could not be attempted lightly. An individual or group would need:

- to have been in contact with the advanced knowledge of the Arabs. Only in this way would they have been privy to the (al)chemical information of Arab culture, to the knowledge of the workings of the *camera obscura* and to the Arab work on optics, derived from the writings of classical times;
- to have been freethinkers at a time when esoteric knowledge and experimentation carried dire punishments. This presupposes a group or Order rich enough and powerful enough to have dared to carry out such 'forbidden' experiments without being overly concerned with censure or proscription;
- to have owned property in or around Jerusalem. This is an absolute prerequisite. It is necessary to account for several otherwise inexplicable forensic aspects of the Shroud, notably the deposits of travertine aragonite limestone found in the Shroud, and for the presence of pollen grains from plant species native to the Jerusalem area. In addition, the images of flowers that occur on the Shroud are also native to Jerusalem and its environs. Given the fresh state of these flowers, the photograph could only have been taken in the neighbourhood of Jerusalem;
- to have possessed an embalmed head that they held in great veneration, and which was considered to be the head of Jesus;
- to have strong connections with the time and location of the first known origin of the Shroud, and with its owners.

Only the Order of the Temple fulfils all the required criteria. Indeed, only the Templars come close. The Templars owned and worshipped a sacred head, which my earlier work has shown they identified as the embalmed head of Jesus. The Templars are the only known Christian group who would have had regular access to, and been able to profit from, the knowledge of the Arabs in the fields of optics and chemistry. They are known to have been far ahead of their time in many areas, such as architecture, engineering, mapmaking and medicine, to name but a few of the fields in which the Knights outstripped their Christian contemporaries.[8] Uniquely, and with papal sanction, the Order had been placed outside both Church and secular law.[9] Although they were nominally answerable to the Pope, in practice they were autonomous and accountable to no one. They were therefore free to follow forbidden paths of esoteric knowledge and to attempt experiments that (while still perilous for any Order in the strict Christian society of the Middle Ages) would have verged on suicidal for any other group in Christendom. The Templars owned huge possessions in Jerusalem and certainly possessed underground strongrooms, dug into the living rock, in which such a precious object as the Shroud could be stored, picking up in the process the rare travertine aragonite limestone which has been found on the Shroud's fibres. The flowers seen on the Shroud would have been easily obtained, and these (plus simple exposure to the air) would account for the pollen species found by Dr Frei's investigations. At the same time, the bright light and high temperatures of the Holy Land would have mitigated any exposure problems with the primitive raw materials they were forced to use. Both would have speeded up the 'filming' process, and the solarograph could be completed long before noticeable decomposition of the crucified body had set in.

The Knights possessed all these – the sacred head, property in the Holy Land, esoteric interests and excellent lines of communications to the Arabs – at *exactly* the time the carbon dating shows that the Shroud of Turin was made. Moreover, this period was a time of crisis in the Sancte Terre, a period when the whole infrastructure of Latin Syria was in imminent danger of collapse, when the very future of a Christian presence in Palestine was increasingly in doubt.[10] Precisely the time that the need for such a photographic record of the head was paramount as an insurance against the capture or destruction of the precious relic. And this period was just the time that, courtesy of the Mamluk Turks, a macabre supply of crucified bodies was available, allowing for a torso for the sacred head which possessed all the requisite scars and marks of crucifixion – the same body on the Shroud whose wounds have so impressed researchers since the time the first negative images of the Shroud became available in 1898.

Moreover, the two main investigations into the Shroud were both orchestrated to culminate on 13 October, the day the Order of the Temple was suppressed. The first known owner of the Shroud, Geoffrey ɪ de Charnay, has recently been shown to have attempted to revive a Templar-like chivalry, the Order of the Star, just before his death. And most tellingly, Geoffrey ɪ was nephew to the Templar Preceptor of Normandy, Geoffrey de Charnay, who admitted the worship of the sacred head, who was burned alive with the Templar Grand Master, and whose right to the Shroud was due to his having 'conquis par feu'.

The Divine Deception

In science, Ockham's razor applies – one must give preference to the theory that covers all the known facts with the simplest explanation. The known facts of the Shroud are far from simple, but I believe that this theory provides the simplest, most comprehensive and most likely explanation for all the information we possess on this enigmatic piece of linen. Of the competing theories, the simple photographic fraud hypothesis comes closest to explaining the Shroud's existence. However, it ignores the undoubted existence of a separate head and body on the Shroud, and the reticence of Geoffrey de Charnay in showing the relic. Nor can it explain why both major scientific reports on the Shroud were engineered to reach their climax on 13 October, the very day the Templars were destroyed.

But if, as the coincidence of 'Templar Day' dates indicates, the Templars are involved, then we are left with the bizarre question of why the Knights were party to the production of a 'relic' that has turned out to be an early photograph of a head and a separate body. Again, if the Templars produced the Shroud, then why was the relic held in secret from the time of its origination (probably in the late thirteenth century) through the destruction of the Order in 1307 until its first public exposition in 1357?

The answer obviously lies in the sacred head the Templars worshipped, a head I have shown to be the embalmed head of Jesus. The head, and its exact copy on the Shroud, both were for the illuminati only, for those initiated into the true secrets of the life and death of Jesus. That the Templars produced the Shroud for gain is an untenable hypothesis – they were fabulously wealthy and, moreover, had in their possession a severed head that could easily have earned them huge amounts if they had chosen to pass it off as a sainted relic. And yet they kept this relic hidden from prying eyes, just as Geoffrey de Charnay held the Shroud in secret and never spoke of its provenance. He had the best of reasons – the Templars with their holy head had been formally suppressed not 50 years before. To admit the relic's connection to either the Order or the head they worshipped would have been to invite ruin and death.

This is the only explanation for the Shroud that fits all the known facts. Unlike other Shroud theories, under this scenario no information on the relic must be buried, no data suppressed or de-emphasised, in order to make the theory work. In addition, it proves the truth of the existence of the sacred head of Christ, the embalmed head of Jesus which the Templars carried to Scotland when the Order was attacked and destroyed in 1307.

The Shroud of Turin is a medieval fake. But it is a fake only insofar as it purports to be the Shroud of the Crucifixion. It is a Divine Deception, a religious truth concealed within a medieval fraud. The Shroud is not the burial cloth of Jesus, but it is something quite as precious, and it deserves the reverence of all Christians. The Shroud is a unique snapshot in time. It allows us to see the appearance of the head the Templars worshipped, to look upon the features of the relic that lies beneath the Apprentice Pillar in Rosslyn Chapel. When we view the Shroud of Turin we see the face of Christ.

NOTES AND REFERENCES

Preface (pp. vii-viii)
1. Laidler, K., *The Head of God*, Orion, 1998.
2. Beattie, Stuart, personal communication, August 1998.
3. Ritchie, John, personal communication, October 1998.

Introduction
A Timeless Mystery (pp. 1–16)
1. Michelet, J., *Procès des Templiers*, I, pp. 89–96.
2. Testimony of Templar Jean de Chalons (see Finke, H., *Papsttum und Untergang des Templerordens*, II, pp. 337–9.
3. Currer-Briggs, N., *The Shroud and the Grail*.
4. See Wilson, Ian, *The Turin Shroud* (Appendix B) for an English translation of the letter by the Revd Herbert Thurston.
5. Wilson, Ian, *The Turin Shroud*.
6. Allen, N. P. L., *The Turin Shroud and the Crystal Lens*.
7. Wilson, Ian, *The Blood and the Shroud*.
8. Ian Wilson's book *The Blood and the Shroud* has a 'Chronology of the Turin Shroud' (pp. 263–313) which, while speculative before 1357, does give an admirably clear and concise account of the Shroud's history from that time to the present.
9. Wilson, Ian, *The Turin Shroud*.
10. Probably the most famous of these was the Besançon Shroud, which was for a time a rival of the Turin relic but which was destroyed during the turmoil of the French Revolution.
11. See Walter McCrone's papers in *The Microscope*, issues 28 and 29 (1980–81). David Sox's book *The Image on the Shroud* covers the most pertinent aspects of the debate that followed McCrone's 'discovery' that the Shroud was painted.

12. The work of Sam Pellicori is probably the most comprehensive research to date. See Pellicori, S. F., 1980, 'Spectral properties of the Shroud of Turin', *Applied Optics*, 19(12): 1913–20, and Pellicori, S. F., and Evans, S. M., 1981, 'The Shroud of Turin through the microscope', *Archeology*, 34(1): 34–43.

13. According to Picknett and Prince (1994), this theory was first mooted by P. W. O'Gorman in 1931. It was proposed again (apparently independently) by John Jackson, the co-founder of STURP (see Wilson, Ian, *The Turin Shroud*, Chapter 24).

14. Zugibe, F. T., *The Cross and the Shroud. A Medical Examiner Investigates the Crucifixion.*

15. Rodante, Dr Sebastiano, 'The Coronation of Thorns in the Light of the Shroud', *Shroud Spectrum* 1, 4–24, 1982.

16. Barbet, P., *A Doctor at Calvary.*

17. Kohlbeck, J. A., and Nitowski, E. L., 'New Evidence May Explain Image on Shroud of Turin', *Biblical Archaeology Review*, p. 21, 1986.

18. Ibid., p. 23.

19. Wilson, Ian, *The Blood and the Shroud*, p. 101.

20. Frei, Max, 'Note a seguito dei primo studi sui prelievi di polvere aderente al lenzuolo della S Sindone', *Sindone*, April 1976.

21. Frei, Max, 'Nine Years of Palynological Studies on the Shroud', *Shroud Spectrum International* (3), 1982.

22. Gove, H. E., *Relic, Icon or Hoax: Carbon dating the Turin Shroud*, Institute of Physics Publishing, 1996.

23. There have been several mis-datings, some of which have been put down to the presence of a 'bioplastic coating', a carbon-rich covering laid down by the action of symbiotic algae and fungi over the centuries. On one occasion a Mayan 'Itzama Tun' carving was dated at AD 400 when, on stylistic grounds, a more probable date was AD 1000. It has since been claimed that a bioplastic coating exists on the fibres of the Turin Shroud, which means that the carbon dating results for the Shroud *may* have been skewed by the presence of the additional carbon in the bioplastic coating. The most obvious answer, to remove the bioplastic coating from the four-centimetre sample of Shroud that remains untested, and then to carbon date this sample, has yet to be undertaken.

24. See Gove, H. E., *Relic, Icon or Hoax.*

25. *Nature*, 16 February 1989.

26. *The Independent*, 14 October 1988.

Chapter One
Jesus and the Cult of the Head (pp. 19–32)

1. Geary, P. J., *Furta Sacra: thefts of relics in the central Middle Ages.*

2. Brooke, R., and Brooke, C., *Popular Religion in the Middle Ages.*

3. Bentley, J., *Restless Bones.*

4. Ibid.

5. Ibid.

6. Gardner, L., *Nexus*.
7. Osman, A., *Stranger in the Valley of the Kings*.
8. Ibid.
9. Toldoth recension of the Strasbourg MS. See also Mead, G. R. S., *Did Jesus Live 100 Years BC?*.
10. Osman, A., *The House of the Messiah*, p. 170.
11. Mead, G. R. S., *Did Jesus Live 100 Years BC?*.
12. Osman, A., *Stranger in the Valley of the Kings*.
13. See Rollefson, G., Simmons, A. H., and Kafafi, Z., *Journal of Field Archaeology*, 19 (1992); Kenyon, K., *Digging Up Jericho* (1957); Yakar and Hershkovitz, 'Atiquot', 18, 59–63 (1988).
14. See Cauvin, J., *Religions Néolithiques de Syro-Palestine*.
15. See Osman, A., *Moses, Pharaoh of Egypt*.
16. Van Seters, J., *The Hyksos*.
17. Redford, D. B., *Akhenaten, the Heretic King*.
18. Rosicrucian teachings are necessarily initiatory, and therefore secret, but this link between Akhenaten and the Great White Brotherhood is generally acknowledged.
19. MacGregor-Mathers, S. L., *The Kabbalah Unveiled*.
20. Laidler, K., *The Head of God*.
21. Freud, S., *Moses and Monotheism*.
22. Ibid.
23. *New Larousse Encyclopaedia of Mythology*, p. 58.
24. Osman, A., *Moses, Pharaoh of Egypt*.
25. Aldred, C., *Akhenaten*.
26. Osman, A., *Moses, Pharaoh of Egypt*.
27. For an overview of this aspect of the Akhenaten mystery, see Laidler, K., *Head of God*, pp. 21–6.
28. Gaballa, G. A., *The Memphite Tomb Chapel of Mose*, p. 23ff.
29. Lillie, A., *In Christendom*, p. 102.
30. Epiphanius, *Panarion*, Haer. xviiiff. This is a diatribe of no small size, written between AD 374 and 377 against 'the poison of the hydra-headed serpents of error', or, put another way, against any person whose idea of Christianity did not accord with those of Epiphanius and the adherents of the Nicene creed.
31. Epiphanius, *Panarion*, Haer. liiiff.

Chapter Two
The Head of God (pp. 33–52)

1. Zias, J., personal communication, September 1997.
2. Roach, W. (ed), *Continuation of the Old French 'Perceval'*, pp. 480–88.
3. Shah, I., *The Sufis*, p. 225.
4. William of Tyre, *A History of Deeds Done Beyond the Sea*.
5. See, for example, Saewulf, *The Pilgrimage of Saewulf to Jerusalem and the Holy Land in the Years 1102 and 1103*, Palestine Pilgrims' Text Society, vol. 4, pp. 8–9, 1982.

Also Barber, M., *The New Knighthood: a history of the order of the temple*, 1994.

6. Ben Dov, Meir, *In the Shadow of the Temple*. Also Silberman, N. A., *Digging for Gold and Country*.
7. Brydon, R., personal communication, December 1997.
8. Baigent, M., Leigh, R., and Lincoln, H., *The Holy Blood and the Holy Grail*.
9. Ibid.
10. Daniell, C., *Death and Burial in Medieval England*, p. 44.
11. Michelet, J., *Procès des Templiers*, I, p. 645.
12. Knight, C., and Lomas, R., *The Hiram Key*.
13. Laidler, K., *The Head of God*, pp. 108–9.
14. Seward, D., *The Monks of War*, p. 84ff.
15. See Martin, E. J., *The Trial of the Knights Templar*, p. 20. Also Meyer, P., *Bibliothèque de l'Ecole de Chartres*, sixth ser., v, p. 484ff.
16. Strayer, J. R., in *Medieval Statecraft and the Perspectives of History*, pp. 239–47. Barber, M., *The Trial of the Templars*.
17. Finke, H., *Papsttum und Untergang des Templerordens*, II, pp. 83–4.
18. Baluze, E., *Vita Paparum Avienonensum*, G. Mollat (ed), vol. III, pp. 58–60, 1914–27.
19. Barber, M., *The Trial of the Templars*.
20. Michelet, J., *Procès des Templiers*, I, pp. 89–96.
21. Ibid.
22. Finke, H., *Papsttum und Untergang des Templerordens*, II, p. 336.
23. Currer-Briggs, N., *The Shroud and the Grail*.
24. Barber, M., *The Trial of the Templars*.
25. Seward, D., *The Monks of War*, pp. 212–13.
26. Delisle, L., *Mémoires sur les opérations financières des Templiers* (Mémoires de l'Institut National de France, Académie des Inscriptions et Belles-Lettres, vol. 33), Paris, 1889.
27. Finke, H., *Papsttum und Untergang des Templerordens*, II, pp. 337–9.
28. Sinclair, A., *The Sword and the Grail*, p. 42.
29. McKenzie, A. M., *Robert Bruce, King of Scots*, p. 220.
30. *The Brus*, Todd, G. E. (trans.)
31. Sinclair, A., *The Sword and the Grail*, p. 46.
32. According to Father R. A. Hay (*Genealogie of the Saintclaires of Rosslyn*, 1835), building began in 1446. Slezer (*Theatrum Scotiae*, 1693) states that work on Rosslyn commenced six years earlier, in 1440.
33. The Earl of Rosslyn, *Rosslyn Chapel*, p. 4.
34. Hay, R. A., *Genealogie of the Saintclaires of Rosslyn*.
35. Frazer, J., *The Golden Bough*, p. 152.
36. Knight, C., and Lomas, R., *The Hiram Key*, p. 414.
37. Begg, E., *The Cult of the Black Virgin*.
38. Delaude, J., *Le Circle d'Ulysse*.
39. Sinclair, A., *The Sword and the Grail*, p. 28.
40. Ibid., p. 49.

41. Curl, J. S., *The Art and Architecture of Freemasonry*.
42. Brydon, R., personal communication. See Laidler, K., *Head of God*, p. 263.
43. MacKay, A. G., *Encyclopaedia of Freemasonry*.
44. The Earl of Rosslyn, *Rosslyn Chapel*, p. 27.
45. *New Larousse Encyclopaedia of Mythology*, p. 257.

Chapter Three
The Divine King (pp. 53–67)
1. Frazer, J., *The Golden Bough*, p. 53.
2. Barker, M., *The Gate of Heaven*.
3. James, E. O., *The Origins of Sacrifice*, p. 78.
4. Williamson, H. R., *The Arrow and the Sword*.
5. Frazer, J., *The Golden Bough*, Chapters 24–6.
6. Ibid.
7. Ibid., p. 331.
8. Ibid., p. 532.
9. Ibid., p. 402.
10. Williamson, H. R., *The Arrow and the Sword*.
11. Godwin, J., *The Mystery of the Seven Vowels*, p. 58.
12. Begg, E., *The Cult of the Black Virgin*.
13. Graves, K., *The World's Sixteen Crucified Saviours*.
14. Söderblom, A., quoted in Williamson, H. R., *The Arrow and the Sword*, p. 71.
15. Williamson, H. R., *The Arrow and the Sword*, p. 71.
16. Mead, G. R. S., *The Hymn of Jesus*, p. 24.
17. Philo, *On the Contemplative Life*.
18. Mead, G. R. S., *The Hymn of Jesus*, p. 41.
19. Ibid., p. 44.
20. Epiphanius, *Panarion*, Williams, F. (trans.), p. 94.
21. Murray, M., *The God of the Witches*.
22. Williamson, H. R., *The Arrow and the Sword*, p. 101.

Chapter Four
By Arrow and by Sword (pp. 69–85)
1. Stoyanov, Y., *The Hidden Tradition in Europe*.
2. Strayer, J., *The Albigensian Crusade*.
3. See, for example, Zoe Oldenbourg's *The Massacre at Montségur*.
4. Murray, M., *The God of the Witches*.
5. *Liber Poenitentialis*, quoted in Williamson, H. R., *The Arrow and the Sword*.
6. *Ecclesiastical Canons of King Edgar*, 959, quoted in Williamson, H. R., *The Arrow and the Sword*.
7. Stevenson, J. (ed), *Chronicles of Lanercost*.
8. Freeman, A., *The Reign of William Rufus*.
9. Williamson, H. R., *The Arrow and the Sword*, p. 91.
10. Epiphanius, *Panarion*, Williams, F. (trans.), p. 86.

11. Freeman, A., *The Reign of William Rufus*.
12. Williamson, H. R., *The Arrow and the Sword*, p. 110.
13. Smythe, B., *Trobador Poets*.
14. Williamson, H. R., *The Arrow and the Sword*, p. 121.
15. Mee, A., *The King's England: Durham*.
16. Weston, J. L., *From Ritual to Romance*.
17. Freeman, A., *The Reign of William Rufus*.
18. Williamson, H. R., *The Arrow and the Sword*, p. 113.
19. See Freeman, A., *The Reign of William Rufus*, vol. ii, p. 502.
20. Stoyanov, Y., *The Hidden Tradition in Europe*.
21. Stokes, M., *Six Months in the Apennines*.
22. Freeman, A., *The Reign of William Rufus*.
23. In a version of this dream the object on the altar is at first a stag and only later changes into a man. The associations of the stag to the horned god (the stag, bull and goat were equally symbols of the god) are obvious. See Freeman, A., *The Reign of William Rufus*.
24. Freeman, A., *The Reign of William Rufus*.
25. These and other examples are recounted in Freeman, A., *The Reign of William Rufus*.
26. Murray, M., *The God of the Witches*.
27. Williamson, H. R., *The Arrow and the Sword*, p. 116.
28. Graves, R., *The White Goddess*, p. 185.
29. Ibid., p. 193.
30. Freeman, A., *The Reign of William Rufus*.
31. Frazer, J., *The Golden Bough*.
32. It is notable that Becket predicted his own death, that he entertained his slayers and that when they left him his monks carried him forcibly to the cathedral for his own protection. Four was an especially sacred number to the Cathars, and Becket climbed four steps as his four killers advanced. Each of the four blows struck were directed at the top of the head. For a fuller account of the symbolism and discrepancies in the orthodox accounts surrounding Becket's death, see Hugh Ross Williamson, *The Arrow and the Sword*, pp. 120–36.
33. Hoare, D. C., personal communication, October 1998.

Chapter Five
Original Christianity (pp. 87–97)

1. J. and W. McQueen, (eds), *Scotichronicon*.
2. Taliesin, in Jowett, G. F., *The Drama of the Lost Disciples*, p. 80.
3. See Laidler, K., *The Head of God*, Chapter 3. In addition, the 'Lost Chapter of Acts', discovered by C. S. Sonnini in the Archives of Constantinople in the late eighteenth century, and purporting to be the final (twenty-ninth) chapter of the Acts of the Apostles, makes some startling statements concerning the Druids. According to this manuscript, Saint Paul was not

executed in Rome after his deportation from Israel, and later preached in Britain. Verse 13 continues: 'And it came to pass that certain of the Druids came unto Paul privately, and showed by their rites and ceremonies they were descended from the Jews which escaped from bondage in the Land of Egypt . . .'

4. Saint Augustine of Hippo, quoted in Williamson, H. R., *The Arrow and the Sword*, p. 41.

5. Wilson, A. N., *Jesus*, pp. 47–8.

6. Brandon, S. G. F., *The Fall of Jerusalem*.

7. Eisenman, R. H., *James the Just in the Habakkuk Pesher*, pp. 8–9, n. 20.

8. It was the continuation and expansion of this latter practice that Josephus blames for the disastrous insurrection by the Jews against Rome in AD 66.

9. Eusebius, *Ecclesiastical History*, Loeb Classical Library, 1926.

10. The Desposyni are said to have asked the Bishop of Rome to confer the bishoprics of Jerusalem, Antioch, Ephesus and Alexandria on Desposyni members, despite the fact that these positions were already filled. They also requested that the tradition of sending money to the Mother Church of Jerusalem be resumed. All such demands were rejected, and at this point the Desposyni disappear from orthodox histories. See Martin, M., *The Decline and Fall of the Roman Church*.

11. Meyer, E., *Ursprung und Anfänge des Christentums*, vol. III, pp. 224–5.

12. Origen remarks that Josephus *ought to have said* that the fall of Jerusalem was caused by the slaying of Jesus. See Brandon, S. G. F., *The Fall of Jerusalem*, p. 114.

13. *Peake's Commentary on the Bible*. See also Knight, C., and Lomas, R., *The Hiram Key*, p. 275.

14. Brandon, S. G. F., *The Fall of Jerusalem*, p. 75.

15. Ibid., p. 75.

16. Ibid., p. 98.

Chapter Six
The Myth of Israel (pp. 99–110)

1. Pfeiffer, J., *The Emergence of Man*.

2. Garraty, J. A., and Gay, P. (eds), *The University History of the World*, Chapter 5.

3. *The Times Atlas of World History*.

4. Bury, J., *History of the Later Roman Empire from the Death of Theodosius I to the Death of Justinian*.

5. Osman, A., *Stranger in the Valley of the Kings*.

6. Williamson, H. R., *The Arrow and the Sword*, p. 64.

7. Capt, E. R., *Missing Links Discovered in Assyrian Tablets*, p. 67.

8. See Lobineau, H., *Dossier Secrets d'Henri Lobineau*.

9. Such an emigration is highly plausible. The poet/scholar Robert Graves notes in his *Greek Myths* the tale of Danaus, a son of King Belus, who is said to have landed in this region with his daughters. Graves believes this is a mythologised telling of 'colonists from Palestine' migrating to Greece. He

goes on to suggest that King Belus is in fact the god Baal (or perhaps the goddess Belial), to whom these colonists owed allegiance. See Graves, R., *Greek Myths*, vol. 1, p. 203, n. 1.

10. Rabinowitz, J. J., *Speculum*, 22.
11. Wallace-Hadrill, J. M., *The Long-Haired Kings*.
12. In the Book of Daniel Javan is three times translated as 'Greece', a designation confirmed in Zechariah and by the Roman historian Josephus.
13. Gawler, J. C., *Dan, the Pioneer of Israel*. Thus we have Danube, Danastris (Dniester), Danapris (Dnieper), the Co-dan Gulf, Dan-Mark (Dan's Land) and Dannonia (Devon). Colonel Gawler gives many other examples.
14. Sailman, B., *Researches in the East*.
15. Gawler, J. C., *Dan, the Pioneer of Israel*, Chapter II.
16. See 9. above.
17. Latham, J., *Ethnology of Europe*, p. 157.
18. Laidler, K., *The Head of God*, p. 78.
19. *Annals of Ireland, by the Four Masters*. Quoted in Gawler, J. C., *Dan, the Pioneer of Israel*, p. 30.
20. Sinclair, A., *The Sword and the Grail*, p. 73.

Chapter Seven
The Pauline Heresy (pp. 111–20)

1. Eusebius, quoting Hegessipus' *Memoirs*. See Routh, G., *Reliquae Sacrae*, pp. 208–9.
2. Brandon, S. G. F., *The Fall of Jerusalem*, p. 20ff.
3. Black, M., *An Aramaic Approach to the Gospels and Acts*, pp. 146–8.
4. Brandon, S. G. F., *The Fall of Jerusalem*, p. 35ff.
5. Ibid., p. 59.
6. Ibid., p. 68.
7. Eisenman, R. H., *James the Just in the Habakkuk Pesher*.
8. Brandon, S. G. F., *The Fall of Jerusalem*, p. 55.
9. Goguel, M., *La Naissance du Christianisme*, p. 248.
10. Brandon, S. G. F., *The Fall of Jerusalem*, p. 151.
11. Baignet, M., Leigh, R., and Lincoln, H., *The Messianic Legacy*, p. 76.
12. The account in Acts of the death of James the Just, and the account given by Hegessipus, are both considered suspect by many scholars. See Brandon, S. G. F., *The Fall of Jerusalem*, pp. 90 and 95.
13. Hassnain, F., *A Search for the Historical Jesus*, pp. 219–20.

Chapter Eight
The Lost Disciples and the Sacred Head (pp. 121–33)

1. Quoted in Jowett, G. F., *The Drama of the Lost Disciples*, pp. 79–80.
2. Cardinal Baronius, Alford, Bishop Ussher, Eusebius of Caesarea, Tertullian of Carthage, Chrysostom of Constantinople and many other authorities have confirmed the history of Britain's early conversion to (non-Roman) Christianity. See Jowett, G. F., *The Drama of the Lost Disciples*, pp. 72–82.

3.   Lewis, L. S., *Joseph of Arimathea at Glastonbury*.

4.   Rawlinson, G., *History of Phoenicia*.

5.   Dobson, C. C., *Did Our Lord Visit Britain?*, p. 19ff.

6.   At Ding Dong Mine in Cornwall there was a saying: 'Jesus worked as a miner'. Another refrain ran: 'Joseph was a tinner, a tinner, a tinner.' Henry Jenner of the British Museum persuaded a foreman to amplify on this chant and he was told: 'We workers in metal are a very old fraternity, and like other handicrafts we have our traditions amongst us. One of these . . . is that Joseph of Arimathea, the rich man of the Gospels, made his money in the tin trade with Cornwall. We have also a story that on one occasion he brought with him the child Christ and his mother and landed them at St Michael's Mount.' Quoted in Seaman, W. De M., *The Dawn of Christianity in the West*, pp. 37–8.

7.   Taylor, J. W., *The Coming of the Saints*, p. 145.

8.   Hunt, R., *Popular Romances of the West Country*.

9.   Lewis, L. S., *Joseph of Arimathea at Glastonbury*, pp. 51–2.

10. Jowett, G. F., *The Drama of the Lost Disciples*, p. 144.

11. Dobson, C. C., *Did Our Lord Visit Britain?* p. 40.

12. Apion, quoted by Josephus, *Contra Apionem*, III, in *Works*.

13. Brandon, S. G. F., *The Fall of Jerusalem*, p. 127.

14. Baigent, M., Leigh, R., and Lincoln, H., *The Holy Blood and the Holy Grail*.

15. Elder, I. H., *Celt, Druid and Culdee*, p. 93.

16. Ibid., p. 95.

17. Bacon, N., *Laws and Government of England*, p. 3.

18. Jowett, G. F., *The Drama of the Lost Disciples*, p. 40.

19. Groves, Dr C. P., personal communication, 1998.

20. Wilson, R. McL., *The Gospel of Philip: Translated from the Coptic Text, with an Introduction and Commentary*. See also *The Nag Hammadi Library in English*, p. 153.

21. Lewis, L. S., *Joseph of Arimathea at Glastonbury*, p. 25.

22. Rabanus, M. MS held at Magdalene College, Oxford.

23. Lewis, L. S., *Joseph of Arimathea at Glastonbury*, p. 43.

24. Loomis, R., *The Grail*, p. 120.

25. Jones, T. G. And G. (Trans), *The Mabinogian*.

26. Gervais of Tilbury, *Otia Imperialia*. See Liebnitz, *Scriptores rerem Brunswicensium*, p. 914.

Chapter Nine
Egyptian Christianity (pp. 135–42)

1.   Brandon, S. G. F., *The Fall of Jerusalem*, pp. 167–8.

2.   Josephus, *Jewish War*, VII; x.

3.   Brandon, S. G. F., *The Fall of Jerusalem*, p. 24.

4.   Godwin, J., *The Mystery of the Seven Vowels*.

5.   Baigent, M., Leigh, R., and Lincoln, H., *The Holy Blood and the Holy Grail*.

6.   Pagels, E. H., *The Gnostic Gospels*.

7.	See also Platt, R. H. (ed), *The Lost Books of the Bible*.

8.	Franzmann, M., *Jesus in the Nag Hammadi Writings*.

9.	Pagels, E. H., and Turner, J. D., *Nag Hammadi Studies* XI, 1 : *The Interpretation of Knowledge*, pp. 21–88. Hedrick.

10.	See Robinson, J. M., 'Jesus as Sophos and Sophia: Wisdom, Tradition and the Gospels', in Wilken, R. L., (ed), *Aspects of Wisdom in Judaism and Early Christianity*, pp. 1–16; Koester, H., 'Apocryphal and Canonical Gospels', *Harvard Theological Review*, 73: 105–130; and Kloppenborg, J. S., ' "Easter Faith" and the Sayings Gospel Q', *Semeia*, 49: 71–99.

11.	Schonfield, H. J., *Secrets of the Dead Scrolls*, pp. 1–7.

12.	Schonfield, H., *The Essene Odyssey*, p. 164.

13.	Hancock, G., *The Sign and the Seal*, p. 334.

14.	Schonfield, H., *The Essene Odyssey*, pp. 162–5.

15.	Fulcanelli, *The Mystery of the Cathedrals*.

Chapter Ten

Lost Photographic Techniques (pp. 145–53)

1.	Bahn, P. and Vertut, J., *Images of the Ice Age*.

2.	Joubert, J., quoted in Pauwels, L. and Bergier, J., *The Dawn of Magic*, p. 48.

3.	Alleau, René, lecture quoted in Pauwels, L. and Bergier, J., *The Dawn of Magic*, pp. 43–52.

4.	Flinder, A., *Secrets of the Bible Seas*, pp. 101–12.

5.	Heron called his invention an aeolipile ('wind ball'). It was essentially a sealed cauldron of boiling water with two bent pipe outlets. Steam issuing from the vents caused the ball to rotate: 'jet propulsion' at around the time of Christ. The 2,000-year-old Baghdad battery is a seven-inch-tall clay jar with a copper cylinder inserted in the neck and sealed at the bottom with asphalt. The top is likewise sealed with asphalt, except for a hole which takes a long iron rod. If the space between the iron and the copper is filled with acid, an electric current flows between the two metals.

6.	Majno, G., *The Healing Hand*.

7.	Alleau, René. Lecture quoted in Pauwels, L. and Bergier, J., *The Dawn of Magic*, pp. 43–52.

8.	James, P., and Thorpe, N., *Ancient Inventions*, pp. 387–9.

9.	Alleau, René. Lecture quoted in Pauwels, L. and Bergier, J., *The Dawn of Magic*, pp. 43–52.

10.	Needham, J., *Science and Civilisation in China*, vol. 2, pp. 192–3.

11.	Ibid.

12.	*Focal Encyclopaedia of Photography*, p. 1006.

13.	Alleau, René. Lecture quoted in Pauwels, L. and Bergier, J., *The Dawn of Magic*, pp. 43–52.

14.	Gutas, D., *Greek Thought, Arab culture: the Graeco-Arab translation movement in Baghdad and early Abbasid society*.

15.	Maalouf, A., *The Crusades through Arab Eyes*.

16. Sarton, G., *Introduction to the History of Science*. Vol. III: *science and learning in the fourteenth century*, p. 141.
17. *Focal Encyclopaedia of Photography*.
18. Eder, J. M., *History of Photography*.
19. Wilson, Ian, *The Blood and the Shroud*.

Chapter Eleven
Could It Be Done? (pp. 155–69)

1. Picknett, L., and Prince, C., *Turin Shroud: in whose image?*, p. 68.
2. Wilson, Ian, *The Blood and the Shroud*, p. 211.
3. Picknett, L., and Prince, C., *Turin Shroud: in whose image?*, p. 188.
4. Wilson, Ian, *The Blood and the Shroud*, p. 211.
5. See Baigent, M., Leigh, R., and Lincoln, H., *The Holy Blood and the Holy Grail*.
6. See Laidler, K., *The Head of God*, p. 254ff; also Delaude, J., *Le Circle d'Ulysse*.
7. Picknett, L., and Prince, C., *Turin Shroud: in whose image?*, p. 155ff.
8. Ibid., p. 168.
9. Allen, N. P. L., *The Methods and Techniques Employed in the Manufacture of the Shroud of Turin*, unpublished D. Phil. dissertation, University of Durban-Westville, 1993.
10. See Allen, N. P. L., 'Is the Shroud of Turin the First Recorded Photograph?', *The South African Journal of Art History*, 11: 23–32, 1993; also Allen, N. P. L., *The Methods and Techniques Employed in the Manufacture of the Shroud of Turin*.
11. Quartz lenses have been discovered in ancient Egyptian sites. See Allen, N. P. L., *The Turin Shroud and the Crystal Lens*, p. 26.
12. Allen, N. P. L., 'Verification of the Nature and Causes of the Photo-Negative Images on the Shroud of Lirey-Chambéry-Turin', *De Arte*, 51, 21–35.
13. Ibid.
14. Pellicori, S. F., and Evans, S. M., 'The Shroud of Turin Through the Microscope', *Archeology*, 34 (1), 34–43, 1981.

Chapter Twelve
Theories and Discrepancies (pp. 171–89)

1. Wilson, Ian, *The Blood and the Shroud*.
2. See Picknett, L., and Prince, C., *Turin Shroud: in whose image?*; Wilson, Ian, *The Blood and the Shroud*.
3. McCrone, W. C., 'Authenticity of Medieval Document Tested by Small-Particle Analysis', *Analytical Chemistry*, 48, 676–9, 1976.
4. Cahill, T. A., et al, 'The Vinland Map Revisited: New Compositional Evidence on Its Ink and Parchment', *Analytical Chemistry*, 59, 829–33, 1987.
5. Morris, R. A., Schwalbe, A., and London, J. R., 'X-Ray Fluorescence Investigation of the Shroud of Turin', *X-Ray Spectrometry*, 9 (2), 1980.
6. Dr Adler found protein traces only in the 'blood' areas of the Shroud. See Heller, J. H., and Adler, A. D., 'Blood on the Shroud of Turin', *Applied Optics*, 19, 12, 1980.

7. Allen, N. P. L., 'Verification of the Nature and Causes of the Photo-Negative Images on the Shroud of Lirey-Chambéry-Turin'.

8. Vignon, P., *Le Saint Suaire de Turin devant la science, l'archaeologie, l'histoire, l'iconographie, la logique,* Paris, 1939.

9. Christopher Knight and Robert Lomas have recently resurrected this theory, claiming that the body of Jacques de Molay, the Templar Grand Master burned to death in 1314, is the origin of the figure on the Shroud, produced by the exudations from his still-living body as a result of torture (Knight, C., and Lomas, R., *The Second Messiah*). This does not seem at all likely. Apart from there being no evidence that Jacques de Molay was ever tortured, and that the resemblance claimed between the Shroud face and that of the Grand Master is based on an artist's impression of de Molay drawn centuries after his death, all the objections concerning image distortion of a draped image are pertinent here.

10. Kersten, H., and Gruber, E. R., *The Jesus Conspiracy*.

11. Wilson, Ian, 'Riddle of the Dead Man's Hand', *Observer Magazine*, 31 January 1988.

12. Nickell, J., *Inquest on the Shroud of Turin*.

13. Volkringer, Jean, *Le Problème de Empreintes devant la Science*, Paris, 1942.

14. Mills, Alan, 'The Russel Effect', lecture to the British Society for the Turin Shroud, 23 October 1991.

15. The fingers on the left hand of the original Shroud image do, however, seem to be unnaturally long.

16. A similar theory had been proposed in 1931 by P. W. O'Gorman. See also Wilson, Ian, *The Turin Shroud*, Chapter 24.

17. Hancill, G., personal communication, 1998.

18. Various implausible theories have been constructed to allow for a Shroud in such a position during the burial of Christ: in one, Jesus is said to have lain in a lidless sarcophagus; in another, blocks of spices are laid around the body and the Shroud draped over the top. The desperation of such hypotheses is eloquent testimony to the serious distortion produced by draping a shroud over a normal body.

19. Wilson, I., *The Blood and the Shroud*, pp. 56–7.

20. Gledhill, Dr T., personal communication, October 1999.

21. During the last century, the White Jews of Cochin were known to contain many individuals with blond hair and blue eyes. See also Israel, B. J., *The Jews of India*.

22. Campbell, A., personal communication, 3 June 1999.

Chapter Thirteen
A Medieval Crucifixion (pp. 191–205)

1. Curtius Rufus, Hist. *Alex.*, 4, 4, 17.

2. Josephus, F., *Antiquities*, xii, 256.

3. Even today crucifixion has not been outlawed. In April 1998 *Catholic World*

News reported that two Catholic priests in the Sudan had been arrested and, if convicted of the charges against them, could face death by crucifixion. See cwnews.com.; also www.domini.org/openbook/sud81204.htm

4. Arberry, A. J., *Sufism*.
5. Bahm, A. J., *The World's Living Religions*, p. 331.
6. Von Grunebaum, G. E., *Medieval Islam: a study in cultural orientation*, p. 133.
7. Jacobs, A., *Sufism*.
8. Shah, I., *The Sufis*.
9. Bahm, A. J., *The World's Living Religions*, p. 331.
10. Massignon, L., *The Passion of al-Hallaj*, p. xxv.
11. Mason, H., *The Death of al-Hallaj*, p. ix.
12. Mead, G. R. S., *Did Jesus Live 100 Years BC?*.
13. Some survived the full punishment: the Melchite Patriarch was still alive after 1,000 stripes, for example.
14. Mantiq, quoted in Massignon, L., *The Passion of al-Hallaj*, p. 602.
15. Testimony of Zanji. See Massignon, L., *The Passion of al-Hallaj*, p. 569.
16. 'Account of Shibli'. See Massignon, L., *The Passion of al-Hallaj*, p. 606.
17. Massignon, L., *The Passion of al-Hallaj*, p. 607.
18. Ibid., p. 608. See also Attar, Farid al-Din, *Muslim, Saints and Mystics*. Arberry, A. J. (trans.).
19. Massignon, L., *The Passion of al-Hallaj*, plate 39, p. 138.
20. Irwin, R., *The Middle East in the Middle Ages*, p. 86. See also Meyerhof, M., and Schacht, J. (eds), *The Theologus Autodidactus of Ibn al-Nafis*.
21. Irwin, R., personal communication, July 1999.
22. Mayerhof, M., and Schacht, J. (eds), *The Theologus Autodidactus of Ibn al-Nafis*.
23. See Kerr, A., *The Crusades*.
24. Straiton, M., 'The Man in the Shroud – a 13th-Century Crucifixion Action-Replay', *Catholic Medical Quarterly*, vol. XL, No. 3 (243), p. 135.
25. Ibid., p. 137.
26. Ibid., p. 137.
27. Seward, D., *The Monks of War*, p. 85ff.

Chapter Fourteen
The Crucified Man (pp. 207–21)

1. Laidler, K., *The Physical and Psychological Development of an Infant Orang-utan*, Unpublished Ph.D. thesis, Durham University, 1978. See also Laidler, K., *The Talking Ape*.
2. Whittaker, J. R., *The Physical Cause of the Death of Our Lord*. An address to the St Luke's Guild, London. Wedessow, U., *Considerazioni ipotetiche sulla causa fisica della morte dell'iliomo della sindone*, 1978.
3. Hynek, R. W., *Science and the Holy Shroud*, Barbet, P., *Les Cinque Plaies du Christ*: Wilson, Ian, *The Turin Shroud*.
4. Zugibe, F. T., 'Pierre Barbet Revisited', *Sindon*, N. S. Quad. No. 8, 1995.
5. Robins, S. L., and Cotran, R. S., *Pathologic Basis of Disease*, p. 112.

6. Josephus, F., *Jewish Wars*, vii, pp. 389–90.
7. Tzaferis, V., 'Jewish Tombs at and near Giv'at Ha-Mivtar', *Israel Exploration Journal*, 20: 31, 1971.
8. Haas, N., 'Anthropological Observations on the Skeletal Remains from Giv'at Ha-Mivtar', *Israel Exploration Journal*, 20: 1–2, 1970.
9. Zias, J., and Sekeles, E., 'The Crucified Man from Giv'at Ha-Mivtar: A Reappraisal', *Israel Exploration Journal*, 35: 22–27, 1985.
10. Zugibe, F. T., 'The Man on the Shroud Was Washed', *Sindon*, N. S. Quad. No. 1, 1989.
11. Sherbok, D. C., 'Jewish Shroud of Turin', *Expository Times*, 1981, quoted in Zugibe, F.T., 'The Man on the Shroud Was Washed', *Sindon*, N. S. Quad. No. 1, 1989.
12. Wilson, Ian, *The Blood and the Shroud*, p. 55.
13. Gansfried, S., *Code of Jewish Law*, vol. IV, pp. 99–100, Goldin, H. E., (trans.)

Chapter Fifteen
A Surfeit of Symbols (pp. 223–33)
1. For example, most of the photographic prints available from STURP photographer Barrie Schwortz have the contrast digitally enhanced. See Shroud of Turin Website: http://www.shroud.com/
2. Whanger, A. D., and Whanger, M., 'Polarised image overlay technique: a new image comparison method and its applications', *Applied Optics*, 24: 766–72, 1985.
3. Whanger, A. D., and Whanger, M., *The Shroud of Turin: an adventure in discovery*, pp. 19–20.
4. Ouspensky, L., *Theology of the Icon*.
5. See, for example, Morgan, R., 'Did the Templars take the Shroud to England? New Evidence from Templecombe', *History, Science, Theology and the Shroud, Symposium Proceedings*, pp. 205–32, 1991.
6. Whanger, A. D., and Whanger, M., *The Shroud of Turin: an adventure in discovery*.
7. Filas, F. L., *The Dating of the Shroud of Turin from Coins of Pontius Pilate*. For contrary views, see Lombatti, A., 'Doubts Concerning the Coins Over the Eyes', Letters to the Editor, *BSTS Newsletter*, no. 45, 1997.
8. Avinoam, D., 'Where Did the Shroud of Turin Originate? A Botanical Quest', *Eretz* magazine, Nov/Dec, 1997. Also Avinoam, D., 'The Origin of the Shroud of Turin from the Near East as Evidenced by Plant Images and Pollen Grains', paper presented at Turin Symposium, 1998.
9. See, for example, pp. 63, 67, 69 and 70: Whanger, A. D., and Whanger, M., *The Shroud of Turin: an adventure in discovery*.
10. Tacitus, *Annals: Nero*, p. 365. See also Baigent, M., Leigh, R., and Lincoln, H., *The Holy Blood and the Holy Grail*, p. 312ff.
11. Mark xvi, 11; Luke xxiv, 11, John xx, 9.
12. Even today, rabbis and ultra-orthodox Jews will scour the site of the terrorist atrocity, 'literally sponging up the blood of the victims which is on the ground to be buried appropriately' (Rabbi Micha Halpern, *In Pursuit of the*

Shroud, Rock Creek Productions/ABC Productions for The Learning Channel, 1998).

13. Whanger, A. D., and Whanger, M., *The Shroud of Turin: an adventure in discovery*, pp. 84 and 94.

14. Ferguson, G., *Signs and Symbols in Christian Art*.

15. The images around the figure on the Turin Shroud form a more than passing resemblance to the Arma Christi (Instruments of the Crucifixion), a favourite subject in some medieval paintings. See Schiller, G., *Iconography of Christian Art*.

Chapter Sixteen
The Secret in the Headboard (pp. 235–43)

1. Whanger, A. D., and Whanger, M., *The Shroud of Turin: an adventure in discovery*, p. 99.

2. Filas, F. L., *The Dating of the Shroud of Turin from Coins of Pontius Pilate*.

3. The two lepta are the same size but apparently show two different designs. Of great interest is the fact that Father Filas's claim was derided by many experts owing to his belief that he could see four letters, UCAI, on one of the coins, whereas all known coins of this type carried the letters UKAI. Over a year later, in 1981, a Pontius Pilate lepton was discovered bearing the letters seen on the Shroud image, UCAI (see Whanger, A. D., and Whanger, M., *The Shroud of Turin: an adventure in discovery*, pp. 23–8.

4. Whanger, A. D., and Whanger, M., *The Shroud of Turin: an adventure in discovery*, pp. 30–31.

Chapter Seventeen
Oviedo's 'Holy Face' (pp. 245–57)

1. Ricci, G., *The Holy Shroud*. Contains a chapter on the Sudarium of Oviedo.

2. Pelagius, Bishop of Oviedo, *Book of Testaments of Oviedo*, and *Chronicon Regum Legionensum*.

3. Asimov, I., *Asimov's Chronology of World History*, p. 123.

4. Ricci, G., *L'Uomo de la Sindone Gesu*.

5. Bentley, J., *Restless Bones*.

6. Quoted in Guscin, M., 'The Sudarium of Oviedo', paper presented at Nice Symposium, May 1997.

7. Rodriguez J., and Chirivella, J. (coordinators), 'El Sudario del Señor – 'Sudarium Domini', *Actas del 1 Congreso Internacional sobreel Sudario de Oviedo*. Ed. Exemo. Cabildo de la S. I. Cathedral Basilica Metropolitana de Oviedo, 1996.

8. Guscin, M., *The Sudarium of Oviedo*.

9. Laidler, K., *Head of God*, p. 85.

10. Guscin, M., *The Sudarium of Oviedo: Its History and Relationship to the Shroud of Turin*.

11. Mourant, A. E., Kopec, A. C., and Domaniewska-Sobczak, K., *The Distribution of the Human Blood Groups and Other Polymorphisms*.

12. Smith, M. T., personal communication, May 1999.

13. Whanger, A. D., and Whanger, M., *The Shroud of Turin: an adventure in discovery*, pp. 57–9.
14. Ibid., p. 59.
15. Clive Prince and Lynn Picknett showed that it was quite possible to use light-sensitive chemical to 'retouch' an already existing image produced by the *camera obscura*, but, given the presence of human blood on the Shroud, it is more likely that actual blood was dribbled, or painted, on to the linen directly.

Chapter Eighteen
The Face of Christ (pp. 259–69)
1. 'Poser' for AppleMac, Fractal Design, 1997.
2. It is not clear that there is any reduction in head size because of spherical aberration. As can be seen in the 50–50 illustration of Professor Allen's model and Mr Perfect (plate 25), both heads fit together perfectly.
3. Wilson, Ian, *The Blood and the Shroud*, p. 20ff.
4. Picknett, L., and Prince, C., *Turin Shroud: in whose image?*, p. 135.
5. Allen, N. P. L., 'Verification of the Nature and Causes of the Photo-Negative Images on the Shroud of Lirey-Chambéry-Turin', *De Arte*, 51, 21–35.

Chapter Nineteen
Epilogue (pp. 271–80)
1. *The Independent*, 14 October 1988.
2. Wilson, Ian, *The Turin Shroud*.
3. Fisher, H. A. L., *A History of Europe*.
4. Bentley, J., *Restless Bones*.
5. The Turin Shroud's most famous 'rival' was the Besançon Shroud, probably produced in the 1500s (Wilson, Ian, *The Turin Shroud*). For a photograph of the Besançon Shroud see Currer-Briggs, N., *The Shroud and the Grail*.
6. Bentley, J., *Restless Bones*.
7. Allen, N. P. L., 'Verification of the Nature and Causes of the Photo-Negative Images on the Shroud of Lirey-Chambéry-Turin', *De Arte*, 51, 21–35.
8. Baigent, M., Leigh, R., and Lincoln, H., *The Holy Blood and the Holy Grail*.
9. Kerr, A., *The Crusades*.

BIBLIOGRAPHY

Aldred, C., *Akhenaten*, Abacus, 1968

Allen, N. P. L., *The Methods and Techniques Employed in the Manufacture of the Shroud of Turin*, unpublished D. Phil. dissertation, University of Durban-Westville, 1993

Allen, N. P. L., 'Is the Shroud of Turin the First Recorded Photograph?', *The South African Journal of Art History*, 11: 23–32, 1993

Allen, N. P. L., 'Verification of the Nature and Causes of the Photo-Negative Images on the Shroud of Lirey-Chambéry-Turin', *De Arte*, 51, 21–35, 1995

Allen, N. P. L., *The Turin Shroud and the Crystal Lens*, Empowerment Technologies Pty Ltd., South Africa, 1998

Arberry, A. J., *Sufism*, George Allen and Unwin, 1950

Asimov, I., *Asimov's Chronology of World History*, HarperCollins, 1991

Attar, Farid al-Din, *Muslim Saints and Mystics*, Arberry, A. J. (trans), Arkana, 1990

Avinoam, D., 'Where Did the Shroud of Turin Originate? A Botanical Quest', *Eretz* Nov/Dec, 1997

Avinoam, D., *The Origin of the Shroud of Turin from the Near East as Evidenced by Plant Images and Pollen Grains*, paper presented at Turin Symposium, 1998

Bahn, P., and Vertut, J., *Images of the Ice Age*, Facts on File, 1988

Bahm, A. J., *The World's Living Religions*, Dell, 1964

Baigent, M., Leigh, R., and Lincoln, H., *The Holy Blood and the Holy Grail*, Jonathan Cape, 1982

Baigent, M., Leigh, R., and Lincoln, H., *The Messianic Legacy*, Jonathan Cape, 1986

Bacon, N., *Laws and Government of England*, quoted in Elder, I. H., *Celt, Druid and Culdee*, p. 98

Baluze, E., *Vita Paparum Avienonensum*, Mollat, G., (ed.), vol. III, 1914–27

Barber, M., *The New Knighthood: a history of the order of the temple*, Cambridge University Press, 1994

Barbet, P., *A Doctor at Calvary*, Doubleday, 1953

Barbet, P., *Les Cinque Plaies du Christ*, 2nd edn, Procure du Carmel de l'Action de Grâce, 1937

Barker, M., *The Gate of Heaven*, SPCK, 1991

Begg, E., *The Cult of the Black Virgin*, Arkana, 1985

Bentley, J., *Restless Bones*, Constable and Co, 1985

Ben Dov, Meir, *In the Shadow of the Temple*, trans. I. Friedman, Harper and Row, 1985.

Black, M., *An Aramaic Approach to the Gospels and Acts*, Oxford University Press, 1946

Brandon, S. G. F., *The Fall of Jerusalem*, SPCK, 1951

Brooke, R., and Brooke, C., *Popular Religion in the Middle Ages*, 1984

The Brus, G. E. Todd (trans), Gowans and Gray, 1907

Bury, J., *History of the Later Roman Empire from the Death of Theodosius I to the Death of Justinian*, 2 vols., Macmillan and Co., 1923

Cahill, T. A., et al, 'The Vinland Map Revisited: New Compositional Evidence on Its Ink and Parchment', *Analytical Chemistry*, 59, 829–33, 1987

Capt, E. R., *Missing Links Discovered in Assyrian Tablets*, Artisan, 1996

Cauvin, J., *Religions Néolithiques de Syro-Palestine*, Publication du Centre de Researches d'Écologie et de Préhistoire 1972

Chronicon de Lanercost, Stevenson, J. (ed.), Edinburgh, 1839

Continuation of the Old French 'Perceval', Roach, W. (ed), 1952

Curl, J. S., *The Art and Architecture of Freemasonry*, Overlook Press, 1993

Currer-Briggs, N., *The Shroud and the Grail*, Weidenfeld & Nicolson, 1987

Curtius Rufus, *History of Alexander the Great*, M. Cooper, 1753

Daniell, C., *Death and Burial in Medieval England*, Routledge, 1997

Delaude, J., *Le Circle d'Ulysse*, Priory of Sion document, 1997

Delisle, L., *Mémoires sur les opérations financières des Templiers*, Mémoires de l'Institut National de France, Académie des Inscriptions et Belles-Lettres, vol. 33, 1889

Dobson, C. C., *Did Our Lord Visit Britain?* Covenant Publishing Co, 1993

Eder, J. M., *History of Photography*, Columbia University Press, 1945

Eisenman, R. H., *James the Just in the Habakkuk Pesher*, Leiden, 1986

Elder, I. H., *Celt, Druid and Culdee*, Covenant Publishing Co, 1994

Emry, S., *Paul and Joseph of Arimathea*, America's Promise Ministries, n.d.

Epiphanius, *Panarion*, Williams, F., (trans.), E. J. Brill, 1987

Eusebius, *Ecclesiastical History*, Loeb Classical Library, 1926

Ferguson, G., *Signs and Symbols in Christian Art*, Oxford University Press, 1954

Filas, F. L., *The Dating of the Shroud of Turin from Coins of Pontius Pilate*, 2nd edn, 1982

Finke, H., *Papsttum und Untergang des Templerordens*, II, Münster, 1907

Fisher, H. A. L., *A History of Europe*, vol. 1, Fontana, 1970

Flinder, A., *Secrets of the Bible Seas*, Severn House, 1985

Focal Encyclopaedia of Photography, Focal Press, 1975

Franzmann, M., *Jesus in the Nag Hammadi Writings*, T. and T. Clark, 1996

Frazer, J., *The Golden Bough* (abridged edn), Penguin, 1996

Freeman, E. A., *The Reign of William Rufus*, Clarendon Press, 1882

Frei, Max, 'Note a seguito dei primo studi sui prelievi di polvere aderente al lenzuolo della S Sindone', *Sindone*, April 1976

Frei, Max, 'Nine Years of Palynological Studies on the Shroud', *Shroud Spectrum International* (3), 1982

Freud, S., *Moses and Monotheism*, The Hogarth Press, 1951

Fulcanelli, *The Mystery of the Cathedrals*, Spearman, 1971

Gaballa, G. A., *The Memphite Tomb Chapel of Mose*, Aris and Philips, 1977

Gansfried, S., *Code of Jewish Law*, vol. IV, Goldin, H. E. (trans.), Hebrew Publishing Co., 1927

Gardner, L., *Nexus*, vol. VI (4), New Times, 1999

Garraty, J. A., and Gay, P., *The University History of the World*, New Orehard Editions, 1985

Gawler, J. C., *Dan, the Pioneer of Israel*, W. H. Guest, 1880

Geary, P. J., *Furta Sacra: thefts of relics in the central Middle Ages*, Princeton University Press, 1978

Godwin, J., *The Mystery of the Seven Vowels*, Phanes Press, 1991

Goguel, M., *La Naissance du Christianisme, The Birth of Christainity*, H. C. Snape (trans.), George Allen and Unwin, 1953

Gove, H. E., *Relic, Icon or Hoax: Carbon Dating the Turin Shroud*, Institute of Physics Publishing, 1996

Graves, K., *The World's Sixteen Crucified Saviours*, Colby and Rich, 1897

Graves, R., *Greek Myths*, Penguin, 1978

Graves, R., *The White Goddess*, Faber and Faber, 1986

Grunebaum, G. E. von, *Medieval Islam: a study in cultural orientation*, University of Chicago, 1946

Guscin, M., *The Sudarium of Oviedo*, paper presented at Nice Symposium, May 1997

Guscin, M., *The Sudarium of Oviedo: Its History and Relationship to the Shroud of Turin*, 1998

Gutas, D., *Greek Thought, Arab Culture: the Graeco-Arab translation movement in Baghdad and early Abbasid society*, Routledge, 1998

Haas, N., 'Anthropological Observations on the Skeletal Remains from Giv'at Ha-Mivtar', *Israel Exploration Journal*, 20 (1–2), 1970

Hancock, G., *The Sign and the Seal*, Mandarin, 1993

Hassnain, F., *A Search for the Historical Jesus*, Gateway, 1994

Hay, R. A., *Genealogie of the Saintclaires of Rosslyn*, 1835

Heller, J. H., and Adler, A. D., 'Blood on the Shroud of Turin', *Applied Optics*, 19, 12, 1980

Hunt, R., *Popular Romances of the West Country*, Chatto and Windus, 1903

Hynek, R. W., *Science and the Holy Shroud*, Benedictine Press, 1936

Independent, The, 14 October 1988

Irwin, R., *The Middle East in the Middle Ages: the Early Mamluk Sultanate 1250–1382*, Croom Helm, 1986

In Pursuit of the Shroud, Rock Creek Productions/ABC Productions for The Learning Channel, 1998

Israel, B. J., *The Jews of India*, New Delhi Centre for Jewish and Inter-Faith Studies, 1982

Jacobs, A., *Sufism*, Encarta Encyclopedia, 1995

James, E. O., *The Origins of Sacrifice*, 1933

James, P., and Thorpe, N., *Ancient Inventions*, O'Mara Books, 1995

Josephus, F., *Antiquities*, XII, in *Works*, H. St J. Thackeray et al (eds), Heinemann 1926

Josephus, F., *Contra Apionem*, III, in *Works*, H. St J. Thackeray et al (eds), Heinemann, 1926

Josephus, F., *Jewish War*, VII, in *Works*, H. St J. Thackeray et al (eds), Heinemann, 1926

Jowett, G. F., *The Drama of the Lost Disciples*, Covenant Publishing Co, 1996

Kenyon, K., *Digging Up Jericho*, Benn, 1957

Kersten, H., and Gruber, E. R., *The Jesus Conspiracy*, Element, 1994

Kerr, A., *The Crusades*, Wheaton, 1966

Kloppenborg, J. S., ' "Easter Faith" and the Sayings Gospel Q', *Semeia*, 49: 71–99, 1990

Koester, H., 'Apocryphal and Canonical Gospels', *Harvard Theological Review*, 73: 105–30, 1980

Knight, C., and Lomas, R., *The Hiram Key*, Century, 1996

Knight, C., and Lomas, R., *The Second Messiah*, Century, 1997

Kohlbeck, J. A. and Nitowski, E. L., 'New Evidence May Explain Image on Shroud of Turin', *Biblical Archaeology Review*, p. 21, 1986

Laidler, K., *The Physical and Psychological Development of an Infant Orang-utan*, unpublished Ph.D. thesis, Durham University, 1978

Laidler, K., *The Talking Ape*, Collins, 1980

Laidler, K., *The Head of God*, Orion, 1998

Latham, R. W., *Ethnology of Europe*, 1852

Lewis, L. S., *Joseph of Arimathea at Glastonbury*, James Clarke, 1922

Lobineau, H., *Dossier Secrets d'Henri Lobineau*, privately published, 1967

Lombatti, A., 'Doubts Concerning the Coins over the Eyes', Letters to the Editor, *BSTS Newsletter*, no. 45, 1997

Loomis, R., *The Grail*, Columbia University Press, 1963

MacGregor-Mathers, S. L., *The Kabbalah Unveiled*, Keegan Paul and Co, 1926

MacKay, A. G., *Lexicon of Freemasonry*, Charles Griffon and Co, 1873

Maalouf, A., *The Crusades through Arab Eyes*, J. Rothschild (trans), Al Saqi, 1984

McCrone, W. C., 'Authenticity of Medieval Document Tested by Small-Particle Analysis', *Analytical Chemistry*, 48, 676–9, 1976

McCrone, W. C., and Skirius, C., 'Light-Microscopical Study of the Turin Shroud', *The Microscope*, 28 and 29, 1980 and 1981

MacKenzie, A. M., *Robert Bruce, King of Scots*, Oliver and Boyd, 1956

Majno, G., *The Healing Hand*, Harvard University Press, 1975

Martin, E. J., *The Trial of the Templars*, Allen and Unwin, 1928

Martin, M., *The Decline and Fall of the Roman Church*, Secker & Warbury, 1982

Mason, H., *The Death of al-Hallaj*, University of Notre Dame Press, 1979

Massignon, L., *The Passion of al-Hallaj*, Princeton University Press, 1982

Mead, G. R. S., *Did Jesus Live 100 Years BC?* Theosophical Publishing Society, 1903

Mead, G. R. S., *The Hymn of Jesus*, Theosophical Publishing Society, 1907

Mee, A., *The King's England: Durham*, Hodder and Stoughton, 1969

Meyer, E., *Ursprung und Anfäng des Christentums*, vol. III, 1921–3

Meyer, P., *Bibliothèque de l'Ecole de Chartres*, sixth ser., v, 1869

Meyerhof, M., and Schacht, J. (eds), *The Theologus Autodidactus of Ibn al-Nafis*, Columbia University Press, 1968

Michelet, J., *Procès des Templiers*, I, 89–96, 1841–51

Mills, Alan, 'The Russel Effect', lecture to the British Society for the Turin Shroud, 23 October 1991

Morgan, R., 'Did the Templars Take the Shroud to England? New Evidence from Templecombe', *History, Science, Theology and the Shroud, Symposium Proceedings*, pp. 205–32, 1991

Morris, R. A., Schwalbe, A., and London, J. R., 'X-Ray Fluorescence Investigation of the Shroud of Turin', *X-Ray Spectrometry*, 9 (2), 1980

Mourant, A. E., Kopec, A. C., and Domaniewska-Sobczak, K., *The Distribution of the Human Blood Groups and Other Polymorphisms*, Oxford University Press, 1976

Murray, M. A., *The God of the Witches*, Faber, 1931

Needham, J., *Science and Civilisation in China*, vol. 2, (6 vols), Cambridge University Press, 1954

New Larousse Encyclopaedia of Mythology, Hamlyn, 1984

Nickell, J., *Inquest on the Shroud of Turin*, Prometheus, 1987

Oldenbourg, Z., *The Massacre at Montségur*, Weidenfeld and Nicolson, 1961

Osman, A., *Moses, Pharaoh of Egypt*, Paladin, 1991

Osman, A., *Stranger in the Valley of the Kings*, Paladin, 1987

Osman, A., *The House of the Messiah*, HarperCollins, 1992

Ouspensky, L., *Theology of the Icon*, St Vladimir's Seminary Press, 1978

Pagels, E. H., *The Gnostic Gospels*, Random House, 1979

Pagels, E. H., and Turner, J. D., *NHC* XI, 1: *The Interpretation of Knowledge*, Hedrick, 1990

Pauwels, L. and Bergier, J., *The Dawn of Magic*, Anthony Gidds and Phillips, 1963

Peake's Commentary on the Bible, T. Nelson, 1962

Pelagius, Bishop of Oviedo, *Book of the Testaments of Oviedo* and *Chronicon Regum Legionensum*, Verbo, 1331

Pellicori, S. F., 'Spectral properties of the Shroud of Turin', *Applied Optics*, 19 (12): 1913–20

Pellicori, S. F., and Evans, S. M., 'The Shroud of Turin through the microscope', *Archeology*, 34 (1): 34–43

Pfeiffer, J., *The Emergence of Man*, Nelson, 1970

Philo, Judaeus, *On the Contemplative Life*, F. W. Tilden (trans), Bloomington, 1922

Picknett, L., and Prince, C., *Turin Shroud: in whose image?*, Bloomsbury, 1994

Platt, R. H. (ed), *The Lost Books of the Bible*, World Publishing Company, 1974

'Poser' for AppleMac, Fractal Design, 1997

Rabanus, M., MS held at Magdalene College, Oxford

Rabinowitz, J. J., *Speculum*, 22, 1947

Rawlinson, G., *History of Phoenicia*, Fisher & Unwin, 1885

Redford, D. B., *Akhenaten, the Heretic King*, Princeton University Press, 1984

Ricci, G., *L'Uomo de la Sindone Gesu*, fifth edn, Edizioni Stadium, 1969

Ricci, G., *The Holy Shroud*, 1981

Robins, S. L., and Cotran, R. S., *Pathologic Basis of Disease*, 2nd edn, W. B. Saunders and Co., 1979

Robinson, J. M., 'Jesus as Sophos and Sophia: Wisdom, Tradition and the Gospels', in *Aspects of Wisdom in Judaism and Early Christianity*, Wilken, R. L. (ed), University of Notre Dame Press, 1975

Rodante, Sebastiano, 'The Coronation of Thorns in the Light of the Shroud', *Shroud Spectrum*, 1, 4–24, 1982

Rodriguez, J., and Chirivella, J. (coordinators), 'El Sudario del Señor – "Sudarium Domini" ', *Actas del 1 Congreso International sobreel Sudario de Oviedo*, ed. Exemo, Cabildo de la S., Cathedral Basilica Metropolitana de Oviedo, 1996

Rollefson, G., Simmons, A. H., and Kafafi, Z., *Journal of Field Archaeology*, 19, 1992

Rosslyn, Earl of, *Rosslyn Chapel*, 1997

Routh, G., *Reliquae Sacrae*, Oxford, 1846

Saewulf, *The Pilgrimage of Saewulf to Jerusalem and the Holy Land in the Years 1102 and 1103*, Palestine Pilgrims' Text Society, vol. 4, 1982

Sailman, B., *Researches in the East*, 1818

Sarton, G., *Introduction to the History of Science. Vol. III: Science and learning in the fourteenth century*, The Williams and Wilkins Co., 1947

Schiller, G., *Iconography of Christian Art*, Lund Humphries, 1971

Schonfield, H. J., *Secrets of the Dead Sea Scrolls*, Element, 1956

Schonfield, H., *The Essene Odyssey*, Element Books, 1984

Scotichronicon, McQueen, J. & W., (eds), 1993

Seaman, W. De M., *The Dawn of Christianity in the West*, The Chrest Foundation, 1993

Seward, D., *The Monks of War*, 1972

Shah, I., *The Sufis*, Cape, 1969

Sherbok, D. C., 'Jewish Shroud of Turin', *Expository Times*, 1981

Silberman, N. A., *Digging for Gold and Country*, Alfred A. Knopf, 1992

Sinclair, A., *The Sword and the Grail*, Century, 1992

Slezer, J., *Theatrum Scotiae*, 1693

Smythe, B., *Trobador Poets*, 1911

Sox, H. D., *The Image on the Shroud*, Unwin Hyman, 1981

Stokes, M., *Six Months in the Apennines*, G. Bell and Sons, 1892

Stoyanov, Y., *The Hidden Tradition in Europe*, Arkana, 1994

Straiton, M., 'The Man in the Shroud – a 13th-Century Crucifixion Action-Replay', *Catholic Medical Quarterly*, vol. XL, no. 3 (243)

Strayer, J. R., *Medieval Statecraft and the Perspectives of History*, Princeton University Press, 1971

Tacitus, *Annals: Nero*, in *The Annals and The Histories*, A. J. Church and W. J. Broadribb (trans), Encyclopaedia Britannia, 1952

Taylor, J. W., *The Coming of the Saints*, Methuen and co, 1906

The Times Atlas of World History, G. Barraclough (ed), Times Books, 1984

Tzaferis, V., 'Jewish Tombs at and near Giv'at Ha-Mivtar', *Israel Exploration Journal*, 20: 31, 1971

Van Seters, J., *The Hyksos*, Yale University Press, 1966

Vignon, P., Le Saint Suaire de Turin devant la science, l'archaeologie, l'histoire, l'iconographie, la logique, Paris, 1939

Volkringer, J., Le Problème de Empreintes devant la Science, Paris, 1942

Wallace-Hadrill, J. M., The Long-Haired Kings, Methuen, 1962

Wedessow, U., Considerazioni ipotetiche sulla causa fisica della morte dell'iliomo della Sindone, 1978

Weston, J. L., From Ritual to Romance, Doubleday, 1957

Whanger, A. D., and Whanger, M., 'Polarised image overlay technique: a new image comparison method and its applications', Applied Optics, 24: 766–72, 1985

Whanger, A. D., and Whanger, M., The Shroud of Turin: an adventure in discovery, Providence House Publishers, 1998

Whittaker, J. R., The Physical Cause of the Death of Our Lord, address to the St Luke's Guild, London

William of Tyre, A History of Deeds Done Beyond the Sea, Columbia University Press, 1941

Williamson, H. R., The Arrow and the Sword, Faber and Faber, 1947

Wilson, A. N., Jesus, Flamingo, 1992

Wilson, I., The Turin Shroud, Gollancz, 1978

Wilson, I., 'Riddle of the Dead Man's Hand', Observer Magazine, 31 January 1988

Wilson, I., The Blood and the Shroud, Weidenfeld & Nicolson, 1998

Wilson, R. McL., The Gospel of Philip: Translated from the Coptic Text, with an Introduction and Commentary. Harper & Row, 1962. See also The Nag Hammadi Library in English, 1977

Yakar and Hershkovitz, 'Atiquot, 18, 59–63, 1988

Zias, J., and Sekeles, E., 'The Crucified Man from Giv'at Ha-Mivtar: A Reappraisal', Israel Exploration Journal, 35: 22–7, 1985

Zugibe, F. T., The Cross and the Shroud. A Medical Examiner Investigates the Crucifixion, Angelus, 1982

Zugibe, F. T., 'Pierre Barbet Revisited', Sindon, N. S., Quad. No. 8, 1995

Zugibe, F. T., 'The Man on the Shroud Was Washed', Sindon, N. S., Quad. No. 1, 1989

PICTURE CREDITS

The author and publishers would like to thank the following individuals and agencies for their kind permission to reproduce the photographs in the plate section:

1, 2, 18a: Photos courtesy of Holy Shroud Guild, Esopus, NY
3, 4, 5: Copyright Liz Laidler
7: Copyright British Library, London/Bridgeman Art Library, London/NY
6: Copyright Robert Brydon
8, 9: Copyright Nicholas P. Allen
10: Copyright H. Corbin
11, 12: Copyright Frederick T. Zugibe
13: Courtesy Saint Catherine's Monastery
14, 15, 16: Copyright Alan Whanger
17, 18b, 19, 20, 23, 24, 25, 26: Copyright Pachyderm Ltd
21, 22: Copyright I. Piczek

Every effort has been made to trace and contact all copyright holders. The author will be glad to rectify any omissions at the earliest opportunity.

INDEX